# Saskatchewan Politicians

## LIVES PAST AND PRESENT

# Saskatchewan Politicians

## LIVES PAST AND PRESENT

*Series Editor*
Brian Mlazgar

*Volume Editor*
Brett Quiring

2004

Canadian Plains Research Center
University of Regina
Regina, Saskatchewan S4S 0A2
Canada
Tel: (306) 585-4758
Fax: (306) 585-4699
e-mail: canadian.plains@uregina.ca
http://www.cprc.uregina.ca


**Library and Archives Canada Cataloguing in Publication**

Saskatchewan politicians : lives past and present / series editor, Brian Mlazgar; volume editor, Brett Quiring.

(TBS, ISSN 1482-9886 ; 14)
ISBN 0-88977-165-0

1. Legislators--Saskatchewan--Biography. 2. Politicians--Saskatchewan--Biography. 3. Saskatchewan--Biography.
I. Quiring, Brett, 1978- II. University of Regina. Canadian Plains Research Center III. Series.

FC3505.S28 2004              971.24'009'9              C2004-906758-3



Cover design: Brian Danchuk Design, Regina
Cover photo courtesy Saskatchewan Archives Board, 88-0913-32
Printed and bound in Canada by Houghton Boston, Saskatoon
Printed on acid-free paper

We gratefully acknowledge the financial support of the following:
• The Government of Canada through the Book Publishing Industry Development Program (BPIDP)
• The Cultural Industries Development Fund, Government of Saskatchewan

# —TABLE OF CONTENTS—

# —PREFACE—

*Series Editor, Brian Mlazgar*

Saskatchewan's provincial motto, *Multis E Gentibus Vires/From Many Peoples, Strength*, is very much in keeping with the philosophy that lies behind the development of the "Saskatchewan Lives Past and Present" book series, to which the present volume belongs.

Over the course of nearly two decades of publishing books about the prairie region, and more specifically Saskatchewan, I have become increasingly concerned about the paucity of information available about the people who helped to build this province. To be sure, almost everyone has heard of Tommy Douglas and John Diefenbaker, and biographies of prominent (mainly political) figures have occasionally been published over the years. Such biographies, however, fail to recognize the countless, lesser-known individuals who often laboured their entire lives in semi-anonymity, tirelessly contributing to the development and enrichment of their communities.

With this in mind, I decided that it would be appropriate for the Canadian Plains Research Center to launch the "Saskatchewan Lives" book series. Inaugurating the series, however, proved to be far easier than actually deciding what—and who—would be included. Our original list included eighteen possible books. Due to a variety of budgetary, editorial and temporal constraints, we were obliged to focus on five titles that will be published in 2004–2005:

- *Saskatchewan Agriculture: Lives Past and Present*, edited by Lisa Dale-Burnett, focuses on Saskatchewan men and women over the past century who were dedicated to building agricultural communities as well as agriculture itself.
- *Saskatchewan First Nations: Lives Past and Present*, edited by Christian Thompson, recognizes and celebrates the vital and ever-growing contributions of First Nations people to this province and its cultural mosaic.
- *Saskatchewan Politicians: Lives Past and Present*, edited by Brett Quiring, includes, by necessity, only a fraction of the many men and women—some quite famous, some infamous—who have held political office in the province over the past one hundred years.
- *Saskatchewan Sports: Lives Past and Present*, edited by Tim Switzer, applauds the sports figures who have consistently allowed this province to achieve successes on the "playing field" far beyond what would be expected from our small population.
- *Saskatchewan Writers: Lives Past and Present*, edited by Heather Hodgson, features many men and women whose writing has at some point been nurtured by the richness of the Saskatchewan landscape and by the vibrant writing community in the province.

Books of this nature must, by necessity, be developed using some sort of selection process. The preface in each volume outlines the criteria used for that particular book, as well as any factors which prevented inclusion of some individuals who would otherwise have "qualified." Readers are invited to contact the publisher directly with suggestions for future, supplementary volumes.

Because we wanted to include in these volumes not only those who are already well-known in their field, but also many who are lesser-known but who have nonetheless contributed much to the province, the individual biographies are relatively brief and ought not, therefore, to be considered as definitive biographies. Rather, they are designed to increase awareness, stimulate interest, and promote further research.

I would like to extend my appreciation to the editors who helped to compile these books, to the CPRC staff who checked facts where necessary, and did the copy-editing, layout, and design. I also want to acknowledge the funding agencies (listed on the copyright page) without whose support the development of these books would not have been possible. Finally, I want to extend my deepest thanks to the hundreds of individuals who voluntarily wrote entries for this book series. Through their collective efforts they have demonstrated, yet again, the wisdom of our provincial motto: *Multis E Gentibus Vires/From Many Peoples, Strength*. Quite simply, in Saskatchewan, this is how things are done.

As Saskatchewan approaches the 100th anniversary of its formation as a province in 2005, it is fitting that its citizens reflect on those whose contributions and accomplishments have created and nurtured the culture and society of this place we call home. It is hoped that this series of books will help, in some small measure, to accomplish that.

# —PREFACE—

*Volume Editor, Brett Quiring*

This book was commissioned as part of a biographical series that covers several important fields in Saskatchewan history. The series is part of the forthcoming *Encyclopedia of Saskatchewan*, and many of the entries in this volume will be included in the encyclopedia. The purpose of *Saskatchewan Politicians: Lives Past and Present* is to provide a reference to students of Saskatchewan politics and those who have an interest in the field.

I have defined politics very narrowly for the purposes of this book; therefore, only lieutenant-governors, members of the Saskatchewan legislature, and Saskatchewan representatives in the House of Commons or the Canadian Senate have been considered for inclusion. As a consequence, people who have only held municipal office have not been included. This is meant in no way to diminish their accomplishments, but is a necessary sacrifice to keep the length of this volume manageable. Further, with the large number of provincial and federal politicians elected throughout Saskatchewan's history, it was impossible to include all of them in the book. As such, criteria was developed to determine the subject list. The following list of positions was used to gauge who should be included:

Premiers;

Federal cabinet ministers representing a Saskatchewan riding;

Provincial cabinet ministers who have held positions of influence in government;

MLAs or MPs who have held important positions within their respective assemblies (i.e. Speaker, leader of the Opposition, leader of a political party);

MLAs or MPs who have been elected to four or more terms of office;

MLAs and MPs who have distinguished themselves in some fashion;

Party activists who have left a lasting mark on their political party;

Lieutenant-governors who made a lasting contribution to Saskatchewan politics.

Some of these criteria are obviously open to interpretation, and inevitably some will question why certain individuals were included while others were not. I have tried to be as inclusive as possible with the entry list. Efforts have been made to include representatives of smaller, less successful political parties, such as Social Credit. These former MLAs and MPs have been included even though no individual may technically meet the selection criteria. I have further tried to select subjects who researchers in Saskatchewan history would likely encounter in their studies and require more information about, even though some of these selectees may have served only a single term or may have been of fleeting importance. Finally, some members who should have been included were not because of a lack of information on their careers. Collecting adequate information was particularly difficult for several MLAs from Saskatchewan's formative years and former members of the Territorial Assembly. Effort has been undertaken to research these individuals, but in some cases completing their biographies proved to be impossible. It is my hope that the entries I have selected serve the purposes of most readers and that additional research will be undertaken into the careers of those who could not be included.

The length of the entries are limited—most are under 500 words—and thus can only provide a brief outline of the subject's career and political achievements. The entries have only compiled existing knowledge and are not meant as the final word on the subject. If large works have been written on an individual the entry will note it, but in most cases entries have been composed from a wide number of sources which may not give a complete record on all aspects of the subject's career. The contributors have invested a great deal of time and effort in preparing these entries, but, because this is the first time a reference work of this type has been compiled, we expect that additional information will come to light and new sources will be found following its publication.

It is my hope that this work, and its sister publications, will serve as the foundation of reference works in Saskatchewan history and that these entries will be built on, expanded and refined over time. I hope that these biographies will spur research into individuals, and from conversing with the contributors I am pleased to report that it is already happening. For this process to continue, I ask readers to contact me with any suggestions, additions, or corrections to this book in the event a second edition is published. With your help, I am sure that we can build reference works that dutifully serve both the books' subjects and the province.

# —NOTES ON SOURCES—

This book used several sources for the biographical information in the individual entries. However, using the "further reading" section at the end of each entry to denote sources that are common to all entries would be repetitive and would restrict the number of entries that could be included. Thus, it is prudent to discuss some of the major sources of information separately. The "further reading" section will list only the secondary literature and the primary sources that are unique to each particular entry.

The two most useful sources of information for all MLAs and MPs are the *Canadian Parliamentary Guide* and *The Saskatchewan Executive and Legislative Directory*. The *Saskatchewan Executive and Legislative Directory* provides a great deal of information on all federal and provincial elected officials from Saskatchewan. The directory lists all members elected to the Saskatchewan Legislature and Saskatchewan members of the House of Commons and Senate, their terms of service, the electoral district and their political party. The directory also provides lists of all legislative positions held, such as Speaker, leader of the Opposition and all appointments to cabinet. The directory is the most reliable source of basic information on elections and positions held by Saskatchewan's elected officials.

The *Parliamentary Guide* is produced yearly and provides short biographical information on all current federal and provincial elected officials. These guides were published long before the Northwest Territories began electing MPs or the territorial council was formed; therefore, information for all periods of Saskatchewan politics can be found in these books. The information these books contain is variable; some entries are long, while some can consist of only two or three lines with the majority of entries consisting of ten to twenty lines. The information in these books is provided by the members themselves and tends to be factual in nature, listing information on the member's education, family, life before politics as well as any official posts they have held in the government. Outside of these criteria, the guide provides no information on the specifics of a member's career such as important legislation they were in charge of, political scandals they were involved in, or any issues and causes the member was interested in. Since the member provides the information for the guide, the guide's information has been used if it was in conflict with other sources.

For the deceased subjects, obituaries usually provide the best information. Saskatchewan obituaries have largely been indexed for all periods prior to the early 1980s. These indexes are held by the Saskatchewan Archives Board and can be consulted there. Largely, the obituaries used have been from the Regina *Leader-Post* and its predecessors, which seem to have the most comprehensive obituaries throughout most of the province's history. Thus, obituaries provided most of the information in entries on deceased subjects; however, since these obituaries tend to contain errors, all information was verified when possible. The best and most reliable obituaries were printed in the proceedings of the Saskatchewan Legislative Assembly. When a former member of the Saskatchewan legislature dies, a tribute is always given to that member in the house. Read

into the record is a short biography of the member, after which the current members give tributes to the deceased. These tributes are a wealth of information on each deceased member and
have been relied upon in this book.

In addition to these sources, several other sources were used in select cases. For cases where
the subject is still alive, authors have often interviewed the subject to gain a greater depth of
information. This project also benefited from being allowed to consult the private candidate files
held and compiled by the Saskatchewan New Democratic Party. These files have been used
extensively for many CCF/NDP MLAs and MPs. This project also benefited from the files of the
Saskatchewan Archives Board, which maintains biographical information on many former
Saskatchewan politicians. These files do not cover all former politicians but do contain information on many of this book's subjects. Finally, in both 1957 and 1969, editions of *Who's Who in
Saskatchewan* were produced. Each book contains short biographical entries on important citizens
of Saskatchewan. These *Who's Who* books are similar to the *Parliamentary Guide*. The information was provided by the individuals themselves, and for the politicians included in these books
the information provided does not usually exceed that of the *Parliamentary Guide*.

The entries for John Maharg, Toby Nollett, George Spence, Gordon Taggart, and Beatrice
Trew were adapted from Volume 3 of *Salute to Saskatchewan Farm Leaders* (Saskatoon:
Saskatchewan Agricultural Hall of Fame, 1995) and the entry for Herb Sparrow was adapted
from the Saskatchewan Agricultural Hall of Fame Citation for Herbert O. Sparrow, 2000.

The entries for T. C. Douglas and Ross Thatcher were condensed and adapted from chapter-
length biographies written for *Saskatchewan Premiers of the Twentieth Century* (Canadian Plains
Research Center, University of Regina, 2004) by Thomas H. McLeod and Ian McLeod (Douglas)
and by Dale Eisler (Thatcher).

# ACKNOWLEDGEMENTS

A book is a large and complex endeavour. It requires the skills and commitment of a variety of individuals, and I therefore have many people to thank. First and foremost, I have to express my gratitude to all the book's contributors. They all volunteered their precious time and expertise to create this and other reference works that Saskatchewan has been lacking for too long. The entries in this book serve as proof of their dedication to their respective subjects and to this work as a whole. Without their contributions, this work could never have been completed.

Secondly, I would like to thank all the support staff I have hounded relentlessly for information and sources. The staff of the Saskatchewan Archives Board, the City of Regina Archives, the Prairie History Room at the Regina Public Library, the University of Saskatchewan Library and the University of Regina Library all provided invaluable service to me in researching this book. I would also like to acknowledge Mark Suggitt, who allowed me access to the private candidate files of the Saskatchewan New Democratic Party, which provided me with a wealth of information. Photos were provided by the Saskatchewan Archives Board, the Saskatchewan New Democratic Party, the Office of the Lieutenant-Governor, the University of Regina's Audio Visual Services, and some individuals (all indicated by a credit line under the photo).

Thirdly, I would like to thank all the former MLAs and MPs who consented to interviews about their careers and gave time to contributors.

Fourthly, I would like to thank the staff of the Canadian Plains Research Center for commissioning this book and for all their help throughout this project. In particular, I am grateful to Brian Mlazgar for allowing me the opportunity to work on this project, and his guidance and advice. Further, I want to acknowledge the contribution of Donna Achtzehner for her work copy-editing and formatting this book, as well as Kristine Douaud who acted as proofreader. I thank Lorraine Nelson for her assistance in co-ordinating the printing and distribution of materials related to this book. Also, I cannot emphasize enough the help that Lisa Dale-Burnett was to me throughout this endeavor. She provided me with help getting the project off the ground and by allowing me to make use of her work on the agricultural biography book. She further helped by providing me support and encouragement throughout the duration of our projects.

Most importantly, I would like to acknowledge my family: my parents Sylvia and Garry who provided me with everything I needed and helped me edit the biographies I wrote and also my sister Wendy who put up with me. I would also like to acknowledge my friends who supported my endeavors and who all patiently listened to the daily trials and tribulations of this book.

# Saskatchewan Politicians

## AGAR, CHARLES

(1882–1961). Born in Belfast, Ontario, on September 5, 1882, Charles Agar was educated in Ontario before he came to Saskatchewan in 1905 to farm. Becoming active in several farmers' organizations, Agar, like many other farmers, gravitated towards the Progressives after the First World War. He first ran as a Progressive in the 1921 election in the constituency of Saskatoon County and was narrowly elected. Re-elected as a Progressive in 1925, Agar, like many Progressives, gravitated back towards the Liberals. In 1927 Agar was convinced by James Gardiner to cross the floor and sit as a Liberal. Contesting the 1929 election, this time as a Liberal, Agar was again re-elected. Ironically, he won because the Progressives did not endorse his Conservative opponent as they had in many places throughout the province.

After spending a term in opposition, Agar was elected in the constituency of Hanley in 1934 as the Liberals swept back to power. In 1938, with the defeat of the current Speaker John Parker, Agar became Speaker due to his long experience in the house. Agar presided over the legislature for six years until 1944, when he was defeated by CCF candidate James Aitken.

Agar retired from politics and died in Saskatoon in January 1961.

BRETT QUIRING

SAB R-A640-2

CHARLES AGAR

## ANDERSON, J. T. M. (1878–1946).

James Thomas Milton Anderson, fifth premier of Saskatchewan, was born in Fairbank, Ontario, on July 23, 1878. After graduation he taught for six years in Ontario and migrated to western Canada in 1906. He taught first in Manitoba, then near Melville, and finally at Grenfell. Here he met and married Edith Redgewick with whom he had a son and a daughter. In 1911 he was appointed Inspector of Schools based in Yorkton, a position he held for seven years. During this time he continued his own education, earning B.A., M.A. and law degrees from the University of Manitoba and a doctorate in pedagogy from the University of Toronto. In 1918 he published his first and only book, *The Education of the New Canadian*, and the Martin government brought him to Regina as a Director of Education, with special responsibility to ensure that school boards and teachers in "ethnic" districts obeyed the law with respect to educating their children in English. The integrity of the public school system was a principal concern of Anderson's, and he might never have turned to politics had he been allowed to remain in his post. He was, however, removed from it in 1922. His bitterness at the demotion may explain in part why he listened to the overtures which led him to the leadership of the provincial Conservative Party two years later.

The Conservative Party in Saskatchewan in the early 1920s was in disarray with no leader, only three members in the legislature, and surpassed in public support by the Progressives. In these circumstances the party turned to Dr. Anderson to lead it at its convention in March 1924. Shortly thereafter, the federal party made him its paid organizer in the province, an arrangement which became the norm for most provincial Conservative leaders into the modern era. Anderson did not turn things around for his party immediately; in fact, the

Conservatives again won a mere three seats in the legislature in the 1925 election. Nevertheless, the party emerged from that election far stronger than in 1921: Anderson won his seat, and the party raised its popular vote considerably. Anderson would need determination and political skill to win the premiership, but it was not beyond the realm of possibility. In the next four years he would receive the help of a new Conservative newspaper in Regina and the co-operation of all those opposed to the Liberal government. There would also arise a number of issues which would split the coalition which had kept the Liberals in power for over two decades.

On June 6, 1929, enough voters in Saskatchewan deviated from their traditional voting patterns to bring the Conservatives to power, albeit in coalition. Several factors combined to bring about this result. The defensive campaign wages by the Liberals, the presence of the Liberal "machine" and the many scandals attributed to it, the belief that the government had stagnated after so many years in office, and the general feeling that it was time for a change all contributed to the Liberal downfall but must be considered of minor importance. Of greater importance was the failure of Premier James Gardiner to gain control of Saskatchewan's natural resources, which had been held back by the federal Liberals in 1905. Gardiner refused the settlement offered by the King government, and found it difficult to counter Anderson's claim that the province would still be better off with the resources than without them. Of even greater significance were Anderson's tireless efforts to ensure that the

opposition vote was not split on election day. Right from the time he took on the Conservative leadership he sought the support of every person, group and party committed to the defeat of the Liberals. Eventually the strategy paid dividends. By 1928 he had an agreement with the provincial Progressives not to oppose each other at the next election; further, in any constituency where neither local party would step aside, an open convention of all those opposed to the Liberals would be held and the candidate who won the nomination would run as an independent. They also agreed that a "co-operative" government consisting of representatives from all parties would be formed should the Liberals be defeated.

Of greatest importance, however, was the sudden appearance of the Ku Klux Klan in Saskatchewan in 1927. Klan speakers charged that the large-scale immigration of people from central and southeastern Europe threatened the province's Anglo-Canadian way of life; that Roman Catholicism posed a danger to the public school system; and that the Gardiner government had turned a blind eye to both in order to attract the "foreign" vote to the Liberal Party. Anderson stated categorically that neither he nor his party had any formal ties to the Klan, but he did promise to promote additional immigration from Great Britain and to amend the *School Act* so that no one in religious garb could teach and no religious emblems could be displayed in public schools. Further, he blamed the Liberals for allowing such emotional and divisive matters to become political issues in the first place and his campaign had the desired effect: on election day, sufficient Anglo-Canadian and Protestant voters

SAB R-A 629(1)

J. T. M. ANDERSON

left the Liberal Party to cut its representation in the legislature in half (to twenty-six plus two elected at deferred contests). The Conservatives elected twenty-four, the Progressives five, and six constituencies returned independents opposed to the Liberals. Three months later, after all Opposition members joined to pass a want-of-confidence motion in the Gardiner government, J. T. M. Anderson became premier.

Anderson's government, which he always referred to as a "co-operative" government, had the misfortune to come to power at the very beginning of the Depression. Although it amended the *School Act*, established a non-partisan public service commission, passed much-needed labour legislation, began an ambitious highway construction program, and concluded an agreement with the Bennett government which brought Saskatchewan's natural resources under provincial control, as the years went by more and more of its time had to be devoted to attempts to alleviate the worst effects of the Depression. To this end, it created the Saskatchewan Relief Commission to administer the province's many relief programs, declared a moratorium on sales of land to pay municipal taxes, established the Debt Adjustment Board to mediate between debtors and creditors, tried to protect the wheat pool, and borrowed from wherever it could to keep farmers operational and to maintain minimum standards in the health and education systems. In fact, it probably did as much as any provincial government could do given the terrible situation in which Saskatchewan found itself during those years. Just the same, none of this saved it at the next election. On June 19, 1934, neither Anderson nor any candidate—Conservative, Progressive or independent—who supported his government won a seat in the legislature, and the

only formal opposition to the Liberals rested with five Farmer Labour members who formed the nucleus of the new CCF.

Thus, in ten years J. T. M. Anderson took his party from the political wilderness to power, himself to the premiership, and both to near oblivion. He deserves credit for the accomplishment, and probably sympathy rather than blame for the defeat. It is most unlikely that anyone or any set of policies would have saved any government of Saskatchewan given the impact of the Depression. Anderson resigned as leader of the Conservative Party in 1936 but continued to urge co-operation with anyone and everyone opposed to the Liberal Party, a legacy of dubious value to his successors. He went into business from 1936 to 1944, and from 1944 until his death was superintendent of the Provincial School for the Deaf. He died on December 28, 1946, and is buried in Saskatoon.

PATRICK KYBA, UNIVERSITY OF GUELPH

**FURTHER READING:** Archer, John H. 1980. *Saskatchewan: A History.* Saskatoon: Western Producer Prairie Books. • Russell, Peter A. 1983. "The Saskatchewan Conservatives, Separate Schools and the 1929 Election." *Prairie Forum* 8, no. 2: 211–23.

## ANDREYCHUK, RAYNELL (b. 1944).

Raynell Andreychuk was born in Saskatoon on August 14, 1944. She completed a B.A. and a law degree from the University of Saskatchewan in 1967, and established a law practice in Moose Jaw. In 1976, she was appointed to the provincial court and helped establish the family court in Regina.

Andreychuk was elected chancellor of the University of Regina in 1977 and served the university for eight years in that position. In 1985, she left the court to begin a career in the civil service as associate deputy minister for Social Services in Saskatchewan.

In 1987, Andreychuk was named high commissioner to Kenya and Uganda, and Ambassador to Somalia until 1990 when she was appointed Ambassador to Portugal. During her diplomatic career she served on several United Nations (UN) committees, including the UN Environmental Programme and the UN Human Rights Commission.

UNIVERSITY OF REGINA AV SERVICES

RAYNELL ANDREYCHUK

In March of 1993, Andreychuk was appointed to the senate by Prime Minister Brain Mulroney, making her the first female senator from Saskatchewan. She has served on a number of important senatorial committees during her tenure in the upper house, including the Special Joint Committee for the Review of Canada's Foreign Policy and the Standing Committee on Legal and Constitutional Affairs.

Outside of the courtroom and the senate, Andreychuk has served on a number of volunteer boards. Between 1975 and 1981 she served as national president and international vice-president of the Young Men's Christian Association and played an active role with the United Way of Canada and Big Sisters Canada.

LEAH SHARPE, REGINA

## ANGUISH, DOUGLAS KEITH (b. 1950).
During much of the 1980s and 1990s, Doug Anguish stood out as a leading New Democratic Party (NDP) politician in the west central part of Saskatchewan. Anguish was born on July 8, 1950, in Meadow Lake to Ann (née Pope) and Willard Earl Anguish. He and his wife Mona Jane (née Karpenko) have four children: Bruce, Ashala, Nikki, and Jordan.

Anguish's full-time involvement in the political arena began with his work as a ministerial assistant, first for Ed Tchorzewski and then for Ted Bowerman. Politically ambitious himself, Anguish won as the NDP Member of Parliament for The Battlefords–Meadow Lake riding in the 1980 general election. After serving one term in Ottawa, he met defeat in the 1984 general election. Anguish successfully ran for the NDP in the constituency of The Battlefords, later known as the North Battleford constituency, in the provincial general election of 1986. As an Opposition member, he helped Roy Romanow rebuild the NDP. Anguish participated in the NDP return to power in 1991. He was re-elected in 1995, but resigned in 1996, part way through his third term.

For a time, while in office, Anguish served on Romanow's executive council. His positions included those of minister of Energy and Mines from January 1993 to February 1995, and minister of Labour beginning in February 1995. He was reappointed to the latter position in November 1995. His duties as minister included responsibilities for the Saskatchewan Energy Conservation Authority, the Saskatchewan Research Council, the Labour Relations Board, and the Workers Compensation Board. Anguish also chaired the boards of SaskPower and SaskEnergy.

Anguish pursued active careers before and after his time in politics. Until his mid-twenties, Anguish worked as a Life Skills coach at various locations in Saskatchewan and Alberta. After his years in public office, he first served as vice-president of marketing for the Northwest Territories Development Corporation and then as manager of corporate communications for Renaissance Energy. Since 2000, Anguish has worked in a company he founded, External Solutions Ltd., a project management company for social development. He currently resides in Calgary, Alberta.

As an elected representative in Ottawa and Regina, Anguish made many contributions to his constituents and other residents of Saskatchewan. He also played an important role in his chosen New Democratic Party, including on the campaigns of other NDP politicians.

DAVID QUIRING, UNIVERSITY OF SASKATCHEWAN

**ARGUE, HAZEN ROBERT** (1921–1991). Saskatchewan's longest serving federal parliamentarian (18 years as a member of Parliament and 25 as a senator) began his career as a member of the Cooperative Commonwealth Federation (CCF) and ended it as a Liberal Senator. Elected to the House of Commons in 1945 at the age of twenty-four, the one-time boy wonder of Saskatchewan politics experienced both the highs and lows of political life.

The son of Howard and Legia Argue was born in Moose Jaw on January 6, 1921. When Hazen was five his father rented out their Kayville farm and moved the family to Avonlea were he operated a farm machinery business. The business was successful until the crash of 1929. The family resources quickly ran out and Howard Argue was forced to seek government help. Upon graduating from high school Hazen took a job,

lack of money forcing him to give up his idea of going to university. In 1940 fate began to shine on Argue. The family financial picture was brighter and Hazen was able to enrol at the University of Saskatchewan. He graduated in 1944 with a Bachelor of Science degree in agriculture. This was the same year the CCF won a stunning election victory in Saskatchewan.

Argue's political career began in 1945. His family's experiences in the early 1930s had caused him to adopt the social reform principles of the CCF. When the 1945 federal election came around Argue decided to run as the CCF candidate for Wood Mountain. He was elected and went to Ottawa, the youngest member to ever enter the House of Commons. For the next thirteen years Argue was an effective and vocal MP, supporting and promoting the concerns of the residents of Saskatchewan and speaking out against high interest rates and the abolition of the Senate.

SASKATCHEWAN NDP PHOTO ARCHIVES

HAZEN ARGUE

In 1958, Argue's hard work and dedication was rewarded when he was the only Saskatchewan Opposition MP to survive the Diefenbaker sweep. In fact, there were only eight CCF MPs elected. With the defeat of M. J. Coldwell, the tiny caucus was in need of a House Leader. In what has been described by some as a ridiculous 3-2-2 vote, Argue was elected House Leader. Two years later Coldwell resigned and Argue was appointed temporary CCF leader. This caused a split among the CCF executive, as many of them believed Argue to be a House Leader with only regional appeal and no knowledge of issues outside agriculture.

In 1961 a union between the CCF and the Canadian Labour Congress (CLC) created the

New Democratic Party (NDP). The leadership contest for the new party was between Argue and long-time Saskatchewan CCF premier, Tommy Douglas. Douglas won a first-ballot victory by the margin of 1391–380. Argue returned to his farm in Saskatchewan were he spent the next six months brooding over his defeat.

From the beginning, controversy was a part of the career of "Blazin' Hazen." When he was first elected it was felt he was too young to be effective. Once in Ottawa he developed what was called a "club-swinging style" of oratory that propelled him into the national spotlight. He once called Diefenbaker Canada's greatest salesman because he had to try to sell the worst product in the world: his own record. Argue was also quoted as saying that the greatest mistake in Liberal history was Lester Pearson. None of this, however, could compare with the controversy that would surround him from 1962 onward.

On February 18, 1962, Argue announced he was leaving the NDP and joining the Liberals. He said he did not believe in the policies of the new party, which he said was being ruled by a small labour clique. Douglas responded by calling Argue a "straight opportunist," while other NDP brass said Argue was leaving because he was angry at losing the NDP leadership contest. Whatever the reason, Argue entered the 1962 federal election as a candidate for the Liberal Party. He held his seat in 1962 but was badly defeated in 1963 and 1965.

In 1966, over the objections of several members of the Liberal caucus, Lester Pearson appointed Argue to the senate. He held this position until his death in 1991. In 1980, in an attempt to regain some support on the prairies, Trudeau named Argue minister of State for the Canadian Wheat Board. Argue served in this capacity until the Liberal defeat of 1984. In 1982 Argue achieved national recognition by arranging a grain deal with the Soviet Union worth about $1.7 billion.

By 1989 the spotlight was once again on Argue, although this time he was deep in controversy. He found himself accused of using Senate funds to hire research assistants and other staff to help his wife Jean attempt to win a federal Liberal nomination. Argue was charged with fraud, theft and breach of trust. The charges were dropped in 1990 when he became seriously ill. Argue died on October 2, 1991.

Controversy continues to follow Hazen Argue even after his death. He has been described as a gifted orator and a lazy House Leader. While he has been called both an opportunist and a prairie populist, the one thing his critics and his supporters can agree upon was his passion for agriculture, Saskatchewan, and its people.

DWAYNE YASINOWSKI, UNIVERSITY OF REGINA

FURTHER READING: McLeod, Thomas H., and Ian McLeod. 1987. *Tommy Douglas: The Road to Jerusalem*. Edmonton: Hurtig Publishers.

## ASELTINE, WALTER MORLEY (1886–1971).

Walter Morley Aseltine was one of the longest serving senators in Canadian history. He was a member for thirty-seven years and in that time he earned the respect of his peers and the people of Rosetown.

Aseltine was born on September 3, 1886, in Napanee, Ontario. He was educated at the Collegiate Institute in Perth, Ontario. After graduation he went on to teach school in Manitoba and Saskatchewan. He decided to return to school, obtaining his B.A. from Wesley College at the University of Manitoba.

In 1913, Aseltine was called to the Saskatchewan Bar, and soon after established a law firm in Rosetown. (He was made King's Council in 1930.) In 1911 he married France Alice Derby. France died in 1919, leaving Walter to care for their son John. In 1923 he married Laura Irene King with whom he had three children.

Aseltine began his public life in 1920, serving on the Rosetown School Board until 1927. From 1930–1934 he served as the town's mayor. In 1921 Walter ran unsuccessfully for the Conservative Party in the Rosetown constituency. Prime Minister R. B. Bennett appointed him to the Senate on December 30, 1933.

From 1958 to 1962 he served as the leader of the government in the Senate. Throughout his career he performed many duties on the international stage including attending the coronation of Queen Elizabeth II as a member of the official Canadian delegation. In 1961 he was made a member of the Privy Council. For twenty-one years he served on the Senate Divorce Committee, ten of which he served as chairman. Upon his retirement Senator Paul Martin remarked jokingly, "When I think of all the things you have done, I just think of the hundreds of couples you have separated."

The people of Rosetown respected Walter Morley Aseltine. Even while he was a member of the Senate he was still very active within his community. Walter was a lifetime member of the Masonic lodge. Between 1925 and 1934 he was the secretary-treasurer of the Rosetown Board of Trade. Walter was also an avid sports fan who enjoyed everything from tennis to hockey.

Walter Morley Aseltine resigned from the Senate in March of 1971 and died on November 14, 1971.

TRENT EVANISKY, DIEFENBAKER CENTRE

**ATKINSON, PATRICIA** (b. 1952). Elected to the legislature for five terms and serving as a key cabinet minister in both the Romanow and Calvert governments, Pat Atkinson was one of Saskatchewan's most visible politicians over the past two decades.

Atkinson was born in Biggar on September 27, 1952. She attended high school in Saskatoon and graduated from the University of Saskatchewan with degrees in Arts and Education. After university, she worked for the Radius Community School in Saskatoon as a teacher therapist and as school principal.

Atkinson took to politics at an early age. She came from a political family. Her father, Roy Atkinson, was a prominent Saskatchewan farmer who was active in a variety of farm organizations. Pat Atkinson became involved in variety of organizations, most notably on the board of the Saskatoon Community Clinic. In 1982, she won the hotly contested NDP nomination in Saskatoon Nutana. However, she was narrowly defeated as the Conservatives swept the province. In 1986, Atkinson had more success as she easily won the seat in the rematch. In Opposition, Atkinson became one of the NDP's most vocal members as the party's health critic.

Re-elected in the constituency of Saskatoon Broadway in 1991, Atkinson was soon appointed to cabinet as minister of Social Services in 1992. A year later she was appointed minister of Education, holding that post for the next five years where she oversaw several important reforms. The Community School program was expanded and she introduced a pre-kindergarten program for children at risk and restructured the school divisions.

Having earned a reputation as a tough, forceful and skilled minister, Atkinson was moved into the department of Health in 1998, where she dealt with the increasing strife

SASKATCHEWAN NDP PHOTO ARCHIVES

PAT ATKINSON

between the health sector unions and government over wage demands. The situation deteriorated in 1999 when the nurse's union went on strike and defied back-to-work legislation. Re-elected in 1999, she remained minister of Health until February 2001 when she was appointed minister of Highways and Transportation in the first Calvert cabinet.

Atkinson left cabinet in October 2001, but returned in 2003 as minister of the Crown Management Board after she was successfully re-elected in Saskatoon Nutana.

BRETT QUIRING

## AXWORTHY, CHRISTOPHER (b. 1947).

Chris Axworthy was a prominent New Democrat MLA, MP, provincial Justice Minister and contender for the leadership of the Saskatchewan NDP, who left the party to seek office for the federal Liberals.

Axworthy was born in Plymouth, England, on March 10, 1947. Educated at City of London College, Axworthy came to Canada in 1970 to study law at McGill University. Earning a Masters of Law, he began his career teaching at the University of New Brunswick and later at Dalhousie. In 1984, Axworthy came to Saskatoon to teach law at the University of Saskatchewan and to serve as the first executive director of the University of Saskatchewan's Centre for the Study of Co-operatives.

First contesting public office in 1988, Axworthy ran for the New Democrats in the federal riding of Saskatoon Clark's Crossing. Easily elected, he served his caucus as critic of Health, Post-secondary Education, Justice and Industry and as deputy House Leader from 1990 to 1992. Narrowly re-elected in 1993, Axworthy was one of only nine NDP MPs to be elected that year. In 1995, he initially campaigned for the leadership of the federal NDP but withdrew from the campaign after it became clear he would be unsuccessful.

Re-elected in 1997 in the new riding of Saskatoon Rosetown-Biggar, Axworthy did not serve out the entire term, resigning in April 1999 to enter provincial politics. Contesting the 1999 by-election in Saskatoon Fairview, Axworthy easily won. Winning in the general election a few months later, Axworthy was immediately appointed to cabinet as minister of Justice and Aboriginal Affairs. After Premier Romanow resigned as NDP leader in 2000, Axworthy was considered an early front runner to replace him. Campaigning on the right wing of the party, Axworthy was unable to overcome the early lead of Lorne Calvert, who defeated Axworthy on the fourth ballot of the leadership vote.

Axworthy remained in cabinet as minister of Justice taking on both the Intergovernmental and Aboriginal Affairs portfolios for a period. He resigned his seat in the legislature in 2002 to return to teaching at the University of Saskatchewan. However, he returned to politics in 2004 to run for the Liberals in Saskatoon-Wanuskewin, but lost.

SASKATCHEWAN NDP PHOTO ARCHIVES

CHRIS AXWORTHY

BRETT QUIRING

## BAKER, HENRY HAROLD PETER (1915–2004).

Henry Baker was the longest serving mayor of Regina and represented the city in the Saskatchewan Legislature for eighteen years.

HENRY BAKER

Born in Lipton on November 24, 1915, Baker was educated in the Lipton and Regina school systems. After high school, he enrolled in the Regina Teachers' College and began teaching in 1934 until the outbreak of the Second World War. Joining the Royal Canadian Air Force, he served two years training Commonwealth aircrews. After completing a business course in Chicago, Baker was appointed secretary of the Saskatchewan Public Service Commission in 1944.

Baker first ran for public office in 1955 when he was elected to Regina City Council. Serving one term on council, Baker ran for mayor three years later and was elected. Baker was re-elected as mayor for the next three terms until 1970 when he was defeated by Harry Walker.

Active in the CCF, Baker first contested the CCF nomination in the constituency of Regina in 1960 but was defeated. Running for nomination again in 1964, Baker was successful in the multi-member constituency of Regina East. Narrowly elected in 1964, Baker was re-elected four more times until 1982.

In 1973, Baker ran for mayor again and recaptured his old post. He was re-elected mayor once more in 1976. During his tenure as mayor, Regina undertook several major projects such as the construction of the Ring Road, the Centre of the Arts and the new City Hall. However, Baker's relationship with council was sometimes difficult. Many councillors were critical of Baker's election as both mayor and an MLA arguing he could not do either job effectively. However, Baker argued that being elected to the legislature allowed him to better represent and more effectively lobby on Regina's behalf.

Baker ran in the 1982 election in the constituency of Regina Victoria but was defeated, ending his twenty-seven year career representing Regina. In 1997, the City of Regina re-named the city council chamber in his honour.

Henry Baker passed away in Regina on March 4, 2004.

BRETT QUIRING

## BAKER, WILLIAM GEORGE (1885–1960).

Long-time MLA for Moose Jaw, William Baker was the first member of the Saskatchewan legislature elected as a Labour representative.

William Baker was born in Owen Sound, Ontario on January 16, 1885, and was educated in the town. Baker came to Saskatchewan in 1906 to work as a brakeman for the Canadian Pacific Railroad (CPR) in Moose Jaw. Later promoted to the position of conductor, Baker became heavily involved in the labour movement. From 1910 to 1921 he was the chairman of the local committee of the Brotherhood of Railroad Trainmen and in 1916 was elected vice-chairman of the General Committee of Trainmen of the CPR Western Lines. An advocate for labour's entry into politics, he founded the Labor Representation League and was president of the organization from 1915 to 1917.

Baker first contested the provincial constituency of Moose Jaw in 1917 but finished third behind both established parties.

Contesting the seat in a 1918 by-election, Baker was again defeated, but he improved his standing significantly when the Conservatives chose not to field a candidate. Again contesting the seat of Moose Jaw in 1921, he was elected. His election was bolstered by the Conservatives only nominating one candidate in the new dual member constituency. During his term, Baker worked closely with the Liberal government and chose to contest the 1925 election as an official Liberal candidate running under the Labor-Liberal banner. Easily topping the ballot in 1925, Baker was a victim of the growing unpopularity of the Liberal government in 1929 when he was defeated by the Conservatives by a mere twenty-eight votes.

Baker attempted to regain his seat in the legislature in 1934, once again running as a Labor candidate. However, Baker finished poorly behind the Liberal, Conservative and newly-formed Farmer–Labor Party. In 1938, Baker again ran in Moose Jaw, this time as Liberal, and was easily elected. In 1944, Baker's political career came to an end as the CCF swept to office. Many of the labour activists had changed their political allegiance and Baker's ties to the Liberal Party became a major liability as he was defeated by Dempster Heming, a trade unionist and railroader, who had previously been an influential supporter.

Baker retired from politics and lived in Moose Jaw until his death on April 9, 1960.

BRETT QUIRING

## BALFOUR, (REGINALD) JAMES (1928–1999).

James Balfour was born on May 22, 1928, to a prestigious legal family in Regina. His grandfather, James Balfour, was a prominent lawyer, sometime School Board trustee and Mayor of Regina, while his father, Reginald M. Balfour, would be appointed to the Saskatchewan Court of Queen's Bench. Balfour was educated in the Regina Public School system and at Luther College in Regina before receiving his law degree from the University of Saskatchewan. In 1952 he joined his grandfather's law practice in Regina.

Balfour was first elected to the House of Commons in 1972 as a Progressive Conservative representing the riding of Regina East and was subsequently re-elected in 1974. Not an outgoing man by nature, he did not thrive in the cut-and-thrust environment of political debate, but instead invested his energies in obscure parliamentary committees and in developing Progressive Conservative party policy. After announcing he would not seek re-election due to health problems, newly elected Conservative leader, Joe Clark, appointed Balfour to chair the platform committee of the party. The committee mapped out the plan of action program for the short-lived Clark government that was elected in 1979. As a reward for his efforts, Clark appointed Balfour to the Senate in September 1979. Balfour remained in the Senate for over twenty years until his death on December 12, 1999.

BRETT QUIRING

## BARRIE, (JAMES) ROSS (1903–1976).

J. Ross Barrie served as Saskatchewan's minister of Natural Resources, and was briefly in charge of the Saskatchewan Indian and Métis Branch in Ross Thatcher's provincial government.

Ross Barrie was born on August 14, 1903, in Morden, Manitoba. After receiving his education in Manitoba and Vancouver, Barrie became a hardware merchant in Kamsack, Saskatchewan. He first entered politics in 1940 when he ran unsuccessfully to represent the Mackenzie riding in the federal election.

ROSS BARRIE

In the 1956 Saskatchewan election, the Pelly constituency elected Ross Barrie to be its Member of the Legislative Assembly. During Barrie's first term in the legislature, he was quite active in the Liberal Party. During the 1959 Liberal leadership race that brought Ross Thatcher to the head of the party, Barrie supported Alexander Cameron in his unsuccessful bid for leadership. Ross Barrie was re-elected in the 1960 general election, but was defeated by the CCF candidate Leonard Larson in 1964. Barrie won back his seat in 1967. At the end of that year, Ross Thatcher appointed him the minister of Natural Resources, and put him in charge of the Saskatchewan Indian and Métis Branch. In both these portfolios, Barrie replaced Dave Steuart, the deputy premier who had just been appointed provincial treasurer. At that same time, Ross Barrie also became the chairman of the Wascana Centre Authority.

As Natural Resources minister, Ross Barrie was also supposed to discover why the Liberal Party lacked support in Northern Saskatchewan, making the North a priority. Ross Thatcher claimed that he chose Barrie as minister of Natural Resources and the Saskatchewan Indian and Métis Branch because the cabinet minister lived in Kamsack, Saskatchewan. Kamsack is near four First Nations reserves, and Thatcher believed that the ministers in charge of both those departments ought to have personal experience with First Nations people and the issues related to them. Barrie was in charge of the Indian and Métis Branch from 1968 to 1969, and during that year he helped to create jobs, especially in the North.

Ross Barrie did not want to seek re-election in the 1971 election, but Ross Thatcher convinced him to run again. Barrie lost that election, again to Leonard Larson. Nearly sixty-eight years old, Ross Barrie left provincial politics after the 1971 election. He died five years later, in November of 1976.

MARYANNE COTCHER, UNIVERSITY OF REGINA

## BASTEDO, FRANK LINDSAY (1886–1973).

Born in Bracebridge, Ontario, in 1886, Frank Bastedo received his law degree from the University of Toronto in 1909. In 1911 he moved to Saskatchewan to join a Regina law firm. He was appointed King's Counsel in 1927 and argued cases before the Supreme Court of Canada and the Judicial Committee of the Privy Council in London. He served as president of the Regina federal Progressive Conservative Association from 1921 to 1924, but twice declined to stand for nomination in the constituency.

Frank Bastedo was appointed eleventh Lieutenant-Governor

FRANK BASTEDO

of Saskatchewan in 1958 by the federal government of John Diefenbaker. He placed great emphasis on the dignity of the office, going against the trend of reduced formality since the closure of Government House in 1945.

On April 8, 1961, during the CCF administration of Woodrow Lloyd, Frank Bastedo made history by reserving royal assent for the Governor General on Bill 56, The Alteration of Certain Mineral Contracts, because he had doubts about its validity and whether it was in the public interest—the first case of reservation in Canada since 1937, the only example in the history of the province, and the last in the country. Mr. Bastedo had not consulted the federal government, and the Diefenbaker government passed an order-in-council giving the legislation royal assent. The incident resulted in cool relations between the Lieutenant-Governor and the CCF/NDP for the next two decades.

MICHAEL JACKSON, REGINA

FURTHER READING: Eager, Evelyn. 1980. *Saskatchewan Government: Politics and Pragmatism.* Saskatoon: Western Producer Prairie Books. • Hryniuk, Margaret, and Garth Pugh. 1991. *"A Tower of Attraction": An Illustrated History of Government House, Regina, Saskatchewan.* Regina: Government House Historical Society/Canadian Plains Research Center. • Leeson, Howard A. (ed.) 2001. *Saskatchewan Politics: Into the Twenty-first Century.* Regina: Canadian Plains Research Center.

**BATTEN, MARY JOHN** (née Fodchuk) (b. 1921). As one of the earliest women elected to the legislature and as one of the first female judges in the province, Mary Batten was instrumental in helping to remove barriers to women in society's highest public offices.

Born August 30, 1921, in Sifton, Manitoba, Batten was educated in Saskatchewan in Calder, Ituna, and Regina. Attending the University of Saskatchewan she earned degrees in both arts and law. Articling under future prime minister John Diefenbaker, she was accepted to the Saskatchewan bar in 1945. Settling in Humboldt, Batten became involved in a variety of community organizations.

Interested in politics, Batten first ran in 1956 in the constituency of Humboldt for the Liberals. She was successful, narrowly defeating CCF cabinet minister Joseph Burton. As the Liberals' only elected lawyer, Batten served in the high-profile

WEST'S STUDIO, REGINA•SAB R-A 10,442

MARY BATTEN

position of Justice critic. A vocal critic of party leader Hammy Macdonald, Batten was instrumental in precipitating Macdonald's resignation, which led to the leadership convention that elected Ross Thatcher.

Re-elected with a large majority in 1960, Batten served out the term before being appointed to the Court of Queen's Bench. At the time, she was only the second woman ever appointed to the court. In the sixties she chaired two provincial royal commissions, the first in 1966 on accounting practices, and the second in 1968 on the cost of living.

In 1983, Batten was appointed Chief Justice of the Court of Queen's Bench, the first female chief justice in Saskatchewan history. Batten remained on the bench until her retirement from the court in 1990, having spent twenty-six years as a judge.

BRETT QUIRING

**BEECHING, WILLIAM** (1913–1990). Journalist, author, and Communist leader William Beeching was born in Regina on June 22, 1913. He died January 4, 1990, also at Regina.

Bill Beeching became active in radical working-class politics during the Great Depression of the 1930s. He embraced the ideas of socialism and joined the Communist Party which he represented in the Youth Congress movement. When the Spanish Civil War erupted in 1936, Beeching was one of the 1,440 young Canadians who volunteered to fight Franco fascism by joining the International Brigades. He served throughout the conflict as a scout, first in the US Abraham Lincoln Brigade and later in the Canadian MacKenzie-Papineau Battalion.

Following his return to Canada in 1939 Beeching became the Saskatchewan Organizer for the Communist Party of Canada. At the outbreak of the Second World War in 1939, the federal government banned the Communist Party and interned many of its leaders, including Bill Beeching. A public outcry prompted the release of the Communist internees upon which Beeching and many of the others joined the Canadian Armed Forces to fight Hitler fascism.

After his discharge from the Canadian Army in 1945, he was re-elected as the provincial organizer of the Communist Party. In 1957, he was elected provincial leader, a post which he held until 1969. During his term as provincial leader, Beeching stood for election to all levels of government and authored numerous articles, tracts and leaflets. He presented briefs to government and was a familiar speaker at public meetings. In 1969 Beeching was elected to the Central Executive Committee of the Communist Party and appointed editor of the *Canadian Tribune*, the party's national newspaper.

During the *War Measures Act* crisis of October 1970, sharp differences over the party's relationships with other forces on the political left arose within the party leadership.

As a result Beeching and several other members of the Central Executive Committee resigned their positions. Beeching returned to Saskatchewan and in 1971 was re-elected provincial leader. Tim Buck, national chairman and former general sectretary of the Communist Party, asked Beeching to edit Buck's biography, which he did in defiance of the party's leadership. As a result, Bill Beeching was expelled from the party in 1978 but the book, *Yours in Struggle*, was published in 1977.

After his expulsion in 1978 the majority of party members in Saskatchewan quit the party and, with the support of other dissident communists across the country, formed the Committee of Canadian Communists (CCC) under Beeching's leadership. Beeching continued to champion the cause of socialism in the province as chairman of the CCC and editor of its newsletter *Focus on Socialism*. During the 1980s Beeching wrote the official memoir of the MacKenzie-Papineau Battalion which was published under the title *Canadian Volunteers in Spain 1936–1939* (Canadian Plains Research Center, 1989). Bill Beeching remained politically active until his death in January 1990.

DAVID GEHL, INDIAN HEAD

**BELANGER, BUCKLEY** (b. 1960). Early in the new millennium, Buckley Belanger stands out as a northern and Métis politician in the Saskatchewan political scene. After a controversial jump from the Liberal Party to the New Democratic Party (NDP), he distinguished himself as a trusted member of the Roy Romanow and Lorne Calvert cabinets. In various positions, he has acted as a powerful spokesman for northerners and aboriginals.

Belanger was born on March 21, 1960, at

Île-à-la-Crosse to Lena Ahenakew and Leo Joseph Belanger. On August 10, 1985, he married Rebecca Pederson. They have three children: Michelle, Kellie, and Taylor.

Success also accompanied Belanger's efforts prior to entering provincial politics. From 1980 to 1995, he pursued a variety of vocational and community interests. These included writing for the aboriginal publication *New Breed*, editing the Île-à-la-Crosse newspaper, and varied roles at Missinipi Broadcasting Corporation. Importantly, he helped a dozen northern communities establish radio and television broadcast facilities. Belanger also became president of his own company, Belanger Communications, and a finalist for the ABEX Business Award. An interest in northern government also grew. From 1988 to 1995, Belanger served three terms as mayor of Ile a la Crosse. He also sat on the board of the Saskatchewan Urban Municipalities Association and chaired the Northwest Saskatchewan Municipal Association.

Belanger's first election to the Saskatchewan Legislature took place in the 1995 general election as a Liberal member for the Athabasca riding. A New Democrat at heart, he resigned the seat and his membership in the Liberal Party on September 2, 1998. While other politicians also have "crossed the floor," few immediately resigned their seat and returned to the electorate for approval of their action. Belanger did so. In the by-election of October 26, 1998, Belanger won Athabasca for the NDP. He again won the same riding for his party in the next general election on September 16, 1999. Belanger joined Roy Romanow's cabinet as the minister

BUCKLEY BELANGER

of the Environment and Resource Management and associate minister for Intergovernmental and Aboriginal Affairs. He held the latter job until February 2001. While continuing as minister of the Environment and Resource Management, beginning in October 2001, he also served as the minister of Northern Affairs in the Lorne Calvert government. His responsibilities expanded further when he became minister of SaskWater in March 2002. In June 2002, Calvert reappointed Belanger as minister for the Environment and Northern Affairs portfolios. Belanger was re-elected in 2003 and continued his role in cabinet as minister of Northern Affairs.

As one of the first aboriginal northerners to hold office in the provincial government, Belanger's political career holds considerable significance. Given the breadth of his knowledge and experience, he has brought valuable insights to designing and implementing northern, environmental, and aboriginal programs. His position as minister responsible for key departments has allowed him to make a difference in the region of his birth.

DAVID QUIRING, UNIVERSITY OF SASKATCHEWAN

**BELL, GEORGE ALEXANDER** (1856–1927). As provincial treasurer and minister of Telephones, George Bell implemented many programs that helped build the basic telephone infrastructure of the province, particularly the early telephone network in rural Saskatchewan.

Born in Brant, Canada West, on August 3, 1856, he was educated in Huron County and apprenticed as a blacksmith shortly after completing school. He moved out west in

1882 to work as a blacksmith for the Canadian Pacific Railroad in Winnipeg. Although only working there for a couple years, he remained in Manitoba and established a blacksmithing shop in Melita. Bell first came to Saskatchewan in 1900 when he was hired as an inspector for the Dominion Lands office in the Estevan district, a position he held until deciding to enter politics.

A life-long Liberal and an ardent advocate for free-trade policies, Bell first contested the constituency of Estevan for the Liberals in the 1908 general election. Spending his first term as a government backbencher, he was re-elected in 1912 and was appointed to cabinet as Provincial Treasurer and six months later as minister of Telephones. As provincial treasurer, Bell continued the policies of his predecessors by not funding lavish economic development projects, which helped Saskatchewan emerge from the first world war in significantly better financial shape than either of the other prairie provinces.

As minister of Telephones, Bell attempted to expand telephone service in rural areas with the help of the government. The government provided local telephone companies, usually not-for-profit companies, with free telephone poles and, later, loans to help facilitate the construction of the lines. This policy led to an explosion of local telephone companies across the province.

An early advocate for the establishment of large-scale power facilities to make use of the Estevan lignite coalfields, Bell helped convince government to enact several investigations into the possibility of exploitation of the resource. Partly as a result of public pressure created by

SAB R-A 248

GEORGE BELL

Bell, interest in the fields increased and with the outbreak of the First World War large-scale private mining began.

In October, 1916, he resigned as provincial treasurer, but remained in the telephone portfolio. Re-elected in 1917, Bell spent one more year in the legislature and resigned his seat in 1918. Later that year Bell was appointed chairman of the Local Government Board, which oversaw the activities of Saskatchewan's municipal governments, a position held until 1926. In retirement Bell was active in the Anti-Tuberculosis League, serving as a director of the organization and as governor of the provincial sanatorium in Fort Qu'Appelle. He died in Regina on September 13, 1927.

BRETT QUIRING

## BENJAMIN, LESLIE GORDON (1925–2003).

Les Benjamin was one of Saskatchewan's most able representatives in the House of Commons. During his twenty-five-year tenure as a New Democratic Party member of Parliament for various Regina ridings, "Boxcar Benjamin" was on the Commons Transport Committee and was outspoken on the subject of grain transportation.

Leslie Gordon Benjamin was born on April 29, 1925, in Medicine Hat, Alberta. He was raised in southwestern Saskatchewan and southeastern Alberta. Benjamin enlisted in the air force during World War II, but the war was over before Benjamin's training was completed. He spent much of his time in the armed forces fixing the Alaskan Highway after the United States Army surrendered control to the Canadian government. After his military service, he worked for the CPR as a telegrapher, station agent and manager. In 1951, he became involved with the political party then called the Cooperative Commonwealth Federation. His early experiences working for the CPR inspired him to become a democratic socialist, he would later say. Benjamin made two unsuccessful runs for provincial office in the riding of Maple Creek, but his lack of initial political success did not dampen his enthusiasm. By 1961 he had become the provincial secretary for the New Democratic Party, a position he held until 1968.

That year, Benjamin ran for federal office in the riding of Regina–Lake Centre. He finally won, beginning a twenty-five-year political career. Over those years, Benjamin represented Regina–Lake Centre, Regina West, and Regina–Lumsden. While in the House of Commons, Benjamin worked on the transportation committee. This was a perfect fit for Benjamin in so many ways: he was a former railroad employee himself who was representing a city that essentially would not have existed without the railroad, in a province that was heavily dependent on the railroad for grain transportation. He resigned from his seat in 1993.

Benjamin was married twice: in 1950 to Marjorie Kathleen McKinnon (Kay), and then to Constance Freisen in 1976. He had three children and two stepchildren. Les Benjamin lost his battle with cancer on June 16, 2003.

DANA TURGEON

**SOURCE:** Benjamin, Les, and James Warren. 1997. *Rolling in the Grass Roots.* Ottawa: Doculink International.

## BENSON, JACOB ("JAKE") (1892–1987).

Jake Benson was born March 13, 1892, in Cumberland, England, and immigrated to Canada with his parents in 1903, homesteading near Last Mountain Lake. Benson attended the University of Saskatchewan for three years but left before completing his studies to begin farming, eventually settling down on a farm near Semans. Benson became active in various farm organizations, such as the Saskatchewan Grain Growers Association (SGGA), and canvassed his township convincing farmers to sign contracts in order to establish the Saskatchewan Wheat Pool. Through his involvement in the farmers' movement, Benson became involved in the Progressive Party. He actively campaigned for the federal Progressives in 1921 and, in 1925 and 1926 he managed the Progressive campaign in the Last Mountain riding. In 1929 he was elected to the Saskatchewan legislature for Last Mountain, defeating prominent Liberal cabinet minister Samuel Latta. Upon election Benson was the only Progressive not to join J. T. M. Anderson's Co-operative government, although throughout the term he gave the government his support.

Benson followed the SGGA successor, the United Farmers of Canada, into politics when it affiliated with the CCF. In 1934 he was narrowly defeated and later unsuccessfully contested the federal riding of Yorkton for the CCF. During this campaign he was publicly endorsed by a group of Social Credit supporters disillusioned with their party's choice of candidate. After the election, party officials mistakenly chastised him for accepting a

SAB R-A 664-2

JAKE BENSON

Social Credit nomination and discussed revoking his party membership. After some hard feelings, the incident was cleared up and Benson again contested the Last Mountain constituency for the CCF in 1938 and was elected. Benson was re-elected in 1944 and 1948, but the relationship between Benson and senior members of the CCF government continued to deteriorate. Always skeptical of party discipline, Benson voted against the government on a number of issues and in 1950 left the CCF to sit as an independent. He contested the 1952 election as an independent but was beaten by the CCF candidate, Russ Brown. Benson continued to farm until 1964 when he retired to Victoria where he died in 1987.

BRETT QUIRING

**BENTLEY, THOMAS J.** (1891–1983). Thomas John Bentley was born in Dartmouth, Nova Scotia, in 1891. He received his education from the Dartmouth public school, the Acadia Villa Boarding School, and the McDonalds Consolidated High School of Middleton, in the Annapolis Valley. After high school he spent two years in Labrador working with the Grand River Pulp and Lumber Company. In 1907 Bentley moved west where he worked in logging camps and on railroad bridge construction. In 1914 he married Nora Chabot. Early in 1915 he was sent overseas with the 66th Battalion from Edmonton. During his tour of duty he received the Distinguished Conduct Medal. Upon his return to Canada he settled in the Preeceville area to farm.

Like many farmers, Bentley quickly became frustrated with the tariffs, low wheat prices, and high freight rates of the period. In response, he became a member of the Saskatchewan Grain Growers Association, and was active in the formation of the local Farmers Union and the United Farmers of Canada, as well as the Saskatchewan Wheat Pool. Bentley was also a supporter of the Saskatchewan Progressive Party, which eventually led to his involvement with the Cooperative Commonwealth Federation (CCF).

By 1926, Bentley had quit farming and was working as an elevator operator with the Wheat Pool. In 1932 he was appointed to the field staff, headquartered first out of Canora and then Swift Current. In 1944 he resigned from his position with the Wheat Pool and began his career as a politician. He was first elected CCF MP for Swift Current in 1945. Bentley served in this capacity until 1949 when he was defeated. His time out of politics was short-lived. In November of that same year he was elected CCF MLA in a by-election for Gull Lake. Bentley would successfully run in the next two provincial elections, finally retiring in 1960.

WEST'S STUDIO, REGINA•SAB R-A 5349-1
THOMAS BENTLEY

During his time in the legislature, Bentley served as minister of Health from 1949 to 1956 and as minister of Social Welfare and Reconstruction from 1956 to 1960. During his career, he expanded many of the programs introduced by T.C. Douglas during his stint as the head of the Department of Health. These included a Saskatchewan hospital services plan, which by 1954 covered 96 percent of the population, free cancer treatment, and an extension of public health nursing services. Bentley is solely responsible for launching the construction of the Moose Jaw training school and the University Hospital, as well as the widespread distribution of Salk polio vaccine in the province.

DWAYNE YASINOWSKI

## BEREZOWSKY, WILLIAM

(1903–1974). Born in western Ukraine on January 5, 1903, Bill Berezowsky immigrated to Canada with his parents in 1908. After spending several years in Winnipeg, Berezowsky's parents homesteaded near Prince Albert. After completing his education in Prince Albert, Berezowsky earned a teaching certificate from the Saskatoon Normal School, and began teaching in number of small

WEST'S STUDIO, REGINA•SAB R-A 8409

WILLIAM BEREZOWSKY

towns around Prince Albert. During his summer breaks he tried his hand at fur trapping and prospecting in the Churchill River Basin. Berezowsky quit teaching in 1927 when he was appointed secretary of the Rural Municipality of Garden River and began farming. Active in his community of Meath Park, he was instrumental in establishing the Greek Orthodox parish in the area and was also active in several co-operative organizations.

Berezowsky became involved in the CCF in 1940, and in 1952 contested the party nomination for the constituency of Cumberland, winning by a single vote. In the 1952 campaign he narrowly defeated the Liberal incumbent. He was re-elected in 1956 and 1960 with increasing margins. During his time in government, Berezowsky developed a reputation as a powerful and forceful speaker. He was a constant advocate for the north and was the government caucus expert on First Nations peoples with whom he had close contact and developed good relationships during his prospecting days.

Re-elected in 1964, he held many key critique duties for the Opposition. Re-elected for the last time in 1967, representing the new constituency of Prince Albert East-Cumberland, Berezowsky took a backseat role in the Opposition, as leader, Woodrow Lloyd, promoted several new young MLAs. It was a move which greatly upset Berezowsky. He retired from the legislature in 1971, but contested the federal riding of Prince Albert in 1972 at which time he was badly beaten by incumbent John Diefenbaker. On January 18, 1974, Berezowsky died at his home.

BRETT QUIRING

## BERNTSON, ERIC ARTHUR (b. 1941).

Eric Arthur Berntson was one of the most formidable members of the Progressive Conservative government of Grant Devine during the 1980s.

Born in Oxbow on May 16, 1941, Berntson quit school in grade nine, but later completed high school in Halifax in order to join the armed forces. He served with the Canadian Navy and Canadian Air Force for eight years. When he left the armed forces he moved to Calgary, where he worked nights in electronic data processing for National Cash Register. He attended university during the day, taking classes in pre-law, pre-medicine, and political science, but he never did finish a degree. He eventually returned to Saskatchewan and began farming near Carievale, a small town in the southeastern part of the province.

Eric Berntson was first elected to the Saskatchewan legislature in the traditionally Conservative rural constituency of Souris-Cannington in 1975, and again in 1978, 1982, and 1986. He was deputy premier and government House Leader from May 1982 until October 1989; minister of Agriculture from May 1982 until July 1983; minister of Economic Development and Trade from July 1983 until December 1985; and minister of Economic Development and Tourism from October 1989 to March 1990. He served on the boards of most Crown corporations during his term in government.

SAB R-PS 82-612-33

ERIC BERNTSON

Berntson resigned his seat in the provincial government on July 19, 1990. On September 27, 1990, he was summoned to the Senate by Brian Mulroney. He was one of Mulroney's "GST senators," added to the Senate to ensure the Goods and Services Tax became law. In January 1994 he was appointed deputy leader of the Opposition in the Senate.

In January 1997, Berntson was charged with several counts of fraud. He was the most prominent of all the Tories charged in "Project Fiddle," the name given the RCMP investigation into the misuse of public money by members of Grant Devine's Conservative government. Berntson was also charged with breach of trust.

Eric Berntson was found guilty of stealing $41,735 through the use of false claims on his Constituency Secretarial and Constituency Office and Services Allowances while he was an MLA. He was acquitted on the charge of committing a breach of trust, and fraud allegations involving another MLA allowance were dismissed.

On March 15, 1999, Eric Berntson, in an emotional address to the court during his sentencing, said: "After thirty years of serving my country and my province with hard work and dedication, this conviction forever will be on the Berntson name. Again, my lord, I apologize."

Berntson was sentenced to a year in jail and ordered to pay full restitution. The Saskatchewan Court of Appeal upheld the conviction. His appeal to the Supreme Court of Canada was dismissed. Eric Berntson resigned his seat in the Senate in February 2001.

GERRY JONES

**BJORNERUD, BOB** (b. 1945). Bob Bjornerud, Saskatchewan Party MLA for Saltcoats, was born in Kelvington on September 8, 1945. Bjornerud's parents moved to Saltcoats in 1948, where Bjornerud completed his education. Bjornerud is married to Patricia and together they have three children: Grant, Garnet and Jodi.

Bjornerud began his career in mining with International Minerals and Chemicals in Esterhazy. Following this, he made the decision to farm near Saltcoats in 1974.

Bjornerud's political career began in 1995 when he was elected as a Liberal to the provincial legislature to represent the Saltcoats constituency, winning the large, rural seat by less than 500 votes. In 1997, Bjornerud, along with three fellow Liberal MLAs, defected to join forces with Conservative caucus members to form the Saskatchewan Party, allowing it to become the Official Opposition. Calls from angry constituents for a by-election led Bjornerud and his colleagues to offer to resign if half of the eligible voters in their respective constituencies signed a recall petition, but that never materialized. Rather, Bjornerud maintained his MLA status for the Saskatchewan Party, and has since served as the party Agriculture critic, Municipal Affairs critic and Opposition whip.

In March 2003, Bjornerud was defeated at a nomination meeting in his riding that attracted over 1,000 people, losing out to Grant Schmidt, a former cabinet minister in Grant Devine's Conservative government. The nomination did not hold, however, as Grant's alleged "off-the-cuff" style as a former minister led him to be seen as a liability by the Saskatchewan Party executive council, who voted 44 to 11 to overturn his nomination just five days later. Schmidt appealed but failed to convince the council to reverse the decision, and the vote was upheld by a count of 43 to 10. Schmidt later announced he would run as an independent in the next provincial election for the Melville-Saltcoats constituency. Bjornerud later won the controversial Saskatchewan Party nomination by acclamation, being the only incumbent MLA to seek the job. In 2003, Bjornerud defeated both Schmidt and NDP candidate Ron Osika and was elected in Melville-Saltcoats.

WINTER FEDYK, KINGSTON, ON

**BLAKENEY, ALLAN EMRYS** (b. 1925). Allan Emrys Blakeney was premier of Saskatchewan between 1971 and 1982. Born in Bridgewater, Nova Scotia, on September 7, 1925, he was a gold medalist in law school at Dalhousie University in Halifax. He won a Rhodes Scholarship to Oxford University, where he studied economics, modern history, and philosophy.

Following his return to Canada, Blakeney went to work for the government of T. C. Douglas. He married Molly Schwartz in Halifax just prior to moving to Regina in 1950. She was to die suddenly in 1957, leaving Blakeney with two young children. He was remarried in 1959 to Anne Gorham, a friend from his university years, and they were to have two more children.

Blakeney occupied increasingly senior posts in the civil service, then in 1960 he won election as an MLA and was soon appointed to cabinet. In 1962, the CCF government introduced North America's first public, tax-financed health care system. Most doctors were opposed, and on July 1 they went on strike. Blakeney played a key role in the negotiations, and when the crisis ended after twenty-two tense days, he was appointed minister of Health with responsibility to get the new system up and working.

The Liberals replaced the CCF in 1964 and won again in 1967. Blakeney succeeded Woodrow Lloyd as NDP leader in 1970, defeating Roy Romanow and two other candidates. Premier Thatcher called an election for June 1971 and campaigned on his record. The NDP offered a detailed program, printed in a slim blue-on-white booklet called "New Deal for People," and on June 23 won forty-five of sixty seats with 55 percent of the popular vote.

Blakeney turned quickly to improving health and social programs—a dental program for children, a prescription drug program, subsidized housing, home care, and a guaranteed income supplement to improve the lot of the elderly poor.

The centerpiece of the agriculture program was a Land Bank, where the government purchased land, usually from older farmers, and leased it back to others, most often family members. The program attracted immediate interest, but it was difficult to administer and fraught with political controversy. The Opposition said that it was a plot to turn farmers into serfs, and used that theme in the 1975 provincial election in which the NDP vote tumbled by 15 percent.

By 1975, Blakeney had concluded that the key to diversification and prosperity lay in Saskatchewan's burgeoning mineral sector. Prices for oil, potash and uranium were rising dramatically, and Saskatchewan had plentiful supplies of each. He created new Crown corporations, such as SaskOil, that became vehicles for government to become a major player in resource development. When potash companies balked at paying increased royalties and refused to pay their taxes, Blakeney responded by buying out half of the industry and creating the Potash Corporation of Saskatchewan to operate the government's mines.

His development strategy paid off in growing prosperity, but despite Saskatchewan's relative affluence some people were being left behind. The tried and trusted social democratic approach of creating universal programs to meet broad social priorities was not suited, for example, to the emerging needs of Native people.

In its first term, the Blakeney government had created a separate department for northern Saskatchewan. Despite many tensions, there was progress in modernizing the north and creating some new jobs. But the majority of Native people lived in the south, and they were moving to the cities where they encountered poverty and discrimination.

Following the NDP's third electoral victory in 1978, Blakeney responded by creating

SAB R-A 23,088

ALLAN BLAKENEY

special programs aimed at Native people and focused mainly on the cities. There was an affirmative action plan for hiring in government, and an economic development corporation providing investment money to Native entrepreneurs and co-operatives.

The thrust in education was to train Native teachers and aides, to develop a curriculum more suitable to Native students, and to create community schools which fostered a closer relationship between parents and schools.

The employment programs were only modestly successful, but there were promising results in education, featuring the community schools and new, Native-controlled post-secondary institutions. The Saskatchewan Indian Federated College became a leader in Indian education, and the Métis operated Gabriel Dumont College.

On the national stage, Blakeney played a significant role in the constitutional debates of the 1980s. Prime Minister Trudeau made known his intention to bring Canada's constitution home from Great Britain, and to add to it a Charter of Rights. Blakeney was apprehensive about Trudeau's charter, which he believed would remove power from elected legislators and hand it to appointed judges. But he played a pivotal role in negotiating a compromise where provinces accepted a Charter of Rights, but one that could be overridden by elected legislatures.

Blakeney seemed poised in 1982 to win a fourth election. His was a clean and competent administration, and one that delivered an unbroken string of budget surpluses despite an activist government agenda.

The Conservatives replied that while the

government might be prosperous, individuals were hurting. Interest rates were at 20 percent; farmers were losing land, and consumers their homes. The Conservatives offered both lower taxes and more spending, a program that was popular but was later to almost bankrupt the province. The NDP suffered a humiliating defeat in 1982, retaining a mere eight seats in the legislature.

Blakeney felt he had an obligation to rebuild the party, and he led the NDP into the 1986 election, which the NDP lost despite receiving marginally more votes than the Conservatives. Blakeney resigned in 1987, and was replaced by Roy Romanow as leader.

Blakeney and his wife Anne then spent two years in Toronto, where he occupied the Bora Laskin Chair in Public Law at Osgoode Hall. They settled in Saskatoon upon their return to Saskatchewan. He accepted the Law Foundation Chair at the university, and then remained as a visiting scholar at the law college where he still keeps a modest office.

Blakeney has remained active, serving on numerous boards of directors and volunteer associations, but his most intense engagement has been with South Africa, where he helped to develop the structures for democratic government following the dismantling of apartheid.

Tommy Douglas, summarizing the contributions of his successor, said that Allan Blakeney proved that social democracy is a practical program and not just an impossible dream.

Blakeney brought to his task as premier an extraordinary mix of intellect, stamina and experience. He was a principled pragmatist, a decent, extremely capable man who provided good, honest and compassionate government, a most valuable contribution in any age.

DENNIS GRUENDING

**FURTHER READING:** Blakeney, Allan, and Sandford Borins. 1992. *Political Management in Canada*. Whitby, Ont: McGraw-Hill Ryerson. • Gruending, Dennis. 1990. *Promises to Keep: A Political Biography of Allan Blakeney*. Saskatoon: Western Producer Prairie Books.

## BOWERMAN, GEORGE REGINALD ANDERSON "TED" (b. 1930).

From the 1960s to the 1980s, Ted Bowerman played a major role as an NDP member of the legislative assembly in Regina. He became one of the highest profile members of the Allan Blakeney NDP government, in which he held several important positions.

Ted Bowerman was born on November 3, 1930, north of Shellbrook in the Rayside school district, to Laura Rosalee (née Anderson) and Edward LeRoy Bowerman. After completing grade eight in the local one-room school, he continued his education by taking correspondence courses and obtaining vocational training in agriculture and resource management. On February 14, 1959, Bowerman married Dagmar Alma Louise (née Christiansen). Their family included three children: Stephen George, Curtis Christin, and Mark Aaron.

Bowerman owned and operated the family farm from the time he was a young man. Since other activities often occupied him, hired managers carried out farm duties for many years. Beginning in the late 1940s, he spent eighteen years in the Saskatchewan public service. While employed by the Department of Natural Resources, Bowerman formed part of the province's early smoke-jumper group and worked with the province's commercial fishing industry. Under his supervision, the development of Kenosee Lake in Moose Mountain Provincial Park took place. For decades, involvement with the community occupied much of Ted's time. He chaired the first Prince Albert Community Health Clinic Board in 1962, during the time leading up to the introduction of medicare and the infamous doctors' strike.

Bowerman's involvement with CCF politics began early in his life. In 1945, he helped his father, Edward LeRoy Bowerman, succeed in his bid to defeat Liberal Prime Minister William Lyon Mackenzie King in the federal riding of Prince Albert. Ted Bowerman's own political career began in 1967 when he successfully contested the provincial Shellbrook constituency for the CCF. Although the federal CCF Party had already reorganized as the New Democratic Party, the provincial party still retained its CCF designation. His constituents re-elected Bowerman in 1971, 1975, and 1978 as an NDP member of the legislative assembly. He served continuously as an MLA until 1982, when he met defeat in the Devine Conservatives' surge to power. From 1971 to 1982, Bowerman held various positions in the Executive Council under Premier Allan Blakeney. His responsibilities included minister responsible for Indian and Métis from June 1971 to May 1972, minister of Mineral Resources from June 1971 to January 1972, minister of Northern Saskatchewan from May 1972 to December 1978, minister of Natural Resources from May 1972 to January 1974, and minister of Environment from December 1978 to 1982.

Blessed with great conviction, energy, and

PHOTO COURTESY TED BOWERMAN

TED BOWERMAN

talent, Ted Bowerman has left his mark on his community and the province of Saskatchewan. Throughout his lengthy and varied career, he earned the respect of supporters and opponents alike.

DAVID QUIRING, UNIVERSITY OF SASKATCHEWAN

**BOYD, BILL** (b. 1956). Bill Boyd was born on August 22, 1956, in Eston. He operates a farm in the Eston area, and is a welder by trade.

He was first elected as MLA for the Kindersley constituency in 1991, and was re-elected in both 1995 and 1999. Boyd became leader of the Progressive Conservative Party of Saskatchewan on November 20, 1994. Less than a year later his party suffered its worst electoral defeat in over twenty years, receiving 18 percent of the popular vote, and electing only five MLAs in the 58-seat legislature. In August 1997, Boyd helped broker a deal between the Progressive Conservative caucus and disaffected members of the Liberal caucus to form the Saskatchewan Party, a right-wing alternative to the governing New Democratic Party. The Saskatchewan Party stunned political observers by garnering 39.61 percent of the popular vote, and electing twenty-five MLAs to the legislature in 1999. Boyd was credited by many as a "driving force" behind the surprisingly quick electoral success of the Saskatchewan Party.

In the legislature, Boyd was a folksy populist, feisty orator, and a strong advocate for his constituency on issues pertaining to agriculture and small business. He held a rugged individualist's view of government. He outlined his views on government in a letter to members of the Progressive Conservative Party during the 1994 PC leadership campaign: "I believe in smaller government, less bureaucracy, less government spending, lower taxes, balanced budgets, eliminating patronage and an end to government handouts." Boyd stepped down as MLA for the Kindersley constituency on April 4, 2002.

JASON NYSTROM

**BRADLEY, JUDY LLEWELLYN** (née Bratt) (b. 1952). Born in Regina on October 18th, 1952, Judy Bradley grew up on the family farm in the Milestone/Gray areas. Ms. Bradley attended Milestone High School, and went on to earn a B.Sc. (Honours) and a B.Ed. (Great Distinction) from the University of Regina. She began her professional career in Regina teaching biology at Sheldon Williams Collegiate, and later returned to Milestone to teach elementary and special education. In 1973 she married Gary Bradley, a farmer and carpenter, with whom she has three children, Holly, Jesse, and Paula.

Judy Bradley was first elected to the Saskatchewan legislature to represent the constituency of Bengough-Milestone in the 1991 general election that saw the Roy Romanow NDP defeat the Grant Devine Tory government. She was re-elected in 1995 to represent the newly redistributed riding of Weyburn-Big Muddy.

On June 27, 1997, Bradley was appointed minister of Highways and Transportation as well as minister responsible for the Status of Women. As the first female minister of Transportation and Highways, Bradley steered the department through a tumultuous period. Road conditions became a major political issue, so the department implemented a policy of returning some minor highways to gravel roads. Ms. Bradley was also a strong advocate for bringing short-line railways to rural communities.

Judy Bradley was defeated in the 1999 provincial election that saw the NDP lose nearly all of their rural seats and led to the first minority government in seventy years. Upon defeat, she returned to Milestone and resumed her teaching career.

DEREK DE VLIEGER, OTTAWA

**BRADSHAW, JOHN ERNEST** (1866–1917). John E. Bradshaw, Member of the Legislative Assembly from 1908 to 1917, was born in Newport on the Isle of Wight on December 13, 1866. Educated at Chelmsford, Essex, he immigrated to Canada with his family as a teenager and worked first in his father's general store in Toronto and later as a bank clerk in Duluth, Minnesota. In 1891 he joined the Hudson's Bay Company, which appointed him manager of its branch in Prince Albert where he met and married his wife, Agnes Thompson, in 1894. They had five children together. After a short time, Bradshaw left the Company to go into business for himself and in 1900 established an insurance business in Prince Albert.

Always active in municipal politics he served as an alderman from 1895 to 1905 and became mayor of the city in 1906. A year later he ran unsuccessfully for the Provincial Rights (Conservative) Party of Sir Frederick Haultain at a by-election in Prince Albert, but defeated the sitting member, W. F. A. Turgeon, at the general election in 1908. He held on to the seat as a Conservative four years later and during his second term achieved a level of notoriety unusual for most Opposition backbenchers.

The two issues which brought him into the limelight were women's suffrage and corruption in government. He raised the question of votes for women in the legislature in 1912, for which he received the grateful thanks of Nellie McClung, and kept pressing it until the Scott government introduced enabling legislation in the 1916 session. In February of that year he turned to the corruption issue, accusing Liberal cabinet ministers and backbenchers of accepting bribes from provincial liquor interests who wanted to defeat prohibition and of diverting public funds from highway construction to pay party organizers. He demanded and won three Royal Commissions to investigate his charges and by the time they reported Premier Scott and four Liberal members had resigned, two others had been expelled from the legislature. Dramatic improvements had also been made in the accounting procedures of several departments, especially Highways.

Nevertheless, the scandals did not lead to the expected favourable results for the Conservative Party. In the election of 1917, Conservative representation at Regina dropped despite an increase in the number of seats in the Assembly, and Bradshaw himself went down to defeat in Prince Albert. It appears that nothing the provincial party did could offset its national counterpart's determination to introduce conscription. In this context, perhaps Bradshaw's recruitment of an infantry battalion during the war and his willingness to act as its colonel, admirable actions in some quarters, did him no good politically. He died suddenly on December 25, 1917, of a heart attack.

PATRICK KYBA, UNIVERSITY OF GUELPH

**SOURCES:** Smith, David E. 1998. *Dictionary of Canadian Biography.* s.v. "Bradshaw, John Ernest." Toronto: University of Toronto Press. • Saskatchewan Archives Board. J. E. Bradshaw Papers. A-35. Saskatoon. • Ward, N., and D. E. Smith. 1990. *Jimmy Gardiner: Relentless Liberal.* Toronto: University of Toronto Press.

## BREITKREUZ, GARRY W. (b. 1945).

Garry Breitkreuz was born in Yorkton on October 21, 1945. Raised in a farming community near Springside, Breitkreuz obtained a Bachelor of Education from the University of Saskatchewan and taught for twenty-four years prior to entering the political arena. His years as a teacher and principal took him to classrooms in Cameroon, on an Indian reserve in northern Saskatchewan, and in Malaita in the Solomon Islands.

Breitkreuz was elected to the House of Commons in October 1993 as Reform member for the riding of Yorkton-Melville in eastern Saskatchewan, and was re-elected in the 1997 and 2000 general elections first for the Canadian Alliance. Breitkreuz was appointed the Official Opposition's Deputy House Leader in January 2004, as well as the Official Opposition's Firearms and Property Rights Critic, and sat on the House of Commons' Procedure and House Affairs Standing Committee.

Breitkreuz served as deputy critic for Aboriginal Affairs; deputy critic to the Solicitor General; and critic for Unemployment Insurance. He served as the deputy whip of the Official Opposition between 2000 and 2003, with a four-month stint in between as chief Opposition whip.

He has been the vice chair of the Standing Committee on Procedure and House Affairs, and has served on a plethora of House of Commons standing committees, including Agriculture and Agri-Food, Justice and Human Rights, and Public Safety and Emergency Preparedness.

Throughout his years in office, Breitkreuz has been a vocal opponent of the Liberal government's firearms registration scheme. Breitkreuz publicly denounced the Firearms Act for what he claims to be an exorbitant and unnecessary public expense in support of privatization. A staunchly pro-life Member of Parliament, he has introduced a series of private member's motions in Parliament to protect the rights of unborn children, to better inform pregnant women, and for the adoption of a definition as to what constitutes a human being. In March 2004, Breitkreuz introduced Private Member's Motion M-560 calling for the government to create a new criminal code protecting unborn children in cases of violence against pregnant women.

TERESA WELSH, TORONTO

## BROCKELBANK, JOHN EDWARD (b. 1931).

Born February 23, 1931, in Tisdale, John Edward Brockelbank spent much of his early childhood in the Bjorkdale district. His father, John Hewgill Brockelbank, was elected to the legislature in 1938, and upon appointment to cabinet in 1944 the family moved to Regina. Completing his education in Regina, Brockelbank attended the Regina campus of the University of Saskatchewan for one year. In 1951, he accepted a position with the British American Oil Company as an instrument technician.

WEST'S STUDIO, REGINA•SAB R-A 8397

JOHN EDWARD BROCKELBANK

Moving to Saskatoon in 1952, Brockelbank was active in the labour movement, holding a variety of posts in his local of the Oil, Chemical and Atomic Workers International Union. Brockelbank was active in the co-operative movement, and served on the board of the Saskatoon Co-op and the Saskatoon Low Rental Housing Authority.

Brockelbank followed his father's path into politics in 1964 when he was elected in the multi-member seat of Saskatoon. Elected at age thirty-three, Brockelbank represented a new generation of CCF MLAs, whose formative political experience was not the depression. His young age placed him in a position of prominence within the CCF caucus anxious to recast itself after its defeat. Re-elected in 1967 in the constituency of Saskatoon-Mayfair, Brockelbank along with several other younger MLAs centered around Roy Romanow, were brought to the front bench and provided the bulk of the NDP's critique of the Thatcher government.

Re-elected in the Blakeney sweep in 1971, he chaired a committee that examined liquor regulations in Saskatchewan. The committee's recommendation led to the wide scale liberalization of the province's liquor laws. Brockelbank was appointed to cabinet in 1972 as minister of Public Works and minister of Government Services. When re-elected in 1975, Brockelbank left cabinet and became Speaker of the House where he remained until 1982. Re-elected again in 1978, Brockelbank was narrowly defeated in Grant Devine's sweep in 1982.

In the fall of 1982, Brockelbank re-entered politics with his election to Saskatoon city council. Serving one term on council, he returned to the legislature in 1986. Brockelbank served one last term in Opposition before retiring from the legislature in 1991.

BRETT QUIRING

## BROCKELBANK, JOHN HEWGILL (1897–1977).

John Brockelbank was instrumental in the formation of the CCF in Saskatchewan, and held several key cabinet posts in the Douglas and Lloyd administrations.

He was born on June 25, 1897, in Grey County, Ontario, moving west in 1911 with his parents, who homesteaded near North Battleford. In 1917 he enlisted in the Princess Patricia Canadian Light Infantry and served in France and Belgium. Upon returning to Canada he began farming near Bjorkdale.

During the 1920s, Brockelbank became active in several of Saskatchewan's various farmers' movements. It was through his involvement in the United Farmers of Canada (Saskatchewan Section) and in various co-operatives, that Brockelbank first became involved in the CCF. Along with Sandy Nicholson, he laid the foundation for the CCF organization in northeastern Saskatchewan. In 1938, he was elected to the legislature from the constituency of Tisdale and he would be re-elected in every election until his retirement in 1967. During his tenure in the legislature, Brockelbank developed a reputation as an accomplished parliamentarian, and because of his intimate knowledge of parliamentary procedure and rules, became the CCF's primary legislative tactician.

In 1941, when CCF leader George Williams enlisted in the military, Brockelbank became leader of the Opposition. Upon the CCF's victory in 1944, he was appointed to Douglas' first cabinet as minister of Municipal Affairs. After the 1948 election, he was appointed minister of Natural Resources, a post he held for fourteen years. During his time as minister, both the potash and oil

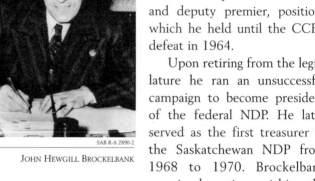

SAB R-A 2890-2

JOHN HEWGILL BROCKELBANK

industries of the province would begin significant growth. His tenure as minister marked the change in the CCF's focus away from government administered development of natural resources towards encouraging development by the private sector. In 1962, the new premier, Woodrow Lloyd, appointed Brockelbank provincial treasurer and deputy premier, positions which he held until the CCF's defeat in 1964.

Upon retiring from the legislature he ran an unsuccessful campaign to become president of the federal NDP. He later served as the first treasurer of the Saskatchewan NDP from 1968 to 1970. Brockelbank remained active within the NDP's organization until his death on May 30, 1977.

BRETT QUIRING

**SOURCES:** Saskatchewan Archives Board. John H. Brockelbank Papers. R-907. Regina. • Richards, John, and Larry Pratt. 1979. *Prairie Capitalism: Power and Influence in the New West*. Toronto: McClelland and Stewart.

**BROWN, ALLAN LISTER SAMUEL** (1917–1985). Long-time CCF MLA from Bengough, Allan Brown was born February 23, 1917, in Readlyn. He was educated in the local rural school before he attended the College of Agriculture at the University of Saskatchewan. He excelled, earning the University Medal upon graduation. Returning to the Readlyn area, Brown established a farm and became active in the local community. Before his first election to the Saskatchewan legislature, Brown served on a variety of community organizations. Particularly involved in the co-operative movement, he served as chairman of the local co-operative and as a director of the local credit union. He was also involved in the Saskatchewan Wheat Pool, and was elected a Wheat Pool delegate in 1941, serving until 1943.

SAB R-B 5445-24

ALLAN BROWN

Brown always had a keen interest in public affairs. He first became involved in politics at the age of sixteen when he joined the CCF's predecessor, the Farmer-Labor Party. Active in the party for the rest of his life, Brown was nominated as the CCF candidate in 1944 in the constituency of Bengough. At the age of twenty-seven, Brown was the youngest CCF candidate and was the second youngest MLA ever elected at the time. He was easily elected in the CCF sweep and was re-elected three more times, in 1948, 1952 and 1956, before retiring from politics in 1960. Although never holding a cabinet position, Brown was influential as an advocate for farm issues within the government. Brown was instrumental in convincing the government to establish crop insurance and was appointed the first chairmen of the Saskatchewan Crop Insurance Program. Brown died January 4, 1985.

BRETT QUIRING

**BROWN, RUSSEL** (1911–1971). Russ Brown was born in Fort William, Ontario, in 1911. His father was heavily involved in the Saskatchewan Wheat Pool and, after moving around the province extensively, the family eventually settled down in Chamberlain.

Prior to the Second World War, Brown worked as a grain buyer for the Wheat Pool and actively organized several co-operatives. He enlisted in the armed forces in 1941 and saw active service in northern Europe. After the war, he returned to Saskatchewan and was employed as an organizer and auditor of the Saskatchewan Department of Co-operation.

In 1948 he began his political career unsuccessfully contesting a seat on the council of the City of Regina for the Co-operative Labour League. In 1950 Brown was appointed provincial secretary of the Saskatchewan CCF and in 1952 was elected to the Saskatchewan legislature representing the constituency of Last Mountain. After his re-election in 1956, he was appointed to cabinet as minister of the Saskatchewan Power Corporation, and in 1957 took on the added responsibility of the Department of Industry and Information. Under his guidance, the Saskatchewan Power Corporation continued its expansion. Negotiations between the corporation and the City of Regina led to the sale of the city's power plant to the Saskatchewan Power Corporation in 1965.

After Brown narrowly lost his seat in the 1964 election, he was hired as the director of Organization for the federal NDP. After organizing the 1965 federal NDP election campaign he resigned, returning to Saskatchewan where he purchased the Empire Hotel in Estevan. In 1967 he ran an unsuccessful campaign for re-election to the legislature in the constituency of Souris–Estevan, but was subsequently successful in the 1971 campaign. Brown unfortunately passed away a couple of months after the 1971 election.

BRETT QUIRING

**BROWN, WALTER GEORGE** (1876–1940). Walter George Brown, born in 1876 in Huntingdon County, Quebec, attended the Presbyterian College in Montreal, where he obtained a Bachelor of Divinity in 1902. After serving as a missionary in the lumber camps of northern Ontario and mining towns of British Columbia, he accepted in 1907 a call from a Presbyterian congregation in Red Deer, Alberta. From there he went to Saskatoon in 1925 where he served as the highly effective and well-respected minister of St. Andrew's Presbyterian Church. With the advent of the Great Depression in 1930, Brown identified himself with the cause of the unemployed. He distributed assistance to the needy, intervened with the City Relief Officer on behalf of relief recipients, and gave speeches calling for a new social order based on the principles of Christianity and cooperation.

He stood as the candidate for the United Reform Movement in a federal by-election in Saskatoon held December 18, 1939. His platform was based on four main issues: monetary and fiscal reform, including "extensive coinage of silver" and "the financing of the war and social services with debt-free money"; extension of social benefits, such as old age pensions, unemployment insurance, and parity prices for farmers; elimination of patronage; and support for the war effort. The power of his personality and unimpeachable integrity brought together a disparate group of supporters from the CCF, Social Credit, the Saskatoon Trades and Labor Council, and, most controversially, the Communist Party. He defeated his sole opponent, Liberal Michael P. Hayes, by a vote of 10,766 to 5,757. The reformers were jubilant and, temporarily, united. They organized a torchlight parade with old brooms dipped in gasoline and placed Brown on top of an old car so that he could deliver his victory speech to cheering supporters. Brown repeated his victory in the general election held March 26, 1940, but his political career was cut short when his health broke down and he died at age sixty-four on April 1, 1940. The United Reformers contested the subsequent by-election, but were unable to hold the seat. Brown's political career demonstrated how the dire effects of the Depression generated powerful grassroots demands for alternatives to the status quo, and how difficult it was to organize such demands into a coherent movement without the unifying effect of a charismatic personality.

JAMES M. PITSULA, UNIVERSITY OF REGINA

**BRYANT, JAMES FRASER** (1877–1945). James Fraser Bryant, minister of Public Works and minister of Telephones and Telegraphs in J. T. M. Anderson's Co-operative government from 1929 to 1934, was born at Glen Allan, Ontario, on May 19, 1877. Educated at Upper Canada College, Queen's University, and the University of Manitoba, he graduated with a Master's degree in Classics and a Bachelor of Laws. After teaching for a year, he articled in Regina in 1902 and became a partner in the law firm of Allan, Gordon, Bryant and Gordon in 1907. A year later he married Myra Boyd of Regina, where they lived for most of Bryant's career.

SAB R-B 3067

JAMES BRYANT

Bryant led a very active life both as a lawyer and in public service. He rose within his profession to become president of the Regina Bar Association and eventually a judge. He also joined several service clubs and held various executive positions in them, such as Grand Master of the Ancient Order of United Workmen, president of the Saskatchewan Institute for the Blind, and president of the Canadian Clubs of both Regina and Saskatoon twenty-five years apart. Nevertheless, education and politics soon came to dominate his extra-professional activities. In the field of education he rose to become chairman of the Regina Public School Board and then president of the Saskatchewan School Trustees Association for seven years. During this time, in 1917, he established the Bryant Oratorical competition which in future years introduced thousands of the province's high school students to the art of public speaking. Also during his presidency, the Trustees came out in opposition to religious instruction in the schools and were in favour of making English the sole language of instruction in Saskatchewan's public schools. These were two of the major issues Bryant brought with him when he sought election to the legislature in the mid- and late-1920s.

Politics proved to be Bryant's other passion. A life-long Conservative, he served as secretary of the provincial association, from 1911 to 1912; president of the Regina association, from 1912 to 1921; and finally president of the provincial Conservative association from 1922 to 1925. Bryant's first attempt at election to the legislature occurred at the general election in 1925 when he stood for one of the two Regina seats. Although he did not win at that time, his campaign added lustre to his reputation as one of his party's pre-eminent spokesmen. Over the next four years he continued to speak out on the issues he believed to be of the utmost importance to the

province—sectarianism in the public school system and corruption in government.

These issues helped defeat the Liberals. In the 1929 election, Bryant won a seat in Lumsden and the Assembly chose him as its new Speaker. A non-confidence vote forced Gardiner to resign, making J. T. M. Anderson premier. Anderson immediately asked Bryant to leave the Speaker's chair to accept two portfolios in his new Co-operative government—Public Works and Telephones and Telegraphs. Bryant quickly became recognized as one of the most important members of Anderson's cabinet. While his portfolios did not provide him with much scope to make a mark, especially with the onset of the Depression, he played an important role in most of the government's major activities. He helped rewrite the *School Act* to ban religious symbols from public schools and to strengthen the position of English as the sole language of instruction and administration. He worked on the agreement which gave the province control over its lands and natural resources held back by Ottawa since 1905. Finally, he led the government's attack on corruption while the Liberals were in office. The so-called "Bryant charges" led to the appointment of two Royal Commissions which showed some of Bryant's accusations to be true, though not all of them, and eventually they faded from public view in face of the disasters wrought by the Depression. Nevertheless, they did lead to the creation of a strong and independent Public Service Commission which within a generation made Saskatchewan's civil service the envy of the country.

Bryant did not survive the defeat of the Anderson government. He lost his seat at the 1934 election, as did every other candidate who ran as one of its supporters. In these circumstances, and seeing little hope for the

Conservative Party in provincial politics in the near future, he accepted appointment to the bench as a judge of the District Court in Saskatoon. He held this position until his death on September 18, 1945.

PATRICK KYBA, UNIVERSITY OF GUELPH

FURTHER READING: Russell, P.A. 1970. "The Co-operative Government in Saskatchewan, 1929–1934." Unpublished M.A. thesis, University of Saskatchewan. • Ward, N., and D. E. Smith. 1990. *Jimmy Gardiner—Relentless Liberal*. Toronto: University of Toronto Press.

## BUCHANAN, NILES (1909–1987).

Niles Buchanan was born in Sussiton county, South Dakota, in 1909. He moved with his family to Canada in 1913. At the age of nineteen he was employed as a teacher in Saskatchewan. He

WEST'S STUDIO, REGINA•SAB R-A 7896-2

NILES BUCHANAN

became an active member of the CCF, and was involved in organizational works from 1932 until 1941. In that year he enlisted in the Canadian Armed Forces to secure paid employment, and also due to a deep hatred of fascism. Because of his socialist leanings he was suspected of being a Communist, and so he was relegated to serve in the department of Homeland Defense. In 1944 he took leave from the army to campaign for the CCF in the Saskatchewan provincial election. He managed to obtain a seat in the Notukeu-Willow Bunch constituency. He kept his position in the armed forces for two terms while serving in the provincial legislature. He joined two other MLAs, Owie Hanson and George Cadbury, on a committee to review the *Professionals Acts* for the premier. In 1947 he advocated the licensing of doctors, but was defeated in caucus. He was re-elected in 1948 for his constituency in Notukeu–Willow Bunch. Later in 1956 he advocated the creation of the grid road system. This system would establish a more efficient distribution of roadways to complement the highways. His motion to to imprement this system was defeated by one vote in caucus, prompting his resignation in 1956, before the election of that year. The grid road system was passed in the next session without him. Initially an enthusiastic MLA, he lost interest in politics as backbenchers were relied upon less for their opinions and more for their votes.

JEREMY MOHR, UNIVERSITY OF WESTERN ONTARIO

SOURCE: Buchanan, Niles L. 1982. Interview by Jean Larmour. Saskatchewan Archives Board, 26 August. Tape recording. SAB R-8340 and R-8341.

## BUCKLE, WALTER CLUTTERBUCK (1886–1955).

Walter Clutterbuck Buckle, minister of Agriculture in the Co-operative government of J. T. M. Anderson from 1929 to 1934, was born in Gloucester, England, in 1886. Following his education at Sir Thomas Rich's School and Brentford College, he immigrated to Canada in 1905, settling in the Tisdale area five years later where he homesteaded and later operated a farm implement business. In 1916 he married Jean Hughes of Tisdale with whom he had a daughter, Maida Evelyn, and two sons, Harry Hughes and Thomas Francis.

Buckle became mayor of Tisdale in 1921, a position he held until his election to the legislature in 1925. As one of only three

SAB R-A 5350

WALTER BUCKLE

Conservatives elected that year he served as his party's Agriculture critic and became minister of Agriculture after the defeat of the Gardiner government in 1929. His career as minister followed a pattern common to most of his colleagues in the Anderson cabinet. First, Buckle attempted to discover and halt the corrupt practices in his department which had been inherited from the previous Liberal regime. He then introduced legislation designed to improve the lot of Saskatchewan's farmers. Finally, he became frustrated as the Depression deepened and the understanding grew that no money would be available for anything other than keeping people alive on their farms and safe from foreclosure. Thus, in 1930 Buckle initiated an audit of the Farm Loan Board. He put an end to the misappropriation of funds and political interference with the Board's operations under the Liberals. The same year he also announced a series of measures aimed at increasing farm revenues, ranging from fruit-growing to moisture conservation. Within two years, however, further investigation of the Liberals seemed pointless and new programmes proved unaffordable as the government tried to cope with the appalling effects of drought, pestilence, and declining private and public revenues. Saskatchewan simply did not have the means to withstand the catastrophe; thus, departments such as Agriculture gave way to new non-partisan institutions such as the Relief Commission and the Debt Adjustment Board. The length and severity of the Depression altered the expected course of the Anderson government completely and left it in a vulnerable position from which to campaign for re-election. In fact, not a single supporter of the Co-operative government won a seat in 1934. Buckle went down to defeat in Tisdale and never made it back to the legislature as a member. In 1946 he retired from business and moved to Victoria, where he lived until his death in 1955.

PATRICK KYBA, UNIVERSITY OF GUELPH

**SOURCE:** Russell, Peter A. 1970. "The Co-operative Government in Saskatchewan, 1929–1934." Unpublished M.A. thesis, University of Saskatchewan.

## BULYEA, GEORGE HEDLEY VICAR

(1859–1929). George Bulyea was an influential Liberal politician and the first Lieutenant-Governor of Alberta. He was born on February 17, 1859, in Gagetown, Queen's County, New Brunswick. His parents, James Albert and Jane (née Blizzard) were prosperous farmers and very active in the local Baptist Church. First in his class in mathematics and French, G.H.V. Bulyea graduated from the University of New Brunswick with honors. He married Annie Blanch Babbitt in 1885 and they had one son, Percy, who died in his fifteenth year.

Bulyea taught grade school in New Brunswick from 1878 to 1882, rising to become principal of the Sheffield Grammar School. At times he was also employed as a surveyor and undertaker. In 1892 he moved west, settling first in Winnipeg and in 1893 in Qu'Appelle, Assiniboia. There, Bulyea ran a general store that sold furniture, flour and feed. He also wrote a pamphlet for the Canadian government extolling the virtues of the North-West

Territories to potential settlers.

Moving into politics, Bulyea unsuccessfully contested the 1891 Territorial election. On his second attempt in 1894 he was elected to the Legislative Assembly of the North-West Territories from South Qu'Appelle. Bulyea quickly established a position of leadership in the non-partisan assembly that was beginning to polarize Liberals and Conservatives. A Liberal and supporter of Sir Wilfrid Laurier, Bulyea joined the first cabinet in 1897 as Territorial Secretary and Commissioner of Agriculture. In 1903 he relinquished these positions to become Commissioner of Public Works. A combination of administrative skill and the support he received from the Liberals in the Assembly—he was their unofficial leader by 1903—made him second only to Premier Frederick Haultain in influence. He served as a special commissioner for the North-West Territories to the Yukon in 1897.

Bulyea originally worked quite closely with Haultain, but Haultain's increasingly partisan Conservative behavior alienated him. He resigned in 1903 when Haultain, attempting to embarrass the federal Liberal government, rejected the federal grant-in-aid to the Territories that Bulyea painstakingly negotiated. Because of his indispensability to both the Liberal Party and the government, Bulyea was quickly persuaded to rejoin the cabinet, but the relationship between the two men was henceforth quite strained. In 1904 when Laurier indicated that the federal government was prepared to negotiate the terms of the North-West Territories' entrance into confederation as provinces, Bulyea became a key member of the cabinet sub-committee that

SAB R-B 3198

GEORGE BULYEA

represented Territorial interests in Ottawa. Bulyea sided with the federal Liberals over a number of issues, ensuring that Alberta and Saskatchewan were created along the lines laid out by the federal cabinet—not by Haultain and the Conservatives. During the provincial elections of 1905, the Liberal "machine" that Bulyea created was one of the keys to the Liberal victory in both provinces.

In recognition of his service to Canada, Laurier appointed Bulyea the first Lieutenant-Governor of Alberta. Bulyea employed his significant political skill in assisting Premier Alexander Rutherford in organizing the first provincial cabinet. He left office on November 20, 1915. Bulyea died on July 28, 1928 at Peachland, British Columbia, and he is buried in the Qu'Appelle Cemetery in Saskatchewan.

Bulyea was instrumental in getting the people of Alberta and Saskatchewan to accept the 1905 constitutions designed by Laurier, particularly the introduction of partisanship in the new legislatures. The organizational advantage the Liberals enjoyed in the new provinces in 1905 elections can be traced to his skilled organization.

MICHAEL THOME, UNIVERSITY OF SASKATCHEWAN

**FURTHER READING:** McDougall, D. Blake, et al. 1991. *Lieutenant-Governors of the Northwest Territories and Alberta, 1876–1991.* Edmonton: Alberta Legislature Library.

## BURTON, JOSEPH WILLIAM (1892–1960).

Joe Burton was born on October 12, 1892, in Pittsburg, Kansas. His early life was one of a pioneer. His father was a farmer who moved his family to North Dakota in 1899 in a covered wagon, and to a homestead four miles north of Humboldt in 1904.

Burton stayed in the Humboldt area for the rest of his life. He became a farmer and was a strong supporter of farmer organizations and co-operative enterprises throughout his life. He was an active member of the United Farmers of Canada, a delegate to the Saskatchewan Wheat Pool, and President of the Humboldt Agriculture Society. He also helped found and was president for many years of a local non-profit rural telephone company. He was a devout Roman Catholic and was the Grand Knight of the Humboldt Council of the Knights of Columbus.

Burton contested five provincial and four federal elections for the Humboldt riding over a 22-year period. Throughout his political career, he was concerned with rural issues such as orderly marketing, rural electrification and rural transportation. He first ran as a Farmer-Labour candidate in the provincial general election of 1934 but was defeated. As a CCF candidate, he was defeated in the federal general election in 1935, a provincial by-election in the same year and the provincial general election of 1938. However, in August of 1938, the Liberal incumbent in Humboldt stepped down to allow the former minister of highways, C. M. Dunn, to gain a seat. Burton surprised many by defeating the former Liberal minister in the by-election and entering the provincial legislature as a part of George Williams' CCF Official Opposition. Burton's by-election heralded an upsurge in the popularity of the CCF that eventually culminated in their election to government in 1944.

WEST'S STUDIO, REGINA•SAB R-A 5351

JOSEPH BURTON

In 1943, Burton resigned his provincial seat to win a federal by-election in Humboldt, forming a part of the CCF caucus in the House of Commons under the leadership of M. J. Coldwell. Burton was re-elected in the general election of 1945, but defeated in 1949. After three years of working on rural electrification as the public relations director for the Saskatchewan Power Corporation, Burton returned to provincial politics and was elected as the MLA for Humboldt in 1952. From 1952 to 1956, he served as provincial secretary and minister responsible for the Bureau of Publications in the Douglas cabinet. He was defeated in the 1956 general election and his health began to fail him soon afterwards. He eventually died of a heart attack on August 1, 1960, at the age of sixty-seven.

DAVID MCGRANE, CARLETON UNIVERSITY

**BYERS, NIEL** (b. 1928). Born December 7, 1928, in Fertile, Niel Byers was raised on his parents' farm near Frobisher. Upon graduating high school in 1949, he attended normal school in Moose Jaw.

He started teaching in several schools in and around Estevan and Broadview before accepting a teaching position at the Foam Lake High School where he remained for the duration of his teaching career. Throughout his teaching career, Byers was very active in the Saskatchewan Teachers' Federation, holding a variety of positions in the organization at both the local and regional levels.

Byers became active in the CCF at an early age. He served as a party organizer in the southeast of the province on two occasions and ran the CCF campaign in the constituency of Moosomin in 1956. Byers first ran for a seat in the legislature in 1964 after he defeated incumbent Cliff Peterson for the CCF nomination in Kelvington. But Byers lost the seat as Ross Thatcher's government came to power. Contesting the seat again in 1967, Byers lost by a mere seven votes. The result was challenged in the courts and in 1969 the result was contraverted and a by-election was called. The by-election proved to be a litmus test for the government. The NDP experimented with a new type of campaigning and tested the issues they would use in the upcoming general election, all with great success as Byers was easily elected.

Byers was re-elected in the 1971 election and was appointed to Blakeney's first cabinet as minister of Highways. In 1972 he was moved to the newly created Department of the Environment. During his tenure as minister, the environmental movement criticized him for being pro-development and for supporting the expansion of the uranium industry. Re-elected in the constituency of Kelvington-Wadena in both 1975 and 1978, Byers was moved out of environment after the 1978 campaign into the new portfolio of Northern Saskatchewan. Byers left cabinet in 1979 and remained in the legislature until his defeat in 1982.

BRETT QUIRING

FURTHER READING: Gruending, Dennis. 1990. *Promises to Keep: A Political Biography of Allan Blakeney*. Saskatoon: Western Producer Prairie Books.

## CADBURY, GEORGE WOODALL (1907 –1995).

George Cadbury was one of the most influential civil servants during the early years of the T. C. Douglas government. Born and raised in Birmingham, England, Cadbury was the eldest grandchild of the Quaker founder of the famous chocolate dynasty. In the 1920s, Cadbury attended King's College at Cambridge to study economics, where he was personally supervised by John Maynard Keynes. Afterwards, he studied at the Wharton School of Business at the University of Pennsylvania.

Before Cadbury arrived in Saskatchewan, he had accumulated years of experience as a managing director of two sizeable food processing enterprises in England. With the outbreak of the Second World War, he was lent to the Ministry of Aircraft Production where he was the deputy director of production for three years. He then worked for the British Air Commission in Washington, DC. Although a business executive, Cadbury had close links with the British Labour Party and was well known in Fabian Society circles. As a result, he got to know a number of Canadian socialists including David Lewis, the future leader of the New Democratic Party. It was Lewis who suggested that Cadbury pay a visit to Saskatchewan to see the newly elected CCF government in Saskatchewan. In the summer of 1945, Cadbury made his way to Regina where he met with various officials in the government and was invited to observe a cabinet meeting. T. C. Douglas and his key officials recognized Cadbury's great experience as a manager and a planner well as his obvious commitment to democratic socialism, and Cadbury was soon extended a job offer.

Cadbury arrived for duty in December. He was soon joined by his wife Barbara, also a committed socialist with much experience in the co-operative movement, along with their two daughters. Premier Tommy Douglas needed Cadbury to bring order to the disorganized group of enterprises that the government had

GEORGE CADBURY

purchased or set up in its first few months of government. He also wanted an effective system for more long-term economic planning. To accomplish both objectives, Cadbury established the Economic Advisory and Planning Board. Although a committee of cabinet, Cadbury became the chair. Through his position, Cadbury provided a stream of advice to cabinet aimed at improving the performance of the government's enterprises. With his growing team of able and enthusiastic experts recruited from all over Canada, the Planning Board soon became the brains trust for the new government. It would soon spin off two additional central agencies, both of which were to have great impact on the evolution of government in Saskatchewan. The first was the Budget Bureau that pioneered a more collective approach to expenditure control as well as acting as an advisory body on the machinery of government more generally. The second was the Government Finance Office, later known as Crown Investments Corporation, a holding company and treasury board for the growing number of Crown corporations in the province.

Through these agencies, Cadbury put Saskatchewan at the cutting edge of innovative government in the world. By the end of the decade, Cadbury felt that the creative part of his job had been completed and he left the province for a long career in the United Nations as an advisor to various developing countries. Upon retiring, he moved to Ontario and returned to political life as the chairman,

and later president, of the national New Democratic Party. He was also active with his wife in the International Planned Parenthood Federation. He died on February 28, 1995.

GREGORY P. MARCHILDON, UNIVERSITY OF REGINA

SOURCES: Cadbury, George Woodall. 1981, 1982. Transcription of oral interview with Jean Larmour. Saskatchewan Archives Board, R-8343 to R-8345 • McLaren, Robert I. 1995. "George Woodall Cadbury: The Fabian Catalyst in Saskatchewan's 'Good Public Administration.'" *Canadian Public Administration*, vol. 38, no. 3: 471–480 • Cadbury, George. 1971. "Planning in Saskatchewan." In *Essays on the Left*, ed. Laurier Lapierre et al., 51–64. Toronto: McClelland and Stewart.

## CALDER, JAMES ALEXANDER (1868–1956).

James Calder was born on a farm in Oxford County, Ontario, on September 17, 1868, to James Calder and Johanna McKay, both of Scottish descent. At age thirteen, Calder moved with his family from Ingersoll to Winnipeg and took his high school there. Calder's father died accidentally shortly thereafter. This meant that the Calder children, in a single parent family, all found jobs to keep the family together.

Calder attended Manitoba College and University of Manitoba, graduating with a B.A. in Science in 1888. He received his teaching certificate the following year from Normal School. He taught in various rural schools until he became principal of the Moose Jaw High School in 1891. Three years later, he became a school inspector.

While he was within the school system, he began to study law. From 1901 to 1905, Calder was Deputy Commissioner (Deputy Minister) of Education in the North-West Territories under the premiership of Frederick Haultain. He was called to the Bar but he never assumed an active law practice.

When the province of Saskatchewan was formed in 1905, Walter Scott received the nod to become premier. After much persuasion by Scott, Calder finally agreed to be the Commissioner (Minister) of Education and Provincial Treasurer in Scott's first cabinet.

The first general election was held on December 13, 1905, and Calder was elected in South Regina. He was defeated in the 1908 general election in Milestone, but within months was back in the Legislative Assembly due to a by-election in the constituency of Saltcoats. He was re-elected in 1912 and 1917. In 1912, Calder became the minister of Railways, Telephones and Highways.

Although Scott was a masterful and successful leader, he suffered from manic depression and was out of the province for up to six months of every year. Calder very ably served as deputy premier in Scott's absence. This was a good partnership with Scott generating the big ideas and long term plans, while Calder was the "detail man" and administrator.

In 1917, Calder resigned his seat in the Legislative Assembly and joined Borden's Union government at the national level. He was elected to the House of Commons representing Moose Jaw and assumed the Immigration and Colonization portfolios. In 1921, Calder was appointed to the Senate as a Conservative, where he served until 1956.

Life was not all politics for Calder. He married Eva Mildred Leslie in 1910 and they had one son, James Alexander. Calder

SAB R-A 246

JAMES CALDER

devoted nearly his entire life to public service. In his roles as school inspector, MLA, cabinet minister, member of the House of Commons and then Senate, he served the people of Saskatchewan and Canada for 62 years. Calder died on July 20, 1956.

GORDON BARNHART, UNIVERSITY OF SASKATCHEWAN

FURTHER READING: Saskatchewan Archives Board. J. A. Calder Papers. Personal recollections. M2-file #63, Saskatoon.

## CALVERT, LORNE ALBERT (b. 1952).

Lorne Calvert was born on December 24, 1952, in Moose Jaw. Given his deep commitment to community and Saskatchewan roots, it is not surprising that he has followed two paths in his public life: religion and politics. Furthermore, his religious background helps to explain the strong social orientation he has brought to his work as an elected official.

After high school, Calvert obtained a Bachelor of Arts in economics at the University of Regina and a Bachelor of Divinity in theology at Saint Andrew's College in Saskatoon. In 1976, he was ordained in the United Church of Canada. Calvert served congregations in various towns in Saskatchewan, including Perdue, Gravelbourg, Bateman, Shamrock, Coderre and Palmer. In the late 1970s, he returned to Moose Jaw to serve as a minister of Zion United Church. He remained in that position until 1986, when he was first elected to the Saskatchewan Legislative Assembly as the New Democratic Party (NDP) representative for the constituency of Moose Jaw South. His decision to join the Saskatchewan NDP was in part influenced by his father who had been a long-time supporter of the Co-operative Commonwealth Federation.

Subsequently, Calvert was re-elected twice

as the Saskatchewan NDP representative for Moose Jaw Wakamow. Between 1992 and 1995, he was appointed to several important cabinet positions, namely associate minister of Health and minister responsible for the Wakamow Valley Authority (1992), minister responsible for SaskPower and SaskEnergy (1992–1993), and minister of Health (1995). In the fall of 1995 he became minister of Social Services. In that capacity, Calvert had to address issues relating to the Public Service Commission, seniors, and eventually disabilities.

SASKATCHEWAN NDP PHOTO ARCHIVES

LORNE CALVERT

In the late 1990s, Calvert decided to take a break from politics to spend more time with his family. After a two-year hiatus, he returned to politics in 2001 to contest the leadership of the Saskatchewan NDP. The leadership convention took place at the end of January in Saskatoon. For the first time in its history, the party was to use a direct form of voting (allowing all registered party members, as opposed to party delegates, to vote) to select its new leader. After four rounds of voting, Calvert finally defeated six challengers, including Nettie Wiebe, an ethics professor at Saint Andrew's College, and Chris Axworthy, the Minister of Justice in Roy Romanow's government. In the last round of voting, he defeated Axworthy with 10, 289 votes (or 57.6 percent of the vote). Calvert officially assumed the duties of premier of Saskatchewan on February 8, 2001, and won Roy Romanow's former seat of Saskatoon-Riverdale one month later.

When Calvert became premier of Saskatchewan, the NDP government was in a coalition with the Liberal Party. As a result of the 1999 provincial election, the NDP found itself with 29 seats, the Saskatchewan Party with 26 seats, and the Liberal Party with 3 seats. Eluding the legislative majority by one seat, the NDP then formed Saskatchewan's first coalition government in almost seventy years with the Liberal Party. Liberal MLAs Jim Melenchuk, Ron Osika, and Jack Hillson were given positions in the Romanow government. After Romanow's retirement from politics, Calvert was able to renew the coalition by appointing Jim Melenchuk as minister of Education and maintaining Ron Osika as the Speaker of the Legislative Assembly. At the time of writing, the two men were sitting as independents and respectively held the Finance and the Government Relations portfolios.

Although Saskatchewan's fiscal situation has dramatically improved since Romanow first became premier in 1991, Calvert's approach to government finances has been cautious. In keeping with his NDP predecessors beginning with Tommy C. Douglas, he has launched several social initiatives while keeping a close eye on the province's finances. Consequently, during his tenure as premier, funds were provided for agricultural revitalization, highway repairs, childcare spaces, training and education opportunities, health care, and renewable energy projects. At the same time, measures such as government re-structuring and tax increases on cigarettes and alcohol were implemented in order to ensure that budgets would remain balanced. Under Calvert's leadership, the NDP won 30 seats in the November 2003 provincial elections and formed the government.

JOCELYNE PRAUD, UNIVERSITY OF REGINA

## CAMERON, ALEXANDER C.

(1907–1996). "Alex" Cameron was a member of the Saskatchewan Legislative Assembly for twenty-three years, serving in Ross Thatcher's government as minister of Mineral Resources and minister of Telephones.

Alex Cameron was born in Avonhurst on June 30, 1907. After receiving his education in Saskatchewan, at Campion College and the University of Saskatchewan, Cameron taught in several schools in southwest Saskatchewan. He ended up in Richmound, where he was principal and was involved in the Saskatchewan Teacher's Federation for several years. In 1941, he and his brother opened up a garage in Richmound, which they ran until 1960. Before entering provincial politics, Cameron was Richmound's mayor, organised credit unions, and was involved in the Swift Current health district.

When Alexander Cameron joined the Liberal Party in the 1940s, there was nearly no Liberal support in his region. A respected member of the community, as well as a charismatic and often colourful speaker, in the 1948 Saskatchewan general election Alex Cameron won a seat representing Maple Creek. Early in his career in provincial politics, Cameron was a vocal member of the legislature, publicly criticising the reigning CCF government, often accusing them of having ties to the Communist Party. Being such a visible and established member of the Saskatchewan Liberal Party, Cameron ran for leadership in the 1959 party leadership race. However, his bid was unsuccessful and Ross Thatcher won.

When the Liberals came to power in Saskatchewan, Premier Ross Thatcher

SAB R-A 10450-3

ALEX CAMERON

appointed Cameron as his minister of Mineral Resources, a position which Cameron held until the Liberals lost the 1971 election. On December 13, 1965, Cameron also took charge of the Department of Telephones. He would also end up in charge of SaskTel, Saskatchewan Government Insurance and the Saskatchewan Transit Company. During his term as Mineral Resources minister, Alex Cameron worked closely with the private sector, encouraging exploration and the development of the industry, especially with petroleum and potash. The 1960s were a time of great oil exploration, as the government and the oil industry hoped for an oil discovery comparable to the one in Leduc, Alberta.

With both of his cabinet positions, Cameron placed a high priority on developing the North. His department introduced telephone service to the thousands of Saskatchewan farms that were still without telephones in the 1960s, while Mineral Resources developed a cost-sharing program to encourage mining in the North.

Alex Cameron lost the Maple Creek constituency in the 1971 general election when Allan Blakeney's NDP came to power. Cameron died on January 16, 1996.

MARYANNE COTCHER, UNIVERSITY OF REGINA

**FURTHER READING:** Eisler, Dale. 1987. *Rumours of Glory: Saskatchewan and the Thatcher Years.* Edmonton: Hurtig Publishers.

## CAMPBELL, MILTON NEIL (1881–1965).

One of the last Progressives in the House of Commons, Milton Campbell was a forceful campaigner for the interests of the western Canadian farmer. He was born in Greenvale, Prince Edward Island, on January 21, 1881. Campbell excelled in school, graduating from Prince of Wales College in 1902. After graduation, he began a career as a telegraph agent for the Canadian Northern Railway, first stationed at Atikokan, Ontario. He first arrived in Saskatchewan in 1905 when he was stationed in Humboldt. In December of that year he settled in Kamsack where he remained until his resignation from the House of Commons in 1933.

In Kamsack, Campbell and two of his brothers went into business with a farm implement dealership and a Ford dealership. They also had an interest in the Pioneer Grain Company elevator at Pelly and became involved in land speculation in the region. The brothers' businesses did well during the war years, but they fell on hard times after the economic boom of the war ended. Outside of business Campbell was active in the local community, serving ten years as chairman of the Pelly School Board and as a town councillor from 1912 to 1920.

Being involved in the farm community and holding a membership in the Saskatchewan Grain Growers Association, Campbell became active in the Progressive Party. Upset by what he thought was unfair treatment of prairie farmers by the federal government and the "old party system," Campbell ran for the Progressives in the Liberal stronghold of Mackenzie. Campbell was elected in 1921 despite opposition from noted Liberal orator, Dr. Michael Clark, who left his seat of Medicine Hat hoping to find a

safer Liberal seat in Saskatchewan.

In the House of Commons, Campbell became a leading speaker for the Progressives on such issues as the proposed Hudson's Bay railway, unfair freight rates, and transportation issues generally. Campbell, who had previously supported the King government, became estranged from King and from the Manitoba "pro-Liberal" wing of his party. In 1924 he voted with a minority of Progressives for a budget amendment proposed by James S. Woodsworth. The amendment had been proposed by the Progressives the year before, but was dropped as the Manitoba wing of the Progressives moved closer to the Liberals, a move that was increasingly unsettling to Campbell.

Campbell was re-elected in 1925 with an increased majority, a feat of some significance seeing as the Progressives lost over two-thirds of their seats. Because neither the Liberals nor Conservatives held a majority of seats, the small Progressive caucus had enormous influence. Campbell managed to pass an amendment to the *Canada Grain Act* which allowed farmers to designate to which terminal elevator their grain was to be sent, an amendment which benefited the Saskatchewan Wheat Pool.

Re-elected in 1926, he became closely involved with the Labour group under Woodsworth. He continued to advocate the Hudson Bay railroad and the abolishment of the protective tariff, but also advocated a more collectivist policy of nationalization of the railroad, public utilities and the brewing industry. Re-elected a final time in 1930, he developed a great deal of sympathy for the

SAB R-A 21321

MILTON CAMPBELL

Bennett government, believing him more apt to rectify the west's grievances. To this end he was appointed to the Tarriff Advisory Board in 1933. Campbell served out his ten-year term before retiring from public life. He retired to London, Ontario, where he died on November 11, 1965.

BRETT QUIRING

FURTHER READING: Thomas, Lewis. 1976. "Milton Campbell-Independent Progressive." In *West and the Nation*, ed. Carl Berger. Toronto: McClelland and Stewart. • Saskatchewan Archives Board. Milton Campbell reminiscences.

## CARMICHAEL, ARCHIBALD MORRISON

(1882–1959). Archibald Carmichael was born in Smithdale, Ontario, on January 4, 1882. His parents had immigrated to Canada from Scotland and were among the first Europeans to settle in Nottawasaga, Ontario. He was educated at the Collingwood Collegiate Institute, the Bradford Model School and the Regina Normal School. Carmichael had obtained a second-class teacher's certificate and taught as a rural school teacher in Nottawa, Ontario, for two years before moving to Manitoba and Saskatchewan where he also taught. In March 1906, Carmichael married his first wife, Mary Magdelene Hahn, with whom he had five children. He re-married in February 1916 to Roxina Anger after moving to Kindersley, Saskatchewan. There he settled on a quarter section where he farmed from 1908 to 1913. Carmichael helped to found the town of Kindersley in 1913, where he opened and taught at its first school. He was the president of the Kindersley District Religious Education Council for two years and also served on the school board for four years.

In 1921, Archibald Carmichael was nominated to be a candidate in the general election for the Progressive Party in the riding of Kindersley, winning his seat with a majority of the vote. Carmichael sat with 65 other Progressive Party members in the fourteenth Parliament of Canada. That election marked the first time that a third party had gained the second largest number of seats in the House of Commons. Because it went against their political philosophy, the Progressives did not take on the role of Official Opposition and instead opted to sit neither in support of nor in opposition to the governing Liberal Party.

The Progressive Party returned to the House of Commons with forty-one fewer members in 1925. Carmichael, who had previously been a Conservative Party supporter, voted along with Sir Arthur Meighen's amendment to censure Mackenzie King's Liberal government for continuing in office even though the Conservative Party had won the largest number of seats in the election. Carmichael and other Conservative-leaning members of the Progressive Party challenged King's government on several other occasions until its ultimate downfall in the 1926 constitutional crisis, which led to the dissolution of parliament.

Carmichael returned to the House of Commons on two more occasions after the 1926 and 1930 election as one of the few remaining independent Progressive members. He sat as a member of Parliament for fourteen years until 1935 when he did not seek re-election. Archibald Carmichael died on August 30, 1959.

SEAN KHERAJ, YORK UNIVERSITY

## CASTLEDEN, GEORGE HUGH (1895–1969).

George Castleden was born in Moosomin on July 23, 1895. Upon completing school in Moosomin, Castleden attended the

Regina Normal School, earning his teaching certificate. Shortly after graduation, he enlisted in the Canadian Air Force. After the First World War, Castleden returned to teaching at Lemberg, before accepting a position at the Yorkton Collegiate Institute in 1937.

Involved in the Saskatchewan Teachers' Federation (STF), Castleden was first elected to the STF executive in 1936 and subsequently re-elected in 1937 and 1938, serving as the organization's vice-president in 1937. Like several other prominent CCF leaders, his experiences as a teacher during the depression and what he perceived as unfair treatment of his profession by government and school boards fueled his political involvement. His grievances were further highlighted when, upon accepting the 1940 CCF nomination in the federal riding of Yorkton, he was promptly fired from his teaching position.

SASKATCHEWAN NDP PHOTO ARCHIVES

GEORGE CASTLEDEN

In the 1940 federal election, Castleden was elected along with five other CCF MPs from Saskatchewan. Unlike many of his caucus colleagues that term, Castleden did not have a high public profile and was content to work behind the scenes representing the CCF on many House of Commons committees.

Castleden was re-elected in 1945, but was later narrowly defeated in 1949. He was appointed director of staff training for the Saskatchewan government, a position he held until he mounted a successful political comeback in 1953. Castleden would be re-elected again in 1957 only to be finally defeated in

Diefenbaker's 1958 sweep.

After retiring from politics, Castleden returned to teaching. He spent five years teaching in Bredenbury and Saltcoats before retiring in 1963. He died at his home in Saltcoats on April 25, 1969.

BRETT QUIRING

**CLINE, ERIC** (b. 1955). Eric Cline was a prominent figure in the NDP governments of Roy Romanow and Lorne Calvert. As minister of Finance from 1997 through 2003, he was arguably Saskatchewan's most important cabinet minister during this period.

Cline was born August 12, 1955. He was raised and educated in Saskatoon, earning degrees in political science (1976) and law (1979) at the University of Saskatchewan. He practiced law with Mitchell, Taylor, Romanow and Ching, an NDP firm that had the future premier as a partner. He married Pauline Melis in 1988.

Cline ran in Regina South in 1975 but was defeated. He was elected MLA for Saskatoon Idylwyld in 1991, was re-elected from Saskatoon Mount Royal in 1995 and 1999, and from Saskatoon Massey Place in 2003. Romanow appointed him to cabinet in 1995 as minister of Health. This post required that he manage the consequences of healthcare cutbacks and reforms implemented during the Romanow government's first term. Having proven himself in this difficult portfolio, he was appointed minister of Finance after the 1997 provincial budget.

Cline's predecessor in Finance, Janice MacKinnon, had balanced Saskatchewan's budget through deep spending cuts and modest tax increases, and had repaid a portion of the provincial debt. In allocating the public funds made available by economic growth and lower debt-servicing costs, Cline advocated the "balanced approach" of dividing surplus revenues equally between spending increases, tax reductions, and debt repayment.

This dispersal of funds allowed the government to do a little bit of everything, but prevented it from concentrating on any major initiatives. The 1998 and 1999 budgets slightly reduced Saskatchewan's income and sales taxes. Funding was partially restored to government programs, but a Department of Finance report showed that, by 1999, public-sector salaries were the only component of provincial expenditure to have been fully restored from the severe cutbacks of the early 1990s.

In the 2000 budget, Cline abandoned the balanced approach in favour of the largest income-tax cuts in Saskatchewan's history. He sought to make Saskatchewan more competitive with other provinces in attracting and retaining high-income individuals and business investment.

Over four years, income-tax rates were cut by nearly a third. By changing Saskatchewan's income tax from being a proportion of federal tax to being a direct tax on income, Cline was also able to reduce the differentials between rates for different income brackets. He recovered about half the cost of these cuts by applying the sales tax to more goods. Historically, the NDP had advocated using a progressive system to tax large incomes at substantially higher rates than small ones. Reducing the differences between tax brackets and shifting the tax base from income to consumption constituted major departures from this policy. On the other hand, Cline made some progressive changes such as increasing tax credits, elimi-

SASKATCHEWAN NDP PHOTO ARCHIVES

ERIC CLINE

nating the 2 percent flat tax, and introducing partial sales tax rebates. Although there are different ways of measuring progressivity, most supporters and opponents of Cline's policy agreed that it reduced progressivity to increase competitiveness.

Also in the 2000 budget, Cline created a Fiscal Stabilization Fund from the retained earnings of Saskatchewan's Liquor and Gaming Authority. The new Fund was intended to absorb small provincial surpluses and deficits, maintaining its value at about 5 percent of provincial revenues. But Cline's tax cuts contributed to a significant gap between revenues and expenditures, which was temporarily filled by depletion of the Fund.

Early in 2003, Calvert removed Cline from Finance and appointed him minister of Justice and Attorney General, and minister of Industry and Resources. After the 2003 election, Cline was re-appointed only to Industry and Resources.

ERIN M. K. WEIR, UNIVERSITY OF CALGARY

FURTHER READING: MacKinnon, Janice. 2003. Minding the Public Purse: The Fiscal Crisis, Political Trade-offs, and Canada's Future. Montreal & Kingston: McGill-Queen's University Press. • Vicq, Jack, Charlie Baldock, and Shelley Brown. 1999. Final Report and Recommendations of the Saskatchewan Personal Income Tax Review Committee. Regina: Government of Saskatchewan.

## CODERRE, LIONEL (1915–1995).

Lionel Coderre was born in Coderre, a town named for his family, on April 15, 1915. He was educated in Coderre, and attended College Mathieu in Gravelbourg.

Coderre became a nurse at the provincial

hospital in Weyburn until he joined the army with the South Saskatchewan Regiment in 1939. He was promoted to Major with command over his own company and fought in the Dieppe Raid during which he was mentioned twice in the official dispatches. Following an honourable discharge in 1945, Coderre married Pauline Graf and returned to Saskatchewan. The couple had three children, Claudia Marie, Richard Edward, and Barbara Anne.

WEST'S STUDIO, REGINA • SAB R-WS65-1134

LIONEL CODERRE

Upon his return from the Second World War, Coderre purchased and operated the local power plant in his hometown of Coderre and later owned and operated his own hardware store. He was active in the Liberal Party, serving as president of the Gravelbourg Liberal Association. First elected to the Saskatchewan legislature in 1956 for the Gravelbourg constituency, Coderre was re-elected in 1960, 1964, and 1967. Following the election of the Liberal government in 1964, Coderre was appointed minister of Labour and minister of Co-operative Development, positions he held until his appointment as minister of Public Works on September 1, 1970.

During his tenure as minister of Labour, relations between the government and labour organizations deteriorated as various legislation enacted by the government was seen to threaten the rights of unions. In March 1966 the Liberal government passed amendments to the *Trade Union Act* which limited the ability of unions in the province to organize and strike. As well, the government passed the *Act Respecting the Continuance of Services Essential to the Public*, also known as the *Essential Services Act*. This *Act* allowed the government to end any strike involving the provincial

utilities, hospitals, or nursing homes if it was deemed that the strike jeopardized life, health, or property. It was Ross Thatcher, not Coderre, who presented the legislation, and Coderre later commented that the *Trade Union Act* was a "gross abuse of compulsory arbitration by our government."

After leaving elected politics following the defeat of the Thatcher Liberals, Coderre remained active in the Liberal Party, working on campaigns and as a volunteer on election days. Coderre died on August 3, 1995, at the age of eighty.

ROBERTA LEXIER, UNIVERSITY OF ALBERTA

**FURTHER READING:** Saskatchewan Archives Board. Lionel Coderre Papers. R24, Regina. • Eisler, Dale. 1987. *Rumours of Glory: Saskatchewan and the Thatcher Years.* Edmonton: Hurtig Publishers. • Snyder, Gordon T. 1997. "Social Justice for Workers." In *Policy Innovation in the Saskatchewan Public Sector, 1971-82,* ed. Eleanor D. Glor, 140–149. North York, Ontario: Captus Press.

**CODY, DON WILLIAM** (b. 1936). Donald William Cody was born on March 28, 1936, in the hamlet of Pilger, a farm community near Humboldt. Upon graduation from the local high school, he went to work as a telegraph operator and agent for Canadian Pacific Railways Co. In 1961, he married Joan Germshield, with whom he had two sons, Scott and Garnet. In 1963, he embarked on a career in insurance, starting as a claims adjuster for Saskatchewan Government Insurance (SGI). Four years later he moved to Co-op Insurance Services, Ltd. to become a claims examiner, and, in 1969, he was promoted to Saskatchewan claims supervisor.

In 1970, Mr. Cody won the provincial

nomination for the New Democratic Party for the constituency of Watrous. A year later he was elected to the Saskatchewan Legislative Assembly as part of Allan Blakeney's NDP team that defeated Ross Thatcher's Liberal government. In 1974, he was appointed as minister of Co-operation and Co-operative Development, which he held until the general election a year later. The 1975 general election saw Cody defeated in the riding of Qu'Appelle, but he was re-elected in the 1978 general election for the constituency of Kinistino. That year he was appointed minister of Telephones and the following year he was reappointed minister of Co-operation and Co-operative Development. Don Cody was defeated in the Progressive Conservative resurgence in 1982.

Since leaving provincial politics, Cody has served as the mayor of Prince Albert from 1994 to 2003, and has been the chair of the board of SGI.

DEREK DE VLIEGER, OTTAWA

# COLDWELL, MAJOR JAMES (1888–1974).
M. J. Coldwell, born in Seaton, England, on December 2, 1888, was a key political figure in the creation of the social democratic Co-operative Commonwealth Federation (CCF) and served as its second federal leader from 1942 to 1960. A former teacher and school principal, he was elected as a Regina alderman and Saskatchewan member of Parliament.

Educated in England, Coldwell arrived in Canada in 1910 to take up his first teaching appointment in Alberta. The next year he was hired as a principal in Sedley, when his new employer mistakenly assumed "Major" meant he was an older, former military officer. Later he was a school principal in North Regina and Regina until 1934.

Active in several teachers' federations from the mid-1920s until the mid-1930s, he served as president of the Saskatchewan Teachers' Alliance and president of the Canadian Teachers' Federation. Coldwell became an alderman in 1921 and generated considerable publicity when he exposed first-hand the deplorable food served to the unemployed. Coldwell served four terms until 1932.

In 1925 Coldwell was a federal candidate for the Progressive Party and also ran in 1934 as a provincial candidate for the Saskatchewan Farmer-Labour Party (a party aligned to the CCF). A year later, Coldwell, campaigning for the federal CCF in Rosetown-Biggar, was victorious and would go on to win four subsequent elections in 1940, 1945, 1953, and 1957, until losing in the Tory landslide of 1958.

In 1931 Coldwell was president of the Independent Labour Party. Selected as the first leader of the Saskatchewan Farmer-Labour Party in 1932, his position was greatly weakened when he did not win a seat in the 1934 provincial election and he was soon displaced as leader by George H. Williams.

Given the controversial pacifism and declining health of J. S. Woodsworth, the CCF's first federal leader, Coldwell increasingly became the de facto spokesman for the party. Following Woodsworth's death in 1942, Coldwell was elected the CCF's leader and remained in the post until 1960.

Coldwell pressed for a more

NATIONAL ARCHIVES OF CANADA C49570

M. J. COLDWELL

centralized professional party and brought in key staffers such as David Lewis. On foreign policy, in contrast to Woodsworth's uncompromising idealism, Coldwell opted for a more realistic response to Hitler's aggression. Coldwell served as a member of the Canadian delegation at the creation of the UN and favoured the formation of NATO in response to the Soviet threat. Far more controversial was Coldwell's adamant support of West Germany's rearmament during the Cold War.

In the more affluent post-war era, Coldwell urged a reassessment of social democratic ideas and by 1956 the more moderate Winnipeg Declaration had been penned to replace the 1930s Regina Manifesto. Coldwell's great respect for parliament is often cited in accounts of the 1956 Pipeline Debate when the Liberal government arbitrarily used closure.

Under Coldwell's tenure, the CCF achieved its greatest gains federally in seats and vote in 1945. Later, the aging and ill Coldwell was no match for the prairie populism of John Diefenbaker and the party's vote and seats fell dramatically in 1958. Following this setback, social democracy would be reborn as the NDP.

Coldwell's decency and gentleness were hallmarks of his career. He acted as a mentor to several politicians. Both Douglas and Coldwell (the "preacher and teacher") had run unsuccessfully in the 1934 provincial election and were first elected to the House of Commons in 1935. Coldwell protected his younger colleague from Williams' efforts to expel Douglas over a Social Credit endorsement. Coldwell had clashed with Williams first in 1934–1935 when Williams had shunted Coldwell aside as provincial leader and then in 1941–1942 when Coldwell encouraged Douglas to displace Williams as CCF provincial leader. Douglas would soon form one of the most successful and influential provincial governments in Canadian history. Clarence Fines, an assistant principal at one of Coldwell's schools, would also become a key figure in the Saskatchewan CCF.

Coldwell was respected by his peers in other political parties and was offered cabinet posts in provincial and federal governments, Speakership of the House of Commons and a Senate seat. He declined all such inducements. In later years, Coldwell was named to the Privy Council (1964) and made a Companion of the Order of Canada (1967). The Douglas-Coldwell Foundation, a left-wing educational organization, is named after two remarkable Saskatchewan political figures.

Coldwell's distinguished record of public service was achieved while caring for an invalid wife for two decades. Coldwell died in Ottawa on August 25, 1974.

ALAN WHITEHORN, ROYAL MILITARY COLLEGE

**FURTHER READING:** Coldwell, M. J. 1945. *Left Turn, Canada.* New York: Duell. • Stewart, Walter. 2000. *M. J: The Life and Times of M. J. Coldwell.* Toronto: Stoddart.

**COLLVER, RICHARD LEE** (b. 1936). Dick Collver is a former leader of the Saskatchewan Progressive Conservative party. He resurrected the party in the mid-seventies, making it a political force in the province for the first time since the depression, and laid the foundation for the Conservative victory in 1982.

Collver was born in Toronto on February 13, 1936. The son of a salesman, Collver moved frequently as a child but eventually settled in Calgary where he completed high school. He earned an arts degree in economics from the University of Alberta and articled as an accountant for Price Waterhouse in Calgary.

Afterward, he worked as a travelling salesman and was business manager of an Edmonton medical clinic.

In 1965 Collver moved to Saskatchewan founding Management Associates Limited. Working as a management consultant, his business quickly expanded into four other western cities. Collver's business interests also expanded. In 1972 he first ran for public office contesting the Saskatoon mayoralty. Although he finished third, his campaign impressed many people. Shortly afterward he was approached to lead the troubled Saskatchewan Progressive Conservative party.

Winning the party leadership in 1973, Collver set out to expand the party which had won under 3 percent of the vote in the previous provincial election. Fielding a full slate of candidates in the 1975 election, Collver's effort paid off as the Conservatives won seven seats and over 28 percent of the vote. During the session the party benefitted from the Liberal party's collapse and assumed the post of Official Opposition after winning two by-elections and convincing two Liberal MLAs to abandon their party.

Collver's promising political career became tainted due to previous business dealings. In 1976, a prominent business partner in his Saskatoon management firm sued Collver over the company's dealings. The suit was settled out of court; however, it took two years to conclude and irreparable damage was done to his political image. Adding to Collver's problems, months after settling the first legal action, Saskatchewan Government Insurance Office (SGIO) launched a law suit suing Collver for debts amassed by a failed construction company of his that SGIO had extensive dealings with. The suit dragged on until 1983 when the government decided to drop the suit.

As the 1978 election approached, Collver was convinced that the Conservatives would win the election. Although the party won over 38 percent of the vote and it elected 17 MLAs, the result was a bitter disappointment and Collver resigned the party leadership six months later. Continuing to serve out the term, Collver left the Conservative party in 1980 to create the short-lived Unionest party which advocated western Canada joining the United States.

Not contesting the 1982 election, Collver left Saskatchewan, purchasing a ranch in Wickenberg, Arizona.

BRETT QUIRING

**COOPER (HUNT), MARJORIE** (née Lovering) (1902–1984). Marjorie Cooper, the

SAB R-A 5352

MARJORIE COOPER

third female member of the Saskatchewan Legislative Assembly, was elected in 1952, served four terms, and retired from politics undefeated in 1967.

Cooper was born Marjorie Lovering in Winnipeg on May 28, 1902, and moved to Regina in 1907. At the age of seventeen she began a teaching career in a one-room schoolhouse in McCord. In 1925 she left teaching and married Ed Cooper. She spent the following three decades raising two daughters and volunteering at the Metropolitan United Church, the Community Chest, the Saskatchewan Mental Health Association, and the John Howard Society. Cooper also served as president of the Regina

YWCA from 1941 to 1943 and the Regina Council of Women from 1946 to 1948. Cooper was appointed to the Labour Relations Board in 1945 and the Public Service Commission in 1951.

In 1952 Cooper won a CCF nomination and a seat in the provincial legislature in the multi-member constituency of Regina. Although never appointed to cabinet, Cooper acted as an unofficial women's advocate and sat on numerous committees including Crown Corporations, Cabinet Planning, Health and Welfare, Public Accounts, and the Law Amendments Committees.

Cooper's non-confrontational nature and gentle challenge to traditional gender roles allowed her to break new ground for women in politics while offending few. While Cooper did not define herself as a feminist, she expressed feminist goals through her community activism and her socialism. This moderate, respectable feminism contributed to her success in politics. Cooper's political career sheds light on notions of acceptable gender roles in the CCF party, Saskatchewan politics, and society in general in the 1950s and 1960s. Her life and career provide clear examples of some of the ways in which women promoted change between the two waves of the feminist movement in Canada.

C. MARIE FENWICK

SOURCE AND FURTHER READING: Fenwick, C. Marie. 2002. "Building the Future in a Steady but Measured Pace: The Respectable Feminism of Marjorie Cooper." *Saskatchewan History*, 54 (1): 18–34. • Fenwick, C. Marie. 1999. A Political Biography of Marjorie Cooper Hunt, 1902-1984. Unpublished M.A. Thesis, University of Regina.

## CORMAN, JOHN WESLEY "JACK"

(1884–1969). Jack Corman was born on a farm at Stoney Creek, Ontario, on August 2, 1884. His parents were William and Lucinda Corman, both devout Methodists of United Empire Loyalist stock. In 1912 Jack Corman graduated from the University of Toronto with a Bachelor of Arts degree in political science. He decided to move west that year to pursue legal studies, and he settled in Moose Jaw where he articled with William Spotton. He married Mabel "Con" Conner of Portage La Prairie in 1914, and in 1915 he was called to the bar. For the next twenty years he built his legal practice in Moose Jaw and raised a family with Con. They had four children, Francis, Dorothy, Fred and Jack (Jr.). Throughout this time Corman was a member of the Liberal Party, occasionally attending conventions and helping to draft resolutions.

Hard times fell on Moose Jaw during the 1930s. The Great Depression ravaged the city's infrastructure and left a quarter of its citizens on relief. As the decade drew to a close, Moose Jaw defaulted on its debenture debt and an air of crisis hung over the city. This spurred Jack Corman to enter the public service. He abandoned the Liberal Party because of its failure to take strong action to meet the crisis, and he joined an organization called the Civic Progressive Association (CPA) that was running candidates in Moose Jaw's municipal elections. In 1937 he was one of five aldermen elected in the city as part of a CPA slate that swept aside several long-serving incumbents. Corman entered provincial politics for the first time during the Saskatchewan provincial election of 1938, running as a last-minute candidate for Social Credit. He and his Social Credit running mate lost handily to their Liberal opponents in this election, and he turned his attention once again to civic politics in Moose Jaw.

In 1939, just a few months after the

Second World War broke out, Corman ran in the Moose Jaw mayoral race and won a landslide victory, polling nearly 50 percent of the total vote despite competing in a field of five candidates. He served as mayor of Moose Jaw for the next four and a half years. During this time he was tireless in his attempts to lobby the provincial and federal governments to locate wartime industry in his city, and he referred to his overriding policy as "Moose Jaw First." He also tried to resolve Moose Jaw's debt crisis by lobbying the provincial government to pass legislation which would, in effect, enforce a settlement between the city and its creditors. His efforts to obtain this legislation proved unsuccessful as long as Saskatchewan continued to have a Liberal government. Nevertheless, by 1944, when he made his second foray into provincial politics, Corman had become one of the most popular mayors in Moose Jaw's history, causing one journalist to observe, "Moose Jaw is Jack Corman, and Jack Corman is Moose Jaw—and one is reflected in the other."

Prior the 1944 provincial election, Cooperative Commonwealth Federation (CCF) leader Tommy Douglas met Corman in his office and asked him to run as a CCF candidate. Douglas promised Corman a cabinet post, with power over legislation that could enforce a settlement of Moose Jaw's debt. Corman eventually agreed, and along with his CCF running mate, Dempster Heming, was elected to the provincial legislature during the party's landslide victory in 1944. On July 10, 1944, Corman was sworn in as Attorney General in the first Douglas cabinet. One of his first acts as Attorney General was to pass the legislation he had long sought as mayor to

SAB R-A 3410

JACK CORMAN

enable a settlement of Moose Jaw's debenture debt. Although, in doing this, Corman was criticized as favouring Moose Jaw, his amendment helped other hard-pressed Saskatchewan municipalities to come to terms with their creditors. Other highlights of Corman's tenure as Attorney General included the passing of the *Farm Security Act* in 1944 (which he also defended successfully when a petition was filed with the federal government to disallow parts of it) and the passing of the Saskatchewan Bill of Rights in 1947. Corman's Bill of Rights was the first of its kind in the British Commonwealth, and it later became a model for subsequent human rights legislation in Canada and abroad. Corman was also a very important figure in the CCF cabinet, and it has been argued that he, Premier Douglas and Provincial Treasurer Clarence Fines ruled Saskatchewan as a triumvirate during the CCF's early years in power. Corman's role within this triumvirate was that of party strategist and propagandist, and he was well known for his "Your Attorney General Speaks" political radio broadcasts between 1946 and 1950. Jack Corman was twice re-elected to the Saskatchewan Legislature and he remained in the CCF cabinet as Attorney General until he retired in 1956. In 1960, he and his wife returned to Moose Jaw where they lived out the rest of their days. John Wesley Corman died on April 29, 1969, at the age of eighty-four years.

ROBERT ALLAN, MOOSE JAW

**COWLEY, ELWOOD** (b. 1944). Elwood Cowley was one of the main political ministers of the Blakeney government, and a key figure in increasing the role of the provincial government in Saskatchewan's resource sector.

Born August 2, 1944, Cowley was raised in Kinley, near Perdue. In 1961 he began studies at the University of Saskatchewan in Saskatoon, completing a Bachelor of Education in 1965 and Bachelor of Arts shortly thereafter. Cowley then began teaching, first in Assinibioa and then later at Thom Collegiate in Regina.

Actively involved in politics at an early age, he was involved with the New Democratic youth club at the University of Saskatchewan, serving as its president from 1963 to 1965 and was also involved in the provincial youth wing, serving as its president in 1965. In 1970, he was uncontested in his bid to replace former premier Woodrow Lloyd as the NDP candidate in Biggar. Cowley was actively involved in the 1970 leadership campaign as a key organizer for Roy Romanow, and at the leadership convention was elected party treasurer.

In 1971 Cowley was easily elected to the legislature, representing Biggar, and was appointed to cabinet in 1972 as minister of Finance. Cowley quickly became a key member of the government. With a sharp political mind, he became one of Blakeney's top advisors. His quick, cynical wit made him one of the government's most effective debaters, and for this reason he was relied upon to handle many of the government's contentious policy initiatives.

In 1975, Cowley was moved to the lighter portfolio of provincial secretary but was also assigned the responsibility of potash to form the Saskatchewan Potash Corporation. Later that year after considerable disagreement

SAB R-A 24786

ELWOOD COWLEY

between the provincial government, the federal government and the potash industry, Cowley introduced highly controversial legislation to nationalize a portion of Saskatchewan's potash industry. Besides expanding the role of government in the potash industry as minister of Mineral Resources, he also expanded the role of government in the oil sector through SaskOil and in the uranium industry through the Saskatchewan Mining Development Corporation.

Cowley's role in cabinet extended beyond resource policy. He was a central member of cabinet's political committee and, along with Gordon MacMurchy, Jack Messer and William Knight, he exercised considerable influence on the government's priorities and strategy. The committee was primarily responsible for the NDP's successful election campaign in 1978. This success cemented their central position in government until 1982 when their electoral strategy resulted in the CCF/NDP's worst defeat since 1934.

In 1982 Cowley was defeated and returned to teaching before he found work as an investment broker in Saskatoon. In 1989 he established his own consulting company which he continues to operate in Saskatoon.

BRETT QUIRING

FURTHER READING: Gruending, Dennis. 1990. *Promises to Keep: A Political Biography of Allan Blakeney.* Saskatoon: Western Producer Prairie Books.

**CROFFORD, JOANNE SHARON** (née Elkin) (b. 1947). Joanne Crofford was born in Regina on October 29, 1947. She graduated from the University of Regina in 1969, having studied Communications and Social Studies. As a youth, Crofford worked with the City of Regina Parks and Recreation department, and for the YWCA.

In 1976, Crofford moved to LaRonge, where she held the position of assistant director of personnel for the Department of Northern Saskatchewan. She also served as the provincial Environment Impact Assessment Secretariat and as business manager of the Kikinahk Indian and Métis Friendship Centre. When she later returned to Regina, Crofford worked for the Rainbow Youth Centre as program co-ordinator and as research co-ordinator for the Faculty of Social Work at the University of Regina.

Crofford was first elected to the Saskatchewan legislature in 1991 as the New Democratic Party MLA for Regina Lake Centre. She was re-elected in 1995 (Regina Centre) and in 1999 (Regina Centre).

In 1995, Crofford was appointed to cabinet as minister responsible for Saskatchewan Property Management Corporation and the Liquor and Gaming Authority. From February 1995 to June 1997, she served as minister responsible for the Status of Women and minister of Indian and Métis Affairs. On February 8, 2001, she was appointed minister of Culture, Youth and Recreation as well as provincial secretary. Throughout her political career, she has also served as minister of Post-Secondary Education and Skills Training, minister of Labour, Wascana Centre Authority, and minister responsible for the Information Highway.

In 2001, Crofford was one of seven candidates who ran in the NDP leadership race in an attempt to replace Roy Romanow, who had stepped down. She was eliminated after the first ballot vote.

Actively involved in her community,

Crofford has worked with a variety of organizations including cultural, human rights, community service, youth, labour and business. In 2000, the World March of Women honoured Crofford for her commitment and dedication to social justice. She is a member of the Cathedral Community Association, the Regina Community Clinic Association and the Saskatchewan Cultural Exchange Society. She also served as chair of the Regina Opening Ceremonies event for the 1995 Grey Cup.

Crofford is a recipient of the Canada 125 and Queen's Golden Jubilee medals. She also holds an Honorary Certificate in Languages from the Saskatchewan Centre of International Languages for her support of international language instruction and its contribution to enhancing trade.

Crofford was re-elected in the constituency of Regina Rosemont in 2003. After the election she was appointed minister of Community Resources.

JENN RUDDY, REGINA

## CROSS, JAMES ALBERT (1876–1952).

Col. J. A. Cross served as Saskatchewan's Attorney-General for much of the 1920s. Cross was born on December 11, 1876, in Caledonia Springs, Ontario. He left Ontario in 1898, coming to Regina to study law under James Balfour and Sir Frederick Haultain. He became a King's Counsellor in 1916, after being called to the bar in 1905. He also had an interest in

SAB R-B 432-2

JAMES CROSS

education, serving on the Regina Public School board for four years, including one year as the board's chairman.

James Cross first joined the Saskatchewan legislature during his service overseas in the First World War. He served as a Major for the Twenty-Eighth and Twenty-Seventh Battalions—Hamilton and City of Winnipeg—and was awarded a Distinguished Service Order. Upon returning from overseas Cross was promoted to Colonel on June 1, 1918, and was given command over the Military District Number 12, Regina, a position that he held until September of 1919, when he retired from the military and returned to law. In the 1917 provincial general election, Cross was elected as a member of the Legislative Assembly, to be the representative of the Saskatchewan soldiers in Great Britain. He held that seat until the dissolution of the legislature in 1921. Although he was a Liberal, Cross ran as an independent for this election.

In the 1921 provincial general election, Cross ran as Premier Martin's running mate for Regina City. Martin and Cross won Regina City's two seats in the Saskatchewan legislature. In April of 1922, after Martin stepped down as premier, Charles Dunning selected Cross to be the new Attorney General and minister in charge of the Bureau of Child Protection. Later that year, Regina City re-elected him as its MLA in a by-election. In the 1925 general election, Cross lost his Regina City seat, but then, later that year in a by-election, he was elected by acclamation as Willow Bunch's MLA. Cross served as Attorney General until December 1927, and left the Saskatchewan legislature in 1929. J. A. Cross died on March 1, 1952, at the age of seventy-five.

MARYANNE COTCHER, UNIVERSITY OF REGINA

**CUELENAERE, JOHN MARCEL** (1910–1967). However brief the Honourable John Marcel Cuelenaere's involvement was in provincial politics, his contributions to the province and specifically to the Prince Albert area were many.

Cuelenaere was born September 9, 1910, at Duck Lake to Emile and Marie (Pirat) Cuelenaere. He attended school at Duck Lake and later at Campion College in Regina. He continued his studies at the University of Saskatchewan where he received his degree in law. Cuelenaere was selected by John G. Diefenbaker from his graduating class to work in the latter's firm. As a lawyer, Cuelenaere offered much to his profession and these contributions prove impressive. They include being president of the Law Society of Saskatchewan in 1962, vice-president of the Canadian Bar Association in 1964, member of the Law Reforms Committee, as well as serving nine years as bencher of the Law Society.

His contributions at the municipal level were no less noteworthy. Cuelenaere was active as an alderman in Prince Albert for three years, later becoming mayor and serving in that capacity for eleven years. During this time he spent eight years as an executive of the Canadian Federation of Mayors. Cuelenaere also found time to serve as the president of Housing Development, as first chairman of the Northeast Saskatchewan Regional Library Board, as a member of the senate of the University of Saskatchewan for

COURTESY OF THE JOHN M. CUELENAERE
PUBLIC LIBRARY, PRINCE ALBERT

JOHN CUELENAERE

six years, and later as governor of the same university for three years.

Cuelenaere was first elected to the provincial legislature in April 1964. He was appointed minister of Natural Resources from May 1964 until October 1966, under the Thatcher Liberal administration. At this time he resigned his post and became a minister without portfolio until his death on February 12, 1967.

John Marcel Cuelenaere was a man deeply dedicated to anything he undertook. His commitment to his profession and to his constituents enabled him to make significant and lasting contributions to the province.

SUZANNE QUIRING, CHRISTOPHER LAKE

## CULLITON, EDWARD MILTON (1906–1991). Ted Culliton was born on April 9, 1906, in Grand Forks, Minnesota, but his family immigrated to Canada that same year and he grew up on a farm near Elbow. After graduating from the University of Saskatchewan, Culliton was accepted into the Saskatchewan bar in 1930 and established his practice in Gravelbourg. In 1935, Culliton was elected member of the Legislative Assembly for Gravelbourg as a Liberal. In 1938, he was re-elected and selected provincial secretary by Premier William Patterson. In 1941 he enlisted in the Canadian Army and served overseas for the duration of the war. He continued to serve in the provincial cabinet until 1944, as minister without portfolio, but lost his seat in the 1944 provincial election, in which the Co-operative Commonwealth Federation (CCF) defeated the Liberals. Culliton contested the

WEST'S STUDIO, REGINA•SAB R-B 7904

TED CULLITON

provincial Liberal leadership in 1946 and, although narrowly defeated by Walter Tucker, he still ran in the 1948 election for the Liberals and was re-elected in Gravelbourg. Culliton served as Liberal finance critic until he left politics in 1951 when he was appointed to the Saskatchewan Court of Appeal. In 1962 he was made Chief Justice for Saskatchewan and held this position until his retirement in 1981. After leaving the bench he chaired a commission on freedom of information and on provincial electoral boundaries. He was also the first chair of the Advisory Council of the Saskatchewan Order of Merit.

In 1952 Culliton was recruited by CCF Premier Tommy Douglas to serve as chair of the Saskatchewan Golden Jubilee Committee, the body responsible for organizing the mammoth celebration of Saskatchewan's fiftieth anniversary in 1955. His appointment was widely viewed as a testament to the high esteem Culliton was held in, as well as Douglas's confidence in his abilities and his desire to insure the celebrations were non-partisan. Culliton also served as a member of the University of Saskatchewan's Board of Governors for 12 years, including two years as chair and from 1962 to 1968 as Chancellor.

Throughout his life Culliton was dedicated to volunteer service and was prominent in such organizations as the Red Cross, the Canadian National Institute for the Blind, the United Appeal, the Canadian Curling Association and the Roman Catholic Church. In recognition of his long career of public service, Culliton received many honours including being named in 1981 as a Companion of the Order of Canada—the nation's highest honour. He also received the

Saskatchewan Order of Merit, an honorary doctorate of laws from the University of Saskatchewan, was inducted into the Canadian Curling Hall of Fame as a builder and was made a Knight Commander of St. Gregory by Pope Paul VI. Culliton passed away on March 14, 1991.

MIKE FEDYK, REGINA

## DANIELSON, GUSTAF HERMAN

(1883–1971). Born in Sweden in 1883, Herman Danielson immigrated to the United States in 1901 and found his way to Saskatchewan in 1904. He homesteaded south of Elbow later that year and began farming. Danielson was very active in local community organizations, especially in the co-operative movement, where he served three years as a Wheat Pool delegate and served on the board of the Davidson Co-operative Association for over forty years. Active in local government, Danielson was elected to the council of the Rural Municipality of Arm River for seven years and served a additional eight years as reeve. He further served the community by spending seven years on the local school board and 38 years on the Davidson Hospital Board.

Danielson was first elected to the Saskatchewan legislature in 1934 as part of the Liberal sweep of the province. In 1938, he narrowly won re-election, defeating Conservative leader John Diefenbaker. In 1944, he was again narrowly re-elected when the CCF threw the Liberals out of office. As only one of five Liberals elected and only one of three with previous legislative experience, Danielson became the Liberals' most effective critic of the new government. Re-elected four more times, Danielson, along with Mindy Lopston, provided the weak and demoralized Liberals with much needed experience and

SAB R-A 692

GUSTAF DANIELSON

continuity. Danielson became the most vocal critic of the government. His attacks on T. C. Douglas' policies and his length of service in the legislature made him a prominent figure in the province. In 1964, Progressive Conservative leader Martin Pedersen defeated Danielson. Ironically, it was the election that saw the Liberals returned to power after twenty years in opposition. In July 1971 Danielson died at his home in Davidson. After thirty years in the legislature, Danielson still remains the chamber's longest serving member.

BRETT QUIRING

## DARLING, JAMES ANDREW (1891–

1979). James Darling was the minister responsible for the modernization of Saskatchewan's basic infrastructure, from expanding telephone service and electrification of Saskatchewan farms to the introduction of natural gas heating

Darling was born in Shotts, Scotland, on May 21, 1891, into a well-to-do family of industrialists. Darling decided against entering the family business and chose to emigrate to Canada to farm. He arrived in Manitoba in 1908 and worked as a farm hand before purchasing a farm near Colonsay in 1911. Darling became active in the community, serving as secretary of the Elstow agricultural society, as a municipal councillor of Colonsay, and lengthy terms on both the local school board and the local telephone board. He also helped in a small way to organize the Saskatchewan Wheat Pool during the twenties and was active within the organization locally.

After the First World War, Darling was caught up in the farmers' protest against the federal government's agricultural policy. His first foray into partisan politics began with the Progressives, whom he helped organize in his region and whom he helped during the 1921 election campaign. Darling joined the CCF shortly after its inception and became the party's candidate for Watrous in 1944.

Darling was elected in the CCF's rise to power, serving the first term as a backbencher. After narrowly being re-elected in 1948, he was appointed to cabinet as the minister of Public Works and as minister of Telephones. In 1949, Darling launched the government's plan to expand and rationalize Saskatchewan's patchwork of electrical services. The existing Power Commission was discontinued and the Saskatchewan Power Corporation (SPC) was formed and began purchasing much of the province's electrical facilities. Under this policy, SPC began to electrify Saskatchewan's farms, allowing Saskatchewan to become the first province to fully electrify its rural areas, and lowering the price of power for consumers around the province. Under Darling's term as minister, Saskatchewan's telephone system was expanded in a similar way.

Re-elected in 1952, Darling fostered the development of the natural gas network in Saskatchewan. By guaranteeing SPC purchases of natural gas extracted from

SAB R-B 6179

JAMES DARLING

Saskatchewan gas fields, the industry expanded markedly. Also during this period, the outline of Saskatchewan's natural gas distribution network began to allow for the large-scale consumption of natural gas for home heating.

Re-elected in 1956, Darling resigned from cabinet and was elected Speaker of the House until his retirement from politics in 1960. Darling retired to Saskatoon and died there on October 18, 1979.

BRETT QUIRING

FURTHER READING: White, Clinton. 1976. *Power for a Province: A History of Saskatchewan Power*. Regina: Canadian Plains Research Center.

**D'AUTREMONT, DAN** (b. 1950). Dan D'Autremont was born December 28, 1950, to Hugh and Violet D'Autremont. Born in Redvers and raised in Alida, D'Autremont attended the University of Calgary, majoring in Engineering. Afterward, he worked for a number of companies in the oil industry including Mobil Oil, Pan Canadian Petroleum, Dome Petroleum and Producers Pipeline Inc. D'Autremont and his wife Heather have farmed in the Redvers area since 1977. Together they have three children: Nicholas, Amanda and Kelly.

D'Autremont was first elected in 1991 as a member of the Progressive Conservatives and then again in 1995. In 1999, D'Autremont was elected as a member of the Saskatchewan Party to represent the Cannington constituency. Since being one of the original eight founding members of the Saskatchewan Party, D'Autremont has served as the Saskatchewan Party Highways critic, Energy and Mines critic and Health critic. As Highways critic, D'Autremont started the "Worst Highways Contest," where Saskatchewan residents registered their vote for the worst highway in the province.

D'Autremont headed the Saskatchewan Party caucus review of government efficiency and served on the Saskatchewan Party caucus executive committee as House Leader. He was a member of the Saskatchewan Party caucus management committee, and sits on the legislature's board of internal economy. In 2003, he was easily re-elected as the Saskatchewan Party MLA for Cannington.

In addition to his MLA duties, D'Autremont is a member of the Saskatchewan Wildlife Federation, The Safari Club International and S. E. Borderline Gun Club.

WINTER FEDYK, KINGSTON, ON

## DAVIES, WILLIAM GWYNNE (BILL)

(1916–1999). An MLA and cabinet minister, Bill Davies was also one of the most prominent and influential labour leaders Saskatchewan has ever produced.

William Gwynne (Bill) Davies was born at Indian Head on February 11, 1916. He took his very early schooling there, then moved with his family to Regina when he was seven. He attended elementary and high school in Regina.

Davies was bright and a good student, but the death of his father forced him to abandon his studies and go to work at an early age to help support his young siblings and widowed mother. His first job was as an office boy at the Regina Daily Star newspaper, which paid him $25 a month.

Davies was interested in political causes from an early age. He attended his first socialist meeting at age

WEST'S STUDIO, REGINA•SAB R-B 8376

WILLIAM DAVIES

sixteen. He was also present at the Regina Riot and was tear-gassed by the police.

A long career in the labour movement began when Davies was working at the Swifts Canadian slaughterhouse in Moose Jaw in the 1940s. Davies, Hub Elkin, and others organized the plant for the United Packinghouse Workers of America.

Davies was a leader in the effort to establish the first Saskatchewan Federation of Labour which was affiliated to the Canadian Congress of Labour. He was named to the Federal Wartime Labour Relations Board and the Saskatchewan Labour Relations Board where he served for almost two decades.

Before the Saskatchewan Federation of Labour had a full-time president, the most prominent labour leader in the province was the executive secretary of the Federation, a position Davies held for twenty-five years. During that time Davies wrote hundreds of submissions, briefs, and policy papers on behalf of organized labour. He, more than anyone else, laid the philosophical and structural groundwork for modern industrial trade unionism in Saskatchewan.

In the early 1950s, when Pat Conroy retired as the top staff person with the Canadian Congress of Labour, CCL president Aaron Mosher and others offered this important national post to Davies. He declined, preferring to remain in Saskatchewan.

Davies also had a very successful political career, first as a member of Moose Jaw city council from 1948 to 1956, and then as a CCF Member of the Legislative Assembly for Moose Jaw from 1956 to 1971. He was appointed to cabinet from 1960 to 1964, serving as Public Works Minister and as minister of Public Health during the introduction of Medicare.

Davies' calm, sensible leadership during the three-week doctors' strike in July 1962, was a significant factor in the successful implementation of Medicare. He recruited physicians from abroad and kept the hospitals open until an agreement could be worked out with the Saskatchewan Medical Association.

During his tenure in municipal government Davies was instrumental in getting established the first low-cost housing program in the province. He was also appointed to the provincial health committee, which recommended a universal, publicly funded medical care plan.

As an MLA, Davies was known as a relentless advocate for working people. He championed causes such as the 40-hour, five-day workweek and three weeks' annual vacation with pay.

Davies was also an environmentalist and advocate for the conservation of the natural landscape. He was an avid walker and had a keen interest in archaeology, Aboriginal culture, and Saskatchewan and trade union history. He also wrote poetry and published a book of verse entitled *The Buffalo Stone*. Davies and Murray Cotterill of the steelworkers union spent many years researching and writing an extensive history of the Saskatchewan trade union movement. This manuscript survives and has formed the basis of subsequent labour histories.

Davies never really left the labour movement, even in retirement. He was constantly available for consultation and advice. He was a respected mentor to many younger trade union activists.

Davies was an accomplished and complex man. He was awarded an honorary doctor of laws degree from the University of Saskatchewan in 1978 and was named a member of the Order of Canada in 1975.

Davies was strongly committed to his leftist and pro-labour principles, and yet he was also one of the better negotiators around. He was forced out of the education system early, but became a widely read working class intellectual.

Just days before he died, Davies did something that was typical of him. From his hospital bed he wrote a letter of encouragement to 190 locked out packinghouse workers on a picket line in Moose Jaw. It was an inspirational message that, when read at an SFL convention a few days later, received a standing ovation from the 600 delegates.

Davies died November 9, 1999, at age 83. The headline in the Saskatchewan Federation of Labour newsletter read "Workers mourn the passing of Labour's Grand Old Man."

GARNET DISHAW, REGINA

**DAVIN, NICHOLAS FLOOD** (1840–1901) (baptized Nicholas Francis). N. F. Davin, lawyer, journalist, author, poet, orator, dandy, and first MP for Assiniboia West, was born in Kilfinane, Ireland. The details of his early life are somewhat unclear; after law studies and journalistic experience in Ireland and London, he came to Toronto to work for the *Globe* in 1872, having already acquired an impressive knowledge of classical and modern languages and literature.

In Toronto Davin soon began to be noticed as an orator and a writer. In speeches he constantly expressed his enthusiasm for Canada and the British Empire and, in his lengthy *The Irishman in Canada* (1877), praised the role played by his countrymen in establishing the new nation. His political aspirations found expression in the Conservative party and he was narrowly defeated in a strong Liberal constituency in 1878, the achievement resulting in a minor political appointment. Two years later, his reputation was enhanced by his brilliant, if losing, defence of the assassin of George Brown. Another patronage post, as secretary to the Royal Commission on the Pacific Railway, brought Davin to Regina in October 1882.

Impressed by the prospects of the new community, Davin sought funding to establish a Conservative newspaper, and the Regina *Leader* began publication on March 1, 1883. Soon in financial difficulties, he appealed to John A. Macdonald, obtaining the post of secretary to the Royal Commission on Chinese Immigration. The 1885 rebellion and the subsequent trial of Louis Riel brought national attention to him and the *Leader*: he succeeded, by disguising himself as a priest, in obtaining a prison-cell interview with Riel.

In Regina, Davin was involved in all aspects of civic, political, legal, and cultural life. His relationship with Kate Simpson Hayes would produce a son and a daughter. In 1886, Davin won the Conservative nomination for the newly-created riding of Assiniboia West. Elected in 1887, he retained the seat in 1891 with an increased majority. In 1896 he won again, though only when a tie was broken by the returning officer. After four years as the lone territorial MP in the Conservative opposition, he was defeated by Walter Scott, to whom he had sold the *Leader* in 1895.

In parliament Davin was known more for his personality and oratory than for his political acumen. He spoke long and often on a wide variety of topics, intervening particularly

SAB R-A 6665

NICHOLAS FLOOD DAVIN

in matters concerning the North-West, such as bilingualism, second homesteads, and the schools question, though he was ambivalent on the matter of the distribution of power between Ottawa and the Territories; in May 1895, he introduced a women's suffrage bill. Ultimately, he was disappointed in his political aspirations, never receiving the cabinet post that he felt he deserved. His *Eos: an Epic of the Dawn and other Poems* (1889) was the first volume of poetry published in the North-West Territories; the rest of his published work consists mainly of his own speeches. His legal career did not progress and other problems compounded his difficulties: he never overcame his alcoholism, and personal vendettas, notably against Edgar Dewdney and NWMP Superintendent Herchmer, punctuated his career. His marriage to Eliza Reid in 1895 does not appear to have been happy. Davin's ambitions thus remained unfulfilled and he died by his own hand in Winnipeg in 1901. However, Davin left his mark on the province and remains the only politician after whom a locality, a school, and a street have been named, and who, fittingly, is the subject of a biography, a play, and an opera.

BRAIN RAINEY, UNIVERSITY OF REGINA

FURTHER READING: Koester, C. B. 1980. *Mr. Davin, M.P.* Saskatoon: Western Producer Prairie Books. • Thompson, John Herd. 1994. "Davin, Nicholas Flood." *Dictionary of Canadian Biography XIII.* Toronto: University of Toronto Press. 248–253.

## DAVIS, THOMAS CLAYTON (1889–1960). Lawyer, mayor, long-time minister,

diplomat and political confidant of Jimmy Gardiner, Thomas Davis was one of the most prominent ministers of the Gardiner and Patterson governments.

Davis was born into a political family on September 6, 1889, in Prince Albert. His father, Thomas Osborne Davis, served two terms as a member of the House of Commons and then several years in the Senate before his death. Davis was educated in Prince Albert before completing university at St. Johns' College in Winnipeg and law school at Osgoode Hall in Toronto. He returned to practice law in Prince Albert where he began his political career in 1916 as a city alderman. After serving two terms as alderman, Davis won the mayoralty in 1921 and served until 1924.

Davis inherited his father's political leanings and contested the 1925 provincial election for the Liberals in Prince Albert. Easily winning the election, he was quickly brought into cabinet when James Gardiner replaced Charles Dunning as premier. Appointed as the province's first minister of Municipal Affairs, his contribution was mainly as Gardiner's minister for Northern Saskatchewan. When Prime Minister W. L. M. King lost his seat in 1926 and chose to run in Prince Albert, Davis was instrumental in convincing King to establish the Prince Albert National Park.

In the 1929 election, Davis narrowly fought off a challenge from a young Prince Albert lawyer, John Diefenbaker. However, the government fell and Davis was relegated to Opposition. He served as one of the government's most vocal opponents. In 1934, he was again re-elected and was re-appointed to cabinet in the new Liberal government as Attorney

SAB R-B 8266

THOMAS CLAYTON DAVIS

General. When Gardiner resigned as premier to accept a cabinet post in the federal government, Davis was widely touted as his replacement. However, Davis did not want the job and remained as Attorney General in the William Patterson government.

Re-elected in 1938, Davis resigned in 1939 to take an appointment on the Saskatchewan Court of Appeal. His term on the bench was short-lived as the next year he was appointed deputy minister of War Services with the federal government. In 1943, he received his first diplomatic appointment as Canadian High Commissioner to Australia. He would serve in several diplomatic posts in China, Japan and West Germany until his retirement in 1957. Retiring to Victoria, he died on January 21, 1960.

BRETT QUIRING

**FURTHER READING:** Ward, Norman, and David Smith. 1990. *Jimmy Gardiner: Relentless Liberal*. Toronto: University of Toronto Press.

## DE JONG, SIMON LEENDERT (b. 1942).

Long-time Regina MP and federal NDP leadership candidate, Simon De Jong was born April 29, 1942. The son of a Dutch official in Indonesia, he was born in a Japanese internment camp during the war. De Jong came to Canada with his parents in 1951.

Very active in politics at an early age, De Jong was elected president of the Saskatchewan CCF youth wing at the age of fifteen. Active in public speaking and debate, he won the Bryant Oratorical contest that same year. Upon completing high school, De Jong enrolled at the Regina Campus of the

University of Saskatchewan and once again took an active role in politics. De Jong led the NDP club on campus for much of his time there and also served as president of the students' union for a year. He was also an accomplished painter and his works appeared in many exhibitions.

After working for the NDP for a short period, he made his first attempt to enter politics in 1968, contesting the NDP nomination in Regina Lake Centre, but lost to future MP Les Benjamin. In 1969 he moved to Vancouver and was co-director of a youth agency. He also helped to establish several co-operatives and a community clinic in that city. Returning to Regina in 1975, he worked in the Saskatchewan public service for three years before establishing a restaurant in Regina. In 1979, he was successful in securing the NDP nomination in Regina East. Elected in 1979, he was re-elected in Regina East in 1980 and 1984. In 1988, when Regina East was split, he was re-elected in the riding of Regina Qu'Appelle. When party leader Ed Broadbent resigned in 1989, De Jong contested the leadership of the party. Finishing fourth out of seven candidates, he made a strong showing but was defeated.

During his years in parliament he served as his party's critic in a wide variety of capacities such as arts, science, youth, and national revenue. Re-elected for a final time in 1993, he was one of the few NDP MPs to win re-election as the party fell from forty-four MPs to only nine. De Jong served out the term and did not contest

SIMON DE JONG

the 1997 election. After the election De Jong retired to California.

BRETT QUIRING

## DEVINE, GRANT (b. 1944).

Grant Devine was born July 5, 1944, in Regina, and was raised on a farm that his grandfather had homesteaded near Lake Valley, not far from Moose Jaw. After high school he enrolled at the University of Saskatchewan, where he earned a Bachelor of Science degree in Agriculture. He pursued post-graduate studies and completed a Ph.D. in Agricultural Economics at Ohio State University in 1976. He joined the faculty of the University of Saskatchewan, where he taught Agricultural Marketing and Consumer Economics.

Devine was drawn to politics at a time when the fortunes of the Saskatchewan Progressive Conservative Party were rising. Dick Collver, who was elected leader in 1973, argued that the Liberals were a spent force provincially and that the only way to dislodge the NDP government was to build an anti-socialist coalition around the Conservatives. His brand of right-wing populism appealed to voters. In the 1978 election, the PCs displaced the Liberals as the official opposition.

The election marked Grant Devine's entry into electoral politics. He contested the constituency of Saskatoon Nutana and was soundly defeated. When Collver stepped down as leader, Devine put his name forward and cruised to victory at the November 1979 convention. He led the party into the provincial election called for April 26, 1982. It soon became evident that the NDP was vulnerable. Interest rates were at 18 percent and there was a feeling that Allan Blakeney's eleven-year-old government was out of touch with the people. On the first day of the campaign,

Devine announced that he would eliminate the provincial tax on gasoline. This was followed by a commitment to guarantee home mortgage rates at 13.25 percent. The conservatives rolled to victory, winning 54.1 percent of the popular vote and 55 out of 64 seats in the legislature.

One of the first actions of the new administration was to organize an "Open for Business" conference in October 1982 to advertise the fact that the "socialist" era was over, and private investment and free enterprise were welcome in Saskatchewan. As an incentive to the oil industry, the government introduced a three-year royalty holiday for new wells and reduced royalties for existing wells. Drilling increased markedly, but at the sacrifice of a lower royalty revenue share of the value of production. The expansion of Crown corporations was curtailed, but there was no large-scale effort to sell them. A notable exception was the Land Bank, which the NDP had set up to facilitate the inter-generational transfer of land. Devine said the government should not be in the business of owning land, and he dismantled the Land Bank, replacing it with 8 percent loans to enable farmers to purchase their own land.

The government ran consecutive deficit budgets, accumulating a debt of over $1.5 billion its first four years in office. Sensing that he might lose the 1986 election, Devine opened the coffers, giving farmers production loans at 6 percent and homeowners $1,500 home-improvement matching grants. The strategy worked. Although he narrowly lost the popular vote to the NDP, Devine won a second term with 38 seats, against 25 for the NDP and one for the Liberals. In doing so, the

SAB 82-773-0024

GRANT DEVINE

PCs ran up a deficit of over $1.2 billion in 1986-87, a far cry from the deficit figure of $389 million that had been presented in the pre-election budget.

The fiscal crisis led to cutbacks in services, cancellation of programs, and firing of employees. The government launched a privatization crusade, disposing of a wide array of Crown corporations from the $15 million Saskminerals company to the Potash Corporation, valued at well over $1 billion. When the government broke its promise not to sell utilities and placed the natural gas division of SaskPower on the block, the NDP brought the legislature to a halt by letting the bells ring for seventeen days. The public sided with the NDP, and the government backed down from the sale.

Although he pledged to get government out of business, Devine gave loans, subsidies, guarantees and other incentives to private business. The results were impressive: two heavy oil upgraders, a fertilizer plant, a paper mill, a pulp mill, and a bacon-processing plant. The Rafferty-Alameda Dams were built as a public works megaproject. However, the government was never able to control the debt it had incurred in its first term. By the end of the 1980s it was running a surplus on operating expenses excluding debt charges, but interest payments drove the province deeper into debt each year. By 1991-92 the accumulated debt was over $15 billion, and annual interest payment exceeded $500 million, the third largest item in the budget after health and education.

On the national scene, Devine reversed the old rule of Saskatchewan politics: pick a fight with Ottawa at election time. He was a staunch supporter of Prime Minister Brian

Mulroney and gave wholehearted support to Mulroney's two main initiatives, the Meech Lake Accord and the Free Trade Agreement with the United States. Mulroney responded with deficiency payments to Saskatchewan farmers who were suffering drought and record-low grain prices. Farmers were not the only beneficiaries: the billion-dollar assistance package announced days before the 1986 provincial election was a key element in Devine's victory.

Devine sought to undo the legacy of CCF/NDP socialism in Saskatchewan and build a pro-business, entrepreneurial culture. His government carried out a massive privatization program, reduced social assistance payments, and curbed the power of labour unions, but private enterprise continued to rely heavily on government financial assistance. The greatest failure of the Devine years was the accumulation of an unprecedented debt, much of it attributable to tax cuts and unwise election spending. The government lost power in 1991, winning only 10 seats and 25 percent of the popular vote. After the election, a scandal came to light, resulting in the conviction of several former Conservative MLAs on fraud charges. Despite setbacks, Devine remained an eternal optimist holding fast to his free enterprise principles and his belief in the potential of Saskatchewan.

JAMES M. PITSULA, UNIVERSITY OF REGINA

---

**FURTHER READING:** Biggs, Lesley, and Mark Stobbe (eds.). 1991. *Devine Rule in Saskatchewan: A Decade of Hope and Hardship.* Saskatoon: Fifth House. • Pitsula, James M., and Ken Rasmussen. 1990. *Privatizing a Province: The New Right in Saskatchewan.* Vancouver: New Star.

## DEWDNEY, EDGAR (1835–1916). Edgar Dewdney held several key public offices that enabled him to play an important role in the political and economic development of Western Canada in the second half of the nineteenth century.

He was born in Bideford, Devonshire, England on November 5, 1835, to a prosperous family. Arriving in Victoria in the Crown Colony of Vancouver Island in May 1859 during a gold rush, he spent more than a decade surveying and building trails through the mountains on the mainland. In 1872, shortly after British Columbia's entry into Confederation, he was elected MP for Yale and became a loyal devotee of John A. Macdonald and the Conservative Party. In Parliament he pursued the narrow agenda of getting the transcontinental railway built with the terminal route via the Fraser Valley, where he happened to have real estate interests.

In 1879 Dewdney became Indian commissioner of the North-West Territories with the immediate task of averting mass starvation and unrest among the Plains Indians following the sudden disappearance of the buffalo. Backed by a small contingent of Indian agents and Mounted Police, he used the distribution of rations as a device to impose state authority on the Native population. Facing hunger and destitution, Natives were compelled to settle on reserves, adopt agriculture and send their children to mission schools. These measures to bring about self-sufficiency and cultural assimilation appeared to be working, but provoked a sullen resentment that could not be repressed in the spring of 1885. Dewdney has often been blamed for the North-West Rebellion, but in truth much of the responsibility lay in policies devised in Ottawa by men unfamiliar with western conditions. He had warned his superiors of the dangers and urged them to resolve Native grievances, but to little avail. He did succeed, however, in limiting Indian involvement in the hostilities by acts of unprecedented generosity with food and presents. Following the rebellion, a policy of strict surveillance and coercive tutelage was imposed, and it endured as his legacy to Indian administration in the region.

In 1881 Dewdney was appointed Lieutenant-Governor of the North-West Territories, a position he held in conjunction with that of Indian commissioner. One of his first significant acts in this role was the selection of Regina as the new territorial capital in 1882. He happened to own land in the vicinity and was widely criticized by Liberal politicians and the press for his attempt to profit from the decision. As Lieutenant-Governor, he exercised real executive power and his authority was independent of the North-West Council, a partly elected, partly appointed body that served as an incipient popular assembly for the region. As the settler population grew, the elected Council members became increasingly insistent on a larger role in decision-making. They demanded a responsible executive, representation in Parliament and ultimately provincial status. The Lieutenant-Governor's policy, in accordance with Prime Minister Macdonald's wishes, was to keep these demands in check while gradually conceding democratic reforms.

In 1888 Dewdney resigned his two positions in Regina and entered Macdonald's federal cabinet as minister of the Interior. His connection with the prairie region remained, in that he was now MP for Assiniboia East and his portfolio included the administration of the North-West Territories. In connection with this, his policy was as before: the gradual devolution of political powers to the Territorial

SAB R-B 48-1

EDGAR DEWDNEY

Assembly (which had replaced the North-West Council in 1888) while resisting the creation of a responsible executive.

Dewdney left Parliament and his cabinet post in October 1892 to take up the lieutenant-governorship of British Columbia, something he had long coveted. His new position was mainly social and ceremonial in nature, and he enjoyed it immensely. Upon completion of his term of office in 1897, he stayed on in Victoria in semi-retirement, pursuing his passion for investments in real estate, mining and railways. He died on August 8, 1916. He was married twice and there were no children from either relationship.

Edgar Dewdney was a representative of a class of immigrant adventurers who saw in the western Canadian frontier an opportunity for self-aggrandizement. He viewed public office as a means to personal wealth and acquired a reputation as a speculative fortune hunter. Yet his dream of sufficient wealth to lead a life of gentlemanly leisure continued to elude him. He was also noted for his intense loyalty to the Conservative Party—a man who readily used his public offices to dispense an enormous array of patronage appointments and government contracts to the party faithful. One of the main thoroughfares in Regina is named in his honour.

BRIAN TITLEY, THE UNIVERSITY OF LETHBRIDGE

## DEWHURST, FREDERICK ARTHUR
(1911–1985). The longest-serving CCF/NDP MLA and the second-longest-serving member in the history of the Saskatchewan legislature, Fred Dewhurst's most notable contribution to Saskatchewan politics was as Speaker.

Born in Regina on March 17, 1911, Dewhurst was raised on a farm near Archerwill. After finishing school, Dewhurst began farming in the area and was involved in many local organizations. First becoming active in the co-operative movement, Dewhurst served on the boards of both the Archerwill Co-op and the Archerwill Credit Union for over twenty-five years. Involved in the CCF, he was part of the nucleus of the party in his region, helping to elect George Williams to the legislature in 1934. When Williams resigned his seat of Wadena in 1945, Dewhurst contested the by-election and won the seat with over eighty percent of the vote. Easily re-elected in 1948, 1952, 1956 and 1960, Dewhurst was elected Deputy Speaker in 1961 and served in that capacity until Speaker Everett Wood was appointed to cabinet the next year, resulting in Dewhurst's election as Speaker. A fierce partisan CCFer while a backbencher, his election as Speaker caused concern for many Liberals over how he would conduct himself. However, in his first years as Speaker, these doubts were found to be unwarranted as he proved himself a tough but fair Speaker to both sides of the house.

Re-elected in 1964, Dewhurst left the Speaker's chair as the Liberals under Ross Thatcher formed government. Re-elected again in 1967 and 1971, Dewhurst re-gained the Speaker's chair as the NDP regained power. As such, Dewhurst was the only Speaker to serve non-consecutive terms. Dewhurst did not contest the 1975

WEST'S STUDIO, REGINA•SAB R-A 8375

FREDERICK DEWHURST

election and retired from politics.

Dewhurst sold his farm in Archerwill and moved to Wynyard in 1967. In retirement he was still active in his community as president of the Wynyard Community Clinic and in many other capacities. Dewhurst died in Wynyard on July 30, 1985.

BRETT QUIRING

**DIEFENBAKER, JOHN GEORGE** (1895–1979). Although long associated with Saskatchewan in the public mind, John Diefenbaker was actually born in Neustadt, Ontario, on September 18, 1895, and came west when much of it was still the North-West Territories. He was the eldest of the two sons of William T. Diefenbaker and his wife Mary (née Bannerman). The family moved to the Fort Carlton district in 1903 because the doctors of the era recommended the dry prairie climate to help his father's breathing problems.

In 1905, the family moved to Hague, Saskatchewan, and in 1906 relocated to a homestead near Borden. In 1910, the Diefenbaker family moved to Saskatoon so that John and his brother Elmer could attend high school. John Diefenbaker graduated from what is now Nutana Collegiate in the spring of 1912, and entered the University of Saskatchewan as a member of the first class to be educated on the new campus.

John Diefenbaker studied economics and politics for his B.A., and began graduate work on an M.A. In 1916, he volunteered for service in World War I, and was granted his M.A. *in absentia*. He was sent to England for training, but was removed from service as an invalid and returned to Canada in 1917. He returned to the University of Saskatchewan to study law, graduating in 1918.

John Diefenbaker was called to the

Saskatchewan Bar in 1919, and opened his own law office in Wakaw on July 1, 1919. He had always been interested in politics, and in 1920 won election as an alderman in Wakaw. In 1922, he won a decision protecting French language rights in Saskatchewan in the case of Boutin *et al* vs. Mackie.

In 1924, Diefenbaker opened a new law office in Prince Albert, beginning his long association with that city. He ran as a Conservative in the federal elections of 1925 and 1926 and in the provincial election of 1929, but was defeated each time. On June 29, 1929, he married Edna Mae Brower, a school teacher who had grown up in Langham.

Diefenbaker ran for mayor of Prince Albert in 1933, but was defeated. He became leader of the provincial Conservative party in 1936 and ran in the provincial election of 1938, but lost again. He considered abandoning politics, but was persuaded to run one last time in the federal election of 1940. He won the riding of Lake Centre, and was elected to every federal Parliament thereafter, although he did switch to the Prince Albert riding in 1953.

He ran for the Conservative party leadership in 1942, but came third to John Bracken, who insisted that the party become the Progressive Conservatives. He again ran for leader in 1948, but lost to George Drew. He lost his wife Edna to leukemia in 1951.

John Diefenbaker married Olive Freeman Palmer on December 8, 1953. He won the leadership of the Progressive Conservatives in 1956. In 1957, he led his party to a surprising election victory, although it was a minority government.

In 1958, Parliament was dissolved and Diefenbaker led his party to the largest

SAB R-B4008

JOHN G. DIEFENBAKER

election victory in Canadian political history. His government lost its majority in the federal election of 1962, but continued as a minority government. In 1963, Lester Pearson led the Liberals to a minority government, and Diefenbaker became leader of the Opposition. He continued in that role until 1967 when he gave way to Robert Stanfield who had been elected leader of the party the year before. Diefenbaker continued to serve as a Member of Parliament until his death in 1979.

The governments led by John Diefenbaker are notable for a number of accomplishments. Diefenbaker was a champion of human rights, and his government passed Canada's first Bill of Rights in 1958. He also appointed the first First Nations senator, James Gladstone of Alberta, and extended the right to vote to First Nations people. Diefenbaker criticized the Soviet Union for its repression of minorities. He headed the movement for racial equality in the Commonwealth, which led to South Africa leaving that organization.

Having grown up on a pioneer farm, Diefenbaker knew the difficulties faced by the agricultural industry. His government brought in an Agricultural Stabilization Act in 1958 which provided for flexible support and minimum prices on commodities. The Diefenbaker government also began wheat sales to China, which opened a huge new market for Canadian farmers. Diefenbaker supported the construction of the South Saskatchewan Dam at Outlook (later named the Gardiner Dam). The lake it created was named Lake Diefenbaker in his honour.

A controversial decision of the Diefenbaker government, which still resonates, was the cancellation of the Avro Arrow airplane. This jet had been developed to intercept Soviet bombers over the Arctic should North America ever be attacked. When the Russians launched Sputnik it was evident that they had missiles which could reach across the world, and the Arrow's task was over before it really began. The Americans and British, who had similar aircraft under development, cancelled their programs in favour of missile systems. After failing to find other customers or uses for the airplane, the Diefenbaker government cancelled the Arrow in 1959.

The defence crisis created by the Soviet missile threat was a contributing factor to the end of the Diefenbaker government. The military insisted on a missile defence system, but the only one available was the already obsolete American Bomarc missile. It was designed to be equipped with a nuclear warhead, and this created a controversy in Canada, which had never had nuclear weapons. John Diefenbaker's government divided on the issue, and he lost the confidence of Parliament. This defeat led to the election of 1963, won by the Pearson Liberals.

Diefenbaker lost his second wife Olive in 1976. He was re-elected to Parliament for a record thirteenth time in 1979. He passed away at his home in Ottawa on August 16, 1979. A state funeral was held in Ottawa, and his body was transported by train across the country, stopping many times for Canadians to pay their respects. He is buried, with Olive, beside the Diefenbaker Canada Centre on the campus of the University of Saskatchewan in Saskatoon.

R. BRUCE SHEPARD, SASKATOON

**FURTHER READING:** Diefenbaker, John G. 1972. *One Canada* (3 vols.) Toronto: Macmillan. • Shepard, R. Bruce, and D.C. Story (eds.) 1998. *The Diefenbaker Legacy: Canadian Law, Politics, and Society Since 1957*. Regina: Canadian Plains Research Center. • Smith, Denis. 1995. *Rogue Tory: The Life and Legend of John G. Diefenbaker*. Toronto: Macfarlane, Walter and Ross.

## DOUGLAS, JAMES MOFFAT (1839–1920).

James Moffat Douglas was born in Linton, Scotland, on May 26, 1839. A year after his arrival into this world, his family emigrated to Upper Canada.

He was ordained a minister of the Presbyterian Church of Canada on October 16, 1867, after studying at the University of Toronto, Knox College, and the Princeton University Seminary. He initially served congregations in Ontario, but he also became a missionary to Indore, India. In 1882 he was assigned to preside over a parish in Marnis, Manitoba. He later served in Brandon, Manitoba, until 1897, and then in Moosomin from 1890 to 1893. He established a homestead called Tantallon (later to serve as the name for the village) with his son John Douglas in the North-West Territories in 1883, but he did not permanently reside there until 1893. In 1894 he was nominated as a candidate for the Patrons of Industry, an agrarian political movement. He ran, and won the seat for Assiniboia East in the federal election of 1896 as a Patron-Liberal. He was deeply involved in agricultural legislation, and he even proposed a bill in 1898 to end the perceived monopoly on the grain trade. He had to introduce this bill three times before the government finally responded by creating a commission to examine the trade. This commission was to recommend the basis for the Manitoba *Grain Act* of 1900. In that same year he was re-elected for his riding in Assiniboia East. In 1906 he was appointed to the Senate and served as chairman of the Senate's committee on agriculture. A member of the Senate until his death on August 19, 1920, he remained an active debater of agrarian and immigration issues.

JEREMY MOHR, UNIVERSITY OF WESTERN ONTARIO

**DOUGLAS, JOHN TAYLOR** (1892–1976). John Douglas was born at Cumberland, Ontario, on October 28, 1892. In 1906, John traveled west with his parents John Douglas, Sr., and Anne Welsh to the Laura district in Saskatchewan. He received a high school education from the province as well as a degree from the University of Saskatchewan's college of Agriculture. Completing his education, Mr. Douglas began farming in the Laura district.

Douglas, a long-time member of the Saskatchewan Legislative Assembly, first became involved with the Progressive movement in 1919. Almost immediately he became actively involved in the movement, taking over the job of secretary of the Rosetown constituency Progressive Association. As the movement slowly evolved into the CCF, Douglas began supporting the policies of the new party. In a taped interview he explains that he liked the CCF because many of the same people who had been involved in the Progressive movement were now involved in the organization of the CCF. Douglas stated that he was also in favor of their "socialist philosophy" and their belief in "Christian socialism."

In 1935 John Douglas managed the campaign in the riding of Rosetown-Biggar, which elected M. J. Coldwell to the House of Commons. From 1936 to 1941, Douglas served on the CCF Saskatchewan council. In 1941 he became the party's provincial organizer. Over the course of the next three years he helped transform a party that had come out of the 1938 provincial election disillusioned and downtrodden into a provincial powerhouse. During these years of organization, he visited almost every riding in the province, stressing the need for poll organization and people of substance for candidates. In 1944 his efforts were rewarded as the CCF swept to power and he was elected to the Legislative Assembly. Douglas would win three more elections and serve a total of sixteen years in the T. C. Douglas administration, retiring in 1960.

In 1944 John Douglas was named minister of Highways and Transportation and minister of Public Works. In 1946 he set up a Royal Commission on Penal Reform and organized the Saskatchewan Transportation Company into a Crown corporation. When he took on the job of Highways minister, he inherited a department that was under-staffed and lacked modern equipment. It was also a well-known fact that the province had some of the worst roads on the continent. During his time in office Douglas made it a priority to hire competent staff as well as update the highway equipment. Working with an undersized budget, he did his best to improve the condition of Saskatchewan's highways.

Douglas passed away February 19, 1976, at the age of eighty-four.

DWAYNE YASINOWSKI, UNIVERSITY OF REGINA

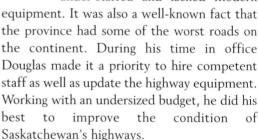

SAB R-A 11520

JOHN TAYLOR DOUGLAS

**FURTHER READING:** McLeod, Thomas H., and Ian McLeod. 1987. *Tommy Douglas: The Road to Jerusalem.* Edmonton: Hurtig Publishers. • Saskatchewan Archives Board. Interview with J T Douglas, tapes R-6086, R-6087.

**DOUGLAS, THOMAS CLEMENT** (1904–1986). Premier and national party leader Tommy Douglas was Saskatchewan's most notable and influential politician. He led the CCF to victory in 1944 and led a government that transformed the role of government in Saskatchewan and across the country.

Douglas was born in Falkirk, Scotland, on October 20, 1904, and grew up in a working-class family. The Scottish Independent Labour Party had heavily influenced his father Tom, and that set the tone for Douglas' political education. Douglas moved with his family to Winnipeg in 1910. At the time, Winnipeg was the centre of a strong working class and social gospel movement. Both these movements had a profound effect on Douglas. He became active in the Labour party and by the early twenties decided to devote his life to social reform through Christian ministry. He first attended Brandon College in 1924. The college served as the training ground for Baptist ministers, and in 1927 Douglas started his first ministry. In 1929, he accepted a full-time ministry at Calvary Baptist Church in Weyburn. While preaching, Douglas finished his Bachelor of Arts in 1930 and Master of Arts from McMaster by correspondence in 1933. He began a doctorate at the University of Chicago but failed to complete all the requirements, preferring to remain ministering in Weyburn.

For Douglas, religion was closely connected with politics. Disinterested in doctrinal disputes and sectarianism of some churches, he believed that the best way to serve God was to create a better, more just society. As a result, Douglas quickly became active in Weyburn politics. He founded a branch of the Independent Labour Party in Weyburn and was active in the formation of the CCF. In 1934, he unsuccessfully contested office for the first time in the provincial election. Douglas tried again in 1935, running in the federal riding of Weyburn, and this time he was narrowly elected.

Going to the House of Commons as one of seven CCF MPs, Douglas soon established himself as one of the CCF's most potent weapons. A gifted orator and debater, Douglas made a name for himself in the House of Commons. Re-elected in 1940, many Saskatchewan CCF activists began calling for Douglas to return to provincial politics and lead the provincial CCF. The local party was embroiled in internal strife as party leader George Williams' style alienated himself from a large section of the party. Douglas challenged Williams for the party presidency in 1941 and won. A year later he won the party leadership over Williams supporter and MLA John H. Brockelbank.

After becoming leader, Douglas set about toppling the Liberal government. Party membership expanded and CCF became more organized. In 1944, Douglas swept the province, winning 47 of the provinces 53 seats and capturing over 53 percent of the vote. During the first term of the government, Douglas put forward an ambitious programme of reform. Labour standards were greatly improved, the educational system was consolidated, legislation was introduced to expand the co-operative sector of the economy and bills were enacted to protect farmers from foreclosure. The government further established many social welfare programs and began to set the foundation of

SAB R-WS15159(1)

T. C. DOUGLAS

socialized medicare. The CCF also began to play a larger role in the economy and the government became involved in a number of business ventures such as a shoe factory, a box factory, and a brick plant. These ventures attracted a great deal of opposition, and after 1948 the government largely retreated from non-utility business ventures.

The Douglas government continued its program and was re-elected four times in 1948, 1952, 1956, and 1960. The Douglas government was largely responsible for the modernization of Saskatchewan by using Crown Corporations to expand electricity and telephone service throughout the province, using natural gas as a heating source, and expanding the province's highway system.

However, Douglas' contribution was most significant in the field of health care. The government provided a province-wide hospitalization programme in 1947, established a medical school at the University of Saskatchewan, and increased the mental health budget many times over. After contesting the 1960 general election on the issue of universal state-run health insurance, Douglas began to set up the parameters of the Medicare system. After a heated consultation process and substantial opposition from the doctors, Douglas moved the Medicare legislation into the legislature. However, Douglas never saw the legislation passed.

In 1961, Douglas returned to the federal arena to lead the New Democratic Party, which had been created after the CCF and the Canadian Labour Congress entered into a new political alliance. Douglas first ran for the party in 1962 in the riding of Regina City but, facing the brunt of the doctors' strike over the Medicare issue, Douglas lost.

Leaving Saskatchewan to contest a by-election in the British Columbia riding of Burnaby-Coquitlam, Douglas returned to the House of Commons. Douglas continued to lead the Federal NDP but would never again represent a Saskatchewan riding. He was re-elected in 1963 and 1965 in Burnaby and, after defeat in 1968, he ran in Nanaimo and won in 1969, 1972, and 1974. In 1972 Douglas resigned as NDP leader, but continued to be a prominent party spokesman until he retired from politics in 1979.

On February 24, 1986, Douglas died in Ottawa.

BRETT QUIRING

**FURTHER READING:** McLeod, Thomas H., and Ian McLeod. 1987. *Tommy Douglas: The Road to Jerusalem.* Edmonton: Hurtig Publishers. • Shackleton, Doris French. 1975. *Tommy Douglas.* Toronto: McClelland and Stewart. • Thomas, Lewis. 1981. "The CCF Victory in Saskatchewan, 1944." *Saskatchewan History.* 34 (1): 1–16.

## DUNCAN, JOAN HEATHER (née Tratch) (b. 1941).

Joan Duncan, along with Patricia Smith, were the first female cabinet ministers appointed in Saskatchewan history.

Born October 30, 1941, in Cudworth, Duncan was educated at the University of Saskatchewan. Before entering politics she owned and operated a drug store in Maple Creek. In 1978, Duncan first contested public office running for the Progressive Conservatives in the constituency of Maple Creek. Easily elected in the general election, Duncan soon took a prominent role

SAB R-P5 82-612-902

JOAN DUNCAN

as the only woman elected to the legislature that term. A vocal member of the Opposition, Duncan was a key member of the Progressive Conservative revitalization and strong supporter of Grant Devine's campaign for party leader.

Easily re-elected in the Conservative sweep of 1982, Duncan was appointed to Devine's first cabinet as minister of Government Services. Although holding a variety of minor cabinet positions during her term, Duncan nevertheless spearheaded several significant initiatives and programs. As minister responsible for Northern Saskatchewan, she shaped the Devine government's policy on the region and oversaw the construction of the LaLoche-Fort McMurray road. While Tourism minister, the government invested significantly in developing the industry through various local initiatives and through building a tourist infrastructure throughout the province.

In 1989, Duncan was dropped from cabinet, a move that proved to be her undoing in more than one way. In retaliation she filed false expense claims to finance a personal trip to Hawaii and to receive a $1,500 kickback. She did not contest the 1991 election, but her false expense claims were uncovered by an RCMP investigation into the financial dealings of the Progressive Conservative caucus office. She was charged, pleaded guilty and was ordered to repay the money plus a $5,000 fine.

BRETT QUIRING

## DUNN, CHARLES MORTON (1892–1975).

Charles Dunn was protégé and heir of James Gardiner's political organization. As an influential minister in the Gardiner and Patterson governments, Dunn was one of the Liberal Party's key political ministers. His political defeats in 1938 marked the decline in power of the Saskatchewan Liberal Party in the years leading up to the CCF victory in 1944.

SAB R-A 639

CHARLES DUNN

Born July 17, 1892, in Granville Ferry, Nova Scotia, Dunn was educated at Annapolis Royal Academy. Coming to Saskatchewan as a young man, Dunn was employed as a life insurance agent for Mutual Life of Canada. Involved in his profession, he became very active in the Life Underwriters Association of Canada, serving as its president.

Active in the Liberal Party, Dunn first ran for public office in 1929 in the constituency of Pheasant Hills. Dunn was successful and served his first term in Opposition as the Liberal government was defeated. In spite of his inexperience, Dunn managed to play an important role in Opposition as one of the party's most vocal critics of the government. Re-elected in 1934, this time in the constituency of Francis, Dunn was immediately appointed to cabinet as minister of Highways. The post was highly influential as the department had historically been the main source of government political patronage and, as such, the position also carried with it the responsibility for the Liberal Party's organizational structure. With the departure of James Gardiner to federal politics in 1935, Dunn assumed responsibility for the party's electoral machine. In 1938, Dunn again changed seats, running in Gardiner's old seat of Melville. However, the Opposition was eager to defeat Dunn and both the local CCF and

Conservative parties chose not to nominate candidates in favour of the Social Credit candidate, John Herman. Consolidation of the anti-Liberal vote proved to be successful as Dunn was narrowly defeated. However, Premier William Patterson was eager to keep Dunn in cabinet and arranged for the Liberal MLA in Humboldt to step down, creating a vacancy for Dunn. Once again only one anti-Liberal contested the seat, as the local Social Credit and Conservative parties supported CCF candidate Joseph Burton. Once again, Dunn was narrowly defeated, ending his political career.

Dunn remained active within the Liberal Party, but never again contested office. He died on November 15, 1975.

BRETT QUIRING

## DUNNING, CHARLES AVERY (1885-1958).
Charles Dunning was born July 31, 1885 in Leicestershire, England. He possessed little formal education, and at the age of sixteen, decided to come to Canada to farm. Dunning arrived in Canada in 1902, penniless and without any prior knowledge of agriculture. Nevertheless he went west, settling in the Yorkton area. He spent the first year working as a farm labourer before he established a homestead near Beaverdale. Finding settlement conditions favorable, he sent word to England for his family and eventually formed a farming partnership with his father.

Dunning's experience in farming led him to disillusionment with the treatment of farmers at the hands of station agents, farm implement dealers,

SAB R-A 631 (2)

CHARLES DUNNING

and all other businessmen; it was this sentiment that first brought him into the farmers' movement. Dunning's first involvement was with the Territorial Grain Growers Association and later the Saskatchewan Grain Growers Association (SGGA) local in Beaverdale. Having a natural speaking ability, Dunning soon established himself as one of the local's most prominent activists and represented them at the 1910 SGGA convention in Prince Albert where he was elected the SGGA district director for his area.

At the following SGGA convention in 1911, Dunning improved his position further when he was elected as the organization's vice-president. As vice-president, Dunning was charged with investigating the country elevator system in Saskatchewan. The 1911 SGGA convention asked Dunning to investigate different grain-handling options in order to remedy faults many saw in the current system. His report sparked great debate within the farmers' movement and in government. Although Dunning preferred a government-run elevator system, a compromise was reached which established the Saskatchewan Co-operative Elevator Company.

Dunning was appointed to the board of directors of the co-op, and after the first general meeting, was appointed its first general manager. Under Dunning's leadership the co-op quickly expanded. Within four years the co-op became the largest grain-handling company in the world, and by 1916, the co-op had built 230 elevators and handled over 28,000,000 bushels of various crops. Aside from his work with the co-op, Dunning was called to serve Saskatchewan agriculture in several other ways. Dunning served on two Royal

Commissions dealing with Saskatchewan agriculture, the Grain Market Commission, which had little lasting influence, and the Agricultural Credit Commission, which eventually led to several largely unsuccessful government experiments in farm credit later during Dunning's political career.

By 1916, Premier Walter Scott was suffering from ill health that severely hampered his ability to lead the province. Also, his government was under siege in a serious corruption scandal. Scott resigned and Regina MP William Martin took over as premier. Martin set about to change the face of government. To this end, he asked Dunning to come into government as provincial treasurer. In the midst of scandal, Martin felt it was important to bolster the Liberal Party's ties to the farm movement and continued the practice of bringing prominent farm leaders into government. Dunning ran in a by-election in the constituency of Kinistino and won by acclamation.

In 1919, Dunning was given added responsibility for the department of Agriculture and during that time he expanded the duties and responsibilities for the Labour Bureau. He used the bureau, which was created in 1911, in an ever-increasing manner to expand exploitation of Saskatchewan's resource base. Dunning promoted the first commercial extraction of sodium sulfate reserves, established the first experimental coal plant near Estevan, and undertook the first extensive prospecting of mineral resource wealth in northern Saskatchewan. While few of these activities immediately impacted on Saskatchewan's economy, all resulted in long-term development, making Dunning one of the first advocates of the diversification of Saskatchewan's agricultural economy with large-scale mineral resource extraction.

In the wave of growing farmer animosity to the federal Liberal party, the Saskatchewan Liberals officially severed ties in order to avoid the creation of a farmers' party in Saskatchewan. However, in the 1921 federal election, Premier Martin had openly supported several federal Liberal candidates. This move upset many in the farmers' movement and caused the resignation of a senior minister. With the SGGA openly discussing the option of forming a third party, Martin's authority was seriously undermined. Martin resigned and many Liberals looked to Dunning to combat the potential farmers' party. Dunning's long history with the farmers' movement placed him in a unique position to win back the support of the SGGA. Dunning attempted to meet the challenge head-on through meeting with the SGGA directly and trying to convince them that he still represented farmers and was not Prime Minister King's pawn. Dunning chose a more passive approach until a series of provincial by-elections all resulted in Liberal victories over independent progressive candidates. In 1924, Dunning's efforts paid off as the SGGA rescinded their call for a new farmers' party. As the federal Progressive Party began to wane, Dunning became more actively involved in federal politics and was eventually able to re-establish formal ties between the provincial and federal levels of the Liberal party.

As premier, Dunning's main issue was the price of wheat, which fell due to the post-war depression. Local farmers seriously opposed the abolishment of the Canadian Wheat Board by the federal government. Dunning supported the wheat board and immediately tried to lobby the federal government to re-establish the board, but to no avail. Dunning tentatively threw his support behind the idea of voluntary pooling. After a rough start, the Saskatchewan Wheat Pool was established in

1924. The Wheat Pool then sought to buy the Saskatchewan Co-operative Elevator Company, a move that was supported by Dunning, who passed the legislation that allowed the sale to take place—this proved to be his last act as premier.

In 1926, Dunning was invited to move to federal politics and became Saskatchewan's representative in federal cabinet. Dunning ran in a by-election in the riding of Regina in March 1926. However, by the time he arrived in Ottawa, the government had fallen and the Conservatives took power. The Conservative government also soon fell, and in September Dunning ran and was re-elected in a general election. This time the Liberals formed a majority government and Dunning was appointed minister of Railways and Canals. A strong proponent of the Hudson's Bay Railway, Dunning was instrumental in the construction of the line and the choice of Churchill as its terminus. In 1929, he was promoted and took on the responsibility as minister of Finance. However, the term was short-lived, for in 1930 the Liberals were defeated and Dunning himself suffered a personal defeat in Regina.

In 1930 he returned to the business world, but this proved to be temporary. The Conservatives lost the 1935 election and Prime Minster King returned to office. King pressured Dunning to return to his government. Dunning accepted and the MP for the riding of Queen's County, Prince Edward Island, resigned, allowing Dunning easy access to the House of Commons. Dunning reassumed his former post as minister of Finance.

In 1938, Dunning suffered a heart attack. Although his actions were severely limited, he struggled to continue in his post, but finally resigned in July 1939, when he returned to his native England to recuperate. He returned to Canada just before the commencement of the Second World War.

Although choosing not to contest the next federal election, Dunning's business experience was nevertheless needed by the government to execute the war effort. Dunning was appointed chair of the National War Loans Committee, which was established to facilitate raising money for the war effort. He also was named chair of the Allied Supplies Limited. The company was established by the federal government to administer and bolster production of munitions and explosives for the British government in Canada. He was also appointed chancellor of Queen's University and continued at this post until his death. After the war Dunning continued his connection with the business community, serving on the board of directors of several companies. Although he continued to remain in possession of several farms in Saskatchewan, Dunning retired to upscale Montreal. He remained in close contact with Saskatchewan, usually returning to Regina once a year until his death. In late September 1958, he entered hospital for a kidney operation and died October 1, 1958.

BRETT QUIRING

FURTHER READING: Brennan, J. W. 1968. "The Public Career of C. A. Dunning in Saskatchewan." Unpublished M.A. thesis, University of Saskatchewan, Regina Campus. • Brennan, J. W. 1969. "C. A Dunning and the Challenge of The Progressives: 1922–1925." *Saskatchewan History* (Winter), 1–12. • Smith, David E. 1975. *Prairie Liberalism: The Liberal Party in Saskatchewan 1905–1971.* Toronto: University of Toronto Press.

**ELHARD, D. WAYNE** (b. 1947). Wayne Elhard was born in Rosthern and has resided in Eastend since 1982. He graduated from the University of Lethbridge in 1971 with a

Bachelor's degree in history and philosophy, and furthered his education with a Master's degree from Baylor University (Waco, Texas) in 1976.

Preceding his entry into politics, Elhard gained experience in a broad range of fields. He worked in the electronic media sector in Alberta, British Columbia, and Texas. During his later years in this arena, he became a director of news and public affairs broadcasts. Elhard also worked as a personnel recruiter for engineering and construction companies, and a farm machinery sales representative.

Wayne Elhard was first elected to the Saskatchewan legislature during a by-election for the Cypress Hills constituency on June 28, 1999. This earned him the title of the first-ever elected member of the Saskatchewan Party. Elhard retained the Cypress Hills seat during the 1999 and 2003 general elections. Towards the start of his political career, he served as Highways critic, gaining a reputation as a key figure in the Saskatchewan Party's opposition to government policy. Elhard often expressed concern that the provincial and federal governments' twinning of the Trans-Canada Highway through Saskatchewan was proceeding too slowly. After the 2003 election he was appointed as the shadow cabinet's critic for Government Relations and deputy-critic of Learning.

JACQUELINE M. ROY, UNIVERSITY OF REGINA

**ELIASON, FRANK** (1883–1956). Frank Eliason was born January 13, 1883, in the province of Dalsland in Sweden. In 1902, when he was nineteen, Eliason emigrated to the United States and lived in Minneapolis until 1910. This was a particularly formative period in Eliason's life. Apparently he never found steady employment, and often faced difficult financial circumstances. He attended meetings where religious, labour and political speakers expounded on a variety of tenets that were then a part of American progressive thought. His American experiences led him to conclude that the producers of wealth, the labourers and the farmers, should unite to build a co-operative society. Eliason remained loyal to that populist principle throughout his life.

In 1910 Eliason came to Wynyard. Soon he was secretary of the Saskatchewan Grain Growers' Association local. The SGGA espoused views that he readily accepted. Later he recalled that the farm organization practiced socialism, but in Saskatchewan they called it cooperation. In the years that followed, Eliason became committed to the co-operative ideology of the farm movement. He coordinated bulk buying for local farmers, supported the organization of the wheat pool and in the 1920s was active in the Progressive Party.

In 1929 Eliason became the provincial secretary of the United Farmers of Canada (Saskatchewan Section), the successor to the SGGA. From its office in Saskatoon he administered the UFC during the Great Depression. Because of a shortage of funds, Eliason was forced to run the UFC almost single-handed. His salary, with which he supported eight children whom he raised alone after the tragic death of his wife in 1921, was greatly reduced. He corresponded with UFC locals and prepared briefs to present to governments. A used clothing depot was established at UFC headquarters, and sixty tons of clothing were distributed. He publicized the social tragedy farm families faced. He reported that in some areas babies were learning to walk without shoes and mothers were making moccasins for them out of old leather gloves.

The UFC voted to enter politics at its annual convention in 1931. The following year the UFC and the Saskatchewan Independent Labour Party met in Saskatoon and created the Farmer-Labour Party, the forerunner of the Saskatchewan CCF. Eliason served a dual role as secretary of both the new party and the UFC and directed day-to-day activities from UFC headquarters. He urged Farmer-Labour supporters to organize their ridings, and he dealt with local constituency problems that invariably arose. He handled requests for speakers, contacting M. J. Coldwell, George Williams, Louise Lucas, Clarence Fines and others who addressed hundreds of meetings in school houses and villages throughout the province. Funds were very limited; frequently he paid postage out of his own pocket so that literature could be mailed to constituencies. No one was more important than Frank Eliason to the life of the Saskatchewan Farmer-Labour Party during its first two years of existence.

Frank Eliason also played an important role in the founding of the national CCF. In 1932 he contacted Canadian farm and labour leaders, inviting them to a meeting in Saskatoon in April to discuss the establishment of a new social order. Because of various circumstances it was held instead in Calgary at the beginning of August. Saskatchewan delegates, including Eliason, attended. He drafted a program based on Saskatchewan Farmer-Labour policies which he took with him to Calgary. The Cooperative Commonwealth Federation was created at the Calgary conference, and Eliason's draft document was accepted as the basis for the eight-point program the party adopted. The following

summer the CCF held its first national convention in Regina. Eliason reported to the convention on behalf of the Saskatchewan Farmer-Labour Party. The delegates debated the famous Regina Manifesto. After it was approved clause by clause, Eliason moved the motion that it be adopted as a whole. The Manifesto was longer and more eloquently written, but much of its content and certainly its spirit was similar to the document Frank Eliason had brought to Calgary the previous summer.

In 1934 the UFC discontinued its direct political involvement in the Farmer-Labour Party. Eliason resigned as party secretary but remained with the UFC. The Farmer-Labour party became the Saskatchewan CCF and moved its head office to Regina with George Williams in control. Eliason remained a fervent supporter of the CCF, but there were policy differences and personal conflicts which contributed to the divisions which plagued the Saskatchewan CCF before 1944. Eliason continued as secretary of the UFC until it was reorganized as the Saskatchewan Farmers' Union in 1949.

During his retirement years Eliason maintained his interest in public affairs. He was immensely proud of the accomplishments of the Douglas governments. In 1953 he presented a brief to the Saskatchewan Royal Commission on Rural Life. He wrote his autobiography which was never published. In the last years of his life Eliason was more convinced than ever that the capitalist financial system was the root of all evils, and he lamented that the CCF had neglected emphasizing banking and monetary reform. He referred to the ideas of the American

SAB R-A 10415

FRANK ELIASON

monetary reformer, William "Coin" Harvey, and recalled that when the old populist died penniless in 1936, the UFC had purchased his books from his widow for $100. Eliason still had a few of them which he donated to the Saskatchewan Archives. Frank Eliason died March 22, 1956, at age seventy-one.

GEORGE HOFFMAN, UNIVERSITY OF REGINA

FURTHER READING: Eliason, Frank. n.d. "Biography of a Swedish Emmigrant" [sic]. Typescript. Saskatchewan Archives Board. • Hoffman, George. 1979. "The Saskatchewan Farmer-Labour Party, 1932–1934: How Radical Was It at Its Origins?" In *Pages From The Past: Essays on Saskatchewan History*, ed. D.H. Bocking, 210–224. Saskatoon: Western Producer Prairie Books.

## ELLIOTT, OTTO BUCHANAN (1886–1979).

Otto Elliott was born on September 2, 1886, at Erin, Wellington County, Ontario. He was the son of Alfred Henry Elliott and Mary E. Buchanan.

Elliott worked as a station agent for the CNR at Alsask and was also a school trustee before entering federal politics. In 1935 he was elected as the Social Credit member of the House of Commons for the riding of Kindersley. He was one of two Saskatchewan members of the group of seventeen Socreds who went to Ottawa.

Elliott was a conscientious member of the House of Commons. He spoke frequently in Parliament, on transportation matters and freight rates. Occasionally, in keeping with Social Credit monetary ideology, he raised questions from the floor about banking, currency and debt matters. Early in 1939 he was predicting the next war and asking how much Canadian scrap metal had been sold to Japan and Germany recently.

Elliott was a member of Parliament for only one term. In 1939 the federal Socreds joined the New Democracy movement headed by W.D. Herridge, a former Canadian ambassador to Washington. Herridge hoped to defeat the Liberals by aligning various anti-government factions with a vague platform promising monetary reform and 'New Deal' policies. Elliott resigned his seat in order for Herridge to gain a seat in the House of Commons by running in his riding during a by-election. However, Mackenzie King refused to call a by-election during that term of parliament. When Herridge ran in the Kindersley riding in the federal election of 1940 he was soundly defeated by the Liberal candidate and his movement quickly folded. Elliott's sacrifice of his office appeared to be have been unnecessary.

Otto Elliott died in Toronto in 1979 and was buried in Bowmanville, Ontario.

DAVID R. ELLIOTT

BIBLIOGRAPHY: Hallett, Mary. 1966. "The Social Credit Party and the New Democracy Movement." *Canadian Historical Review*: 301–325.

## ENS, GERHARD (1863–1952).

Gerhard Ens was Saskatchewan's first MLA to be neither Anglo-Saxon nor Canadian-born. Ens was born on December 28, 1863, in Ekaterinoslaw, which was then in the southern part of the Russian Empire. He received his education and was married in Russia, emigrating to Canada in 1891.

Ens settled in the Rosthern area, and as he was one of its first settlers, many consider him to be the town's founder. He was certainly instrumental in bringing settlers to the Rosthern area. He especially focused upon bringing settlers from Mennonite communities, although Ens himself became a Swedenborgian.

GERHARD ENS

Ens farmed and became president of the Rosthern Realty Company; he also worked as an Immigration Agent for the Canadian government for nine years. In 1905 Rosthern elected Ens, running for the Liberal Party, as its first Member of the Legislative Assembly. He became the government whip, and remained in the legislature until 1913. In 1916, Ens was one of the eight MLAs who J. E. Bradshaw accused of having taken bribes to oppose the "Banish-the-Bar" bill in 1913; the Supreme Court found him not guilty of these charges.

After leaving provincial politics, Ens continued to help the Mennonite community. In the early 1920s he worked to have the ban on Mennonite immigration lifted. This ban had been put in effect by an Order-in-Council as a result of Mennonite pacifism during the First World War. Gerhard Ens died on January 2, 1952.

MARYANNE COTCHER, UNIVERSITY OF REGINA

## ERB, JACOB WALTER (1909–1990).

Walter Erb was a CCF MLA and minister of Public Health. His defection from the CCF to join the Liberals during the height of the Medicare debate significantly threatened the implementation of the program.

Born January 16, 1909, near Yellow Grass, Erb was educated in Yellow Grass and at Luther College in Regina. After high school he attended the University of Manitoba where he received a B.A. in 1933. The following year he won a two-year scholarship in singing at the Chicago Conservatory of Music. In 1942 he was appointed Dean of Boys and teacher of music at Luther College, a position he held until 1946. In 1943 he was commissioned in the RCAF Air Cadet program and remained involved until June 1945 when he began farming near Lang. He quickly became involved in the local community and the co-operative movement. Erb was elected to the Lang School Board as a trustee.

In 1948, Erb was first elected to the Saskatchewan legislature as the CCF member from the constituency of Milestone. He was re-elected in 1952 and 1956. After the 1956 election, Erb was appointed to cabinet as minister of Public Health after several ministers were defeated that year. Erb had developed a close personal relationship with Premier T. C. Douglas, but many within caucus, especially education minster Woodrow Lloyd, questioned his ability and his commitment to the CCF and to Medicare. Erb was re-elected in 1960 and was given responsibility for the implementation of Medicare. After extensive consultation he appointed the Thompson Commission, which endeavored to develop a process by which Medicare could be imple-

WALTER ERB

mented. However, in 1961, Erb was shuffled out of Health and moved to Public Works when Lloyd replaced Douglas as premier. This move was interpreted as a demotion by Erb, and the suspicion with which Lloyd and Erb viewed each other led to the estrangement of Erb from the government. On May 2, 1962, less than a month before Medicare was to come into effect, Erb resigned from cabinet and joined the Liberal Party in opposition to Medicare. Erb's defection was a huge boost to the anti-medicare forces which were putting tremendous pressure on the government to abandon the program. However, the government did not relent and the program was implemented.

Erb contested the 1964 campaign as a Liberal, but changed seats, trying to use his profile to dislodge the dual-member seat of Regina East from the CCF. However, he lost by a narrow margin. Newly elected Premier Ross Thatcher appointed him chair of the Workmen's Compensation Board, a post he held until 1972. In 1972, he was elected president of the Workman's Compensation Board of Canada. Retiring in 1984, he died in Los Angeles, California, on January 1, 1990.

BRETT QUIRING

## ESTEY, CLARENCE LESLIE BALDWIN
(1917–1995). Clarence Estey served in Ross Thatcher's cabinet in several different departments: as the minister for Municipal Affairs, the Indian and Métis Branch, Industry and Commerce, and in charge of the Saskatchewan Power Corporation.

Estey was born on June 29, 1917, the son of James Wilfred Estey, a former provincial cabinet minister and justice of the Supreme Court of Canada. Educated entirely in Saskatoon, Clarence Estey became a lawyer but briefly left law to serve in the Canadian Army during the Second World War. After being stationed in England for a few years, Estey was injured by "friendly fire" after only a brief time

SAB R-B 7142-1

CLARENCE ESTEY

fighting in France. Estey returned to Canada after his injury. He then joined Moxon and Schmidt, his father's former law firm, and remained there until he ran as a Liberal for the provincial legislature in 1967. Saskatoon Nutana Centre elected Clarence Estey as its Member of the Legislative Assembly in the general election of 1967, and in November of that year Ross Thatcher appointed Estey as the minister of Municipal Affairs.

Clarence Estey is probably best remembered for his activities with the Indian and Métis Branch, a position he held from 1969 to 1971. In 1970 his department helped the Saskatchewan government to make hiring a percentage of First Nations and Métis employees mandatory for government agencies and Crown corporations. The department also worked with private companies to encourage First Nations and Métis hiring, creating 1886 jobs in that year.

A cabinet shuffle in September 1970 moved Estey from his positions as minister of Municipal Affairs and the Indian and Métis Branch to a new role as minister of Industry and Commerce. During that last year in the provincial cabinet, one of the projects that fell under Estey's authority was Homecoming '71, a tourism campaign that invited former Saskatchewan residents to visit the province.

In the 1971 Saskatchewan general election, Estey lost his position in cabinet, and his seat representing Saskatoon Nutana Centre. He returned to his law practice, being appointed to the Court of Queen's Bench in 1974. Clarence Estey retired in 1992, and died in Saskatoon on March 5, 1995.

MARYANNE COTCHER,

UNIVERSITY OF REGINA

**ESTEY, JAMES WILFRED** (1889–1956). Former Attorney-General and supreme court justice, James Estey was born in Keswick Ridge, New Brunswick, on December 1, 1889. After graduating from the University of New Brunswick in 1910 he studied at Harvard, earning a law degree. Estey came to Saskatchewan in 1915 to lecture in law and economics at the University of Saskatchewan, a position he held for ten years. In 1917 he helped establish the law practice of Estey, Moxon, Schmitt & McDonald, and remained with the firm until he was appointed Crown Prosecutor in Saskatoon from 1921 until 1929. Estey was appointed to the board of governors of the University of Saskatchewan in 1926, remaining in the position until he was first elected.

SAB R-A 642

JAMES ESTEY

In 1929, Estey first ran for public office for the Liberals in the constituency of Saskatoon City. However, he was soundly defeated by Conservative premier, J. T. M. Anderson. Returning to private practice, Estey again contested the seat in 1934 and was successful as the Conservatives were swept out of office. Estey's high profile assured him of a cabinet position in the new government, and he was appointed minister of Education. Like many other ministers during the depression years, his main struggle was to keep the department operating. In the previous years school grants had been cut, some local boards were unable to collect property taxes, and some teachers had not been paid by their local boards. Over his term in Education, which ended in 1941, these issues were gradually dealt with as the economy rebounded and government revenue increased.

Re-elected in 1938, Estey took on the responsibility of Attorney-General when T.C. Davis was appointed to the Court of Appeal. During his term as Attorney-General, Estey redrafted debt legislation in Saskatchewan under the *Debt Adjustment Act*. The aim of the *Act* was to give greater protection to debtors who faced seizure of property, particularly farm land, as a result of the effects of the depression. The primary purpose of this legislation was to find a better balance between the debtor and creditor, and to counter the CCF's calls for increased debtor protection.

Estey was defeated in the CCF electoral sweep in June 1944. In October he was appointed to the Supreme Court. He served on the court for eleven years until his death on January 22, 1956. Estey's son, Clarence Estey, would follow in his father's footsteps, also becoming a cabinet minister and judge.

BRETT QUIRING

**FANSHER, WILLIAM RUSSEL** (1876–1957). As a Progressive MP who was subsequently involved in the CCF, William Fansher's career illustrates the link between the radical element of the Progressive Party and the formation of the CCF.

Born in Florence, Ontario, on February 26, 1876, Fansher was educated in Ridgetown, Ontario, and attended the agricultural college in Guelph. Fansher moved to Regina in 1904 and two years later established a farm near Govan, where he became a prominent livestock producer in the area. Fansher soon took to politics through his farming activities. He came from a political family and, in 1921, his younger brother Wendell Fansher was elected to the House of Commons from the Ontario riding of Lambton East as a Progressive. In 1925, William Fansher first contested public office by being elected as a Progressive in the federal riding of Last Mountain. Because the election resulted in a minority government, Fansher held considerable sway as Prime Minister W. L. M. King tried to keep his government in power with the help of Progressives like Fansher. Although initially favorable toward King, Fansher's opinion of King deteriorated during the session. However, Fansher was concerned that instability in Parliament would affect important changes to the Grain and *Farm Loan Acts*, so he supported the government. During the debate over the customs scandal, in which Liberal ministers were charged with knowing of corruption within the customs department, Fansher tried to soften a Conservative motion calling for the censure and defeat of the government.

In 1926, the government did fall and Fansher was again elected. During this term, Fansher become closely involved with a group of Labour and Progressive MPs under the leadership of J. S. Woodsworth. This group would later form the core of the CCF. Fansher was defeated in the 1930 election. During the early thirties, Fansher became closely involved in the formation of the CCF. He ran for the party in 1935 in the new riding of Lake Centre but finished a poor

SAB R-A 3649

WILLIAM FANSHER

third. Running again in 1940, he increased his vote but again finished third in a tight three-way race with John F. Johnson and John Diefenbaker. Undeterred, Fansher ran a final time for the CCF in the provincial constituency of Arm River. Although the CCF swept to power, Fansher was again defeated, this time by a mere ninety votes.

Fansher remained involved in the CCF, but never ran for public office again. He died in Govan on February 28, 1957.

BRETT QUIRING

## FEDORUK, SYLVIA OLGA (b. 1927).

Born in Canora on May 5, 1927, and educated at the University of Saskatchewan, Sylvia Fedoruk pursued a distinguished career in medical physics, specializing in radiation therapy for cancer patients. For thirty-five years, Fedoruk was associated with the Saskatoon Cancer Clinic, where she served as Chief Medical Physicist, and the Saskatchewan Cancer Foundation, where she was Director of Physics Services. Fedoruk held the positions of Professor of Oncology and Associate Member in Physics at the University of Saskatchewan. At the end of 1986 she took early retirement.

OFFICE OF THE LIEUTENANT GOVERNOR

SYLVIA FEDORUK

Sylvia Fedoruk was involved in the development of the world's first Cobalt 60 unit and one of the first nuclear medicine scanning machines. She was the first woman member of the Atomic Energy Control Board of Canada.

— 81 —

She also served as a consultant in nuclear medicine to the International Atomic Energy Agency in Vienna. An avid sportswoman and curler, Sylvia Fedoruk was inducted into the Canadian Curling Hall of Fame in 1986. She was Chancellor of the University of Saskatchewan from 1986 to 1989. In 1986 she was voted Saskatoon's YWCA Woman of the Year and was appointed to the Saskatchewan Order of Merit. In 1987 she was named an Officer of the Order of Canada. She was the first woman Lieutenant-Governor of Saskatchewan, from 1988 to 1994.

Like her predecessor, Frederick Johnson, Sylvia Fedoruk faced the issue of the use of special warrants by the Progressive Conservative government of Grant Devine. In June 1991, the government neared the end of its constitutional five-year mandate; faced with the possibility of losing a vote of confidence, it prorogued the legislature in June without allowing the vote, much to the discomfort of the Lieutenant-Governor. Since a budget had not been passed, the government resorted to a series of special warrants to finance its expenditures. Fedoruk came under considerable pressure to refuse her signature to the warrants but concluded that it was up to the electorate to render final judgement. Continuing as Lieutenant-Governor during the NDP administration of Roy Romanow, she and the premier agreed that they would hold regular monthly meetings; Saskatchewan thus became the only province where the practice existed.

MICHAEL JACKSON, REGINA

FURTHER READINGS: Hryniuk, Margaret and Garth Pugh. 1991. "A Tower of Attraction": An Illustrated History of Government House, Regina, Saskatchewan. Regina: Government House Historical Society/Canadian Plains Research Center. • Leeson, Howard A. (ed.). 2001. Saskatchewan Politics: Into the Twenty-first Century. Regina: Canadian Plains Research Center.

**FINES, CLARENCE MELVIN** (1905–1993). Clarence Melvin Fines was born August 16, 1905, in Darlingford, Manitoba. Although initially a school teacher, Fines became involved with the newly formed CCF Party, chairing the CCF's organizing convention in 1932 in Calgary and later becoming the Saskatchewan CCF president in 1942. As party fundraiser, he played a key role in the fledgling party. Fines made his first entry into politics as a city alderman for Regina in 1934. He decided to run in the provincial election in 1944 and both he and the party emerged victorious, as the CCF won forty-seven of the fifty-three seats in the provincial legislature.

Throughout his political career, Fines had a close relationship with Tommy Douglas and both were key factors for the success of the first CCF government. They first met in 1933 when Douglas won the CCF nomination for Weyburn in 1933. Fines was a practical man with great administrative skills and managerial toughness that complemented Douglas' strong oratical skills and charisma. Their excellent relationship served both Tommy and Clarence well, and it was no surprise that when Douglas shut himself away to create his first cabinet, Fines was there with him to provide advice.

When the cabinet was announced, Clarence Fines was named the Provincial Treasurer. As party fundraiser, the role of Provincial Treasurer for the new CCF government was a natural step. Although he held numerous other cabinet posts, Fines is best known for his work as Provincial Treasurer. At the age of thirty-six when he was appointed minister of Finance, Fines had the arduous task of reviving the province's dreadful economy, while at the same time trying to finance many of the social policies the CCF had promised to institute. On top of this, he had to convince many of the banks and lending institutes in eastern Canada and in the United States that the newly elected 'socialist menace' would keep paying its debts. Shortly after assuming office, Fines flew to New York, Toronto, and Montreal to convince the financial houses that the province would continue paying its debts and succeeded in shoring up Saskatchewan's credit rating. Through his great managerial skill and fiscal prudence, Fines was able to bring down a consecutive budget in his first year as treasurer, while continuing to finance increased social spending. In fact, Fines brought down sixteen consecutive balanced budgets in his tenure as Provincial Treasurer, a record unparalleled by any other province at this time. On budget day, Fines was famous for wearing his horn-of-plenty tie to represent the increased social programs the CCF government was able to finance while still maintaining a balanced budget. When Fines assumed office, the province had a $177 million debt; when he retired from politics, the debt had been reduced to $50 million.

Fines also had an important role in creating the Saskatchewan Government Insurance Office (SGIO and later SGI) and was the minister responsible for SGIO from 1948 to 1960. From his experiences as city alderman, Fines saw the problems of trying to obtain insurance. The price was extremely high and the profits went outside of the province. Fines saw a way to solve both problems by creating government insurance. For his work on the creation of government insurance in Saskatchewan, the SGI head office in Regina on 11th Avenue, erected in 1979, is named after him.

Fines' legacy will be his work as Provincial

SAB R-A 2889-1

CLARENCE FINES

Treasurer. Fines restored the province's credit and established a record of financial prudence while at the same time finding money to provide for vastly expanded and newly created social programs. He retired from politics in 1960 to a comfortable life in Florida where he died on October 27, 1993, at the age of eighty-eight, the last surviving member of Tommy Douglas' original 1944 cabinet.

JAY KASPERSKI, REGINA

**FINLAYSON, DONALD** (1852–1934). Donald Matheson Finlayson was born in Elgin County, Ontario, on August 9, 1852, to Duncan Finlayson and Anabell Matheson. He was educated at Criman Public School. He married his wife Katie in June 1881 and together they raised a family of six children.

In 1879 Donald Finlayson moved to Battleford after a forty-two day trip from Winnipeg. He marketed the first wheat grown in and shipped out of Battleford in 1881. Finlayson and his family were warned about the 1885 rebellion by a First Nations woman they had helped the previous winter. They barely escaped the attack. Three hours after fleeing their home, it was ravaged. Finlayson served with local troops throughout the rebellion. He and his family lived at the Barracks for two and a half months under police protection due to the

SAB R-A 663

DONALD FINLAYSON

dangers of the rebellion.

Finlayson was president of the North Battleford Agricultural Society. Running as a Liberal candidate, he was elected to the Saskatchewan legislature for North Battleford in 1908 and re-elected in 1912. In 1917, Finlayson was elected for Jackfish Lake and re-elected in 1921, 1925, and 1929. He passed away on December 30, 1934.

HEATHER WILSON

## FORGET, AMÉDÉE EMMANUEL

(1847– 1923). Born on November 12, 1847, at Marieville, Canada East, where he was later educated, Amédée Forget made his career in the North-West Territories. For more than forty years he sat close to the centres of non-elected power. Secretary to the Territories' governor, clerk of its Council, a commissioner of Métis land claims (1885) and, later, assistant and then Com-missioner of Indian Affairs for Manitoba and the North-West Territories, he was named Lieutenant-Governor of the Territories in 1898. From there his transition to the office of Lieutenant-Governor of Saskatchewan might have been expected. Still, it was controversial. Under the *Constitution Act* of 1867, lieutenant-governors are appointed by the Governor in Council in Ottawa, on recommendation of the prime minister. Patronage appointments raise opponents' ire as a matter of course, but in this case the stakes were high indeed: the new Saskatchewan Lieutenant-Governor (and the same was true of his Alberta counterpart) was in a privileged position to influence the composition of the province's first government. The *Mail and Empire* termed Forget's

SAB R-B 622

AMÉDÉE EMMANUEL FORGET

appointment "A Crime Against the West," because he was "an instrument in the hands of Sir Wilfrid Laurier," an assertion the appoint-ment of Walter Scott (former Liberal Member of Parliament for Assiniboia West, 1900 –1905) as premier did nothing to counter.

The partisan attacks gradually abated as Forget and his wife, Henriette (née Drolet), established the routine of vice-regal events and ceremonies that their counterparts a cen-tury later still follow: hosting, welcoming, presenting, swear-ing-in and laying (cornerstones). Lieutenant-Governor between September 1, 1905, and October 13, 1910, Forget had only seven months out of public office before he was called to the Senate in May 1911, a posi-tion he held at the time of his death on June 8, 1923.

DAVID E. SMITH,
UNIVERSITY OF SASKATCHEWAN

## GANTEFOER, ROD (b. 1947). Liberal

MLA turned founding member of the Saskatchewan Party and party leadership can-didate, Rod Gantefoer was a prominent mem-ber of the Saskatchewan Party during its form-ative years.

Gantefoer was born on May 15, 1947, in Watson. After completing three years in post-secondary education, he moved to Kelvington and worked on a mixed farming operation in the area. Settling in Melfort, he became heav-ily involved in the business community. He was the founding president of a poultry com-pany and operated two fast food franchises in town. He served as president of the Melfort and District Chamber of Commerce, and was involved in a variety of other local issues.

Gantefoer was first elected to the Melfort School Board and served for a time as its chair. His first foray into provincial politics was in 1991 when he ran for the Liberals in the constituency of Melfort; however, he finished a distant third. He tried again in 1995 in the new constituency of Melfort-Tisdale and this time was successful. Gantefoer held a prominent role in the Opposition, which lacked much legislative experience. He served as the party's House Leader and chaired the Public Accounts Committee. When Liberal leader Lynda Haverstock resigned, Gantefoer was widely touted as a possible successor but later decided against running.

With the election of Jim Melenchuk as party leader, Liberal fortunes started to slip and several MLAs, including Gantefoer, became disgruntled. Gantefoer was part of the talks between these Liberals and the members of the Progressive Conservative Party who, in August of 1997, formed the Saskatchewan Party. Gantefoer contested the leadership of the party but finished behind former MP Elwin Hermanson. Gantefoer continued to hold key positions in the party, serving as the party critic on a variety of high profile portfolios such as Health and Finance. Gantefoer was re-elected in 1999 and 2003.

BRETT QUIRING

## GARDINER, JAMES GARFIELD (1883–
1962). James Garfield Gardiner, born November 30, 1883, on a farm near Farquhar, Ontario, where the counties of Perth and Huron meet, was one of a legion of southern Ontarians to come west (in his case by harvest excursion in 1901) and stay to leave their political mark on the Canadian prairies. William Aberhart, John Diefenbaker, William Martin, Arthur Meighen and Walter Scott were others to make the trek. Raised under Protestant and Victorian influences, all were born in the country but all (except Gardiner) moved to the city. First elected in a provincial by-election in 1914, Gardiner spent two decades in office in Regina and, after entering Mackenzie King's cabinet and later Louis St. Laurent's as minister of Agriculture, another twenty-two years in Ottawa. Nonetheless, his heart remained rooted in agriculture. He bought his farm at Lemberg during the First World War, and supervised its operation under his son or a close associate for more than four decades. When he was defeated in the general election of 1958, he returned to the farm, and it was there that he died January 2, 1962.

Gardiner's agrarian interests permeated his politics, most certainly during the still-unprecedented span in which he held one federal portfolio. The *Prairie Farm Assistance Act* (1939), which statutorily recognized federal government responsibility for the economic well-being of prairie grain farmers, proved to be the forerunner of a score of national agricultural initiatives with the same objective. The disruption to overseas markets caused by the Second World War demanded immediate and continuous adjustments in all areas of agriculture over all regions of Canada. Gardiner's administrative talents during this crisis were acknowledged by political friend and foe alike. Following the war, Mackenzie King announced that he would step down as leader of the Liberal Party of Canada. Gardiner sought but lost the leadership in 1948, coming second to St. Laurent but ahead of C. G. (Chubby) Power. Although national party leadership and the office of prime minister had long been his ambitions, he could not translate his reputation for unswerving loyalty and administrative competence into support from the convention.

The explanation for this failure lay in those very qualities Gardiner offered the Liberal delegates—loyalty and experience. For Gardiner's reputation, established in Saskatchewan first as a back-bencher, then minister and finally as premier, was as that of a relentless partisan who would brook no compromise. Following the cleavage in the Liberal Party over Union Government and conscription, events which saw Gardiner and a tiny minority of Liberals stand by Laurier and against the *Military Service Act* (1917), Gardiner took command of the Liberal Party organization in Saskatchewan and made it a near invincible electoral force. Between 1914 and 1958, Gardiner personally won every election contest he entered, except the last. The provincial party, between 1914 and the Cooperative Commonwealth Federation victory in 1944, won every election except that of 1929, although even then it won more seats and votes than any other party. In addition to its provincial prowess, Gardiner's organization saw that Mackenzie King won the federal seat of Prince Albert in a by-election in 1926 and that he kept that seat in five more contests until 1945. Prince Albert was the only seat in King's political career that he retained as an incumbent.

The Liberal Party organization under Gardiner entered the realm of myth as "the machine" largely due to an academic article written by Escott Reid, "The Saskatchewan Liberal Machine before 1929," in the *Canadian Journal of Economics and Political Science*, 2, no. 1 (1936). This is not to say that the organization was fictitious, but to stress that Reid's depiction depreciated the extent of popular participation by rank-and-file Liberals

JAMES G. GARDINER

that made the organization so electorally successful. In his capacity as Highways minister and then as premier, Gardiner stood at its head overseeing a platoon of government "inspectors" who, while on the public payroll, had the interests of the party as their first priority. But the party required more than a leader to make it succeed, as its slow deterioration once Gardiner departed from Regina demonstrated.

Gardiner's administrative and organizational skills explain his electoral and departmental achievements. They did not contribute to an outstanding career in public policy, either as a provincial cabinet minister or as premier. He succeeded Charles Dunning in the latter office in 1926. Between then and the Liberals' defeat in 1929, the economy was good, and there were no decisions in which Gardiner had a hand that exercised long-term influence on the province. Similarly, after he led the Liberals back to power in 1934 (thereby becoming the only Saskatchewan premier to hold the office twice), his eyes were on a federal cabinet appointment. Except for undoing the Cooperative government's civil service reforms and disbanding its Relief Commission, in both instances handing power back to the politicians, where he believed it belonged, depression and drought limited any policy initiative Gardiner might have attempted.

The singular event of Gardiner's first ministry was the electoral defeat of 1929. That election saw the Ku Klux Klan play a determinative role in coalescing previously fragmented opposition to the Liberals. For the anti-Liberals, the major issue was the government's purportedly loose administration of the separate schools and excessive influence exercised by the Roman Catholic Church. In his traditionally pedagogic platform style, Gardiner attempted to refute the charges with statistics and by appeals to tolerance for minorities. But his arguments were to no avail. For the first time (and the last until 1999), a coalition, on this occasion composed of Conservatives, Progressives and Independents, formed a government under J. T. M. Anderson as premier. In his long career as backbencher, cabinet minister, leader of the Opposition, federal cabinet minister or federal backbencher, Gardiner never willingly relinquished power; however, he maintained until the end of his life that the outcome of that contest was "an honourable defeat" and that the Liberal Party emerged the stronger for its electorally unpopular position.

DAVID E. SMITH, UNIVERSITY OF SASKATCHEWAN

**GARDINER, JAMES WILFRID** (1924–2002). James "Wilf" Gardiner was born July 27, 1924, in Regina to future premier and federal minister of agriculture, Jimmy Gardiner. As the son of a prominent provincial (and later federal) politician, Wilf Gardiner attended several different schools in Regina, Lemberg and Ottawa. He attended university at Queen's in Kingston. Upon completion of his degree he returned to Saskatchewan and began a promising political career.

Gardiner first sought public office in 1948 at the age of twenty-four, when he carried the Liberal banner in the strong CCF seat of Last Mountain. He again contested the Last Mountain constituency in 1952. In 1954 Gardiner ran for leader of the Saskatchewan Liberal Party after leader Walter Tucker returned to federal politics, but

Gardiner lost to Hammy McDonald. In 1956 Gardiner was finally successful in his attempt to capture public office, being elected to the constituency of Melville, which overlapped with his father's riding of the same name. Gardiner once again contested the Liberal leadership in 1959, but finished third behind Ross Thatcher and Alex Cameron.

Gardiner was re-elected in 1960 and again in 1964. When Thatcher formed government in 1964, he initially offered Gardiner the position of Speaker, but Gardiner viewed this as an insult and refused. This forced Thatcher to reluctantly appoint him as minister of Public Works. In 1967 Gardiner was defeated in Melville. Thatcher appointed him deputy minister of Co-operative Development. Gardiner held this position for a year, until he resigned to unsuccessfully contest the Liberal nomination in the federal riding of Assiniboia. He returned to the Saskatchewan government to organize Thatcher's promotional program for "Homecoming '71." Disagreement soon erupted between Gardiner and Thatcher, when Thatcher demanded that he personally approve all expenditures and thus reneged on a promise to allow Gardiner a free hand in the project. Gardiner refused and was fired.

Gardiner publicly demanded the resignations of Thatcher, David Steuart and Clarence Estey. When they refused, Gardiner denounced Thatcher and his governing style on a Regina radio station. Despite this disagreement, Gardiner still contested the seat of Regina Northeast for the Liberals in 1971. Although there was little chance of the Liberals winning this seat, his presence proved to be a constant irritant for Thatcher.

After 1971, Gardiner operated

SAB R-A 7432

WILF GARDINER

several hotels throughout the province. He ran for election again in 1974 in the federal riding of Qu'Appelle-Moose Mountain as an independent, but was only successful in capturing a couple hundred votes. He died in Regina on October 5, 2002.

BRETT QUIRING

**GIBSON, JAMES WILLIAM** (1888–1965). Farmer, co-operator, and school chairman, Jim Gibson was a talented political orator who formed a bridge between the old Progressive tradition and the formation of the CCF.

Born in Edinburgh, Scotland, in 1888, Gibson emigrated to Canada in 1904. He settled with his parents on a farm near Caron. At a young age, he settled his own farm in the Grayburn district and took an interest in local government. At the age of twenty-one he held his first public post as secretary-treasurer of his local school district, and for much of the rest of his life he would continue to hold various elected offices.

In 1921, he first became politically active in the Progressive Party, helping to organize the party in his area. Gibson was later active in other farmers' movements after he returned to Caron in 1929. He was elected to the Caron Wheat Pool committee, to the council of the rural municipality and became active in the co-operative movement as director of the Moose Jaw Co-operative Association.

SAB R-B5445-4

JAMES GIBSON

Gibson followed the United Farmers of Canada (Saskatchewan Section) into politics in 1932 and played a founding role, helping to lay the groundwork for the CCF in his region. He was elected the first president of the Thunder Creek constituency and helped build that party's organization, which allowed the party a respectable showing in the 1934 election. Gibson continued to hold many positions within the party.

In 1946, he was elected the first chairman of the Moose Jaw Larger School District, a post he held until his term expired in 1951. Later in 1946, he first entered provincial office when he successfully contested the constituency of Morse in a by-election after the sitting CCF MLA resigned. Gibson was re-elected three times in 1948, 1952 and 1956. He retired from politics in 1960, returning to Caron where he died on January 28, 1965.

BRETT QUIRING

**GLEAVE, ALFRED P.** (1911–1999). Alfred Gleave was born in Zorra Township, Ontario, on June 6, 1911, and died in Ottawa, Ontario, on August 19, 1999. It seemed that political radicalism was in his bones when Alf Gleave was growing up. His English father had emigrated west from Ontario as part of the great prairie settlement project of the early twentieth century, and in his growing-up years he learned the tales of English co-operatives.

By the time he graduated from high school in 1929 and went to work on the family farm near Perdue, the Depression had started, the dust bowl was just around the corner and the United Farmers of Canada, Saskatchewan Section, was arguing for more farmer market power and new recruits. Gleave was an easy convert: "I was involved in farm organizations and political activity from 1932 onwards," he later wrote. That activism led him from a role in the failed 1946 farmer strike on the prairies to a leading role in the UFC(SS) by the late 1940s, the presidency of the Saskatchewan Farmers Union in 1951 and the position of first president of the National Farmers Union in the 1960s. He led the fight to organize farmer-controlled marketing boards, to support the Canadian Wheat Board and to devise international wheat agreements that would control production and strengthen prices. Twice, he was a member of the Canadian delegation to an International Wheat Agreement negotiation. The first time, in 1959 in Geneva, he met a secretary for the British delegation and wooed her by letters to London for two years. He married Mary Rees in 1961. He had a son, Sheldon, from an earlier marriage.

Politically, Gleave achieved his highest position when he served for Saskatoon–Biggar from 1968 to 1974 as an MP for the New Democratic Party. He had been defeated in 1965. He was NDP caucus chair and agriculture critic, leading the party fight against the Liberal plan in 1970 to react to low prices and surpluses by paying farmers to take land out of wheat production: the Lower Inventories for Tomorrow (LIFT) Program. Gleave argued that LIFT forced too great a burden on farmers. He was able to exact some political revenge two years later when purchases by the Soviet Union drove prices up but Canadian farmers were unable to cash in because of low inventories. In 1971-72, he led the NDP to support Liberal government legislation that allowed creation of farmer-controlled marketing boards with the power to extract higher prices from the market. In Saskatchewan, he had led unsuccessful campaigns to organize cattle and hog marketing boards. Gleave was defeated in 1974 by future PC Justice minister and Governor General Ray Hnatyshyn. He

ran a final time in the Kindersley–Lloydminster riding and was defeated by Progressive Conservative and future Agriculture minister Bill McKnight in 1979.

Beyond his federal election successes and farm movement influence, Gleave also played a pivotal role in 1962 by acting as a mediator between doctors and the Saskatchewan government during the tumultuous introduction of medicare in the province and the resulting doctors' strike. He was a close confidant of CCF Premier Woodrow Lloyd from nearby Biggar.

Gleave served as a member of the Economic Council of Canada and was an early advocate of public broadcasting through the Canadian Broadcasting Corporation.

BARRY WILSON, LOW, QUEBEC

FURTHER READING: Gleave, Alfred P. 1991. *United We Stand*. Toronto: Lugus Publications.

## GOODALE, RALPH EDWARD (b. 1949).

Ralph Goodale was born on May 10, 1949, and was raised on his family's farm near Wilcox. In 1972 he received a law degree from the University of Saskatchewan and was called to the Saskatchewan bar the following year. After working as a special assistant to federal Justice Minister Otto Lang, Goodale was elected as a Liberal in the riding of Assiniboia in the 1974 federal election but was defeated in the 1979 federal election. After failing to win the seat back in the 1980 federal election, Goodale switched to provincial politics and was elected leader of the provincial Liberal Party in 1981.

Goodale led the Liberals during a difficult period. They were wiped out of the provincial legislature in the 1978 provincial election and were suffering due to the unpopularity of the federal Liberal government. In the 1982 provincial election the Liberals' popular vote plummeted and Goodale was defeated in the constituency of Assiniboia-Gravelbourg. In the 1986 provincial election Goodale campaigned on fiscal responsibility in opposition to the large deficits rung up by the governing PCs and the expensive campaign promises made by both the PCs and NDP. Although the Liberals remained in third place, their popular vote improved and Goodale was elected MLA for Assiniboia–Gravelbourg.

Goodale resigned as provincial Liberal leader and as a MLA in 1988 in order to contest the riding of Regina-Wascana in the federal election that year. Although Liberal fortunes improved during this election it was not enough to help Goodale, who lost and temporarily left politics to work in the private sector. Goodale returned in 1993 and won the Liberal nomination in Regina-Wascana. He was subsequently elected in the 1993 federal election and was appointed minister of Agriculture and minister responsible for the Canadian Wheat Board in the majority Liberal government of Prime Minister Jean Chretien.

Under Goodale's guidance the historic freight subsidies paid to Canadian railways, known as the Crow Rate, were eliminated. This move and other problems in the agricultural economy earned Goodale the ire of many in the agricultural sector and contributed to dissatisfaction with the federal Liberal government in western Canada. As a result, there was an upswing in support in Saskatchewan for the Reform Party in the 1997 federal election, and then for its successor, the Alliance Party, in the 2000 federal election. In spite of these trends Goodale was re-elected with comfortable margins in both elections.

Following the 1997 election Goodale was shifted from Agriculture to Natural Resources while still retaining responsibility for the Wheat Board. Goodale continued as Natural Resources minister until 2002, when he briefly became government House Leader. Later in 2002, however, Chretien moved Goodale into the Department of Public Works and Government Services to deal with a scandal that involved inappropriate rewarding of government tendering and advertising contracts. Goodale acted quickly and effectively to diffuse the scandal and his performance in the department further cemented his reputation as one of the government's most capable and credible ministers. Goodale's fortunes continued to rise in 2003 when Paul Martin succeeded Chretien as leader of the federal Liberals and prime minister. Goodale, a long-time ally of Martin, was appointed minister of Finance, a position that made him the most powerful Saskatchewan politician in the federal government since John Diefenbaker. In 2004 Goodale was re-elected.

MIKE FEDYK, REGINA

**GOOHSEN, JACK** (b. 1942). Jack Goohsen was a two-term MLA whose sex scandal made national headlines when he was found with an underage prostitute.

Goohsen was born in Gull Lake on November 7, 1942. He received his early education in the area and attended the University of Saskatchewan, completing a program in agricultural management. He returned to Gull Lake, establishing a farm in the area. He first entered public office as a municipal councillor for the rural municipality of Carmichael, and then served as its reeve from 1981 until 1992.

Goohsen was first elected to the legislature as the Progressive Conservative MLA for the constituency of Maple Creek in 1991. He was narrowly re-elected in 1995 in the new constituency of Cypress Hills. As the election reduced the PC caucus to only five members, Goohsen began taking on more responsibility in caucus and became a more visible critic of the government. However, in April 1997, the RCMP caught him in his parked car with a fourteen-year-old prostitute at an abandoned factory. He was immediately charged, although he claimed only to be driving the girl home. Goohsen resigned from his duties within the PC caucus, and became an independent member a few months later when his caucus colleagues formed the Saskatchewan Party.

Gooshen's trial attracted a great deal of national media attention. In April 1999, he was found guilty of buying sex from an underage prostitute. The next day the legislature undertook impeachment proceedings; however, Goohsen quickly resigned his seat.

BRETT QUIRING

## GOULD, OLIVER ROBERT (1874–1951).

Oliver Gould was born in Hants, England, on April 4, 1874, and was educated in Hampshire until he emigrated to Canada in 1882. There he continued his education in Forest, Ontario, before moving to the province of Saskatchewan. Gould married Sarah Elizabeth Hindmarch in Manor and had seven children. He was a town councillor in Manor as well as a carpenter and farmer.

Gould was first elected to parliament in 1919 in a by-election for the riding of Assiniboia. Oliver Gould was the first member nominated by the Saskatchewan Grain Growers to go to Ottawa under the banner of the United Farmers. Until then, farmers' associations in the prairie West had been reluctant to take independent political action, but the failures of the Union government of Sir Robert Borden to meet the demands of farmers had prompted these associations to seek out their own representation within the House of Commons. Gould managed to defeat his Liberal opponent, W. R. Motherwell, with a majority of over 5,000 votes.

Gould's election to the House of Commons became the subject of some controversy when it was revealed that he had signed a recall agreement with his nomination committee. The practice of signing a recall agreement gave Gould's committee the option of demanding his resignation should he take action against the wishes of his constituents. Other members of parliament from the traditional parties opposed this measure and attempted to declare it illegal under the Dominion Franchise Bill, but failed in their efforts. Many members from the Progressive Party signed similar agreements after the 1921 general election.

Oliver Gould was one of the first farmer representatives to join with T. A. Crerar's agrarian group in parliament in 1920 along with three other United Farmers and three Western Unionist members. This group formed the first permanent core that established the foundation of the Progressive Party for the 1921 general election. Gould sat as a Progressive member until his defeat in the 1925 election, when the Progressive Party lost forty-one seats and were relegated primarily to the three prairie provinces. Oliver Gould passed away on October 7, 1951.

SEAN KHERAJ, YORK UNIVERSITY

## GOULET, KEITH NAPOLEON (b. 1946).

Keith Goulet, a Cree Métis educator and provincial politician from northern Saskatchewan, has left his mark on the province. The son of Veronique (née Carriere) and Arthur (Archie) Goulet, Keith was born on April 3, 1946, at Cumberland House. Today, Keith Goulet's family includes his wife, Linda May Hemingway, and two daughters, Koonu and Danis.

Goulet left his home community at a young age. Since Cumberland House had no high school, he completed grade twelve in Prince Albert. He attended teacher's college in Ontario before studying education at the University of Saskatchewan, where he obtained a Bachelor of Education in 1974. A Master of Education degree from the University of Regina followed in 1986.

Before entering politics, Goulet distinguished himself as an educator. After teaching in several elementary schools in Ontario, he lectured at the University of Saskatchewan and also worked to develop teaching of the Cree language. Goulet then worked as a coordinator and developer at NORTEP, served as principal of the La Ronge Region Community College, and held the position of executive director of the Gabriel Dumont Institute's Saskatchewan Urban Native Teacher Education Program (SUNTEP).

The voters of the Cumberland constituency first elected Goulet to the provincial legislature in the 1986 general election. As a member of the New Democratic Party (NDP) caucus, on September 29, 1992, he became provincial secretary, a position he held until January 8, 1993. That honour distinguished him as the first aboriginal person to serve as a Saskatchewan cabinet minister. From 1993 to 1995, Goulet's responsibilities included those of associate minister of Education and minister responsible for Saskatchewan Government Insurance. On November 22, 1995, Goulet

SASKATCHEWAN NDP PHOTO ARCHIVES

KEITH GOULET

became minister of Northern Affairs, a position he held until 2001. Although he continued as an MLA in 2003, he had announced his upcoming retirement from politics.

No one understands the needs of the north and its people as well as northerners do. In his various roles, Goulet has worked for his people and the northern region. His most visible achievements came during his time in the provincial cabinet. He promoted signing of the Treaty Land Entitlement Agreement in 1992 and the *Métis Act* in 2001. In many ways, Goulet helped create educational and employment opportunities for northern aboriginal people. He also worked to restore the viability of activities such as fishing and trapping. During his time in government, aboriginal people increasingly participated in the mining and forestry sectors. In northern Saskatchewan, dependence on welfare programs decreased and living standards improved. Goulet's efforts contributed to the construction of new water and sewage systems and highways in the north. Construction of the desperately needed bridge to Cumberland House, finally built in 1996, ranks among his most satisfying achievements.

DAVID QUIRING, UNIVERSITY OF SASKATCHEWAN

**GRANT, GORDON** (1910–2001). Gordon Grant was born September 13, 1910, in Regina, to parents William and Margaret. He received a Bachelor of Arts from the University of Saskatchewan in 1933, and with his wife Eileen had three children, Donald, Sharon, and Linda. Grant worked as an insurance broker and was president of Walter M.

Logan Company Limited, General Insurance. He was very active in the Regina community, serving as president and district governor of the Kinsmen Club, president of the Saskatchewan Division of the Canadian Cancer Society, president of the Regina Exhibition Association, president of the Regina Chamber of Commerce, and president of the Saskatchewan Urban Municipalities Association. Grant also sat on the board of governors and was chair for the Regina General Hospital. He served as a member of the advisory boards of the Regina Grey Nuns' Hospital, the Salvation Army, and the Y.W.C.A. Grant was also an elder of the Westminster United Church, served on the Public School Board for two years, and was an alderman on the Regina City Council for six years. Grant became the first native-born mayor of Regina in 1952 and held the position for two years.

SAB R-B 7013

GORDON GRANT

Following his years on the Regina City Council, Grant was elected to the Saskatchewan legislature in 1964, 1967, and 1971 as a Liberal candidate from the Regina Whitmore Park constituency. He acted as minister of Highways and Transportation from May 1964 to October 1966, at which time he was appointed minister of Industry and Commerce, a position he held until December 1967. Grant also served as minister in charge of SaskPower Corporation and minister of Telephones, and held the portfolio for Public Health from October 1966 to June 1971.

As minister of Highways and Transportation, Grant oversaw the continued expansion of the highways in the province and the increasing investments in roadway construction. However, it was through his position of minister of Public Health that Grant remains memorable. It was during his tenure that the Liberal government introduced utilization or deterrent fees for hospital and medical services in what has been referred to as the Black Friday Budget. These fees meant that all citizens of Saskatchewan would be required to pay $2.50 for each day in the hospital and $1.50 for each visit to a physician's office. Grant also oversaw the decision to close eleven rural hospitals which were seen as redundant and, despite continued protest and opposition, he continued with the plan to eliminate the hospitals.

Following the defeat of the Liberal government in 1971, Grant served as Opposition whip from 1971 to 1975. After serving his city and province for many years, he retired to the Hawthorn Park retirement center in Kelowna, British Columbia, and was later diagnosed with Parkinson's disease. Grant died from pneumonia on January 16, 2001.

FURTHER READING: Eisler, Dale. 1987. *Rumours of Glory: Saskatchewan and the Thatcher Years*. Edmonton: Hurtig Publishers. • Grant, Gordon. Papers. R45. Saskatchewan Archives Board, Regina.

## GRASSICK, JAMES (1868–1956). James Grassick was born at Fergus, Ontario, on March 2, 1868. At the age of fourteen, he arrived with his father in what was about to become Regina. In 1885 he was the youngest of on hundred teamsters hauling supplies to Prince Albert during the Riel Rebellion. He would later be active in its veterans' association. In later life he claimed he could speak Cree.

JAMES GRASSICK

Grassick was active in many lines of business over a long career, from hauling milk and running a livery to founding the Capital Ice Company. In 1897 he married Jessie Ann Beattie, from Ontario. They had three children. Grassick held nearly every civic office in Regina, from the Exhibition, school, and hospital boards to two terms as mayor (1920–1922, 1940–1941). A founding member and long-time office holder of Knox Presbyterian Church, Grassick, like the overwhelming majority of Presbyterians in Saskatchewan, joined with Methodists and Congregationalists in 1925 to form the United Church of Canada.

In 1929 Grassick was elected as a Conservative to the Saskatchewan legislature. Conservative Party leader J. T. M. Anderson formed a "Co-operative government" with the support of Progressive and Independent MLAs. A partisan Tory, Grassick opposed the creation of an independent civil service commission, calling it "one of the greatest mistakes the government made." In 1931 he was one of four Conservatives to vote against a government bill to award special pensions to two former senior public servants. However, Grassick very seldom voted against his own government's legislation. In 1933 he was even instrumental in defeating a bill from the government's "left wing" to promote gasoline price competition in the Regina area.

In 1934, like every other member of the Co-operative government, Grassick was defeated. After his death on August 4, 1956

(in a traffic accident), he was remembered by his city as one of its founding members and most dedicated public servants.

PETER A. RUSSELL, OKANAGAN UNIVERSITY COLLEGE

**GUSTAFSON, LEONARD** (b. 1933). Leonard Joe Gustafson was born November 10, 1933, in Macoun. He married Alice Ardeen of Macoun in 1952, and they have four children. Gustafson is active in the Macoun Cooperative Association and the Evangelical Church, including the Evangelize China Fellowship. A grains and oilseeds farmer who, with his sons, owns more than 10,000 acres of cropland, he was first elected to Parliament in 1979 as a Progressive Conservative MP from the Souris Moose Mountain riding. He was re-elected in 1980, 1984 and 1988. For nine years (1984–1993), Gustafson was parliamentary secretary to the prime minister, a Canadian parliamentary record for longevity. In Ottawa during the Mulroney governments, he was dubbed "the prime minister's shadow," always present when Mulroney entered the House of Commons and available daily for a briefing of the prime minister before the House of Commons Question Period. Mulroney once credited the MP with influencing more farmer-friendly western policy than the various agriculture ministers who served during the nine years of PC government. He helped win federal farm aid in 1986, drought aid in 1988 and the highest level of farm spending in history, $4 billion, in 1992. The next year, western voters defeated every PC candidate in western Canada. "That was my biggest disappointment," Gustafson said. On May 26, 1993, he was appointed to the Senate by Prime Minister Brian Mulroney.

His connection to Mulroney began in 1981 after Conservative prime minister Joe Clark had won government in 1979 when Gustafson first was elected, and then lost government nine months later. The rookie MP was disgruntled, met Mulroney and agreed to act in Clark's caucus as Mulroney's unofficial agent. By 1983 when a leadership convention was held, he had helped convince 24 MPs to abandon their leader for Mulroney. He nominated the Montreal lawyer to be leader and became one of Mulroney's most trusted advisors in return.

Gustafson maintains his hands-on connection to the family farm but he can serve in the Senate until November 10, 2008, and expects to serve out his term. "I love politics," he says. He served for years as chair of the Senate agriculture committee and teamed up with former Liberal agriculture minister and foe Eugene Whelan to challenge and ultimately defeat introduction of the dairy growth hormone BST into the Canadian dairy herd.

During his years in Parliament, Gustafson promoted the idea that the Canadian government should buy food to distribute to hungry developing world countries. He argued that it would help support Canadian farm commodity prices and fulfill Canada's oft-repeated commitment to combat world hunger. Gustafson's campaign won media attention but no government commitment.

BARRY WILSON, LOW, QUEBEC

**GUY, ALLAN RAY** (b. 1926). Allan Guy was born in the small farming community of Senlac on May 18, 1926, to John and Villa Guy. Educated at Senlac schools, Guy worked on the family farm before attending the Saskatoon Teacher's College and the University of Saskatchewan. After teaching for a number of years, he became a school principal in La Ronge. Guy was active in both the Saskatchewan Teachers Federation and the La Ronge Chamber of Commerce. He married Sylvia Evangeline Harach of Radisson on August 11, 1951, with a second marriage to Marjorie Hastings in October 1967. Guy had three children: Marcine, Murray, and Maureen.

Guy was first elected as the Liberal candidate from Athabasca to the Saskatchewan legislature in 1960, acting as the Opposition critic for Northern Affairs and Indian issues. He was re-elected in 1964, 1967, 1971, and in a by-election in 1972. He also ran as a candidate for the Rosthern constituency in 1975 but was not elected. Guy served in the cabinet of Ross Thatcher as minister of Public Works from November 1967 to September 1970, at which time he was appointed minister of Municipal Affairs and minister of the Department of Indian and Métis Affairs, positions he held until June 1971, when the Liberal government was defeated. Guy also served on the Saskatchewan Water Resources Commission and the Saskatchewan Water Supply Board.

Prior to serving as minister of the Department of Indian and Métis Affairs, Guy served as the legislative secretary attached to the minister of Natural Resources in charge of

WEST'S STUDIO, REGINA • SAB R-W568-712-2

ALLAN GUY

the Indian and Métis Affairs Branch of the Department. Ross Thatcher established the Department of Indian and Métis Affairs as a separate department in 1969 in an attempt to address the issues of poverty facing First Nations reserves throughout Saskatchewan, but primarily in the northern parts of the province. This was an important issue for Ross Thatcher and much time and attention was given to finding ways to improve the conditions on reserves. As minister in charge of the Department, Guy was responsible for coordinating employment and training programs and establishing electrical and telephone services on reserves.

Guy was also the subject of a controversy with the University of Saskatchewan Regina Campus students when it was exposed that he had received a student loan while serving as minister of Public Works. While it was becoming more difficult to obtain a student loan from the government, students at the Regina Campus were infuriated to find that a cabinet member could receive funding when many students could not.

ROBERTA LEXIER, UNIVERSITY OF ALBERTA

**FURTHER READING:** Eisler, Dale. 1987. *Rumours of Glory: Saskatchewan and the Thatcher Years.* Edmonton: Hurtig Publishers.
• Saskatchewan Archives Board. Allan Guy Papers. R 9171 to R 9173 , Regina.

## HAGEL, GLENN JOSEPH (b. 1949). Born in Beiseker, Alberta, on August 17, 1949, Glenn Hagel became interested in politics at an early age. He realized in a ninth grade Canadian Studies class that the obligation of citizenship is to seek office. Educated at the University of Manitoba and the University of Regina, Hagel received a B.A. in Philosophy and Psychology and also took classes toward a degree in Social Work. Hagel eventually settled in Moose Jaw.

Although his first attempt at electoral politics in 1982 was unsuccessful, Hagel's second attempt in 1986 led to his election. He went on to win the Moose Jaw North seat in five straight elections (1986, 1991, 1995, 1999,

2003). During his time in office, Hagel was NDP caucus chair from 1988–1996 and was Saskatchewan's first Speaker of the House to be elected by a ballot of all of the members of the house. As Speaker, he inaugurated the Speaker's Parliamentary Outreach programme, which included trips to various schools in the province to increase awareness of parliamentary democracy and political involvement.

In 1999, Hagel was appointed minister of Post Secondary and Skills Training. In 2001, he was moved into Community Resources and Employment, with added responsibility as minister responsible for Disability Issues and minister of Gaming. In addition to this, he was chair of the

SASKATCHEWAN NDP PHOTO ARCHIVES

GLENN HAGEL

Planning and Priorities Committee which was the government's core planning committee for the long term. Furthermore, he was the deputy House Leader, helping with the strategic management of the house. After the 2003 election Hagel left cabinet and was appointed legislative secretary in charge of Saskatchewan's Centenary.

COURTNEY ENGLAND

## HAMILTON, CHARLES MCGILL (1878–1952). C. M. Hamilton was involved in many different aspects of Saskatchewan agriculture, most significantly as Saskatchewan's minister of Agriculture for most of the 1920s.

Born on January 17, 1878, in Whitechurch, Ontario, a seventeen-year-old Hamilton came with his family to farm in Saskatchewan in 1895. In 1901 Hamilton began homesteading near Weyburn, after four years of teaching; later he also became involved in agricultural organisations. In the years before his election, Hamilton served in high positions in several different organisations, like Saskatchewan's Western Municipal Hail Insurance Association, and the Western Municipal council. He served as the president of his local chapter of the Saskatchewan Grain Growers' Association, and for seven years was the president of the Saskatchewan Association of Rural Municipalities. One year before his election to the Saskatchewan government, Hamilton was also appointed to, and briefly held, a position as director for the Canadian Northern Railway.

The Weyburn constituency elected C. M. Hamilton, running as a candidate for the Liberal Party, to the provincial legislature in a by-election on June 15, 1919. Less than a year later, in April 1920, Premier Dunning appointed Hamilton minister of Agriculture. It is likely that Hamilton's role as a farmer, and his involvement in Saskatchewan agricultural organisations—especially in the Saskatchewan Grain Grower's Association—had some influence on Dunning's decision. Farmers' organisations were then gaining influence on the prairies. During his time in the provincial cabinet, Hamilton also held the positions of minister of Municipal Affairs, minister of Highways, and minister of the *Child Welfare Act*, sometimes holding several positions at the same time.

In the early part of the 1920s, drought plagued parts of Saskatchewan, and some of the new settlers experienced many successive crop failures. This problem was especially common in the southwest of the province. Many of these settlers turned to Hamilton, their minister of Agriculture, wanting to transfer to another area. At the same time, other farmers came to the provincial government seeking relief because of the drought. At that time, the Saskatchewan government was limited in ways it could help these farmers— the National Department of the Interior controlled Saskatchewan's land. Meanwhile, relief was considered the concern of municipalities and non-governmental organisations like the Red Cross and the Homemakers' Clubs. The provincial government did, at times, subsidise part of the freight costs of those settlers trying to move to a different area because of crop failure. Hamilton worked to help provide relief for the farmers seeking assistance, both as minister of Agriculture and minister of Municipal Affairs. In 1922 the Saskatchewan government enacted the *Municipal Seed Grain Act*, which allowed municipalities to borrow money from the provincial government for the purpose of relief, in the form of feed and seed.

In 1929, the Progressive Party member R. S. Leslie defeated Hamilton in the provincial election. Hamilton resigned from the cabinet and accepted a place on the Board of Grain Commissioners, along with E. B. Ramsay and D. A. MacGibbon. Hamilton sat on that board for nineteen years. He assisted in overhauling the *Grain Act* in 1929, a job the federal government gave over to these new commissioners. In the Canadian Grain Commission, Hamilton is best remembered for his efforts in introducing the rust-resistant Thatcher wheat to Europe in 1938.

C. M. Hamilton retired from the Board of Grain Commissioners in January 1948 and died four years later on May 3, 1952, in Winnipeg, having committed most of his life to Saskatchewan and prairie agriculture.

MARYANNE COTCHER, UNIVERSITY OF REGINA

**SOURCES AND FURTHER READING:** Blanchard, J. 1987. *A History of the Canadian Grain Commission.* Winnipeg: Canadian Grain Commission. • Brennan, J. W. 1976. "A political history of Saskatchewan, 1905–1929." Unpublished Ph.D. dissertation, University of Alberta. • Saskatchewan Archives Board. C. M. Hamilton Papers. Saskatoon.

## HAMILTON, DOREEN ELLEN (b. 1951).

Doreen Ellen Hamilton (née Munholland) was born in Regina on May 17, 1951. She attended the University of Regina, where she earned her Education Standard A Certificate and landed her first teaching position in Southey. In 1972, she married Robert Gordon Hamilton and moved to British Columbia, where she taught kindergarten in the community of Burn Lake until she returned to Saskatchewan in 1975.

Hamilton was elected to the Regina City Council in 1985 and re-elected in 1988. As a city councillor, she was chairperson of the Mayor's Task Force on Women's Issues and a member of the Mayor's Board of Inquiry on Hunger. She also served as interim mayor of Regina for one month in 1988, a position that no woman had previously held.

First elected to the Saskatchewan legislature in 1991 as the New Democratic Party MLA for the Regina Wascana Plains constituency, Hamilton was re-elected in 1995 and 1999. In 1998, Hamilton was appointed to Premier Romanow's cabinet as minister of Saskatchewan Liquor and Gaming, and minister responsible for the Saskatchewan Property Management Corporation, the Public Service Commission, and the Wascana Centre Authority.

After Lorne Calvert assumed the duties of premier in February 2001, Hamilton held ministerial positions responsible for Saskatchewan Liquor and Gaming, the Saskatchewan Property Management Corporation, and the Status of Women until October 2001.

In April 2003, Hamilton was appointed as legislative secretary to the premier and chair of the Voluntary Sector Initiative, established to strengthen the relationship between the public and volunteer sectors in Saskatchewan.

Actively involved in her community, Hamilton is a member of Broadway United Church and serves on the Worship and Membership Committee. She has also served on the Boothill Community Association, which established the first pre-school program in 1982. Hamilton was re-elected in the 2003 provincial election.

JENN RUDDY, REGINA

## HAMILTON, FRANCIS ALVIN GEORGE

(1912–2004). Alvin Hamilton, leader of the Progressive Conservative Party in Saskatchewan from 1949 to 1957 and cabinet minister in the Diefenbaker government, was born in Kenora, Ontario, on March 30, 1912. Orphaned at the age of fifteen, he was taken in by his father's family in Delisle, where he completed his high school education. He attended the University of Saskatchewan from 1934 to 1938 and finished with degrees in both Arts and Education. During his third year he married his high-school sweetheart, Beulah Major, with whom he had two sons—Robert and William—and then taught at Nutana Collegiate in Saskatoon until 1941 when he enlisted in the Royal Canadian Air Force. He served as a navigator in Canada, Britain, and the Far East and after the war returned to teaching for three years until he accepted the job of Director of Organization for the national Progressive Conservative Party in Saskatchewan in 1948. A year later the provincial party elected him leader and he continued in this dual capacity for eight years. As head of what had become a "third" party in a very competitive two-party province, Hamilton faced enormous difficulties during his leadership, but managed to keep the Conservatives alive through two elections and laid the groundwork for the eventual success of the party a generation later.

Hamilton's victory in Qu'Appelle at the federal election of 1957 took him to Ottawa and to the position of minister of Northern Affairs and National Resources in the first Diefenbaker government. His early work there produced the "New National Policy"—a development programme designed to foster economic prosperity and social justice in all regions of the country. This became the "Vision" of Canada which Diefenbaker used to obtain his huge majority in the 1958 election. Under its auspices the government constructed "roads to resources," built the South Saskatchewan River Dam and a regional power grid in the Atlantic provinces, initiated programmes which opened the North to mining and oil and gas exploration, and created Canada's first Department of Forestry. The government also passed the *Agricultural Rehabilitation and Development Act* (ARDA) and the *Prairie Farm Rehabilitation Act* (PFRA), and hosted the "Resources for Tomorrow" conference which established the Canadian Council of Resource and Environmental Ministers—an intergovernmental policy coordination mechanism which remains important today.

In 1960 Diefenbaker moved Hamilton to the Department of Agriculture to tackle the manifold problems of Canada's farm population and to restore the Conservative Party's fortunes among the rural electorate. The massive grain sales to China which followed quickly on his appointment, and increased exports to other Communist countries despite the opposition of the United States, made his task on the prairies relatively easy. ARDA addressed the difficulties of the farm population on a national scale and, as Hamilton's personal popularity rose, especially in the west, so did that of his party. He came to be known as "the best Minister of Agriculture in Canadian history." He left a legacy of support for the Progressive Conservative Party in rural Canada which lasted for three decades, and the window to China which he helped open in the early sixties remains open to Canadian business today.

Hamilton remained active in national politics for another quarter of a century after the defeat of the Diefenbaker government in 1963. He served as Opposition critic for Agriculture, then Finance, in the mid-sixties, as well as chairman of the Caucus Policy-Making Committee—a tribute to his reputation as the "ideas man" of the Progressive Conservative Party. He ran for the leadership of the party in 1967 but lost to Robert Stanfield. He also lost his parliamentary seat to "Trudeaumania" in 1968, but returned to the House in 1972 and remained the Member for Qu'Appelle-Moose Mountain through three more elections until he decided to retire prior to the election of 1988. During these sixteen years he acted as his party's energy critic, continued to pave the way for Canadian business through his contacts in China, and supported a former assistant, Brian Mulroney, in his attempt to replace Joe Clark as leader of the Progressive Conservative Party. Hamilton did not receive a post in Mulroney's first cabinet, but used his status as mentor and friend to advance his views on the proper direction of national policy in a host of areas.

Alvin Hamilton was a "career" politician. He spent six years in the federal cabinet, twenty-seven years as a member of Parliament, and more than forty years in the service of his party at both the provincial and national levels. He made significant contributions to the governance of his country and his career provides a standard of public service against which to measure other politicians—past, present, and future. Hamilton lived in Manotick, Ontario, a few miles upriver from the House of Commons he loved and served so well, until his death on June 29, 2004.

PATRICK KYBA, UNIVERSITY OF GUELPH

**FURTHER READING:** Kyba, Patrick. 1989. *Alvin: A Biography of the Hon. Alvin Hamilton, P.C.* Regina: Canadian Plains Research Center. • Newman, Peter C. 1963. *Renegade in Power.* Toronto: McClelland & Stewart • Smith, Denis. 1995. *Rogue Tory.* Toronto: Macfarlane Walter & Ross.

**HANBIDGE, ROBERT LEITH** (1891–1974). Robert Leith (Dinny) Hanbidge, MLA, MP, and Lieutenant-Governor of Saskatchewan, was born in Southampton, Ontario, on March 16, 1891. Educated in Bruce and Grey counties, he moved west to Regina in 1909 to article in the law firm of Sir Frederick Haultain, then leader of the Provincial Rights (Conservative) Party and later Chief Justice of the province. An avid sportsman, Hanbidge played for the Regina Rugby Club, forerunner of the Roughriders, during his years in the capital, but on completion of his legal studies left for Kerrobert to join his brother Jack's law firm in 1914. A year later he married Jane Mitchell of Francis with whom he had four daughters and a son.

Hanbidge, as with so many of his generation, had an abiding interest in politics and a firm belief in the importance of public service. Thus, he served first on the council and later as mayor of Kerrobert. He then contested and won a seat in the legislature in 1929 and acted as Conservative Party whip throughout the Anderson government's five-year term of office. Defeated with all other supporters of the Co-operative government in 1934, he returned to his law practice but continued to participate in Conservative Party activities for the next quarter of a century. In 1945, for example, he contested but lost the Kindersley seat for the new Progressive Conservative Party at the federal general election. During these years, one prominent friend and constant correspondent was John Diefenbaker and, after he won the national party leadership, Diefenbaker urged Hanbidge to join him in Ottawa. This he did in 1958, winning Kindersley and repeating his victory in 1962. While a Member of the House of Commons he represented Canada at both NATO and Commonwealth conferences.

SAB R-PS62-979-03

ROBERT HANBIDGE

Hanbidge might have been expected to run again in the election of 1963 but, by this time, he had accepted Diefenbaker's invitation to become Lieutenant-Governor of Saskatchewan, a position he filled with distinction for an unusual seven-year term. The University of Saskatchewan recognized his many contributions to the province with an Honorary Doctorate of Laws in 1968 and he maintained his interest in all aspects of Saskatchewan society, especially sports, until his death on July 25, 1974.

PATRICK KYBA, UNIVERSITY OF GUELPH

**FURTHER READING:** Leeson, H. (ed.). 2001. *Saskatchewan Politics:*

*Into the Twenty-first Century.* Regina: Canadian Plains Research Center • Eager, E. 1980. *Saskatchewan Government.* Saskatoon: Western Producer Prairie Books.

## HANTELMAN, LOUIS HENRY (1884–1966).

Louis Henry Hantelman was born in Dubuque, Iowa, on May 20, 1884, and was educated there. Like many other Americans at that time, he came north in search of a homestead, and settled at Rouleau in 1905. A successful farmer, he was a pioneer in the mechanization of agriculture; he owned and operated a 110-horsepower steam giant and later an "Oil Pull" on his farm. He organized and managed one of Saskatchewan's earliest baseball clubs.

Hantelman enlisted in the Canadian Army shortly after war broke out in 1914. He organized and trained the Rouleau detachment which became part of the 46th Battalion of the Canadian Expeditionary Force. To remain with his men when they went to France, he reverted from the rank of captain to that of lieutenant. He was wounded in battle and was discharged in Moose Jaw in June 1919.

Following the war he began farming near Plato and developed a very successful farming enterprise. He participated actively in the work of the agricultural societies and junior clubs and established a "grain club" for students even before the 4H movement got underway.

In the larger sphere of public service, he had a distinguished record. He was one of five Farmer-Labor members, the precursor of the CCF Party, elected to the Saskatchewan legislature in 1934 (for Kindersley). In 1938 he was the successful CCF candidate for Elrose.

SAB R-A 700

LOUIS HANTELMAN

He served for two terms (nine years). He was appointed first chairman of the University Hospital Board in 1945, to plan for the new University Hospital and became a a member of the University of Saskatchewan Board of Governors in 1946. His contributions to the University and the Hospital were recognized by the award of an honorary LLD at the convocation of May 1955.

He was very interested in students and assisted many worthy students financially, usually as an anonymous donor. When he died he left $500,000 to the University of Saskatchewan. Two-thirds of the legacy was directed to agricultural research, and one-sixth each for agricultural scholarships and for scholarships in the humanities and social sciences. In all his endeavors Lou Hantelman was supported by his wife Florence ("Dolly") who shared his great interest in agriculture and the university; she continued her financial support after her husband's death.

The citation given by Dr. V. E. Graham, Dean of the College of Agriculture at the May 1955 University of Saskatchewan convocation sums up his life:

"He was in the district [Rouleau] on the day that Saskatchewan was proclaimed a province... He represents the pioneer whom Saskatchewan is honouring this year... He is a leader in the field of farming, and the progress and stability of agriculture; he had a distinguished record of public service; he helped many and few knew where the help came from; he is a man of wisdom and generous heart."

Lou Hantelman died on January 6, 1969.

LOUIS HORLICK, UNIVERSITY OF SASKATCHEWAN

## HAULTAIN, SIR FREDERICK WILLIAM GORDON

(1857–1942). Sir Frederick Haultain was born near Woolwich, England, on November 25, 1857. In 1860, his family emigrated to Peterborough, Upper Canada. In 1861 his father, Frederick Haultain, a retired officer in the Royal Artillery, was elected to the legislature of the Province of Canada, as a supporter of George Brown's Clear Grits.

The younger Haultain graduated the University of Toronto in 1876 and was called to the Ontario Bar in 1882. Haultain practiced law in Toronto and Kingston until moving to the North-West Territories in 1884. Haultain established his practice in the frontier town of Fort McLeod in the District of Alberta. By 1887 the Fort McLeod area's population was sufficient to be entitled representation in the Territorial Assembly. Due largely to his reputation as a community leader, Haultain won a hard-fought and narrow election and was sent to represent the constituency in Regina, the Territorial capital. Haultain won or was acclaimed in every Territorial election after this and represented the constituency until the creation of the provinces of Saskatchewan and Alberta in 1905.

At the beginning of Haultain's political career the Territorial Assembly had very little authority because control over the Territorial budget rested in the hands of the federal government in the person of the Lieutenant-Governor. The majority of the assembly, which consisted of both Liberals and Conservatives, felt that the Lieutenant-Governor's authority denied the North-West Territories responsible government. Haultain, nominally a Conservative, aligned himself with the majority and used the issue of responsible government to create a loose non-partisan coalition to campaign for increased assembly control over the Territorial finances. Haultain became the recognized leader of this group and maneuvered, lobbied and pressured the federal government to grant responsible government. It was not until 1897, however, that the Lieutenant-Governor was excluded from the executive committee (cabinet) and control over the Territorial budget was turned over to the Assembly. Haultain's efforts were widely credited with the achievement of responsible government and after 1897 he became the first premier of the North-West Territories.

Haultain selected an executive committee with both Liberal and Conservative members and advocated non-partisanship in Territorial matters. He argued that the North-West Territories would be better off without the acrimony of partisan politics. The financial demands caused by rapidly increasing settlement, in particular the need for more roads and schools, challenged Haultain's administration and led to a call for provincial status for the North-West Territories. Haultain seized on the issue of provincial status because it would provide the Territories with increased taxing authority and it provided a focus for unity among the Liberals and Conservatives in the Assembly. The issue proved more problematic as a unifying force than responsible government had because of various regional loyalties and aspirations. These led some people to favour two or more provinces being created out of the Territories rather than only one province, as Haultain wanted. As a result, Haultain faced opposition from several quarters but most notably from the Calgary

SAB R-B 3200

FREDERICK HAULTAIN

area, where numerous leaders hoped that their city could become the capital of one of the new provinces.

The non-partisan unity created by the issue of provincial status was further undermined by Haultain himself, who increasingly became identified with the Conservative Party. In 1903, Haultain accepted an honorary position with the Territorial Conservative Association and openly campaigned for the Conservatives in the federal election that year. Although both parties promised the Territories provincial status if they were elected, Haultain appeared at numerous Conservative events, both in the Territories and in Ontario, arguing that only the Tories could be trusted to grant provincial status. Following the re-election of the Liberals, Haultain was shut out of all planning related to provincial status. In 1905 the federal Liberal government passed legislation that not only created two provinces but also allowed the federal government to retain control over each province's natural resources and guaranteed minority (Roman Catholic) rights through a separate school system. Haultain vehemently attacked the legislation and argued that two provinces weakened the North-West's position within Confederation and that the natural resources and the separate school provisions were an intrusion on provincial rights as established in the *British North America Act*.

Due to Haultain's opposition to the federal government's decisions regarding the new provinces, he was not appointed as provisional premier for either of the provinces and was not even acknowledged in the ceremonies marking their creation. Haultain chose to live in Saskatchewan instead of Alberta because he had lived in Regina for most of his time in the North-West. Haultain transformed the Conservative Party into the Provincial Rights

Party and challenged the provisional Liberal premier, Walter Scott, in the 1905 Saskatchewan provincial election. Haultain portrayed the Provincial Rights Party as non-partisan and attracted a number of prominent Liberals as candidates. He campaigned against what he considered the federal government's intrusion into provincial affairs but his position on education was interpreted as anti-Catholic, which alienated a significant number of voters. The Provincial Rights Party lost the popular vote by a very narrow margin and Haultain, who was elected in the constituency of South Qu'Appelle, became Saskatchewan's first leader of the Opposition.

Haultain contested the 1908 election as the leader of the Provincial Rights Party and the 1912 election as leader of the Conservative Party, but although in both cases he made a strong showing, he was never able to defeat Scott and the Liberals. In 1912 he retired from politics and was appointed the Chief Justice of Saskatchewan. He held that position until his retirement in 1937. He was knighted in 1916 and served as Chancellor of the University of Saskatchewan from 1917 until 1939. He received honorary degrees from the University of Toronto and the University of Saskatchewan and was made an honorary Cree Chief. Haultain retired to Montreal where he passed away on January 30, 1942.

MIKE FEDYK, REGINA

**FURTHER READING:** MacEwan, Grant. 1985. *Frederick Haultain: Frontier Statesman of the Canadian Northwest.* Saskatoon: Western Producer Prairie Books. • Thomas, Lewis. 1970. "The Political and Private Life of F. W. G. Haultain." *Saskatchewan History* 23 (2): 50–58. • Stanley, Gordon. 1981. "F. W. G. Haultain, Territorial Politics and the Quasi-party System." *Prairie Forum* 6 (1): 1–15. • Bocking, D. H. 1964. "Saskatchewan's First Provincial Election." *Saskatchewan History* 17 (2): 41–54.

**HAVERSTOCK, LYNDA MAUREEN** (b. 1948). As both an MLA and Lieutenant-Governor, Lynda Haverstock was best known as a leader of the Saskatchewan Liberal party. She led the party back into Saskatchewan's political scene after a fifteen-year absence. However, her leadership was mired in party infighting that forced her out of the party.

OFFICE OF THE LIEUTENANT GOVERNOR

LYNDA HAVERSTOCK

Haverstock was born in Swift Current on September 16, 1948. She left high school before completion, but later returned to finish as an adult. She attended the University of Saskatchewan, earning bachelor's and master's degrees in education and completing a Ph.D. in clinical psychology. She worked as psychologist in private practice and as a lecturer for both the Universities of Saskatchewan and New Brunswick. Before entering politics, she worked for the Centre for Agricultural Medicine in Saskatoon specializing in farm stress. She was a noted authority on the subject, giving many lectures, authoring several journal articles, and editing a book on the subject.

Haverstock came from a political family. Her brother, Dennis Ham, served two terms as a Conservative in the legislature. She was active in the Liberal party in the 1980s, and in 1989 was approached to contest the beleaguered party's leadership after former leader Ralph Goodale resigned to seek federal office. She was elected leader and served as the first woman to lead a Saskatchewan political party. Without any seats in the legislature, Haverstock sought to increase the party's profile. In 1991, Liberal support more than doubled to over 23 percent of the total vote. Although only a couple of percentage points behind the Conservatives, the Liberal party failed to elected any MLAs besides Haverstock, who was victorious in Saskatoon-Greystone.

During the term, the Liberals seemed to be gaining momentum when NDP MLA Glen McPherson crossed the floor to the Liberals and the Liberals won the 1994 by-election in Regina Northwest. Liberal hopes were high for the 1995 election. However, the party never seriously challenged the ruling New Democrats for power. Besides making major breakthroughs, capturing eleven seats, and increasing its vote to almost 35 percent, Haverstock's leadership was challenged. Haverstock was forced out as leader shortly after the election and remained in the legislature for the rest of the term as an independent.

Haverstock did not contest the 1999 election, and began a short career as a radio talk show host. In 2000, she was rewarded for service to the Liberal party by Prime Minister Jean Chrétien, who appointed her Saskatchewan's Lieutenant-Governor.

BRETT QUIRING

**FURTHER READING:** Haverstock, Lynda. 2001. "The Saskatchewan Liberal Party." in Howard Leeson (ed.), *Saskatchewan Politics: Into the Twenty-first Century*. Regina: Canadian Plains Research Center. 199–250.

**HEMING, DEMPSTER HENRY RATCLIFFE** (1885–1967). Dempster Heming was born November 30, 1885, in London, England, and attended Westminster school and later King's College, University of London. He came to Canada in 1905 and homesteaded near Arcola.

While in Arcola he was employed by the Canadian Pacific Railroad (CPR) which first exposed him to the labour movement. In 1912 he sold his farm and began to work for the CPR full-time in the Moose Jaw yards. In Moose Jaw he became more active in the trade unions, participating on several union committees and becoming active in Moose Jaw's labour community. In 1916, Heming helped form Saskatchewan's first Labour Representative League which contested the Moose Jaw constituency, eventually electing William Baker in 1921. Continuing his involvement in the labour movement, Heming allowed his name to stand in 1937 for Moose Jaw city council and was elected as the reformist slate swept the election. Heming remained on city council until 1947, serving on every city committee and as deputy mayor. He took special interest in recreation: he founded the city's recreation and parks committee and was involved in many local sporting events.

In 1944, he was first elected to the Saskatchewan legislature representing the dual member constituency of Moose Jaw with the city's mayor, Jack Corman. Taking office as the CCF won a massive electoral victory, Heming would remain a backbencher for his entire career. He was re-elected with substantial majorities in 1948, 1952, and 1956. He retired from the legislature in 1960 when he did not contest the election. In retirement he remained in Moose Jaw where he died on April 20, 1967.

SAB R-B 5445-11

BRETT QUIRING

DEMPSTER HEMING

**HEPPNER, BENJAMIN D.** (b. 1943). Ben Heppner was born and raised in Waldheim. He attended Briercrest Bible Institute at Caronport and the University of Saskatchewan, graduating with a Bachelor of Arts and a Bachelor of Education. Following the completion of his schooling, Heppner taught in both the rural school system and city collegiate system for 22 years, including 14 years in school administration. In addition, Heppner served on church boards, the army cadets, the Seager Wheeler Farm Committee and the Community Bond Corporation. He was also a partner in a farm equipment dealership in Rosthern.

Heppner currently resides in Rosthern with his wife Arlene, and together they have three children, Ken, Nancy, and Lana, as well as three grandchildren.

Heppner's political career began when he served as town councilor in Rosthern. In 1988, Heppner was elected mayor. Heppner was elected to the provincial legislature in 1995 and served as the Progressive Conservative Opposition critic for Education, Municipal Affairs and the Saskatchewan Liquor and Gaming Authority.

In 1997, Heppner defected with three fellow MLAs from the Progressive Conservative Party and four MLAs from the Liberal Party to form the Saskatchewan Party. Heppner served as the Justice critic and chair of the Saskatchewan Party caucus. He was also critic for the Crown Investments Corporation, Intergovernmental Affairs, Saskatchewan Liquor and Gaming Authority and Saskatchewan Property Management Corporation. Heppner was re-elected for Rosthern in 1999 and in the new constituency of Martensville in 2003.

WINTER FEDYK, KINGSTON, ON

**HEPWORTH, LORNE HENRY** (b. 1947). Lorne Hepworth was a member of the inner circle of Grant Devine's Progressive Conservative government in the 1980s.

Hepworth was born on December 20, 1947, in Assiniboia. He attended the University of Saskatchewan, graduating as a Doctor of Veterinary Medicine in 1970. He married Fern Dianne Margeurite in 1970. They have two children, Alana and Graeme. The Hepworth family settled in Weyburn, where Hepworth practised as a veterinarian from 1971 to 1982. He was a member of the Council for the Saskatchewan Veterinary Medical Association (1974–1982), a member of the Weyburn Chamber of Commerce and the Weyburn Agricultural Society, and a member of the Canadian Veterinary Medical Association. In 1982, Hepworth ran for the provincial legislature in Weyburn; Tommy Douglas's former constituency went to the young Progressive Conservative veterinarian.

Hepworth became minister of Agriculture in 1983, a position he held until 1985. From 1985 to 1986 he was the minister of Energy and Mines. From 1986 to 1989 he was the minister of Education; from 1986 to 1987 he also held the portfolio of Advanced Education and Manpower. Hepworth was then given the portfolios of Public Participation (1989–1990), Finance (1989–1991) and Saskatchewan Property Management Corporation (1990–1991).

Hepworth's role as Education Minister and Advanced Education and Manpower Minister coincided with the underreporting of the government's deficit in 1986 and the subsequent gutting of post-secondary programs. One hundred and forty-two instructors and seventy-four non-teaching staff were laid off from Saskatchewan's technical institutes, which were then merged to form the Saskatchewan Institute of Applied Science and Technology (SIAST). This opened the post-secondary educational market to private technical schools. Budget cuts implemented by Hepworth also resulted in raised tuition at the province's two universities and led to the professors' strike at the University of Saskatchewan in 1988.

Hepworth also played a role in the privatization of many of Saskatchewan's Crown corporations. The Public Participation portfolio that Hepworth controlled from 1989 to 1990 was created to oversee the privatization of Saskatchewan's Crowns. Hepworth took over the portfolio after a disastrous year in which the government was forced to invoke closure on one bill (PCS), listened to the bells ringing over the attempt to privatize SaskEnergy, and faced a lawsuit from SGI employees over its privatization of the general insurance wing. His appointment was supposed to herald a new era where the government would listen to the people instead of trying to control public opinion.

Lorne Hepworth lost his seat in the 1991 general election. He became president of Croplife Canada, the trade association that represents manufacturers, developers and distributors of pest control products and plant biotechnology.

DANA TURGEON, REGINA

**BIBLIOGRAPHY:** Biggs, Lesley, and Mark Stobbe (eds.). 1991. *Devine Rule in Saskatchewan: A Decade of Hope and Hardship.* Saskatoon: Fifth House Publishers.

**HERMAN, JOHN FREDERICK** (1889–1950). John Herman was born April 11, 1889, in Bradford, Ontario. At the age of four, he traveled west to Rocanville with his parents Frederick William and Sarah Etta (née Roach)

Herman. John Herman was sent back to his parents' hometown in Ontario, where he received his elementary schooling. He eventually returned to Saskatchewan, where he graduated from the Moosomin High School. Herman then continued his education at the Regina Normal School, graduating in 1908. Upon completion of his program in Regina, Herman taught school at Yellow Grass and near Vandura.

On March 2, 1922 John married Eva Chilcott of Winnipeg. The couple had four children: Frederick, Phyliss, Gwendolyn and Stewart.

John F. Herman first threw his hat into the political arena in 1934 when he was elected president of the United Farmers of Canada. He would serve in this capacity for two years. He was unsuccessful in his attempts to win a seat in the Saskatchewan legislature in 1934 for the new Farmer-Labor Party in Moosomin. In 1935 he ran for the House of Commons as the CCF candidate in the riding of Qu'Appelle, but again was unsuccessful. In 1938 Herman's political fortunes changed. He ran as the Social Credit candidate, with support from both the local CCF and Conservative parties, for the Melville constituency, defeating Charles M. Dunn by 11 votes. Herman sat as the MLA for Melville until 1944, when he decided not to contest the election.

Outside of the political sphere, John F. Herman led an active life. He farmed in the Rocanville area for several years, where he was also involved in numerous organizations. Just prior to his death, Herman was working with the local district improvement branch of the department of municipal affairs at Loon Lake. John Frederick Herman passed away in February of 1950.

DWAYNE YASINOWSKI, UNIVERSITY OF REGINA

**HERMANSON, ELWIN NORRIS** (b. 1952). Elwin Hermanson was born August 22, 1952, in Swift Current to parents Elvinus Agator and Helen Lucille (née Fett). Raised near Beechy, Hermanson, at the age of nineteen, enrolled at the Full Gospel Bible Institute in Eston where he attained a three-year diploma. In 1975, Hermanson took over the family grain and beef cattle farm which he operates to this day. During this time, Hermanson met his future wife Gail and the couple now has three teenaged children together: Ehren, Byron, and Marlyn.

From 1979 through 1994, Hermanson served on the board of directors of the Full Gospel Bible Institute, of which he was chair from 1987 until 1991. He was also a part of the Beechy-Demaine Economic Development Committee.

In 1988, Hermanson's interest in politics led him to run for a seat in the federal Parliament as one of the first Reform Party candidates in Canada. Hermanson served three terms on the Reform Party's National Executive Council and was elected as the Member of Parliament for the riding of Kindersley–Lloydminster in 1993. During this time he served as chief Agriculture critic as well as Reform House Leader from 1993 to 1995.

Hermanson lost his federal seat in the June 1997 election, but quickly moved into provincial politics. He agreed to take a leave of absence from his job as the federal Reform Party's national election readiness manager to serve as one of the initial members of the Saskatchewan Party Steering Committee. The Saskatchewan Party was founded in August 1997 when four Conservative members of the legislature and four Liberals defected to form a right-wing alternative to the NDP who were united by a platform to cut taxes, create jobs, crack down on crime, improve health care, fix roads, and introduce workfare. The party got a boost just a few months later when the Conservative Party, mired by a corruption scandal that witnessed 13 former legislators convicted of fraud, decided to put off running any candidates for two elections. On August 21, 1997, the Saskatchewan Party, given that it had more seats than the Liberals, the Official Opposition, was given the status of Official Opposition.

Initially, some supporters of the new party were concerned when Hermanson announced his intention to run as party leader. Many felt that Hermanson's staunch religious beliefs and Reform roots would be subjects of continuous scrutiny by the governing New Democratic Party (NDP). However, Hermanson's strong appeal to Reformers and provincial Progressive Conservatives helped him in the end. On April 20, 1998, Hermanson became the first elected leader of the Saskatchewan Party. At the second ballot, 1,836 of 3,344 party members voted for Hermanson with Melfort–Tisdale MLA Rod Gantefoer, a former Liberal, receiving 1,508 votes. Former Snowbird commander and Progressive Conservative candidate Yogi Huyghebaert, third in the leadership race, was dropped after the first ballot when he received only 454 votes.

On September 16, 1999, the Saskatchewan Party captured 26 of 58 seats in the provincial election, receiving more of the popular vote than the governing NDP. Completely shut out in Saskatchewan's twenty-six city constituencies, the Saskatchewan Party secured all but a handful of thirty-two rural seats meaning that, though the NDP won the election, it was relegated to a minority government. Hermanson defeated the NDP incumbent and was elected as MLA for the Rosetown-Biggar constituency and

leader of the Official Opposition.

During his tenure as Saskatchewan Party leader, Hermanson embarked on a platform designed to increase Saskatchewan's population by 100,000 people in a decade. Hermanson and his party believe that such growth would occur via several avenues, such as strategic tax reduction and eliminating all direct government involvement and investment in the provincial economy. However, the Saskatchewan Party narrowly lost the 2003 election—although Hermanson was re-elected in Rosetown-Elrose. The party's inability to win urban seats proved to be its downfall. After two narrow defeats, Hermanson resigned as leader.

WINTER FEDYK, KINGSTON, ON

**HILSON, JOHN DONALD** (b. 1945). North Battleford MLA, cabinet minister and Liberal leadership candidate, "Jack" Hilson was one of the most prominent Liberal members in the late nineties.

Born February 26, 1945, on the family farm near Briercrest, he completed high school at Briercrest and continued his studies at the University of Saskatchewan. At university, Hilson earned both a B.A. and an M.A. in Political Studies, as well as a law degree. Hilson began his legal career in 1974, establishing a private practice in Melville which he maintained until being appointed director of Legal Aid in North Battleford in 1986.

Actively involved in the Liberal Party since university, Hilson first ran for political office in 1994 when he was elected to North Battleford city council. In 1996, he ran for the Liberal Party in the constituency of North Battleford when NDP cabinet minister Doug Anguish resigned the seat. Hilson was narrowly elected in an upset victory, which bolstered the Liberal Party in the wake of very vicious and public internal party disputes.

In 1997, many Liberal MLAs left the party to join with the remaining Conservative MLAs to form the Saskatchewan Party. Hilson remained with the Liberals, becoming one of the party's most prominent spokesmen as the party's deputy leader. Re-elected in 1999, Hilson joined Liberals Jim Melenchuk and Ron Osika in a coalition government with Roy Romanow's NDP. Hilson was appointed minister of Intergovernmental and Aboriginal Affairs and a year later also took on the responsibility as minister of Municipal Affairs.

In February 2001, Hilson resigned from the government, critical that the Liberals had lost their identity within the coalition. He ran for party leader later that year but finished behind David Karwacki. Hilson contested the 2003 election in the new constituency of the Battlefords, but was soundly defeated as the Liberals failed to elect a single MLA.

BRETT QUIRING

## HNATYSHYN, RAMON JOHN (1934–2002).

Ramon "Ray" Hnatyshyn was an important figure in Canadian political history for his longevity in the public sphere, his renowned sense of humour, and his ability to transcend boundaries of provincialism, regionalism, and partisan loyalties. He practiced law, served as a cabinet minister in the Clark and Mulroney governments, and served as the twenty-fourth Governor General of Canada between 1990 and 1995. Born in Saskatoon on March 16, 1934, Hnatyshyn followed in his father John's footsteps and entered the

RAY HNATYSHYN

legal field. John Hnatyshyn, a lawyer by trade, was also Canada's first Ukrainian-born senator. Ramon graduated from the University of Saskatchewan in 1956 and was called to the Saskatchewan Bar in 1957. He practiced privately for two years, following which time he moved to Ottawa to work as an executive assistant for the government's senate leader.

In 1960 Hnatyshyn returned to Saskatoon, married Gerda Andreasen, and resumed the practice of law. He began to build a political base in the city and in 1964 ran unsuccessfully as a Conservative in the provincial election. Following his defeat, he taught law at the University of Saskatchewan for ten years until entering the political arena.

In the 1974 federal election, Hnatyshyn defeated Alf Gleave in Saskatoon-West. His first mandate in Ottawa, in which the House of Commons was dominated by Trudeau's second majority government, was largely focused on constituency matters.

When the Progressive Conservative Party won a minority government in 1979, Hnatyshyn was appointed to the Energy, Mines and Resources portfolio and was minister of state for Science and Technology. In 1984, following the landslide Brian Mulroney majority, Hnatyshyn was appointed Government House Leader. In the two years that followed, Hnatyshyn was involved in a series of important parliamentary reforms, including the introduction of the secret ballot for elections of the Speaker of the House, and a more streamlined Question Period.

Hnatyshyn was named president of the Privy Council in 1985 and minister of Justice and Attorney General in 1986. Under his tenure several important pieces of legislation were enacted on child abuse, police seizure procedures, judicial authority in victim compensation, and for the allowance of suspected Nazi criminals to be tried in Canada.

In 1988, however, Hnatyshyn was overwhelmingly defeated by the NDP candidate, Chris Axworthy, a loss he credited to the free trade debate. Temporarily removed from the political eye, he re-entered legal practice with the firm of Gowling Strathy and Henderson, where he specialized in trade law and mediation. That year Hnatyshyn was also honoured with the appointment as Queen's Counsel (QC) for Canada. One year later, he was granted an honorary life membership with the Law Society of Saskatchewan.

In late 1989, Mulroney appointed Hnatyshyn Governor General, and he was sworn in in January 1990. Hnatyshyn's term as Governor General was marked by a high level of activity and a spirit of openness. He travelled the country widely throughout his tenure, reopened Rideau Hall's doors to the public, and specifically opened grounds and rooms of the official residence of the Governor General to public events, activities, and tours. New and returning special events at Rideau Hall included the Governor General's Summer Concert Series and the reopening of the Hall's historic skating rink. At the end of his term as Governor General in 1995, Hnatyshyn returned to his legal practice in Ottawa. He became a senior partner with the legal firm Gowling Lafleur Henderson.

Throughout his career in politics, Hnatyshyn exhibited an ardent commitment to the community. He founded the Governor General's awards for the Performing Arts in 1992, and the Ramon John Hnatyshyn Award for Voluntarism in the Arts. He was also a long-standing supporter of youth and educa-tion, having created the Fight for Freedom literacy award, the Canadian Bar Association's Hnatyshyn Award, and scholarships in Environmental Engineering and Science. Hnatyshyn was also a long-term supporter of the YMCA's youth programs.

Mr. Hnatyshyn died at the age of 68 of complications from pancreatitis on December 18, 2002, and is survived by his wife Gerda, and sons John and Carl. At the time of his death, Hnatyshyn was serving as Chancellor of Carleton University.

TERESA WELSH, TORONTO

## HODGINS, GRANT MILTON (b. 1955).
As minister and government House Leader for the Devine government, Hodgins resigned from government because of the Fair Share Saskatchewan program which provided a major blow to the government just prior to the 1991 election.

Grant Hodgins was born July 22, 1955, in Prince Albert. After completing high school in Melfort, he attended the University of Saskatchewan, completing a Bachelor's degree in Commerce. Active in politics at an early age, Hodgins first ran for the Progressive Conservatives in the 1982 election at the age of twenty-six. Contesting the traditionally safe CCF-NDP seat of Melfort, he was easily elected in the Tory sweep.

In 1985, Hodgins was first appointed to cabinet as minister of Highways and Transportation. Easily re-elected in 1986, Hodgins was given added responsibility by taking on the Indian and Native Affairs portfolio. In 1989, Hodgins was moved out of Highways and took over as minister of Environment. He was also given the added responsibility of government House Leader, piloting the government's legislation through the legislature.

In 1991, Hodgins became upset with government policy, in particular the program called "Fair Share Saskatchewan." This rural revitalization program, which would have seen the dispersal of government offices from Regina to various centres across Saskatchewan, was a highly contentious proposal. Hodgins sided with the plan's opponents, who saw the legislation as nothing more than an economically dubious venture that sought to buy votes in rural Saskatchewan at the expense of the NDP stronghold of Regina. In protest, Hodgins resigned from the government and served out the legislative session as an independent.

Hodgins did not seek re-election in 1991, choosing instead to take over the family auctioneering business in Melfort. In 1995, Hodgins was caught in the Tory fraud scandals and charged with fraud under $5,000 for filing a false expense account. He was found guilty, granted a conditional discharge, ordered to repay the money, and sentenced to community service.

BRETT QUIRING

## HOPFNER, MICHAEL ALFRED (b. 1947).

As government whip for much of the Devine government, Michael Hopfner was one of the central figures in the Tory fraud scandal.

Hopfner was born January 25, 1947, in Humboldt, and educated in Lake Lenore. Hopfner graduated form the Moose Jaw Technical school and established himself as a hotel owner and electrical contractor in Lashburn.

Elected as a Progressive Conservative in 1982 representing the constituency of Cut Knife–Lloydminster, Hopfner was part of the Grant Devine government, serving the first term as deputy government whip. Re-elected

SAB R-PS 82-612-942
MICHAEL HOPFNER

in 1986, Hopfner was promoted to government whip, a position that exercised considerable influence over the day-to-day operations of government caucus office.

Hopfner was defeated in 1991 as the Conservative government fell. As the RCMP began to investigate the operations of the Conservative caucus office, Hopfner came under investigation for his actions. In 1995, he was charged with filing false expense claims for $57,348 and conspiracy to commit fraud totaling $837,000. Hopfner's highly publicized trial created considerable drama as Hopfner, defending himself, called Senator Eric Berntson to the stand, who initially tried to use parliamentary privilege to avoid testifying. The trial ended with the judge finding Hopfner guilty of fraud, although he was acquitted of conspiracy to commit fraud. He was sentenced to jail for eighteen months and ordered to pay restitution.

BRETT QUIRING

FURTHER READING: Jones, Gerry. 2000. SaskScandal. Calgary: Fifth House.

## HORSMAN, JOHN WHITMORE (1888–1976). John Horsman was born in Grand Falls, New Brunswick, on September 24, 1888. Educated locally, he moved west in 1907 to homestead in the Unity district. Active in the farming community, he spent many years in local government. In 1918 he began serving as

the secretary-treasurer of the rural municipal-ity of Green Lake, a position he held for twen-ty years. In 1938, he was elected as a council-lor and in 1941 as a reeve, a position held until his election as MLA. Also serving on the Unity School Board and Hospital Board, Horsman developed a strong record in local gov-ernment that led him to provincial politics. Critical of the poli-cies of the CCF gov-ernment, Horsman contested the 1948 election for the Liberals in the constituency of Wilkie. Elected in 1948, he was re-elected three more times in 1952, 1956 and 1960. A strong critic of Jack Corman and Clarence Fines, Horsman provided the demoralized and fractured Liberal Party with continuity during his time in the legislature. Horsman retired from politics in 1964 on the eve of Liberal vic-tory, after 46 years of public service. Returning to his farm in retirement, Horsman died in Saskatoon in June 1976.

SAB R-B 5445-26

JOHN HORSMAN

BRETT QUIRING

**HOVDEBO, STANLEY J.** (b. 1925). Stan Hovdebo was born July 20, 1925, in Domremy. Raised in a political family that was very active in the co-operative movement, Hovdebo became active in the CCF at an early age. Educated locally, Hovdebo later graduat-ed with a B.Ed. from the University of Saskatchewan in 1950 and received his M.Ed. from the University of Toronto in 1959. Hovdebo taught at a variety of schools in northern Saskatchewan, Yukon, Ontario, Quebec and New Zealand before he was appointed director of education of the Prince Albert Public School Board in 1965. From 1971 to 1975, Hovdebo served as the educa-tion advisor for the Kano state government in Nigeria through the Canadian International Development Agency. Returning to Saskatchewan in 1975, he was appointed the superintendent and CEO of the Northern School Board, a position he held until his elec-tion to the House of Commons.

Hovdebo first contested political office in 1979, challenging former Prime Minister John Diefenbaker in the riding of Prince Albert for the NDP. This was the first time since the for-ties that Diefenbaker had been seriously chal-lenged, and he worried that he could be defeated. Although Hovdebo fell short, he nearly doubled the NDP vote in the riding and cut Diefenbaker's majority from over 11,000 votes to under 4,500 votes. When Diefenbaker died a few months later, Hovdebo contested the by-election and this time narrowly defeated his Conservative chal-lenger. Contesting three elections within the course of ten months, Hovdebo was re-elected in 1980 after the fall of the Clark government. He took part in the constitution debates dur-ing this session, actively breaking with his cau-cus and siding with Allan Blakeney's initial reservations of the proposed constitution.

Hovdebo was elected again in 1984. He was re-elected for the last time in 1988, this time in the riding of Saskatoon–Humboldt because of redistribution. During most of his time in Parliament, Hovdebo served as his party's critic of the Wheat Board, Co-opera-tives and Rural Affairs. In 1989, he was elect-ed vice-chair of the NDP caucus, a position he held until 1993.

Hovdebo did not contest the 1993 election

and retired from politics. He continued his involvement in international development, serving on the board of directors and later as chairman of the Canadian Organization for Development through Education (CODE), which primarily promotes literacy in the developing world.

BRETT QUIRING

**HOWE, PETER ANTON** (1888–1976). Peter Howe was born in Warren, Minnesota, on January 1, 1888. Educated in Warren, he came north with his parents, who homesteaded near Foam Lake in 1904. Two years later he homesteaded near his parents' farm, beginning his lifelong career in farming.

SAB R-B 5445-7

PETER HOWE

It wasn't long before Howe became involved in the co-operative movement and in civic politics. In 1911 he joined with several of his neighbors in the creation of the Co-operative Elevator Company's elevator in Leslie; he also belonged to numerous other co-operatives. He led the drive to create the Leslie Rural Telephone Company in 1916 and served on its board for three years. In 1917 he was elected trustee of the school district, a position he held until 1931 when he was elected as the Saskatchewan Wheat Pool delegate for his district.

Howe became politically active in 1920 when he joined the Progressives and served as secretary for his local riding association. He was active in the CCF almost from its inception. In 1938 he ran as the CCF candidate in Kelvington and was elected as one of the eleven CCF members that session. He was re-elected in 1944 in the CCF sweep and was appointed government whip, a position he held until his retirement. Re-elected three more times, he retired from the legislature in 1960 and died in 1976.

BRETT QUIRING

**JOHNSON, FREDERICK WILLIAM** (1917–1993). Frederick Johnson was born in Staffordshire, England, in 1917, emigrating to Canada with his family in 1928. After attending Regina Normal School he taught for four years in Saskatchewan schools. He joined the Canadian Army in 1941, served overseas as an artillery officer and was discharged with the rank of major in 1946. He then took his law degree at the University of Saskatchewan and began the practice of law in Regina in 1950. Mr. Johnson served as chairman of a provincial royal commission on government administration in 1964, and in 1965 was appointed to the Court of Queen's Bench, becoming Chief Justice of the court in 1977.

In 1983, Frederick Johnson was appointed by the Trudeau Liberal government as sixteenth Lieutenant-Governor of Saskatchewan. His swearing-in was a major ceremony, televised from the legislative chamber for the first time. The government of Grant Devine returned the Lieutenant-Governor's office to Government House in 1984, after nearly forty years in the Hotel Saskatchewan, and Frederic Johnson restored much of the dignity and prestige of the position. His wife Joyce was the first Saskatchewan vice-regal spouse to receive the title "Her Honour." He faced a constitutional controversy in 1987 when the Conservative government chose not to recall the legislature and to present its budget after the beginning of the fiscal year. The government resorted to special warrants, normally used only for unforeseen expenditures. The Lieutenant-Governor, although urged to intervene, was unwilling to test the reserve powers of the Crown in this case. Frederick Johnson was named an Officer of the Order of Canada in 1990 and a Member of the Saskatchewan Order of Merit—of which he had been the first chancellor—in 1991.

OFFICE OF THE LIEUTENANT GOVERNOR

FREDERICK W. JOHNSON

MICHAEL JACKSON

**FURTHER READING:** Hryniuk, Margaret, and Garth Pugh. 1991. *"A Tower of Attraction": An Illustrated History of Government House, Regina, Saskatchewan.* Regina: Government House Historical Society/Canadian Plains Research Center. • Leeson, Howard A. (ed.). 2001. *Saskatchewan Politics: Into the Twenty-first Century.* Regina: Canadian Plains Research Center.

## JOHNSTON, JOHN FREDERICK (1876–1948).

The political career of John F. Johnston represents the experience of many of the moderate Progressives, and he was instrumental in returning the bulk of the Progressive movement into the fold of the Liberal Party.

Johnston was born on July 16, 1876, to a successful business family in Bogarttown, Ontario, near Newmarket. He was well-educated and came from a prosperous family that ran a number of lumber and flour mills in Simcoe County, Ontario. He came to Saskatchewan around 1905, first stopping near Yellow Grass before finally settling on a large farm near Bladworth. Here he became successful both as a farmer and as a businessman. He owned the lumber yard and hardware store in Bladworth, as well as a string of general stores as far away as Outlook and Kerrobert.

In 1917 Johnston was elected to the House of Commons, representing Last Mountain, as a Unionist-Liberal supporting the current Borden government. The relationship between Johnston and other Liberals deteriorated in the following years to the point where, upon arriving at the 1919 Liberal leadership convention, he was denied his delegate credentials. Johnston broke with the Liberals and later in the year voted against the Unionist budget because of its failure to lower tariffs. He joined with the new T. A. Crerar-led Progressive group within the House of Commons. In 1921, Johnston won the Progressive nomination and was convincingly re-elected in Last Mountain. Later in the year Johnston was elected the chief whip of the Progressive group, an election that marked the ascendancy of the Liberal-sympathizing "Manitoba wing" of the party. This move angered many of the MPs from Alberta who believed the party should avoid adopting the structure of a traditional party. Johnston was a proponent of Progressive cooperation with the Mackenzie King Liberal government. In 1923 he was the only Progressive to vote with Liberals and Conservatives against a Progressive-led motion which aimed to fundamentally alter how Parliament functioned. Although Johnston remained with the Progressives, it was clear that he was gravitating towards the Liberals.

Johnston contested the 1925 election as a Progressive and was re-elected handily. However, shortly thereafter he was convinced by King to leave the party to sit as a Liberal.

He was re-elected as a Liberal in the 1926 election and in 1929 was rewarded with an appointment as deputy Speaker by Prime Minister King. In 1930, Johnston lost his seat as the Conservatives defeated the King government. Johnston returned to his farm, but made a political comeback in 1935 when he was elected to represent the riding of Lake Centre. Johnston finished his term and was again defeated in 1940, this time by Conservative John Diefenbaker. Three years later, Johnston received an appointment to the Senate where he served until his death on May 9, 1948.

BRETT QUIRING

FURTHER READING: Morton, W. L. 1950. *The Progressive Party in Canada.* Toronto: University of Toronto Press.

## JOHNSTON, JOHN KENNETH (1865–1945).

Born in Elgin County, Ontario, in June 1865, John Kenneth Johnston was educated in Glencoe before he began teaching at the age of seventeen. He returned to school, attending Queen's University in the sciences and eventually attaining a Master of Arts degree.

He moved west in 1900, taking the position of principal of the Calgary High School. In 1903, he decided to enter farming and bought two sections of land, one near Kamsack and the other near Veregin. While farming, he studied law during the winters and eventually established two law offices, one in Canora and the other in Kamsack. In 1908, Johnston was elected to the Saskatchewan legislature as a Liberal representing the constituency of Pelly. He was re-elected for the last time in 1912, and he retired from the legislature in 1917. He attended the 1919 Liberal leadership convention, but soon fell out of favour with the Liberal Party. He contested

the 1929 election as an independent, backed by both the Conservatives and Progressives. Although defeated, he continued to remain involved in farmers' organizations. In 1929, he was elected as a Wheat Pool delegate, a post he held until 1936. In 1942, he participated as a member of the "On-to-Ottawa" farmers' delegation that demanded the King government address the depressed price of wheat. Johnston retired from farming in 1940 and died at his home in Kamsack in May 1945.

BRETT QUIRING

## JOHNSTON, TOM (1881–1969).

Pioneer and founding member of the CCF, Tom Johnston's greatest contribution was as Saskatchewan's longest-serving Speaker of the legislature.

Born in Birmingham, England, on June 19, 1881, Johnson left school at the age of thirteen and worked a variety of odd jobs. He emigrated to Canada in 1901 and, after spending a couple of years in Manitoba, came to Saskatchewan in 1903. Establishing a farm near Cymric, Johnston became a very successful farmer with substantial landholdings in the region. His activities in a variety of farmer organizations led to his eventual turn to politics. Involved in the formation of United Farmers of Canada (Saskatchewan Section), Johnston was an advocate for the organization's entry into electoral politics.

SAB R-B 4071

TOM JOHNSTON

In 1934, Johnston first contested public

office running in the constituency of Lumsden for the CCF predecessor, the Farmer-Labor Party, but finished a poor third. In 1935 he challenged Liberal leader William Lyon Mackenzie King in the federal riding of Prince Albert, but was again defeated. Johnston again ran for the CCF in the 1938 provincial election in the constituency of Touchwood and was elected as one of ten CCF MLAs elected that year.

Easily re-elected in the CCF sweep of 1944, Johnston, as one of the few CCF MLAs with prior legislative experience, was asked to serve as Speaker. Facing a house that had little legislative experience was a challenge during his first term as Speaker, and he developed a reputation as a strict but evenhanded chair. Re-elected in both 1948 and 1952, he continued as Speaker for both of those sessions, spending a record twelve years in the Speaker's chair. On one occasion, Johnston took the extraordinary step to leave the Speaker's chair to enter into debate when he felt his constituency's interests were not being represented, a right rarely exercised by Speakers.

Johnston retired from office in 1956, but remained politically active. At the age of eighty he decided to sail around the world on an ocean freighter to get a better understanding of the problems of the developing world. Returning to Saskatchewan, he became vocally critical of the foreign aid system and called for the developed world to face the problems of abject poverty in developing nations. Johnston died in Regina on September 11, 1969.

BRETT QUIRING

**JULÉ, ARLENE G.** (b. 1946). Born in Saskatoon, Arlene Julé was raised in the Humboldt constituency where her family operated a small business near Peterson. Following the completion of her education in Bruno, Julé and her husband Robert spent their time running a mixed farming operation and raising six children.

Prior to entering provincial politics, Julé was a teacher associate for special needs children and sat as a member of St. Peter's Abbacy Rural Life Committee. She also served as Social Justice Representative for the St. Agnes Parish and trained as a Pastoral Care Worker and Lay Presider.

Julé was first elected to the Saskatchewan legislature as a Liberal MLA for the Humboldt constituency in 1995. During her time as a Liberal, Julé began her work on becoming an advocate on social justice issues like child prostitution and foster care, introducing a private member's bill to combat child prostitution and campaigning for a sex offender registry in the province. Julé was the only woman to enter the Liberal leadership race in the summer of 1996, but she withdrew from the campaign just a few months later. Eventually, Julé left the Liberals altogether over differences of policy and leadership to sit as an independent. After 18 months as an independent, Julé joined the Saskatchewan Party in November 1998 and later assumed the position of Indian and Métis Affairs critic. She has also served as critic of Social Services and Human Rights, as Ombudsman, and as deputy critic of Agriculture, Environment, and Education.

Julé was best known for her work as co-chair, with MLA Peter Prebble, on the Special Committee to Prevent the Abuse and Exploitation of Children Through the Sex Trade. In December 1999, a special all-party committee was appointed to address and make recommendations on the issue of child sexual exploitation. The Committee's final report contains recommendations grouped under four themes: deterring offenders; protective services for children and youth; root causes; and prevention/early intervention. Julé did not seek re-election in 2003.

WINTER FEDYK, KINGSTON, ON

**JUNOR, JUDY** (b. 1948). Born in North Battleford in 1948, Judy Junor was raised in Saskatoon. After completing secondary school, she entered the nursing profession with a diploma from St. Paul's School of Nursing in 1969. Working as a nurse in Saskatoon, she was involved in the Saskatchewan Union of Nurses (SUN) and was elected its president in 1993. Continuing as SUN president, she took on further responsibility as vice-president of the Saskatchewan Federation of Labour in 1997.

As tension grew between the healthcare unions and the government over contract negotiations, the government looked for a potential solution. Hoping that Junor could help broker a deal between the government and the union without large-scale strikes, the New Democrats courted Junor as a potential candidate. She agreed to run for the NDP in a by-election in the constituency of Saskatoon Eastview, which had been recently vacated by NDP MLA Bob Pringle. Her nomination as candidate was seen as a coup for the party, but Junor faced a stiff challenge from Liberal leader Jim Melenchuk for the seat.

Junor won the highly publicized by-election. She was immediately appointed to cabinet as associate minister of Health with the hope that her appointment would help alleviate labour tension. It did not, however, so in 1999 SUN went on a particularly bitter strike. Junor supported the government's back-to-work order, which led to considerable criticism leveled at her by her former colleagues in SUN.

In 1999, Junor was re-elected in Saskatoon Eastview. She was removed from cabinet when Lorne Calvert became premier on February 8, 2001, but was re-appointed to cabinet as minister responsible for Women and as provincial secretary in October. She remained in cabinet until March 2002, when she was removed again. In February 2003, she was re-appointed minister of Learning. Junor again contested Saskatoon Eastview in the 2003 election, easily winning. Junor, however, was dropped from cabinet again after the government was re-elected.

BRETT QUIRING

**KARWACKI, DAVID** (b. 1965). David Karwacki, Saskatoon business person and leader of the provincial Liberal Party, grew up in Saskatoon. Karwacki is married to Laurie, an educator, and has four children: Jonathan, Alix, Sarah and Luke.

Karwacki attended the University of Saskatchewan, graduating from the College of Commerce in 1989. He currently continues his education through enrolment in the Birthing of Giants programme at M.I.T. in Boston.

In 1990, Karwacki and three business partners founded Star Produce Ltd., an international fresh produce distribution company. Karwacki has served as chief operating officer of the company, and is currently CEO. In the community, Karwacki served as the president of the Huskie Basketball Alumni Association, acted as the founding board member of the University of Saskatchewan Athletic Endowment Fund, and participated as a member of the St. Anne's faith community.

Although he had no formal political experience prior to being elected as leader of Saskatchewan Liberals in October 2001, Karwacki won a decisive victory over opponent Jack Hillson by a vote of 430 to 248, inheriting what many believed to be a troubled party. Prior to Karwacki's leadership win, the Liberal Party, which hasn't been in power since 1971 under the leadership of Ross Thatcher, had steadily seen its membership decline. Though it won 11 seats in the 1995 provincial election, five members defected to join the Saskatchewan Party and one left to join the New Democratic Party (NDP). In the 1999 election, the Liberals were reduced to just three seats. Soon after, the party called the vote after the previous leader, Dr. Jim Melenchuk, decided to maintain an NDP-Liberal coalition government instead of forcing the NDP to govern with a minority in the legislature. As a result, one of Karwacki's first jobs as Liberal leader was to attempt to end to the coalition government by having Dr. Jim Melenchuk and Ron Osika forgo their alliance with the NDP and return to their previous posts. Melenchuk and Osika instead agreed to serve as independent MLAs and remain in the coalition cabinet.

Karwacki led the Liberals into the 2003 election. The election was a disaster for Karwacki, who went down to personal defeat in Saskatoon Meewasin. The party also failed to elect any of its candidates, its worst electoral defeat since 1982.

WINTER FEDYK, KINGSTON, ON

## KERPAN, ALLAN EDWARD JOSEPH (b. 1954).

As a Reform Party MP and Saskatchewan Party MLA, Allan Kerpan was involved in building the foundations of both parties in the province.

Kerpan was born December 9, 1954, in Kenaston. He was educated in the town and at St. Peter's College in Muenster. He was involved in farming at an early age, eventually establishing his own farm near Kenaston.

Kerpan was involved in the burgeoning Reform Party and in 1993 ran as the party's candidate in the riding of Moose Jaw–Lake Centre. He narrowly won the election, one of the first four Reform MPs elected in Saskatchewan in the wake of the Progressive Conservative collapse. In 1997 he was re-elected in the new riding of Blackstrap. A prominent figure on the province's political right, Kerpan was involved in the formation of the Saskatchewan Party in August 1997. He was regarded as a potential leader, but he later decided against running for the position. Kerpan's focus, however, was increasingly on provincial politics. He offered to resign his federal seat and run for the Saskatchewan Party in 1999 if the result of the Saskatoon Southeast constituency were contraverted.

Kerpan came under increasing criticism over his attendance record in the House of Commons, for which the federal political newspaper, *The Hill Times*, named him the country's laziest MP. He retired from federal politics in 2000, deciding not to seek re-election. He contested a number of Saskatchewan Party nominations but failed until 2003, when he won the nomination in the constituency of Carrot River Valley after the death of the former Saskatchewan Party MLA. He easily won the by-election and again won the seat in the general election several months later by a much-reduced margin.

BRETT QUIRING

## KERR, WILLIAM FRANKLIN (1876–1968).

William Kerr was born on October 25,

1876, in Goderich, Ontario, and educated in St. Thomas. Upon completion of his studies, he worked for the Canadian Pacific Railway (CPR) and quickly rose within the corporation.

SAB R-A 635

WILLIAM KERR

In 1898, after seven years with the CPR, Kerr moved west, taking a position as assistant to the managing editor of the Winnipeg *Free Press*. In 1902, Walter Scott offered Kerr the editorship of the Regina *Leader*. When Scott was appointed premier in 1905, he sold the paper to Kerr. Under Kerr's leadership the Regina *Leader* abandoned its weekly format and became a daily paper. Kerr also helped found the Western Associated Press, Canada's first newsgathering service and predecessor of the Canadian Press. In 1920 he left the paper to head the Red Cross in Saskatchewan, and in 1924 was appointed legislative librarian and provincial archivist.

Kerr first ran for office in 1934 in Regina City as a Liberal, and won easily in the Liberal sweep of that year. Kerr was appointed to cabinet the following year when William Patterson took over as premier. Appointed as minister of Natural Resources, his tenure in that post saw the first large-scale attempts to find commercially viable oil fields in Saskatchewan. In 1938 Kerr changed seats, leaving Regina to run for re-election in the constituency of Turtleford. After narrowly fending off a strong challenge by the Social Credit candidate, Kerr was re-elected and continued in the Natural Resources portfolio where he remained until 1944. That year he

was defeated as the CCF came to power.

After his political career, Kerr became involved in many local organizations, serving on the boards of local chapters of the Y.M.C.A, Boy Scouts and the Canadian Institute for the Blind. Kerr died in Regina on March 11, 1968.

BRETT QUIRING

**KING, CARLYLE** (1907–1988). As a long-time CCF activist and party president, Carlyle King left an indelible mark on the formation and development of the CCF in Saskatchewan.

King was born November 24, 1907 in Cooksville, Ontario, and moved with his family to Saskatchewan in 1912. After earning a B.A. at the University of Saskatchewan, King went on to earn an M.A. and Ph.D. from the University of Toronto. He returned to Saskatchewan in 1929 to take an appointment teaching English at the University of Saskatchewan, where he continued to teach and hold a variety of administrative positions until his retirement in 1975.

King was an ardent pacifist and socialist. Through his involvement in the socialist and intellectually-based League for Social Reconstruction, King became involved in the CCF. In 1938 he resurrected the Saskatoon CCF, after expunging the organization of members of the Communist Party. He helped lay the foundation of the CCF, which dominated Saskatoon politics until the late sixties.

King rose to prominence within the party by challenging party leader George H. Williams for the presidency of the party in 1940. King had grown weary of Williams' autocratic leadership style and his unwavering support for the war. Although King lost, his strong showing undermined Williams' leadership, paving the way for Tommy Douglas to unseat Williams in 1942.

Although an effective organizer, King was by nature oriented towards policy development. He spent a great deal of his energy developing and writing party policy documents. He was given the task of developing the party's program for the 1944 election and wrote a plethora of other party documents, including the nationally-distributed pamphlet "What is Democratic Socialism?"

In 1945 King assumed the presidency of the party, a position he held until 1960. Even though King did not initially trust Douglas, the two eventually developed a close relationship. During his term as premier, Douglas relied on King to advise him on the party's views and concerns on current political issues. King became one of Douglas' closest and most trusted advisors even though King was critical of the government's abandonment of nationalization as its primary tool for economic development.

Although never elected to public office, King's intellectual and organizational skills left a lasting mark on the CCF. King took responsibility for making sure the party developed and kept an active party organization, which was pivotal for the continuing success of the CCF and NDP in Saskatchewan. King died on March 19, 1988.

BRETT QUIRING

FURTHER READING: King, Carlyle. 1984. "A Beginning in Politics: Saskatoon CCF 1938–1943." *Saskatchewan History.* 102–114. • King, Carlyle. 1981. "The CCF in Saskatchewan." In *Western Canadian Politics: The Radical Tradition.* Donald C. Kerr, editor. Edmonton: NeWest Press. 31–41 • Kerr, Donald C., and Stan Hanson. 1998. "Pacifism and the Saskatchewan CCF at the outbreak of World War II." *Prairie Forum* 23, no. 2: 211–243.

## KING, WILLIAM LYON MACKENZIE

(1874–1950). William Lyon Mackenzie King was Canada's longest-serving prime minister (1921–1925; 1926–1930; 1935–1948). King is best remembered as a lacklustre but effective politician who emphasized compromise, conciliation, and brokerage politics. His middle-of-the-road brand of politics and successful quest to maintain national unity resulted in a period of Liberal government that dominated the vast majority of the twentieth century. Mackenzie King successfully reunited a divided Liberal Party after the divisive conscription crisis of 1917; he weathered the agrarian revolt that created the largely western-based Progressive Party and wooed many of the disgruntled back into the Liberal fold; he was fortunate enough to lose office during the bulk of the Great Depression and he returned to power in 1935 to lead a united Canada through the Second World War and another crisis over conscription.

SAB R-B-8254

W. L. M. KING

When Mackenzie King succeeded Sir Wilfrid Laurier as leader of the Liberal Party in 1919, the most significant threat to national unity came from the Prairie West. King set off to rebuild Liberal support in the frustrated region by supporting the Prairie position on such critical issues as tariffs, freight rates, natural resources, railways, and immigration. He lured former Liberal–Progressives back into party ranks, made sure to offer federal cabinet posts to the influential leaders, and sought to form strong relationships with the provincial governments of Alberta, Manitoba, and most specifically the ardently Liberal province of Saskatchewan under premiers Charles Dunning and Jimmy Gardiner. Both premiers ended up as influential ministers in King's federal cabinets.

Part of King's strategy in rebuilding Liberal fortunes in the west included representing a Saskatchewan riding. After being defeated in the 1925 general election in the Ontario riding of North York, King was elected to represent the federal riding of Prince Albert in a by-election on February 15, 1926. King held the Saskatchewan riding for the majority of his career and was instrumental in the creation of the Prince Albert National Park in 1926. He was defeated in the riding in the general election on June 11, 1945, and held the seat of Glengarry, Ontario, for the remaining three years of his career.

ROBERT WARDHAUGH, UNIVERSITY OF WESTERN ONTARIO

**FURTHER READING:** Wardhaugh, Robert. 2000. *Mackenzie King and the Prairie West*. Toronto: University of Toronto Press.

## KNIGHT, ROBERT ROSS "ROY" (1891–

1971). High school teacher turned Saskatoon MP, Roy Knight became one of the more noteworthy parliamentary orators for the CCF during the fifties. Knight was born into a wealthy family on December 12, 1891, in Cookstown in the County of Tyrone, Northern Ireland. After completing school, he was lured to the Canadian west by the promise of adventure, arriving in Manitoba in 1909. After a year working as a farm hand, he finally settled in Saskatchewan, homesteading in the Meeting Lake district. In 1921 he left the farm to begin a career teaching in Eston and later in Delisle. He left Saskatchewan for a year in 1929 to complete a degree at Queen's University; upon his return, he began teaching at City Park Collegiate in Saskatoon.

Knight's political interests were cultivated in the Progressive movement. While farming, he became active in the co-operative movement and in other community activities. While in Saskatoon, Knight became heavily involved in many organizations, serving as president of the Saskatoon High School Teachers' Association, the Saskatoon Teachers' Credit Union, and the Saskatoon Co-operative Association. He also served on the boards of the Family Welfare Association of Saskatoon and the Third Avenue United Church.

Knight was first elected to the House of Commons in 1945 when the CCF swept 18 of Saskatchewan's 21 seats, but was one of only five CCF MPs who managed to be re-elected in 1949. With colorful language and wit, Knight developed a reputation as one of the premier CCF orators, especially after the party's setback in 1949. He was elected again in 1953, but was narrowly defeated in 1957. He attempted a political comeback in 1958, but was drowned by the Diefenbaker sweep.

He retired in 1958, continuing to live in Saskatoon and remaining active within the CCF-NDP. He died while visiting family in Calgary on September 11, 1971.

BRETT QUIRING

## KNIGHT, WILLIAM G. (b. 1947). As a key

NDP organizer and MP, Bill Knight was a major figure within the NDP at both the provincial and federal levels during the 1970s and 1980s.

Born in Estevan on October 24, 1947, Knight grew up in a strong CCF family. After completing high school, he went to the University in Regina, completing a B.A. in

1968 and a B.Ed. in 1969. While at university he became increasingly involved in the CCF-NDP. He was elected president of the Regina Campus NDP club and started to distinguish himself as a party organizer during the 1968 federal campaign and the 1969 Kelvington by-election. In 1970, he was appointed one of Allan Blakeney's key organizers, helping Blakeney secure the leadership of the Saskatchewan NDP.

In the fall of 1971, Knight accepted a teaching position at Weyburn High School. His teaching career was cut short when in early 1971, the Liberal incumbent in Assiniboia, A. B. Douglas, died. Knight won a hotly contested NDP nomination and then won the seat on November 8, 1971. Knight was re-elected during the general election of the following year and took a leadership role in caucus as Finance critic and as party whip, which was especially important during a minority government. Knight helped to press the government for major electoral reform, which resulted in the *Election Expenses Act*, as a condition of NDP support for the government.

Narrowly defeated in the 1974 election, Knight took a position in the head office of the Saskatchewan NDP, organizing the upcoming election campaign. In January 1975, he was appointed provincial secretary, the party's top administrative job. He ran the provincial campaigns in the 1975 and 1978 elections and had significant influence on government policy as one of the government's senior political advisors. In 1979, he contested the riding of Assiniboia but was again defeated. After his defeat, he became an advisor to Allan Blakeney until 1982. In 1982, he again ran the NDP's provincial election campaign but, unlike 1975 and 1978, he was not successful and the government was swept out of office.

Upon defeat, Knight left Saskatchewan to take a position as an advisor to federal NDP leader Ed Broadbent, a position he held until 1988. After a short stint as federal secretary, he was appointed director of government relations for Credit Union Central of Canada in Ottawa. From 1990 to 1991, Knight served on the Royal Commission on Electoral Reform and Party Finance (Lortie Commission). In 1995, he became president and CEO of Credit Union Central, a position he held until he was appointed Commissioner of the Financial Consumer Agency of Canada in 2001.

BRETT QUIRING

## KNOWLES, WILLIAM ERSKINE (1872–1951).

Born in Allison, Ontario, on November 28, 1872, Knowles studied law at McGill and at Osgoode Hall in Toronto. Knowles established a small law practice in Toronto before moving to Moose Jaw in 1904.

Active politically, Knowles quickly established himself in Saskatchewan political life. In 1905, Knowles was acclaimed in the by-election in the federal riding of Assinibioa West, a seat which had been vacated by Walter Scott when he became premier of the new province. Knowles was re-elected easily in both 1908 and 1911.

Knowles did not contest the 1917 federal election; instead, he vacated the seat for James Calder and served as a minister in Robert Borden's Unionist government. When the Conservative MLA for Moose Jaw, Wellington Willoughby, was called to the Senate, the Conservatives did not oppose Knowles in the provincial by-election for vacating his federal seat for Calder. Knowles was appointed to cabinet immediately as provincial secretary and a year later was given the added responsibility for Telephones. However, Knowles experienced difficulties in the party as the farmers' movement became politically active. As the provincial Liberal Party attempted to distance itself from its federal counterpart, Knowles' fierce Liberal partisanship did not sit well with many in the farmers' movement whom the party was trying to satisfy.

SAB R-A 23621

WILLIAM KNOWLES

Knowles wanted to return to federal politics so when Calder was appointed to the Senate, Knowles resigned his seat in the legislature and contested his old federal seat. In the 1921 election, Knowles was defeated for the first time in his career, losing to Progressive candidate Robert Johnson. Knowles contested the seat again two years later when the Supreme Court voided the 1921 result because Johnson failed to disclose some election expenses. However, the result was the same: Knowles lost out to the Progressive candidate again.

Knowles made one last attempt for public office and was elected in the 1925 provincial election in the constituency of Moose Jaw. He served two years on the government backbench before resigning in 1927 to accept an appointment to the Court of King's Bench. He remained on the bench until 1938 when he suffered a stroke. Knowles moved back to Toronto and died on July 17, 1951.

BRETT QUIRING

**KNOX, ANDREW** (1866–1946). Andrew Knox was born in Ballymoral, Ireland, on April 26, 1866, and emigrated to Canada in 1890. Knox's family was prominently connected with agriculture in Ulster, and he himself became a farmer in Prince Albert. There he married Elizabeth Short in July 1900, with whom he had three children. Knox was also the director of the Saskatchewan Grain Growers from 1907 to 1918. In 1915, Andrew Knox was elected mayor of Prince Albert and served for two years.

Knox was first elected to the dominion parliament in 1917 as a Liberal Unionist in the riding of Prince Albert, one of five farmer candidates. Several Liberal Party supporters had split with the party over the matter of conscription, which was vehemently opposed by the Quebec members. The proposal by Prime Minister Robert Borden to form a Union government that would be non-partisan appealed to many western Liberals, like Knox, who eventually joined the Union government in the 1917 wartime election.

The Union government had focused much of its attention on winning the Great War and had somewhat neglected the interests of the western Liberal Unionists. The dissatisfaction with Borden's government resulted in a split within the Unionists led by T. A. Crerar. Several western Liberal Unionists, including Andrew Knox, left the government to form the Progressive Party. Knox was re-elected in 1921 along with sixty-four other Progressive Party members in the first third party to obtain the second largest number of seats in the House of Commons. Knox was one of many Progressive candidates to be defeated in the 1925 election in his Prince Albert riding, which was one year later, taken over by Prime Minister Mackenzie King.

Andrew Knox did not seek re-election

after his 1925 defeat. He died on August 4, 1946, in Chilliwack, British Columbia.

SEAN KHERAJ, YORK UNIVERSITY

## KOHALY, ROBERT (1921–2001).

Elected in a 1953 by-election, Robert Kohaly was one of only two Progressive Conservatives to be elected to the legislature between 1929 and 1975.

Born in Fredericton, New Brunswick, on July 9, 1921, Kohaly grew up in Toronto and Winnipeg before moving to Saskatoon while still in high school. Enlisting in the South Saskatchewan Regiment at the outbreak of the Second World War, Kohaly saw active service in Europe and was wounded in 1942 during the Dieppe raid.

After returning to Saskatchewan, he attended the University of Saskatchewan where he obtained a B.A. in 1948 and a law degree in 1950. He articled in Estevan and eventually established his own practice in that city. He was nominated as the Progressive Conservative candidate in the 1953 by-election in the constituency of Souris-Estevan and was easily elected, becoming the first Conservative elected to the Saskatchewan legislature since 1930. An active opponent of the Saskatchewan Government Insurance Office and the government's economic policies generally, Kohaly distinguished himself as a vocal and prominent critic of the government. Conservative leader Alvin Hamilton even tendered his resignation to allow Kohaly to become leader, but Kohaly turned him down.

Kohaly's election led to an apparent revival in the fortunes of the Conservative Party; however, it was not to be. The Social Credit parties of Alberta and British Columbia were anxious to establish themselves in Saskatchewan and in 1954 met with Kohaly. They offered Kohaly a coalition, giving him leadership of the new party and half a million dollars to run a campaign, the only stipulation being that the party had to adopt the Social Credit name. Loyal to the Conservatives and Hamilton, Kohaly turned them down. Many Conservatives were upset with the decision to remain an independent party and several constituency associations left the party in protest. In 1956 the Social Credit candidates severely cut into Conservative support. This was one of the factors which contributed to Kohaly's personal defeat.

After his defeat, Kohaly returned to his law practice. Also involved in the Canadian Legion, Kohaly served as president of the Saskatchewan branch in 1961 and as national president in 1968. He died on October 24, 2001.

SAB R-B 5445-23
ROBERT KOHALY

BRETT QUIRING

FURTHER READING: Kyba, Patrick. 1989. *Alvin: A Biography of Alvin Hamilton*. Regina: Canadian Plains Research Center.

## KORCHINSKI, STANLEY JAMES (1929–2000).

Korchinski was born on January 29, 1929, in Rama, where he lived and farmed throughout his life. Korchinski had both Polish and Ukrainian roots, and could speak both languages. He attended primary school in Rama, and then went on to take high school in nearby Canora. Stan then took classes at the University of Saskatchewan. After completing one year of study, he had to return home to run the family farm as his father had passed away a few years earlier. Korchinski married Marcella Ron on November 10, 1962. Together they had four children.

From 1952 to 1958 he served as reeve of the rural municipality of Invermay. He first ran federally for the Progressive Conservative Party in 1957. Korchinski was not initially very interested in running for Parliament but was convinced to do so by members of the area's Progressive Conservative association. This was the first time in twenty-two years that the Progressive Conservatives had put forward a serious effort to win the Mackenzie riding, and a year later the effort of Korchinski and others paid off. One of his major goals at that time was to bring farmers back to the Mackenzie area.

Stan Korchinski served for twenty-six years as a member of Parliament for the riding of Mackenzie. He was elected eight times to the House of Commons. His career ended in a difficult nomination battle in 1984, in which he lost the Progressive Conservative nomination. Stanley James Korchinski died on May 13, 2000, at age seventy-one.

TRENT EVANISKY, DIEFENBAKER CENTRE

## KOSKIE, MURRAY JAMES

(1929–2004). Murray Koskie, a twenty-year veteran of provincial politics, was one of the longest serving members of the Saskatchewan legislature.

Koskie was born at Sinnett on November 5, 1929. He was raised on his parents' farm. After graduation from Humboldt Collegiate, he enrolled at the University of Saskatchewan, where he earned an education degree. He taught

SASKATCHEWAN NDP PHOTO ARCHIVES

MURRAY KOSKIE

school in various parts of the province before returning to the University of Saskatchewan to study law. He practised law in the Yukon, and in Regina and Humboldt.

Koskie first ran for public office in 1967 as the NDP candidate in Regina South-West, but was defeated. Koskie was elected as the NDP member for the rural constituency of Quill Lake in 1975. He served in both Allan Blakeney's and Roy Romanow's cabinets. In the Blakeney years, Koskie served as minister of Social Services from June 1979 to December 1980; minister of Consumer Affairs from December 1980 to March 1981; minister of Consumer and Commercial Affairs from March 1981 to May 1982. After the Progressive Conservatives, led by Grant Devine, won the 1982 provincial election, Koskie served as Opposition whip, as well as caucus critic for Justice and Rural Affairs. In 1992, a year after the New Democrats returned to power, under the leadership of Roy Romanow, Koskie served as minister of Highways and Transportation. He held that position from September 1992 until June 1993.

He was forced to resign his cabinet post when the RCMP began investigating an allegation that he received a kickback. He was accused of using false expense claims to get money through one of his MLA allowances. He was charged with two counts of fraud over $1,000 and two counts of breach of trust. In February 1995, he was found guilty of both counts of fraud, while the breach of trust charges were stayed. He was ordered to pay a $5,000 fine and to make restitution of $2,400 to the provincial government. He was also sentenced to a day in jail but the judge deemed the time had been served by his appearances in court. Koskie resigned his seat in the legislature immediately following the sentencing. The Saskatchewan Court of appeal threw out the conviction on one of the fraud charges, but upheld the other one. The Supreme Court of Canada rejected his application to appeal.

Murray Koskie passed away on March 14, 2004.

GERRY JONES, REGINA

**KOWALCHUK, JOHN RUSSELL** (1921–2000). John Kowalchuk was born August 30, 1921, in Goodeve where he would spend most of his life. After completing high school, he was educated at the normal school in Regina and took correspondence courses from the University of Saskatchewan, earning a teaching certificate. In 1942, he began his teaching career in a number of small-town schools around Melville. Kowalchuk quit teaching in 1956 to run a grocery store, locker plant and insurance business in Goodeve and in 1961 began farming.

Kowalchuk was elected to his first public office in 1959, when he was elected to the Melville school unit. He held this position until 1967, serving five years as unit chairman. In 1964, he was elected reeve of the rural municipality of Stanley, a position he held until 1966. In 1967, he was elected to the legislature as the CCF-NDP member from Melville after unexpectedly defeating cabinet minister Wilf Gardiner. During his first term, Kowalchuk became associated with a new group of young MLAs, led by Roy Romanow and Jack Messer, who increasingly challenged the existing leadership of the party.

Easily re-elected in 1971, Kowalchuk was appointed to cabinet as minister of Natural Resources in 1974, but was forced to step down from cabinet after the 1975 election due to continuing health problems. While an MLA, he continued to be actively involved in his local community, serving as mayor of Goodeve from 1973 to 1985 and in the local Ukrainian community and in the Greek Orthodox Church. He was re-elected for the last time in 1978 and served out the term before retiring from politics. After politics, he continued to farm at Goodeve until 1986 when he retired to Melville. Kowalchuk died in Melville on August 18, 2000.

BRETT QUIRING

**KOWALSKY, MYRON** (b. 1941). Myron Kowalsky, member for Prince Albert Carlton and Speaker of the Legislative Assembly of Saskatchewan, was born in North Battleford on July 11, 1941. He attended high school at the North Battleford Collegiate Institute and Nutana Collegiate in Saskatoon. He later obtained a B.A., B.Ed (with distinction) and a post-graduate diploma in Curriculum Studies from the University of Saskatchewan. Kowalsky is married to Olesia and together they have two daughters, Lisa and Lara, and one grandchild, Sam Wilkinson.

Kowalsky began teaching in 1961, and during his career as an educator was active with the Unity and Prince Albert Lions Club and the Saskatchewan Teachers Federation at both the local and provincial levels. Kowalsky spent time in Gambia on "Project Overseas," a project aimed at strengthening professional skills of teachers. He taught at Quill Lake High School, Unity Composite School, Riverside Collegiate in Prince Albert and at Carlton Comprehensive High School in Prince Albert. Later, Kowalsky assisted in the operation of the family farms and was employed as a crop hail adjuster and in home construction.

Kowalsky was first elected to the legislature in 1986, and was re-elected in 1991, 1995, 1999 and 2003. In 1994, Kowalsky published a book tracing the history of Saskatchewan MLAs with a Ukrainian background, like himself. Although never a member of cabinet in his four terms as the MLA for Prince Albert Carlton, on March 20, 2001, Kowalsky was elected Speaker of the Legislative Assembly of Saskatchewan, replacing Liberal Ron Osika who resigned to become Municipal Affairs minister in the NDP–Liberal coalition government. For only the second time since the Speaker became an elected position ten years prior did members of the legislature have more than one candidate from which to choose. A special legislative rules committee decided in 1991 that the Speaker should be elected by all members of the legislature rather than appointed by the premier's office.

Kowalsky initially faced competition for the job from NDP MLAs Lindy Kasperski and Judy Junor, although Junor later changed her mind about running. Kowalsky, more experienced than competitor Kasperski by nine years, served as government whip and on various committees, including as chair of the Special Committee on Tobacco Control, chair of the all-party Board of Internal Economy and the estimates committee. As Speaker, Kowalsky is responsible for order and decorum in the legislature.

WINTER FEDYK, KINGSTON, ON

**KRAMER, EILING** (1914–1999). Rancher, auctioneer and outspoken eight-term MLA of the Battlefords, Eiling Kramer was one of the more colourful members ever elected to the Saskatchewan legislature.

Kramer was born July 14, 1914, in Highworth. After completing his schooling in Highworth, Kramer worked a variety of odd jobs before purchasing a ranch in the area and began raising cattle. In 1949, he formed a successful auctioneering business, which complemented his imposing stature and booming voice.

WEST'S STUDIO, REGINA•SAB R-A 8395

EILING KRAMER

During the thirties, Kramer became active in the United Farmers of Canada at the local level and by extension was involved in the Farmer–Labor Party/CCF from its inception. Kramer was appointed CCF organizer of northwestern Saskatchewan in 1946 and was very active in the organization of the Saskatchewan Farmers' Union (SFU) in 1950. In 1951, he was elected SFU vice-president and served until his election to the legislature.

Kramer was first elected to the Saskatchewan legislature in 1952, representing the Battlefords where he would be re-elected seven times. Woodrow Lloyd appointed him to cabinet as minister of natural resources in 1962, a position he held until the CCF was defeated in 1964. In Opposition, Kramer was a forceful critic of the government's highway policy. In one celebrated incident, he personally installed a stop sign at an intersection he believed was dangerous after the government failed to act on his recommendation. After the 1967 election, he was one of the few CCFers to bitterly fight for the party to retain the CCF name and not change it to the NDP.

In 1971, Kramer was again appointed to cabinet as the NDP regained power and served as one of Blakeney's key advisors on rural Saskatchewan. He assumed his old portfolio of Natural Resources until he was moved to Highways and Transportation in 1972. He remained in charge of Highways until his retirement in 1980. During his term as minister, the department undertook some of the greatest capital expenditures in its history, nearly completing the paving of the provincial highway system.

Kramer retired from politics in 1980, settling in North Battleford. He relocated to Regina shortly before his death on May 5, 1999.

BRETT QUIRING

## KRAWETZ, KENNETH PATRICK

(b. 1951). Ken Krawetz was the Liberal, and later Saskatchewan Party MLA, for Canora–Pelly. Ken and wife Gail resided on the family farm near Invermay and together they have two children: Bryce and Lindsay.

Krawetz received a Bachelor of Education degree from the University of Saskatchewan. He taught school for eleven years in Invermay, served nine years on the Canora School Board, and spent six years on the Saskatchewan School Trustees Association, serving two years as its president. In addition, Krawetz owned and operated an insurance brokerage from 1983 to 1993 in Invermay and continued to operate the family farm. In his leisure time, Ken plays on his hometown hockey team and is a provincially-registered official for hockey and volleyball.

Krawetz was first elected MLA for Canora-Pelly as a Liberal in 1995. In 1996, after just four years as a member of the Liberal Party, Krawetz ran against Tom Henegan and Jim Melenchuk for leadership of the Liberal Party. The party, which jumped from one to 11 seats in the June 1995 election, had been without an official leader since Lynda Haverstock resigned the post. Though at times it seemed possible Krawetz might win, he eventually was forced to drop out of the race after the second ballot, allowing Melenchuk, family doctor and Liberal Party vice-president, to defeat Henegan by a margin of 554 to 367. Melenchuk, who didn't have a seat in the legislature, chose Krawetz to be his voice as leader of the Official Opposition.

In 1997, Krawetz, along with three fellow Liberal MLAs, defected to join forces with Conservative caucus members to form the Saskatchewan Party, allowing it to become the Official Opposition. Krawetz was chosen by his caucus mates to serve as interim leader of the Saskatchewan Party until the election of Saskatchewan Party leader Elwin Hermanson in 1998. Since then, Ken has served as deputy leader of the Official Opposition and as the Saskatchewan Party's finance critic. Ken's shadow cabinet duties have included Education Critic, Executive Council Critic, and Post Secondary Education & Skills Training Critic. Krawetz was re-elected in Canora-Pelly in 1999 and 2003.

WINTER FEDYK, KINGSTON, ON

## KUZIAK, ALEX GORDON (b. 1908). A

prominent CCF spokesman and cabinet minister, Alex Kuziak was the first person of Ukrainian origin to serve in a Canadian cabinet.

Born October 15, 1908, in Canora, Kuziak was educated in Canora, Yorkton, and Saskatoon. After spending a couple of years employed in odd jobs in Canada and the United States, he returned to Saskatchewan in

1930 to attend normal school in Regina. Kuziak returned to Canora to teach, although he left teaching five years later to become secretary-treasurer of the rural municipality of Keys. Also a successful businessman, he operated a real estate and insurance office in Canora. He was also the senior partner of the Canora Electric and Heating Co.

Like many other MLAs, he had an extensive record of holding public offices at the local level before his election to the legislature. He served on the Canora School Board, the board of the Canora Union Hospital and on the boards of several local co-operatives. Active in the CCF from its formation, Kuziak was one of the driving forces in the Canora constituency CCF association. When CCF MLA Myron Freely chose not to contest the 1948 election, Kuziak replaced him in the legislature. Re-elected in 1952, Kuziak was appointed to cabinet as minister of Telephones and minister in charge of the Government Finance Office, the holding company for most of Saskatchewan's Crown corporations. After re-election in 1956, Kuziak was moved to the Mineral Resources portfolio where he remained until his defeat. As minister in charge of provincial parks, the system expanded significantly under his stewardship. Kuziak was also instrumental in the creation of the Saskatchewan Fisheries Co-operative which helped to expand Saskatchewan's northern fishing industry. Kuziuk's greatest contribution was as a fierce partisan and one of the most forceful oratorical weapons of the government.

Although re-elected in 1960, Kuziak was narrowly defeated in 1964 as the Thatcher government came to power. In 1965, Kuziak

WEST'S STUDIO, REGINA•SAB R-A 7977

ALEX KUZIAK

ran for office again as the NDP candidate in the federal riding of Yorkton. In a hard-fought campaign, Kuziak could not break the Conservatives' stranglehold on the province. Although he significantly improved the NDP vote in the riding, he was nevertheless defeated. Kuziak was once again elected to public office in 1970 when he was elected an alderman for the city of Yorkton. He served only one term as alderman, ending in 1973.

BRETT QUIRING

**LAIRD, DAVID** (1833–1914). David Laird was born in 1833 in New Glasgow, Prince Edward Island. He was educated at the Presbyterian Theological Seminary at Tutor, Nova Scotia. Laird continued his family's tradition of political involvement. In 1859 he founded, edited, and published the newspaper entitled *Protestant and Evangelical Witness*, later renamed *The Patriot* in 1865. His paper was the leading Liberal journal of the island.

Laird's political career began in 1860 when he was elected to the city council of

SAB R-A 1

DAVID LAIRD

Charlottetown. He became a member of the house of assembly for the Liberal Party in 1871 for Queen's county. In 1873 he took part in the negotiations to incorporate Prince Edward Island into confederation, the success of which secured him a seat in the House of Commons in Ottawa.

He played an active role in Parliament as a member of the Haythorne Administration from 1872 to 1873, and his vote helped to topple John A. McDonald's Conservatives. He was made minister of the Interior in 1894, and immediately set about trying to assist the expansion of the railway west. He was successful in his endeavors when he managed to obtain 75,000 square miles of territory in the Qu'Appelle Valley region through Treaty No. 4 and Treaty No. 5. In 1876 his department created the *Indian Act* which stressed assimilation and the paternalistic form of address to manage native relations. In that year he became the Lieutenant-Governor of the North-West Territories as well as superintendent of Indian Affairs. In 1877 he negotiated Treaty No. 7 with the Blackfoot and several other tribes in the area that is now south Alberta, and removed the last barrier to the expansion of the Pacific railway. He remained Lieutenant-Governor even after the Liberal defeat in 1878, but left office in 1881. Due to the difficulties of transportation at this time, the Territorial Council was forced to relinquish most of its powers of administration to Laird. This increase in power came with little financial benefit. In fact, Laird was forced to house his own assistant and had to feed visiting Native leaders from his own larder. At this time he had little interest in territorial government, making little effort to discuss constitutional problems with the federal government. He used his position as Lieutenant-Governor to secure funding to develop local schools, and to help pay for public works. In 1882 he attempted to run for federal office in Saskatchewan but failed to win his riding. In 1898 he was appointed as Indian Commissioner for Manitoba and the North-West Territories, and he presided over three more treaties, No. 8 in 1900, No. 9 in 1905,

and No. 10 in 1906. He resigned his position as Commissioner in 1909 and became an advisor to the federal government on aboriginal issues. He was a very able and well regarded administrator despite being disadvantaged by distance, poor communication, an inadequate staff, and a lack of funds. He died January 12, 1914.

JEREMY MOHR, UNIVERSITY OF WESTERN ONTARIO

**SOURCES:** Robb, Andrew. 1965. *Dictionary of Canadian Biography.* s.v. "Laird, David." 578–581. Toronto: University of Toronto Press. • Weeks, Blair (ed.). 2002. *Minding the House: A Biographical Guide to Prince Edward Island MLAs 1873–1993.* Charlottetown: Acorn Press. • Thomas, Lewis H. 1978. *The Struggle for Responsible Government in the North-West Territories 1870-97.* Toronto: University of Toronto Press.

## LAKE, SIR RICHARD S. (1860–1950).

Sir Richard Lake was born in Preston, Lancashire, England, on July 10, 1860. He was a member of the British civil service for three years, working for the Admiralty in Cyprus until 1883. He came to Saskatchewan in that year to homestead near Grenfell with his younger brother Richard and their parents. He retained his involvement in the civil service while in Saskatchewan, becoming the vice-president of the Territorial Grain Growers Association, and a Justice of the Peace for the region.

Lake was also active in the political arena becoming a member of the North-West Territories Assembly as a Conservative in 1898. He retained his position in that assembly for seven years after a brief, but failed, attempt to win a seat in Ottawa in 1900. He was not successful in winning his riding until 1904 and served for the Conservatives in the House of Commons until 1911. After his defeat in that year he served on the Public Service Commission until 1915 when he was appointed Lieutenant-

Governor of Saskatch-
ewan. His designation in
that position came at a difficult time for the allied
war effort. The casualty
lists from the front had
been eroding Canadian
support for the war. Lake
was appointed to reawaken
the commitment to the
war effort on the home
front. He was deemed
suitable for this task, as his
father was a noted British
war hero and his older
brother Percy was serving
with great distinction in
the military, and later would be knighted. He
made significant contributions in this area,
being the first president of the Regina
Recruiting League and the provincial president
of the Red Cross. He improved the prominence of the latter organisation to the point
that Saskatchewan became the world leader in
per-capita donations to the Red Cross in 1918.
His term as Lieutenant-Governor also saw
some political controversy. In February of
1916 the Conservative opposition accused
Walter Scott's Liberal government of corruption. They requested Lake to appoint a Royal
Commission to investigate the matter. Three
committees were created and found that,
while there was little evidence of bribery, the
liquor interests had spent money to delay
liquor legislation. The Speaker of the House
promptly resigned due to these accusations.
The investigation also found that another
member of the assembly and a high-ranking
official were found to be guilty of corruption
involving the Department of Highways. These
charges brought harsh punishments, including
jail terms, to those involved.

SAB R-B 450

RICHARD LAKE

After being requested to serve a second term as Lieutenant-Governor, Lake
declined in 1921 and moved to Victoria.
He continued to play an active role in
the Red Cross and the Canadian military
effort in World War II. Also of note was
his near brush with death on the
*Athenia*, a passenger liner which was tor-
pedoed by the Germans on September
3, 1939. Lake died on April 23, 1950.
The service of Sir Richard Lake, first
during times of growth and later during
times of trouble, truly illustrates his
importance in the province of
Saskatchewan.

JEREMY MOHR, UNIVERSITY OF WESTERN ONTARIO

**LALIBERTE, RICHARD** (b. 1958). Richard
(Rick) Laliberte was born in Île-à-la-Crosse,
Saskatchewan on September 13, 1958, and
grew up in the predominantly Métis community of Beauval. After graduating from high
school, Laliberte became extremely active in
the local community. He was especially interested in the development of community
media and culture and he was instrumental in
the creation of the radio/television station in
Beauval and in organizing the annual Beauval
Jamboree and the Northern Music Festival.
Rick served for twelve years as a school trustee
and one term as chair of the Northern Lights
School Division. He also served on the Board
of Governors of the Northern Teacher
Education Program.

Laliberte's first foray into federal politics
came in 1993 when he ran as an independent
in the Prince Albert-Churchill River riding.
Although he turned in a creditable performance, it was obvious that he would need the
endorsement of one of the major political parties to be successful. In the 1997 election he

sought the New Democratic Party nomination in the riding, in part because he believed that the New Democratic philosophy of government reflected the traditional practices of Aboriginal people. After a close race, Laliberte won the seat and became one of the first Aboriginal people to represent Saskatchewan in the House of Commons.

As a novice parliamentarian Rick served on a number of committees, but he raised the ire of his colleagues just before the federal election of 2000 when he defected from the New Democrats to the governing Liberal Party. Laliberte explained his move as "a wake-up call to the NDP that they can't form government," and added, to "be in government is a crucial instrument to making change."

Laliberte confounded his critics by winning re-election in the 2000 general election, largely due to the support of Aboriginal people in northern Saskatchewan. It was not his last brush with controversy, however, as it was revealed in 2003 that Laliberte had accumulated the largest travel expense bill of any MP in the country. Furthermore, it became evident that his attendance at parliamentary sessions and committee meetings was not outstanding. Laliberte lost the Liberal nomination in 2004. He contested the 2004 election as an independent and lost.

MICHAEL COTTRELL, UNIVERSITY OF SASKATCHEWAN

## LAMONT, JOHN HENDERSON (1865–1936).

John Lamont was born on November 12, 1865, to Duncan Carmichael Lamont and Margaret Robson Henderson, both of Scottish descent. He grew up and received his education in Dufferin County, Ontario. He graduated from the University of Toronto with a B.A. in 1892 and a LL.B. from Osgoode Hall a year later. He was called to the Ontario Bar in 1893. He practiced law in Toronto for six years before moving to Prince Albert, where he founded a law practice with W. F. A. Turgeon. In 1902, he became a Crown Prosecutor. On October 21, 1899, he married Margaret Murray Johnston and they had one daughter.

In 1904, Lamont was elected to the Canadian House of Commons for the territorial district of Saskatchewan. He quickly formed a friendship with fellow Liberal member Walter Scott. Within a year of being elected, Lamont resigned his seat on speculation that he would be elected to the new Legislative Assembly of Saskatchewan. With his legal background and Liberal beliefs, he was a logical choice as the province's first Attorney General. It was a small cabinet of four (Walter Scott, J. H. Motherwell, J. A. Calder and Lamont) that faced huge challenges in the new province.

After only two years in the Scott government, Lamont resigned from Saskatchewan politics to receive an appointment to the Saskatchewan Court of Appeal. Lamont was replaced by Turgeon, his former law partner from Prince Albert. Lamont served on the Court of Appeal for nearly twenty years before being appointed to the Supreme Court on April 2, 1927, where he served for eight years.

Even though Lamont left active partisan politics when he was appointed to the bench, he again had contact with the Saskatchewan government in 1916, when he was appointed to the Haultain Royal Commission. This commission was chaired by Frederick Haultain, with Judge Newlands and Lamont as members. They were appointed to investigate charges of corruption on the Scott government in the construction of the Battleford asylum, the Regina jail and a building for the

Department of Telephones. The Haultain Commission was one of the three commissions established to investigate the Scott government. Even though Scott and his cabinet were cleared of these accusations, several public servants and MLAs were found guilty of corruption and were punished.

Even though Lamont only spent approximately three years in the House and Legislature, he continued to serve the people of the province and Canada as an Appeal judge for twenty-eight years. Even though the name Lamont is not well known in Saskatchewan history, he provided professional service to his country as a lawyer, elected member, Saskatchewan's first Attorney General and as a distinguished member of the Bench. He died on March 10, 1936, at the age of seventy.

GORDON BARNHART, UNIVERSITY OF SASKATCHEWAN

**LANE, JOHN GARY** (b. 1942). John Gary Lane was a member of the controversial and scandal-plagued governments of Grant Devine. Lane held numerous portfolios during this time and played a vital role in the privatization of several of Saskatchewan's Crown corporations.

Gary Lane was born in Saskatoon on May 2, 1942. He received a Bachelor of Arts in history in 1963 and a Bachelor of Laws in 1966, articling in Saskatoon before joining the Department of the Attorney General as a Crown Solicitor and executive assistant to the Attorney General. In 1971 he founded the firm Lane and Whitmore. Lane was elected as the Liberal Member of the Legislative Assembly for Qu'Appelle-

SAB R-PS 82-612-871

GARY LANE

Lumsden in 1971. Re-elected in 1975, Lane was widely touted as a potential successor to David Steuart. However, Lane was concerned about the provincial Liberals' connections to the increasingly unpopular federal Liberals. After the surge of Conservative support in the 1975 election, Lane, along with Colin Thatcher, abandoned the Liberals in favour of the Conservatives. After the Progressive Conservatives swept into power in 1982, Lane became minister of Justice and Attorney General. In 1984 he was given the additional responsibility of the Employment Development Agency.

In 1985 Lane became the minister of Finance. He was also given responsibility for the Potash Corporation of Saskatchewan (PCS). Thus began the privatization of some of Saskatchewan's Crown corporations. Lane was appointed to the Cabinet Planning and Priorities Committee as well as to the board of the Crown Investments Corporation, which oversaw Crown corporations in the province. In this capacity Lane oversaw the privatization of PCS in 1989. This decision was massively unpopular. The company was a profitable enterprise, and its sale prompted the New Democratic Party to filibuster in the legislature. It was the longest debate over legislation in Saskatchewan's history, and ultimately the government forced closure on the issue, a first for Saskatchewan.

Lane was instrumental in establishing the Saskatchewan Pension Plan. The first of its kind in North America, the Saskatchewan Pension Plan made it possible for homemakers, farmers and small business owners to contribute to a registered pension plan. Lane also oversaw the establishment of individual line telephone service to rural Saskatchewan households. This eliminated the familiar "party line" telephones that rural residents had once shared with neighbours on the same service grid.

Lane was also appointed as the minister responsible for Saskatchewan Telecommunications, a portfolio he held in 1982 and 1983 and then again from 1986 to 1991. In 1989, Lane was returned to minister of Justice and Attorney General. On September 10, 1991, he was appointed to the Saskatchewan Court of Appeal.

DANA TURGEON, REGINA

BIBLIOGRAPHY: Saskatchewan Archives Board. J. Gary Lane Fonds. GR 634, Regina.

**LANG, OTTO EMIL** (b. 1932). Otto Lang was a central figure in the Saskatchewan Liberal party, serving as a federal cabinet minister and the political minister for the prairie provinces during the Trudeau government. During his term as minister, relations between the federal government and the west reached an historic low point.

Born May 14, 1932, in Handel, Lang was raised and educated in the Humboldt area. Gifted academically, Lang earned degrees in arts and law from the University of Saskatchewan. In 1953, he won the prestigious Rhodes Scholarship and spent the next two years studying at Exeter College, Oxford. Returning to Saskatchewan, Lang was appointed professor of law at the University of Saskatchewan and became dean of the College of Law before his thirtieth birthday.

Active in the Liberal party, Lang was an early proponent for the establishment of a federal Liberal party in the province that would have a degree of independence from the provincial party. The move threatened the power of Ross Thatcher, who maintained tight control over the Liberal organization and brought the two men into conflict a number of times throughout their careers. In 1963, Prime Minster Lester Pearson appointed Lang as the Saskatchewan campaign manager for the 1963 federal campaign. Although the campaign was unsuccessful as the Liberals failed to elect a single MP in Saskatchewan, it nevertheless solidified Lang's position as the Liberals' main federal organizer in the province.

Lang was convinced by Pierre Trudeau to contest the 1968 election in the riding of Saskatoon-Humboldt. He narrowly defeated New Democrat George Taylor and was immediately appointed to cabinet as Saskatchewan's lone representative.

Initially appointed as a minister without portfolio, Lang took over responsibility for the Canadian Wheat Board in 1969, a position he held until his political defeat. As minister of the wheat board, Lang was responsible for dealing with the emerging farm crisis as low prices and a massive surplus of wheat crippled the industry. Lang introduced the widely unpopular Lower Inventories For Tomorrow (LIFT) program. LIFT sought to decrease the acreage of wheat by providing incentives for farmers to grow other crops or take land out of production. The policy marked the most significant shift in Canadian wheat policy since the inception of the wheat board. LIFT and the seemingly callous manner in which Trudeau dealt with the crisis created substantial animosity between the government and farmers.

While minister of the Canadian Wheat Board, Lang took on several other cabinet posts beginning with the Manpower and Immigration portfolio in 1970 and Justice in 1972 after he was re-elected. Elected again in

1974, Lang was appointed minister of Transportation in 1975. As minister, he was faced with a particularly bitter strike by airline pilots and air traffic controllers over government bilingualism legislation that would have allowed French to be used in air traffic control.

Facing the intense unpopularity of the Trudeau government in the west, Lang was defeated in 1979 in the new riding of Saskatoon East by New Democrat Bob Ogle. Lang ended his political career and later, in 1979, moved to Winnipeg and was appointed vice president of Pioneer Grain Company.

BRETT QUIRING

**FURTHER READING:** Wilson, Barry. 1980. *Politics of Defeat: The Decline of the Liberal Party in Saskatchewan.* Saskatoon: Western Producer Books. • Smith, David E. 1981. *The Regional Decline of a National Party: Liberals on the Prairies.* Toronto: University of Toronto Press. • Saskatchewan Archives Board. Gary Lane Fonds. GR 634, Regina.

**LANGLEY, GEORGE** (1852–1933). George Langley was born on November 10, 1852, in Essex, England. He came to Canada in 1893 and homesteaded near Rosthern, later establishing a large farm in the Maymont district. He was elected to the first Saskatchewan legislature in 1905, representing the constituency of Redberry. Langley became deeply involved in the farmers' movement and, along with Charles Dunning, represented the inseparable links between the Saskatchewan Grain Grower's Association (SGGA) and the early Saskatchewan Liberal governments.

Langley became active in the SGGA shortly after his first election to the legislature. In 1910 he was elected to the executive of the SGGA as a director-at-large, a position he held until 1917. His dual positions in the SGGA and in the Saskatchewan Liberal Party made him the natural mediator between the two groups. He was utilized by Premier Walter Scott to negotiate with the Interprovincial Council of Grain Growers, who demanded that the government address the increasing problem of proper grain storage facilities throughout the province. Langley was appointed to the Saskatchewan Commission of Inquiry to investigate the elevator system. The report recommended the province provide some of the financial backing for a farmer-run co-operative to construct and operate their own elevator company. The report's recommendations represented a compromise between the SGGA's demand for a government run elevator system and the government's desire to stay out of the business as much as possible. After selling his report to both parties, the Saskatchewan Co-operative Elevator Company was incorporated by act of the legislature in 1911. Langley was elected to the co-operative's board of directors at its first general meeting, and in 1914 was elected vice-president. In 1921 he assumed the presidency which he held until 1924.

SAB R-A 250

GEORGE LANGLEY

Walter Scott appointed Langley to cabinet in 1912 as minister of Municipal Affairs, a position he held until his resignation in 1921. During his tenure as minister he revamped the hail insurance system, providing farmers greater protection and enabling rural municipalities greater leeway in responding to extensive hail damage.

Langley was a strong proponent of the Canadian Wheat

Board, piloting a motion through the legislature in 1920, calling on the federal government to re-establish the board. Like many in the farmers' movement, once it became clear the federal government was not going to reinstate the board, he began to advocate the pooling of Saskatchewan grain and the amalgamation of existing farmers' co-operatives.

Langley was defeated in 1921 in Redberry but then successfully contested a deferred election in Cumberland. However, shortly thereafter, Premier Martin asked Langley for his resignation when he learned that Langley had attempted to exert pressure on a provincial magistrate to exonerate a police officer from Halford whose conduct was called into question. Langley resigned from cabinet and a year later resigned from the legislature. He defended his actions because he felt the police officer had been wrongly accused. Langley's relationship with the Liberal Party steadily deteriorated after this point. He vocally supported the federal Progressive Party and wrote several articles criticizing the policies of former colleagues William Martin and William Motherwell. In 1925 he returned to the SGGA executive as vice-president and advocated the organization of field candidates in the provincial election, a position he steadfastly opposed while in the Liberal Party.

Langley attempted a political comeback in 1929, when he again contested the Redberry constituency. This time he contested the seat as an independent Liberal and only lost by a small margin to the official Liberal candidate.

George Langley died on August 26, 1933.

BRETT QUIRING

## LARSON, LEONARD (1912–1977).

Leonard Larson was a man of intense conviction, an energetic campaigner and the last of

the CCF-NDP's politicians inspired by the hardships of the depression.

Larson was born on November 11, 1912, on a farm near Stornoway. He remained on the farm almost his entire life and was deeply involved in the farmers' movement. He first became involved in the United Farmers of Canada in the 1940s and later in its successor organization, the Saskatchewan Farmers' Union. Like so many in the farmers' movement, Larson was a vigorous proponent of co-operation and a supporter of the co-operative movement. He sat on the board of directors of many co-operatives and helped found the Kamsack Credit Union in 1952 and the Kamsack Community Clinic in 1960.

SAB R-A 8389

LEONARD LARSON

Larson's work in the farmers' and co-operative movements led him into politics. He became involved in the CCF at an early age. He ran for the CCF nomination in Pelly in 1960 but was unsuccessful. In both 1962 and 1963 he represented the NDP in the federal riding of Yorkton, losing badly on both occasions. He was finally successful in 1964 when he was elected to the Saskatchewan legislature representing the constituency of Pelly. Larson was narrowly defeated in 1967, but returned to the legislature in 1971 and again in 1975. Both within the legislature and within the CCF-NDP, Larson quickly developed a reputation as a frank and straight-forward politician who loved political debate and discussion. He thrived on campaigning and continuously canvassed his constituency discussing politics with as many people as he could. Leonard Larson died in March 1977, while still a member of the legislature.

BRETT QUIRING

## LATTA, SAMUEL (1866–1946).

Samuel Latta was born in London, Ontario, on April 3, 1866 . After graduating high school, he attended Western University but left before completing a degree. In 1886 he graduated from the Ottawa Normal School, and in 1895 from the Ontario School of Arts. He began his teaching career in 1894 and taught in a number of schools in Ontario. An accomplished artist, Latta authored *Latta's Drawing Book* which was used as the standard drawing textbook in Ontario for over fifty years.

Latta moved to Saskatchewan in 1905, enticed by the opportunities of a newly settled land. He homesteaded near Govan and began farming. In 1907 Latta founded the weekly newspaper, the *Govan Prairie News,* and remained editor of the paper until 1929.

Upon arriving in Saskatchewan, Latta almost immediately became involved in politics. He was first elected councillor and later served as secretary-treasurer of the rural municipality of Last Mountain Valley before contesting the 1908 Saskatchewan election for the Liberals in Last Mountain. Although he was defeated in 1908, he was successful four years later in 1912, and upon re-election in 1917 was appointed to cabinet as minister of Highways. Under his term as minister, the department's role as distributor of Liberal political patronage appointments began to diminish because Latta was not as intimately

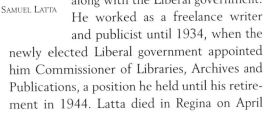

SAB R-A 247
SAMUEL LATTA

connected to the Liberal Party's political organization as his predecessors had been. In 1921, Latta was moved out of the Highways portfolio and into the area of his primary interest, Education. The education department expanded during his tenure, but he faced his most difficult challenge in dealing with the ever politically hot topic of foreign language instruction in the Saskatchewan school system. Trying to appease the Anglo-Saxon elites and the ethnic groups loyal to the Liberal Party proved to be difficult and ultimately led to the Liberal's undoing in 1929. Disagreement over government policy on foreign language instruction between Latta and the government's Director of Education, J. T. M. Anderson, led to Anderson's demotion in 1922, which likely led to his entry into politics a few years later.

In 1929 Latta was defeated along with the Liberal government. He worked as a freelance writer and publicist until 1934, when the newly elected Liberal government appointed him Commissioner of Libraries, Archives and Publications, a position he held until his retirement in 1944. Latta died in Regina on April 22, 1946.

BRETT QUIRING

## LAUTERMILCH, ELDON FLOYD (b. 1949).

Eldon Lautermilch has held several important ministerial positions in the New Democratic Party administration, allowing him to make significant contributions to the growth of Saskatchewan's economy.

Eldon Lautermilch was born September 9, 1949, in the small town of Lafleche. His parents, Milton and Selma Helen (Hauser)

Lautermilch, farmed and owned a small business in that community. He attended Woodrow Public School and Lafleche Central High. The family left that community when Lautermilch was eighteen, and he completed his high school education at the Moose Jaw Technical School. Despite having no political aspirations at the time, he served as president of the student council in his high school years.

ELDON LAUTERMILCH

Lautermilch later studied electronics and worked briefly in Regina. In 1970, he moved to Prince Albert where he still resides. It was here that he started a business in electronic sales and service. Eventually he moved into retail food sales. He married Loretta Brooks on October 17, 1970. They have three children: RaeAnne, Eldon Stacey and JoAnne.

Lautermilch first entered the political arena in 1986 as an elected New Democratic Party representative for the Prince Albert-Duck Lake riding. He was re-elected in 1991, 1995 and 1999 as the MLA for Prince Albert Northcote. During this time he held many ministerial posts in the cabinet. He was appointed the minister of Natural Resources and Rural Development in 1992 and was also responsible for the Saskatchewan Property Management Corporation. In March 1993 he assumed responsibility for the Saskatchewan Liquor and Gaming Authority, and in February 1995 he was made minister of Energy and Mines with responsibility for Saskatchewan Energy, Saskatchewan Power, the Saskatchewan Water Corporation, the Saskatchewan Research Council and Saskatchewan Forest Products. Lautermilch became government House Leader and minister of Economic and Co-operative Development in March 2001. It was at this time that the portfolios for Economic and Co-operative Development and Energy and Mines amalgamated into the Department of Industry and Resources. He continued to be minister of this new department. In February 2003 Lautermilch became the minister of Intergovernmental and Aboriginal Affairs and retained the duties of government House Leader. After he was re-elected in the 2003 election, Lautermich left cabinet.

As an elected member in Regina, Lautermilch has made many contributions to the province of Saskatchewan. He played an important role in the establishment of an Aboriginal Gaming agreement and in revamping the oil and gas royalty taxation structure. He has worked at ensuring that the resource sector in Saskatchewan is competitive.

SUZANNE QUIRING, CHRISTOPHER LAKE

## LEITH, GEORGE GORDON (1923–1996).

George Gordon Leith was born in Saskatoon on June 18, 1923, and died in Winnipeg in 1996. Leith was educated at the University of Saskatchewan and moved to a grain farm in the Glamis district of east-central Saskatchewan. He was enlisted in the Canadian army from 1943 to 1944 and in the Royal Canadian Air

GEORGE LEITH

Force from 1944 to 45. After the war, he returned to the farm and married Beryl Philion of Saskatoon. They had three children.

Leith served two terms as a Liberal MLA for the Elrose constituency (1964–1971). He was defeated in the 1971 election and also in the 1972 federal election when he ran as a Liberal. He came to represent the reformist wing of the Liberal Party of Saskatchewan when in 1966 he was the lone government member to criticize labour legislation aimed at limiting the rights of union members when the government deemed a strike was harming the public interest. By the late 1960s, Leith was one of a handful of MLAs meeting privately and informally to complain about the policies and top-down leadership style of Premier Ross Thatcher.

In 1971 after Thatcher died, Leith became one of three to run for the Liberal leadership in Opposition. He based his campaign on the need for the party to broaden its policy base and to move closer to the political center in order to challenge the governing New Democratic Party. Although he placed a disappointing third on the first ballot with just 171 votes, his campaign and the reformers he attracted to the party influenced Liberal policy renewal through the 1970s. His supporters were informally called the "171 Club" coming out of the convention. Dave Steuart, who won the leadership, credited Leith's role. "George Leith made this convention," he said later. "He offered an alternative ... and it was his campaign that showed us we were probably too far away from being a middle-of-the-road party." The 1972 federal election was Leith's last campaign. In 1973, he was appointed special envoy for western agricultural issues by federal Liberal agriculture minister Eugene Whelan. In 1976, Whelan appointed him to the Canadian Grain Commission in Winnipeg

and he served as chief commissioner from 1986 to 1989. In 1990, Leith chaired the National Committee on Grain Transportation, seeking solutions to declining railway investment and grain freight rate issues.

BARRY WILSON, LOW, QUEBEC

## LINGENFELTER, DWAIN MATTHEW

(b. 1949). Dwain Lingenfelter was born on February 27, 1949, in Shaunavon. He studied at the University of Saskatchewan, where he earned a political science degree. Lingenfelter operates his own farm near Shaunavon and worked for Canada Customs at the border south of Climax prior to running for office.

SASKATCHEWAN NDP PHOTO ARCHIVES

DWAIN LINGENFELTER

Lingenfelter was first elected as MLA for the Shaunavon constituency in 1978, and was re-elected in 1982. He served as minister of Social Services in the Allan Blakeney government from 1980 to 1982. On April 26, 1982, he stunned most political observers by surviving the Progressive Conservative landslide, winning the Shaunavon constituency by only 167 votes. From 1982 to 1986, Lingenfelter was Opposition House Leader. He earned the moniker "one man NDP rat pack" for the way he hounded various ministers in Grant Devine's Progressive Conservative government during Question Period. In 1986, Lingenfelter was defeated. While he lost the seat, he did manage to increase his share of the popular vote by 4 percent compared to 1982. Lingenfelter did not stay away from politics for long. He was elected president of the Saskatchewan New Democratic Party in June 1987 and won the Regina Elphinstone seat vacated by Allan Blakeney, receiving 78 percent of the popular vote in the by-election held on May 4, 1988. Upon returning to the legislature in 1988, Lingenfelter became Opposition House Leader and Opposition critic for Privatization and Saskatchewan Government Insurance. Reflecting on his responsibilities as an MLA, Lingenfelter said at the time: "I see my role as bringing important issues into the house on behalf of the people of the province."

In 1991, Lingenfelter was re-elected. He was appointed minister of Economic Diversification and Trade in the eleven-member "war cabinet" of the newly formed NDP government. He also became government House Leader. For him, the government's precarious financial position in the early 1990s could not permit state intervention to stimulate the economy. Rather, he felt that economic growth required a collaborative effort between the public and private sectors of the economy: "Business—whether it's co-operative, Crown or private—will have to be responsible for the recovery that we're all expecting [...] Government isn't going to pull us out of the mess that we're presently in. Government can only be a facilitator," he explained shortly after his appointment to cabinet. In 1995, Lingenfelter became deputy premier, and was appointed minister of the Crown Investments Corporation in 1997. The 1999 provincial election cost the NDP nearly all of its rural seats. Due to his farming background, Lingenfelter was appointed minister of Agriculture and Food on September 30, 1999. He set out a clear vision for his portfolio: "Over the longer term I want to make sure we have the roads, schools, and other services

needed to support development of the rural economy," he said. Less than a year later, Lingenfelter shocked Saskatchewan's political circles when he resigned on July 4, 2000 to embark on a new career in the resource industry. He became vice-president of government relations for Nexxen—an international oil and gas company.

JASON NYSTROM, REGINA

## LLOYD, WOODROW STANLEY (1913–1972).
Woodrow Lloyd was born in Webb on July 16, 1913. He was the youngest of twelve children born to Welsh settlers.

He completed elementary school in five years starting high school at age eleven and in September 1929, just sixteen, he enrolled at the School of Engineering, University of Saskatchewan. However, due to the depression, he was unable to return after the first year. In 1931, after a year spent working on the family farm, he trained as a teacher, hoping to earn enough by teaching to finance his eventual return to university.

A fundamental part of Lloyd's education came from his family's passionate interest in politics. When the Saskatchewan Teachers' Federation (STF) was formed in 1933, Lloyd became involved and the following year became a councillor representing the Swift Current area. At a local STF meeting he met Victoria Leinan, who was to become his wife.

They married in 1936, and between 1937 and 1954 had two daughters and two sons. They settled in Vanguard where Lloyd became principal of the four-room school. Every summer for the next four years he completed another course towards his B.A. and every winter, despite a heavy work load and his commitment to politics and community, he studied another subject by correspondence.

Finally, in 1940, he was awarded the degree of Bachelor of Arts and the following year received his Permanent Certificate for high school teaching. He enrolled in the RCAF during the war, but poor eyesight meant he was restricted to the drilling of cadets.

First elected to the presidency of the STF in 1940, he held the position for four years. In the fall of 1941, Woodrow and Vicki moved to Biggar where he became vice-principal of the high school. He made contact with the local CCF and joined Tommy Douglas' task force established to work out a blueprint for the future of provincial education.

Lloyd was elected in 1944 when the CCF captured 47 seats. His appointment as minister of Education made him Canada's youngest cabinet minister to date. As the MLA for Biggar, he won the six subsequent elections, until he stepped down in 1971.

Lloyd's main preoccupation between 1944 and 1960 was the creation of a new provincial educational system. This involved the establishment of the controversial Larger School Units (LSU) which brought changes to rural communities and a new system of taxation for education. A scheme of loans and bursaries to students, the first of its kind in Canada, also became a vital part of his program, and was soon copied by other provincial governments. Lloyd was a member of the Treasury Board and, in 1954, represented the province at the Commonwealth Parliamentary Association Convention in Africa.

Following the 1960 election, Lloyd became provincial treasurer and, in his first and only budget, demonstrated his belief that tax dollars were good dollars. Barely four months

WEST'S STUDIO, REGINA • SAB R-WS 15163

WOODROW LLOYD

later, Tommy Douglas was elected national leader of the NDP and Lloyd became leader of the provincial NDP.

Medicare, the event that Canadian newspapermen voted "The News Story of the Decade," brought tension and suspicion between the politicians and the doctors. A special session of the Saskatchewan legislature was called for October 11, 1961, to consider the Medical Care Insurance Bill. On the same day, the doctors held an emergency general meeting and voted 295 to 5 against co-operating with the plan. A doctors' strike started on July 1 while the government imported doctors to staff hastily established Community Clinics. An agreement was finally reached on July 23, through a mediator. On July 1, 1968, the National Medicare Act became law and by 1971 Medicare had become universally available across Canada.

During his term of office, Lloyd addressed other important issues. He campaigned against the Columbia River Treaty, believing that natural resources were the rightful heritage of all the people. He was a firm believer in a united Canada and advocated more regular meetings between heads of governments. He believed that the affairs of the country's First Nations people should be dealt with provincially. He supported the development of the Wascana Centre in Regina and laid the cornerstone of the first building on the University of Regina campus. He bombarded Prime Minister Diefenbaker with letters urging him to postpone the planned abandonment of stretches of the Canadian Pacific Railway lines in Saskatchewan, a strategy that delayed such closures, in some cases, by up to twelve years.

He was horrified at Prime Minister Pearson's intentions of acquiring nuclear weapons for Canada and objected to the proposed construction of anti-ballistic missiles just over the American border.

In the 1964 provincial election, after twenty years in power, the CCF lost to the Liberals. As leader of the Opposition, Lloyd led his party in constructive criticism of the new government's policies and began to rebuild the party and reassess the CCF philosophy. Despite being better prepared, they lost again in 1967.

Lloyd's support of the so-called "Waffle Manifesto" that concerned itself with the ownership of Canadian resources gave those party members who were discontented by their seeming inability to get elected an opportunity to attack his leadership. On March 30, 1970, he tendered his resignation to the House but continued as an MLA until an election was called the following year.

From the spring of 1970, for twenty months, Lloyd was involved in an unhappy and frustrating relationship with the United Nations Development program which, although offering him a position as a resident representative, was unable to settle the arrangements. Finally, in February 1972, he arrived in South Korea to begin work, but within two months he suffered an aneurysm and died on April 7.

On a memorial near the legislative building, a poem exemplifies his life:

Two roads diverged in the wood, and I,
I took the one less traveled by,
And that has made all the difference.
　　—from "The Road Not Taken" by Robert Frost

DIANNE LLOYD NORTON

FURTHER READING: Lloyd, Dianne. 1979. *Woodrow: A Biography of W. S. Lloyd*. Woodrow Lloyd Memorial Fund. • Koester, C. B. 1976. *The Measure of the Man: Selected Speeches of Woodrow Stanley Lloyd*. Saskatoon: Western Producer Prairie Books.

## LOPTSON, ASMUNDUR "MINDY"

(1887–1972). Mindy Loptson distinguished himself over his twenty-year career in the legislature by being one of the most forceful critics of the T. C. Douglas government within the Legislative Assembly.

Born in Iceland in 1887, he moved with his parents to Winnipeg shortly after his birth. In 1891, he came to Saskatchewan when his parents began homesteading near Chruchbridge. After completing school, he trained to become a harness-maker before moving to Selkirk, Manitoba, to apprentice for a short time as a jeweller. In 1909, Loptson moved to Bredenbury where he opened a general store. His store soon grew in scope as he expanded into lumber, farm implements and automotive sales. His enterprises even expanded into telephone and road contracting before his entry into politics.

SAB R-A 709

ASMUNDUR LOPTSON

Loptson first became involved in local politics serving on the council of the rural municipality of Saltcoats for fourteen years, four of which were as reeve. He also served on the town council of Saltcoats, serving as mayor for a short time as well as many years on the Saltcoats school board. In 1929, Loptson was first elected to the Saskatchewan legislature representing the constituency of Saltcoats. As a Liberal, he was one of a handful of new Liberals elected in 1929 as twenty-four years of Liberal government in Saskatchewan came to an end. It was during this session that Loptson developed a close bond with James Gardiner, a man Loptson would remain loyal to throughout his political career. Loptson was easily re-elected in the Liberal sweep of 1934, but lost his seat in 1938 to CCF maverick Joseph Phelps.

Loptson returned to farming in 1938 until his retirement in 1945. In 1948 he again contested Phelps for the Saltcoats constituency, narrowly edging him out. Loptson's experience immediately gave him a position of leadership in the fractured and demoralized Saskatchewan Liberal Party. Along with Gustaf Herman Danielson, Loptson was the party's most vocal critic of the CCF government. His charismatic oratory and sarcastic humour solidified his position as one of the Liberal's chief weapons against T. C. Douglas. After re-election in 1952, Loptson served as the Liberal Party's interim leader, and leader of the Official Opposition, after Walter Tucker returned to the House of Commons. He was re-elected once more in 1956 before retiring from politics in 1960. He retired to Yorkton, and died in Winnipeg on February 28, 1972.

BRETT QUIRING

**LORJÉ, PAT** (b. 1947). Pat Lorjé was born in Eastend in 1947 and raised in Caron. She attended the University of Saskatchewan where she was active on the student council. Completing her studies with a Master of Arts in psychology, she entered the psychiatric profession specializing in psychological counseling. In 1985 she was appointed chief psychologist for the Saskatoon Mental Health Centre, a position she held for the next sixteen years.

Lorjé was elected to Saskatoon city council in 1979 and was subsequently re-elected four times. During her term as councillor she served on a variety of boards including the Saskatoon City Hospital board and was a founding member of the City of Saskatoon race relations committee.

In 1991 Lorjé was elected to the Saskatchewan legislature for the Saskatoon-Wildwood constituency. She quickly developed a reputation as a one of the legislature's more flamboyant and outspoken members. She was re-elected by a slight margin in 1995 and again in 1999 before being appointed to Lorne Calvert's first cabinet as minister of Aboriginal Affairs in February 2001. Upon appointment to cabinet, she made a series of politically damaging statements that undermined her credibility. In May 2002 she stepped down from cabinet after one of her employees accused her of assault. After an investigation, Lorjé was cleared and reinstated to cabinet. Lorjé once again tendered her resignation the next day after speaking to the media about the incident, breaching a confidentiality agreement she had signed with her accuser.

Lorjé was appointed legislative secretary for immigration in 2003. Shortly after, she announced her retirement from politics and chose not to contest the 2003 election.

BRETT QUIRING

**MACDONALD, CYRIL PIUS** (b. 1928). Cyril "Cy" MacDonald was best known as minister of Welfare and Youth Agency from October 1966 until Premier Ross Thatcher's defeat in 1971.

Cy MacDonald was born in Humboldt on February 29, 1928. After receiving his secondary education in Saskatoon, MacDonald took his Bachelor of Arts at Notre Dame College in Wilcox, and then his Bachelor of Education at St. Francis Xavier University in Antigonish, Nova Scotia. MacDonald taught history, first in Yorkton, and then back at Notre Dame College in 1953.

It was during his time teaching that Cy MacDonald became involved in the Liberal Party. In 1960 he ran unsuccessfully in the Saskatchewan general election; the constituency of Milestone elected him as its Member of the Legislative Assembly first in the 1964 general election. Before becoming a cabinet minister, MacDonald was quite active in the provincial legislature: he was the legislature's chief spokesman and acted as legislative secretary to Health Minister David Steuart. Just before Ross Thatcher appointed him to the provincial cabinet, MacDonald formed the Saskatchewan Youth Agency.

On August 6, 1966, at the age of thirty-eight, MacDonald became Saskatchewan's minister of Industry and Commerce. He replaced Gordon Grant, who had held the post temporarily while also acting as Highways Minister. While assuming his new cabinet position, MacDonald also retained responsibility over the Youth Agency. On October 18, 1966, he left the Department of Industry and Commerce to become minister of Welfare and Youth Agency. He remained the Welfare and Youth Agency Minister until the Liberals lost the June 1971 general election.

MacDonald's activities as Welfare Minister reveal a belief in the role of the community in the process of healing and rehabilitation. His department helped to establish a new group home for adults with mental disabilities in

WEST'S STUDIO, REGINA • SAB R-W 567-298.1

CYRIL MACDONALD

Saskatoon; its program emphasized integration into the community over institutionalising its patients. MacDonald applied this same philosophy to prisoners, asking the community in Prince Albert to play a role in rehabilitation.

In the general election of 1978 he lost his seat, then known as Indian Head-Wolsley, in the provincial legislature to Progressive Conservative Graham Taylor. After leaving the legislature, MacDonald has taken part in various governmental commissions, like the Barber Commission, especially after he joined the Progressive Conservative Party. In 1994, as the chairman of CMC Television Services, Cy MacDonald took part in a failed bid to make Regina the home of Canada's first specialty country music cable television channel. He has remained a visible figure in Saskatchewan, even after leaving the provincial legislature.

MARYANNE COTCHER, UNIVERSITY OF REGINA

**SOURCES AND FURTHER READING:** C. P. MacDonald Papers. Saskatchewan Archives Board, Regina. • "Cy MacDonald into Cabinet." 1966. *Leader-Post.* August 15: 1, 8. • Pilon, Bernard. "Group Loses Cable Bid: No 'Nashville North' for Regina." 1994. *Leader-Post.* June 7: A7.

**MACKINNON, JANICE** (b. 1947). Janice MacKinnon was born in Kitchener, Ontario, on January 1, 1947. Her academic background, which included a Ph.D., brought her to Saskatoon to teach at the University of Saskatchewan. Prior to entering politics, she served as president of the Saskatoon Co-Operative Association.

In 1991, MacKinnon was recruited by Roy

Romanow to run for the NDP, and handily defeated Myron Luczka to claim the constituency of Saskatoon–Westmount. She was named minister of Social Services following the election, then elevated to Finance Minister in January 1993 when Ed Tchorzewski resigned from the post. Nicknamed "Combat Barbie" for her tough stand on fiscal matters, Mackinnon's first budget in 1993, which set a precedent of long-term deficit targets, represented one of the Romanow government's strongest steps in reining in the provincial budget deficit.

In the 1995 election, MacKinnon's constituency changed to Saskatoon Idylwyld, but the election results remained the same: she defeated Bonnye Georgia to retain her seat, and held the post of Finance Minister until 1997. MacKinnon remained in cabinet as minister for Economic and Co-operative Development (1997-2001), minister for the Information Highway (1998-2001), and minister for Crown Investments Corporation (2001), and also held the post of government House Leader.

JANICE MACKINNON

Long considered one of the favourites to succeed Romanow as premier, MacKinnon did not pursue the leadership in 2001, and chose to give up her seat later that year out of concern with the fiscal direction of the NDP. MacKinnon did not return to politics, despite interest from both Lorne Calvert's Saskatchewan NDP and Paul Martin's federal Liberal Party.

MacKinnon's political philosophy, both in office and in private life, often ran contrary to traditional NDP positions and to those of her own party leaders. In her third book, *Minding the Public Purse: The Fiscal Crisis, Political Trade-offs and Canada's Future*, MacKinnon noted that much of the opposition to her decisions as Finance Minister came from the NDP itself as well as traditional party supporters, rather than from opposition parties. MacKinnon gave Romanow credit for forcing reluctant party members to unite behind deficit-reduction measures. After the Romanow report on health care was released, however, MacKinnon criticized the former premier's conclusions in failing to allow for private-sector involvement and user fees.

After leaving politics, MacKinnon remained in the public eye as a professor at the University of Saskatchewan, as the author of *Minding the Public Purse* and two other books, and as a board member for International Road Dynamics and for the Institute for Research on Public Policy.

GREG FINGAS, REGINA

**BIBLIOGRAPHY:** MacKinnon, Janice. 2003. *Minding the Public Purse: The Fiscal Crisis, Political Trade-Offs, and Canada's Future.* Montreal: McGill-Queen's University Press.

**MACLEAN, DONALD** (1877–1947). Donald Maclean, leader of the Conservative Party and His Majesty's Loyal Opposition from 1918 to 1921, was born in 1877.

A lawyer by profession, he first won election to the legislature in the war-time election of 1917, one of only seven successful Conservatives at a time when his party expected to do much better given a Conservative government in power at Ottawa. Also, the reports of two royal commissions the previous year had confirmed the charges of Liberal corruption levelled at the Scott Administration by the Conservative Member for Prince Albert, J. E. Bradshaw.

A year later, when W. B. Willoughby resigned his seat to accept an appointment to the Senate, the remaining Conservative MLAs chose Maclean as leader. The major issue Maclean raised in the egislature concerned language, in particular the need to make English the paramount language of instruction in the schools of the province, and Premier Martin did amend the *School Act* to severely limit the use of other languages in the province's schools. Nevertheless, this issue alone was not sufficient to bring down the government or even turn the Conservative Party into a viable contender for power. In fact, events had overtaken Maclean and his tiny band of followers by the early twenties. By this time activists in the farm movement had decided to enter provincial politics directly and public opinion shifted to their political arm, the Progressives, as the more likely group to defeat the Liberals. Maclean saw the "writing on the wall" and in April of 1921, two months before the upcoming election, he resigned his seat and the leadership of his party to accept an appointment to the bench where he remained until his death in 1947.

PATRICK KYBA, UNIVERSITY OF GUELPH

**BIBLIOGRAPHY:** Smith, David E. 1975. *Prairie Liberalism: The Liberal Party in Saskatchewan 1905–1971.* Toronto: University of Toronto Press.

## MACMILLAN, FRANK ROLAND (1881–1948).

Frank MacMillan was born in Chicago, Illinois, on May 15, 1881. As a child he moved to Toronto with his parents and came to Saskatoon as a traveling salesman before starting a men's wear business in 1908. His business, MacMillan's, expanded rapidly and was one of the major department store retailers in Saskatoon until he sold it to Eaton's in 1927.

MacMillan's first foray into politics occurred in 1913 when he was elected to city council. He remained on council until 1915, and in 1919 successfully challenged incumbent Mayor Alexander Young. MacMillan's one-year term as mayor was marred by the political turmoil that swept Canada after the First World War. In June, many of Saskatoon's labour unions conducted a sympathetic strike in support of workers in Winnipeg. MacMillan managed to avoid many of the troubles of other western cities as a result of the strike by successfully controlling the anti-labour business elites and granting minor concessions to the workers. However, MacMillan was defeated in the 1920 mayoral race by the previous mayor, Alexander Young.

MacMillan first attempted to enter federal politics in 1925, but was once again narrowly defeated by Young and again in the 1926 rematch. However, in 1930 MacMillan unseated Young and was elected, representing Saskatoon in the House of Commons. Although serving only one term, MacMillan was successful in securing several major depression relief public works projects for Saskatoon and area, including the Broadway Bridge in Saskatoon and the CP Bridge at Borden.

SAB R-A 26038

FRANK MacMILLAN

Upon retirement from elected politics,

MacMillan continued to remain active in Saskatoon community life, serving as president of the Saskatoon Club, the Saskatoon Board of Trade, and the Conservative Association of Saskatchewan. MacMillan died while on vacation in Vancouver on April 7, 1948.

BRETT QUIRING

**MACMURCHY, GORDON** (b. 1926). Gordon MacMurchy was born in Semans on July 4, 1926. MacMurchy developed his political philosophy from his father, Edward, who had been active in the co-operative movement and an early supporter of the Progressive Party. He inherited the family farm, a one-section wheat farm near Semans, in 1962.

MacMurchy's first foray into public office occurred in 1962 when he was elected trustee of the Govan school unit. He would serve in this capacity until 1971, serving the last two-and-a-half years as chairman of the district. In 1967, he ran as the CCF-NDP candidate in the Last Mountain constituency, but lost by a narrow margin. However, he established himself as a vigorous campaigner with a talent for party organization and in 1969 was appointed provincial director of organization for the Saskatchewan NDP. His term as director of organization was quickly mired in controversy as the party became internally divided over the Waffle, a caucus of NDP members which sought to transform the party into a more left wing and socialist party. Wafflers charged that MacMurchy, and the provincial office generally, were hostile to their movement and that he used his position in the party and party funds

SAB R-A 9410

GORDON MACMURCHY

to organize against the Waffle. The issue came to a head when MacMurchy ran for party president at the 1970 leadership convention, unseating incumbent president and Waffle sympathizer, Bev Currie, by a significant margin.

In 1971, MacMurchy again ran for the NDP in Last Mountain and this time was successful. He was appointed to Allan Blakeney's first cabinet as minister of Education, the only member of cabinet who did not have previous legislative experience. As minister of Education, he institutionalized the salary aspects of the collective bargaining process between teachers and school districts as the direct responsibility of the provincial government. He was minister of education until 1975 when he was appointed minister of Municipal Affairs.

MacMurchy quickly entered the inner circle of the Blakeney cabinet. Blakeney relied on MacMurchy as one of his top political advisors. MacMurchy was appointed to the powerful Political Committee of Cabinet and, along with Elwood Cowley and Bill Knight, increasingly took control of party matters, including running the party's election campaigns. MacMurchy was instrumental in the 1978 election campaign which saw the NDP adopt different campaigning techniques, including the use of polling and television ads.

The results of the 1978 campaign were positive, but the NDP began lagging behind in the rural constituencies. To help rectify this problem, MacMurchy was appointed as minister of Agriculture in 1979. MacMurchy's appointment in agriculture marked a shift in the Blakeney government's focus to agriculture and transportation issues. During his tenure as minister, MacMurchy primarily fought for the implementation of the Hall Commission on Grain Handling and Transportation. The Hall Commission called for the retention of the Crow Rate, the country elevator system, and an end to rail line abandonment. To this end, the government helped purchase a fleet of grain hopper cars with Alberta and Manitoba. During his term as minister, MacMurchy also established the Farm Lab program which allowed the College of Agriculture to conduct research with farmers away from the purely university environment, helping to open up communication between the farmers and researchers. He also established the Saskatchewan Beef Commission, which allowed for the voluntary orderly marketing of beef.

After his defeat in 1982, MacMurchy returned to Semans and became more active in the community. He helped establish the Family Farm Foundation, which encouraged research into the family farm and public education on farm issues. He was elected mayor of Semans in 1982 and held that position until 1997. In 1986, he made one more attempt at provincial political office when he again contested the Last Mountain constituency, but was narrowly defeated. He remained in Semans, keeping involved in the local community by helping to form a local senior's education committee and by keeping active in the his local church.

BRETT QUIRING

## MACPHERSON, MURDOCH ALEXANDER

(1891–1966). As an MLA, a cabinet minister, a two-time federal leadership candidate, and a continual provincial and federal candidate, Murdoch MacPherson left an indelible mark on the Conservative Party both provincially and federally.

MacPherson was born at Grande Anse on the island of Cape Breton on April 16, 1891. He was raised on his parents' farm and was sent to be educated in Richmond and Pictou. After graduation, he taught school for a brief period until he raised enough money to attend law school at Dalhousie University in Halifax.

SAB R-B 3835

MURDOCH MACPHERSON

In 1913 he moved west, establishing a law practice in Swift Current. His law practice ended in 1916 when he enlisted in the Canadian Expeditionary Force. MacPherson saw combat service in France and Belgium and was wounded in April 1917. After the war, he received an appointment as solicitor to the Soldier Settlement Board, which helped demobilized soldiers homestead.

MacPherson settled in Regina and established a successful law practice. He first ran for office in 1921, when he challenged Liberal William Motherwell in the riding of Regina. Although he lost, he proved to be the most successful Conservative candidate in Saskatchewan, finishing second with only 1,700 votes less than Motherwell. In 1925 MacPherson was successful in the provincial election, defeating Attorney General James Cross in the Regina constituency. MacPherson, along with J. T. M. Anderson and Walter Buckle, were the only successful Conservatives in 1925. They provided the nucleus of the party as support grew, and led the party to power in 1929.

Upon re-election in 1929, MacPherson played a pivotal role in the new Anderson government, becoming the province's Attorney General. During his tenure as minister, he was largely responsible for negotiating with the federal government for the transfer of natural resource rights which were kept from Saskatchewan and Alberta after they entered Confederation in 1905. This issue had been a sore point among many on the prairies, who saw it as tangible proof that Saskatchewan was a second-class province.

As one of the few government members with legislative experience and a legal background, MacPherson's leadership in the legislature was instrumental to the government's proper functioning. As the depression began to take hold, MacPherson took on responsibility for the increasingly difficult portfolio of Provincial Treasurer. In the face of plummeting tax revenues and increased need for relief programs, MacPherson tried to keep the government solvent. Only with the help of loans from the Dominion government was this possible.

In 1934, MacPherson, along with all other members of the Anderson government, was defeated. After a brief federal appointment, he returned to his law practice in Regina. Not done with politics, he ran for the leadership of the federal Conservative Party after the retirement of R. B. Bennett in 1938. MacPherson made a strong showing in the race, finishing a close second to Robert Manion and surprising many with a strong surge on the last ballot. He contested the 1940 federal election in Regina, finishing a respectable second place—a result that was significant considering the Conservative's poor results across the province. After the conservative leadership became vacant again in 1942, MacPherson made a second attempt to lead the party, but finished a distant second behind Manitoba premier, John Bracken.

After the Second World War, he represented the Saskatchewan's CCF government as legal counsel in its attempts to stop the railways from raising freight rates and attempting to circumvent the Crowsnest Pass agreement. In a succession of court cases dealing with freight rates, MacPherson became a sharp adversary of the rail companies and an advocate of the western cause for low freight rates on exported grains. In 1959, Prime Minister John Diefenbaker appointed MacPherson to the Royal Commission, commonly referred to as the MacPherson Commission, which examined the railway and freight rate problems in the country.

MacPherson made one more attempt at a political comeback in 1960 when he contested a seat in the legislature representing Regina. He finished poorly, bringing an end to his political career. In 1961 he was named a bencher of the Law Society of Saskatchewan and received an honorary doctorate from the University of Saskatchewan. He continued to practice law until his death on June 11, 1966.

BRETT QUIRING

## MAHARG, JOHN ARCHIBALD (1872–1944).

A pioneer farm leader in Saskatchewan, John Maharg was born at Orangeville, Ontario, in 1872. He came west to settle near Moose Jaw in 1890, taking up grain farming and the breeding of registered cattle.

He was one of the organizers of the Saskatchewan Grain Growers Association (SGGA) and was elected its first president, a post he held from 1910 to 1923. To give farmers some say in the marketplace the SGGA obtained Saskatchewan government loans to build farmer-owned grain elevators. The Saskatchewan Co-operative Elevator Company was formed to operate these elevators and Maharg again was first president. Within fifteen years the company had 450 country elevators, two terminals, and it ran a grain-exporting business.

JOHN MAHARG

Maharg also served as president of the Canadian Council of Agriculture from 1915 to 1917.

In 1917 he was elected Member of Parliament for Maple Creek as an independent supporting the wartime Unionist government. A year later he crossed to the Opposition with a group that was to help found the Progressive party. In 1921 he left federal politics to become minister of Agriculture for Saskatchewan. He ran and was elected provincially as independent member for Morse constituency. He continued in the cabinet until fall, when he resigned in a confrontation which also resulted in the resignation of Premier W. M. Martin. From then until 1924, when he left political life, Maharg served as leader of the Opposition.

Returning to his farming and off-farm interests, he represented the Co-operative Elevator Company on the provisional board of the newly-formed Saskatchewan Wheat Pool. Maharg remained active with the Co-operative Elevator Company until its assets were sold in 1928 to the Pool. He then returned to farming and remained there until his death in November 1944.

LISA DALE-BURNETT

**MALONE, EDWARD CYRIL** (b. 1937). As leader of the Saskatchewan Liberal Party, Ted Malone presided over the Liberal Party during its electoral collapse.

Born in Regina on July 17, 1937, Malone was raised in a political household. His father had been involved in the Liberal Party, and his maternal grandfather was James Grassick, one-time Regina MLA and mayor. Malone was educated at the University of Saskatchewan, and graduated from the college of law in 1962. Malone became actively involved in the Liberal Party as part of a small group of young lawyers who helped organize the federal Liberal Party in Saskatchewan for Otto Lang.

Active in his local Liberal association, Malone served as the Liberal campaign manager in Regina Lakeview during the 1967 and 1971 election campaigns. When Liberal MLA Don McPherson suddenly died in 1973, Malone was nominated as the Liberal candidate and was easily elected in the resulting by-election. He was re-elected in the 1975 election and quickly became a touted leadership candidate for the beleaguered party. When party leader Dave Steuart was called to the Senate in 1976, Malone ran for party leadership against fellow lawyer and Regina MLA

TED MALONE

Tony Merchant. The election was hard fought and bitterly divided the party, creating a rift between the Malone and Merchant camps. Malone easily won the leadership, but inherited a difficult position. The party lost two of the seats they had won in the 1975 campaign in by-elections and two Liberals, Colin Thatcher and Gary Lane, abandoned the party in favour of the upstart Progressive Conservatives. The movement from the Liberals to the Conservatives resulted in Malone having to share Official Opposition status with the Conservatives.

The 1978 campaign was a disaster for Malone and the Liberals. Facing responsibility for unpopular federal Liberal positions and beset by internal strife, the Liberals failed to elect a single member to the legislature for the first time in the party's history. Although personally defeated, Malone remained leader until 1981 when he was appointed to the Court of Queen's Bench in Regina.

BRETT QUIRING

## MARTENS, HAROLD ARTHUR (b. 1941).

In 1977, Harold Arthur Martens was awarded the Queen's Silver Jubilee Medal for his contribution to local government in Saskatchewan.

Martens had a long and distinguished career in local government before switching to provincial politics. He was councillor and reeve of the Rural Municipality of Saskatchewan Landing and sat on the board of directors with the Saskatchewan Association of Rural Municipalities. He was also a member of the Saskatchewan Federation of Agriculture and a member of the Rail Line Abandonment Committee.

Martens was elected to the Legislative Assembly in 1982 as the Progressive Conservative member for the rural constituency of Morse, in southwestern Saskatchewan. His family operated a ranch in the constituency, near Swift Current. Martens served as associate minister of Agriculture and Food from October 3, 1989, until November 1, 1991. During that time, he was also the minister responsible for the Saskatchewan Water Corporation, Agricultural Credit Corporation of Saskatchewan, and the Saskatchewan Horse Racing Commission.

In April 1995, he was charged with two counts of fraud. Martens was one of a handful of sitting Tory MLAs who were charged in "Project Fiddle," the name given to the RCMP investigation into the misuse of public money by Conservatives during the 1980s. He was accused of using two false expense claims to get money from one of his MLA allowances. Martens did not seek re-election in the 1995 provincial election. In February 1996 he was found guilty on both fraud charges. Martens was granted a conditional discharge and placed on probation for a year. He was ordered to repay $5,850, and to perform 240 hours of community service work.

GERRY JONES, REGINA

## MARTIN, WILLIAM MELVILLE (1876–1970).

Politician and jurist William Melville Martin was born August 23, 1876, in Norwich, Ontario, and died June 22, 1970, in Regina. He was a member of Parliament from 1908 until 1916 and served as premier of Saskatchewan from 1916 until 1922, when he was appointed to the Saskatchewan Court of Appeal, serving from 1922 until 1961. He married Violette Florence Thompson of Mitchell, Ontario, in 1905. They had three sons; Walter Melville Martin who also studied law and later became a judge, Douglas Thompson Martin, and William Kenneth Martin, both medical doctors. Mrs. Martin predeceased her husband in 1946.

Martin's parents were of Scottish ancestry and his father, also named William Martin, served as a minister in several Ontario

Presbyterian churches. Young William received his early education in the Exeter public school and the Clinton Collegiate in Huron County. In 1894 he entered the University of Toronto where he distinguished himself, both as a scholar and an athlete who earned awards in lacrosse and several other university sports. He graduated in 1898 with an honours degree in classics, and then attended the Ontario School of Pedagogy in Hamilton where he obtained a teacher's certificate. He taught for two years in Wellington County before returning to study law at Osgoode Hall. In 1903 he followed the call of the west to join the law firm of his cousin, James Balfour, in Regina. Both the Martin and Balfour families had been active in Reform/Liberal politics in Ontario, and the Balfour law firm was also active in Liberal politics. In 1905 Walter Scott, the federal Member of Parliament for the vast riding of Assiniboia West which included the City of Regina, resigned his seat to become the first premier of the newly created Province of Saskatchewan. William Martin was invited, but decided not to seek the nomination in the ensuing by-election. The Assiniboia West riding was divided in 1906, and in the 1908 federal election William Martin was nominated and won the newly created Regina riding.

SAB RB 4621

WILLIAM MARTIN

In Parliament, William Martin became an effective spokesman for western interests, including the need for more railways, reduced freight rates, the incorporation of grain growers' organizations, and a variety of other economic, legal and farm related issues. He also addressed local Regina concerns which included a number of matters related to law reforms

and the North-West Mounted Police, which had its western headquarters in the city. He easily won re-election in 1911, strongly supporting the Liberal Unrestricted Reciprocity policy. He also advocated federal assistance for the construction of a proposed railway to Hudson Bay.

In 1916 the Saskatchewan provincial government became embroiled in charges of patronage, political corruption, and a bitter school policy dispute with some Protestant church leaders. In addition, Premier Scott suffered ill health. He resigned as premier in October 1916. James Calder, who was widely regarded as the logical successor, was tainted by the scandal allegations and declined an invitation to form the government. The party then turned to William Martin who was not contaminated by allegations of scandal and who, as a devout and committed Presbyterian, was expected to heal the rift which had developed between Premier Scott and prominent Presbyterians.

The Martin government established several Royal Commissions and dealt decisively with those found guilty of inappropriate behaviour. Martin established and maintained a scandal-free administration. The most notable policies of the new government included granting women the right to vote in provincial elections, major reforms of the educational system which required all children between the ages of seven and fourteen to attend an approved school, establishment of a government mortgage-lending organization for farmers, reform of the provincial courts, and passage of a Saskatchewan Bill of Rights which demanded federal tariff reductions and the transfer to the province of crown lands and resources.

In his first election as premier in 1917, Martin and his Liberal Party won 50 of the 59 seats in the legislature. Later that year, Martin endorsed a decision by some federal Liberals to join with the governing Conservatives to form a Union government which was committed to a more aggressive war effort and to the introduction of a policy of military conscription. The Union government, however, also followed tariff and some other domestic policies which were not popular in Saskatchewan. That led to the organization of a new western protest party—the Progressive Party of Canada—to represent the interest of farmers. Provincially the Progressives were elected as minority governments in Ontario and Manitoba, and to a strong majority government in Alberta. Martin and the Saskatchewan Liberals blunted the Progressive appeal by bringing prominent farm leaders into the government, introducing legislation advocated by the Progressives, and calling a provincial election in June of 1921 before the provincial Progressives were well organized.

The Liberals won the 1921 provincial election with a large majority, but faced a crisis in the federal election which was held later in 1921. The federal contest in Saskatchewan pitted Progressives against Liberals in many constituencies. Martin made several speeches in support of Liberal candidates in which he also declared his personal opposition to many of the most cherished policies of the Progressives. That led to the resignation of J. A. Maharg, the provincial Agriculture Minister and a strong supporter of Progressives. The resulting tensions in the cabinet and caucus culminated in Martin's resignation as premier at the relatively young age of forty-six. His successor, James Dunning, was a former farm leader and enjoyed the support of members who supported the Progressives federally.

William Martin was appointed as a judge in the Saskatchewan Court of Appeal shortly after his resignation as premier. There he joined Chief Justice Sir Frederick Haultain, the Territorial premier before 1905. Martin succeeded Haultain as Chief Justice in 1941 and served in that capacity until his retirement in 1961 at the age of eighty-four. Two men—Haultain and Martin—thus dominated Saskatchewan's highest court. They, more than anyone else, shaped and interpreted provincial law during the first fifty-five years of the province's history. During the war, Martin also served as custodian of Enemy Alien Property in Canada, and in 1949 he was chairman of a commission assigned the task of revising the Canadian Criminal Code.

At the time of his retirement, Martin was described as an architect of Saskatchewan's greatness. The characteristics of his influence, in politics and as a judge, were described as integrity, dependability and a great sense of confidence. In an editorial written at the time of his death, Regina's largest newspaper, the *Leader*, described Martin as "the grand old man of the west" who was "never afraid to face an issue, unpleasant though it may have been, his sense of justice, tempered with mercy, characterized much of the daily pattern of his life."

TED REGEHR, UNIVERSITY OF CALGARY

## MATSALLA, ADOLPH SYLVESTER (b. 1926).

Born March 22, 1926, in Buchanan, Adolph Matsalla was raised on a farm close to town. Educated in Buchanan and in Yorkton, Matsalla attended Teachers' College in Saskatoon, earning a teaching certificate. He later attended the University of

Saskatchewan, completing the municipal administration program. Matsalla began his teaching career in 1943 and taught in several schools near Canora. In 1953, he left teaching and was hired as secretary-treasurer of the rural municipality of Buchanan and later worked in a variety of municipal administration positions.

Becoming active in the CCF in the early fifties, he held a variety of positions in the Canora CCF association including president from 1964 to 1967. In 1967, Matsalla was first elected to the legislature representing Canora, defeating the Liberal incumbent. In caucus he was part of a new younger group eager to leave their mark on the party, centered around Roy Romanow. Easily re-elected three times in 1971, 1975, and again in 1978, he was appointed to cabinet as minister of Tourism and Renewable Resources in 1975. He remained at that post until 1979 when he was moved out of cabinet to make way for several new ministers. He retired from the legislature and did not contest the 1982 election.

After leaving the legislature, Matsalla returned to his career in municipal administration, becoming the administrator of the rural municipality of Sliding Hills. He would also briefly return to local politics in 1983, serving two years on Canora's town council. Matsalla retired in 1987.

BRETT QUIRING

**MAXWELL, COLIN** (b. 1943). Colin Maxwell was born in Tillicoultry, Scotland, on December 16, 1943. He graduated from Jordanhill College of Education in Glasgow in 1966 and received his Bachelor of Education degree from the University of Regina in 1975.

In July 1966 he married Cherry Harvey and the newlyweds emigrated to Canada, where Colin served as an elementary school principal, university lecturer and high school principal. While principal of Spiritwood High School, he was also a member of the union hospital board and the volunteer fire brigade, and secretary of the Spiritwood Chamber of Commerce. He served two terms as mayor of Spiritwood before being elected as a Progressive Conservative member for Turtleford in the Saskatchewan legislature in 1982. He was re-elected in 1986. He held the portfolios of minister of Advanced Education and Manpower and of Culture and Recreation, but he is best remembered for his achievements as minister of Parks and Renewable Resources (PRR).

As minister of PRR, Colin oversaw designation of about 1.75 million acres of Crown land under the *Critical Wildlife Habitat Protection Act*. By 1990, the Fish and Wildlife Development Fund held more than 95,000 acres of important wildlife habitat. Saskatchewan was the first province to participate in and commit funding to the North American Waterfowl Management Plan. Colin founded the Wildlife Minister's Council of Canada and helped establish the Saskatchewan Round Table on the Environment and Economy. He increased fines for wildlife poaching and trafficking and created a special investigations unit. During his tenure the department cooperated with the World Wildlife Fund, Ducks Unlimited, Saskatchewan Wildlife Federation, Wildlife Habitat Canada, and the Saskatchewan Natural History Society. He was at odds with his cabinet colleagues on a number of issues, including their lack of an Environmental Impact Assessment of the Rafferty-Alameda Dam. He told the annual meeting of the Wildlife Federation that "wildlife and the environment are more important than politics and politicians." In June 1990, he resigned from government to become executive vice-president of the Canadian Wildlife Federation, which he led successfully to its strongest fiscal position, with improved programs. He has served on national bodies that are too numerous to name.

C. STUART HOUSTON, SASKATOON

**MCCONNELL, HOWARD** (1886–1957). Howard McConnell was born in Springbrook, Ontario, on January 27, 1886. He worked briefly as a teacher after graduating from high school and then moved in 1907 to Saskatoon to join his parents who had relocated earlier. He showed an early flair for politics while a student at the University of Saskatchewan and became the first president of the Student Representative Council in 1911. After graduating from the University of Saskatchewan, he completed a law degree at Osgoode Hall in Toronto and he was called to the Saskatchewan Bar in 1916. He operated an independent legal practice in Saskatoon from 1916 until after World War Two and was appointed King's Council in 1929.

McConnell entered civic politics in 1919, serving three consecutive terms on Saskatoon City Council between 1919 and 1922. Following this he served two terms as mayor of Saskatoon in 1922 and 1923. His competent performance in these positions and active involvement in local Conservative organizations provided a springboard into provincial politics, and in 1927 he ran successfully for the Conservatives in a Saskatoon by-election. McConnell took his seat at a time of increasing fragmentation and bitterness in Saskatchewan politics as the rise of the

SAB R-A 628

HOWARD MCCONNELL

Progressive Party and the brief appearance of the Ku Klux Klan polarized the electorate on the emotional issues of religion, race, language, and education. This fragmentation brought more than two decades of Liberal dominance to an end in the 1929 provincial election and their replacement by a Conservative-Progressive coalition led by J. T. M. Anderson.

Anderson's government had the misfortune to come to power at the onset of the Great Depression and McConnell had the further misfortune of being trusted with two different portfolios, first as Provincial Treasurer and later as minister of Municipal Affairs. In the former capacity he struggled with plummeting revenues to maintain even basic services, and in the latter he attempted through the Saskatchewan Relief Commission to coordinate relief programs. Although McConnell and his colleagues probably performed as well as was possible under the appalling circumstances, they were nevertheless held responsible for the catastrophe, and in the 1934 election every single government supporter was defeated.

McConnell returned to his private law practice after his time in government and he remained active in various community service capacities for the remainder of his life. He was a member of the University of Saskatchewan senate for twenty-three years and was also active in the United Church, serving as an elder and member of the Board of Session. He was a Mason and Master of Saskatchewan Lodge #16. McConnell passed away in Saskatoon on October 9, 1957.

MICHAEL COTTRELL, UNIVERSITY OF SASKATCHEWAN

**MCDONALD, ALEXANDER HAMILTON**
(1919–1980). "Hammy" McDonald was born
on March 16, 1919, and grew up in Fleming.
He was the son of G. C. McDonald and Ada
H. Clark. In the Second World War,
McDonald served as a Flight Lieutenant for
the Royal Canadian Air Force from 1940 to
1945. Near the end of his service, on
December 16, 1944, Hammy married
Madeline Anne Casey. Madeline and Hammy
had three children: Maureen Anne, Patrick
Neil, and Hamilton Charles. McDonald
worked as a farmer and later became a businessman in Moosomin and Regina.

Following the war, McDonald's political
activity began locally in his home town of
Moosomin, where his involvement in the community included membership at the Canadian
Legion and the Caterpillar Club, as well as
participation in the United Church. Only
three years after returning from war service,
McDonald sought public office in the
Saskatchewan provincial election of 1948.
Tommy Douglas' CCF government returned
for a second term, but Liberal candidate
Hammy McDonald won his seat as a Liberal
MLA for the Moosomin constituency. He held
this seat for five consecutive elections from
1948 to 1963 and resigned on May 25, 1965.

McDonald's long service and commitment
to the Liberal Party of Saskatchewan made
him an excellent candidate for party leadership, which he assumed on November 26,
1954, and retained until 1959. Following his
role as Liberal leader and Opposition leader in
the Saskatchewan legislature, McDonald acted
as provincial Agriculture minister and deputy
premier in Premier Ross Thatcher's cabinet.
Before finishing the term, however, McDonald
resigned his seat, but did not end his political
activities. Less than three months later, Pierre
Elliot Trudeau summoned McDonald to the
Senate, where McDonald continued his political work on the national and international
stages.

In 1966 McDonald was sworn into the
Senate and publicly congratulated by Speaker
of the Senate, and fellow Saskatchewan
Liberal, Senator Sydney Smith from Regina.
McDonald's role as a Canadian senator broad-
ened his political expertise where he served on
a number of committees representing Canada.
In his first year at the Senate, McDonald traveled as a member of the Commonwealth
Parliamentary Association to the Far East,
along with United Nations delegates, to
review technical aid provided to underdevel-
oped countries. In 1968 Senator McDonald
participated on a National Capital Commission making contributions to long range
planning for the Ottawa River district. In the
fall of 1968, McDonald was hounoured once
again when House Leader Paul Martin
appointed McDonald as deputy government
leader in the Senate, making him responsible
for steering all legislation through the Senate.
By 1969 McDonald added chief whip to his
list of responsibilities. His contributions to the
Senate continued to reflect his political
expertise and astute administrative capabili-
ties.

After a long struggle with heart problems,
McDonald succumbed to a heart attack on
March 31, 1980, shortly after delivering a
speech in the Senate. McDonald dedicated
nearly thirty years to Saskatchewan and
Canadian politics.

ERIKA DYCK, MCMASTER UNIVERSITY

**MCFARLANE, DOUGLAS** (1918–1999).
Douglas McFarlane was born in Wolseley on
January 4, 1918, to parents Andrew and Ella.
Educated in Summerberry, McFarlane worked

on the family farm with his father until 1940 when he joined the Royal Canadian Air Force, attaining the rank of sergeant. Returning to civilian life in 1945, McFarlane continued to farm in the Peebles district. On April 15, 1944, he married Frances Davidson from North Battleford. The couple had four sons: Robert, Douglas, Larry, and Donald.

McFarlane was active in a number of organizations in Saskatchewan. He held the position of director of the Saskatchewan Farmers' Union and was chairman of the local Wheat Pool Committee. McFarlane was also involved in the Canadian Legion, the Glenavon Board of Trade, various livestock associations, and was a member of the agricultural board for the Indian Head District. He was a board member of the local United Church and a leader of the 4-H clubs in his area.

McFarlane first ran for the Saskatchewan legislature as a Liberal candidate in the Qu'Appelle-Wolseley constituency in 1952, but was defeated. He was elected to the legislature in 1956 and was re-elected in 1960, 1964, and 1967. He served in Ross Thatcher's cabinet as minister of Municipal Affairs from May 1964 to July 1965, at which time he was appointed minister of Agriculture, a position he held until his electoral defeat in 1971.

As minister of Agriculture, McFarlane held one of the most important cabinet positions in the provincial government. Despite Wheat Agreements signed with China and the Soviet Union, which provided new markets for Saskatchewan crops, wheat exports continued to decline throughout McFarlane's time in office. Exports for the year ending July 31, 1968, were 336 million bushels compared to 515 million bushels the year before. By 1970, they had dropped to 305 million bushels. Although Saskatchewan farmers produced excellent crops during these years, farm cash income continued to decline, reaching $398 million in 1970, the lowest since 1960. Increasing prices for farm equipment and supplies and decreasing income from wheat exports left farmers in Saskatchewan feeling the effects of a struggling agricultural industry.

In an attempt to counter the impact of decreasing wheat exports, the Liberals advocated a policy of diversification of Saskatchewan agriculture. McFarlane's department presented legislation that promoted the expansion of the livestock industry in the province, such as the *Live Stock Loans Guarantee Act*, the *Cattle Marketing Voluntary Deductions Act*, and amendments to the *Live Stock Purchase and Sale Act*. However, Saskatchewan farmers continued to struggle throughout the late 1960s and early 1970s.

In 1971, after a failed attempt at re-election, McFarlane was appointed to the War Veterans Appeal Board in Ottawa and later moved to Charlottetown when the Appeal Board was relocated to that city. He retired to Winnipeg in 1983 and was presented with a Senior Officer's Retirement Certificate by Governor General E. Schreyer in recognition of long and excellent service. After a distinguished career in the public service, McFarlane died May 6, 1999.

ROBERTA LEXIER, UNIVERSITY OF ALBERTA

FURTHER READING: Saskatchewan Archives Board. Douglas McFarlane Papers. GR 424. Regina.

## MCINTOSH, C. IRWIN (1926–1988).

Cameron Irwin McIntosh was born in North Battleford on July 1, 1926, and educated at the University of Saskatchewan. His father, Cameron Ross McIntosh, was a Liberal MP from 1925 to 1940. In 1952 Irwin McIntosh took over from his father as president and publisher of McIntosh Publishing in North Battleford.

In 1978, when Lieutenant-Governor George Porteous died in office, the federal Liberal government of Pierre Trudeau appointed Irwin McIntosh as fifteenth Lieutenant-Governor of Saskatchewan. His tenure began in controversy when he expressed a public opinion in favour of capital punishment and was criticized by the premier for doing so. However, he gradually restored positive relations between the vice-regal office and the NDP administration of Allan Blakeney, which had been cool since the time of Frank Bastedo. This was accomplished mainly through his support of the national unity campaign, following the election in 1977 of the first Parti québécois government in Quebec, and his active participation in the provincial 75th anniversary program—"Celebrate Saskatchewan"—in 1980.

SAB R-A 23476

CAMERON IRWIN MCINTOSH

In 1981 McIntosh inaugurated the provincial vice-regal flag, based on a national pattern. Although he presided at the opening of the restored Government House in 1980, the office of the Lieutenant-Governor remained at the Hotel Saskatchewan. At the end of his tenure Mr. McIntosh publicly appealed for better accommodation for his successor.

Irwin McIntosh died on September 24, 1988.

MICHAEL JACKSON, REGINA

FURTHER READING: Hryniuk, Margaret, and Garth Pugh. 1991. "A Tower of Attraction": An Illustrated History of Government House, Regina, Saskatchewan. Regina: Government House Historical Society/Canadian Plains Research Center. • Leeson, Howard A. (ed.). 2001. Saskatchewan Politics: Into the Twenty-first Century. Regina: Canadian Plains Research Center.

## MCINTOSH, CAMERON ROSS (1871–1971).

An educator and a newspaper man, Cameron Ross McIntosh represented the almost inseparable links between the early Saskatchewan press and politics.

Born in Grey County, Ontario, on July 7, 1971, McIntosh was educated in Grey County, receiving a teaching certificate from the Owen Sound normal school. Later receiving a B.A. from Queen's University, McIntosh became principal of several schools across Ontario in Grey, Bruce and Middlesex counties. He came to Saskatchewan in the 1910s and established himself as a journalist, printer and publisher. He established the North Battleford News Ltd. which introduced local newspapers in North Battleford, St. Walburg and Turtleford. Actively involved in the newspaper industry, he served on the executive of the Canadian Weekly Newspaper Association and as president of the association's Saskatchewan branch.

Like many other publishers of the time, McIntosh used his newspaper business as a launching pad for his political career. Taking advantage of the Progressives' decline, McIntosh contested the riding of North Battleford for the Liberal Party in 1925. Easily elected, McIntosh was re-elected in 1926, 1930 and 1935. However, in 1940 McIntosh was defeated when a coalition of Conservatives, CCFers, Social Crediters and Communists jointly nominated Dories Nielsen as a Unity candidate against him. McIntosh attempted to take the seat back in 1945 but finished last in a field of six candidates. McIntosh returned to his newspaper business. McIntosh died in 1971 at the age of one hundred. His son, Cameron Irwin McIntosh, would later become Lieutenant-Governor of Saskatchewan.

BRETT QUIRING

## MCINTOSH, JOHN ("JACK") (1909–1988).
John Diefenbaker once said, "Jack McIntosh was never a pussy footer on Parliament Hill." Born on May 18, 1909, in Caithness, Scotland, his parents emigrated to Swift Current in 1911. As a young man he was an outstanding athlete who set provincial records in track and field. He attended schools in Swift Current as well as the Madison School for Boys at Tampa, Florida. He received his post-secondary education from the Royal Military College in Kingston, Ontario. On Christmas day in 1935 he was married to Helen Mary Burroughs of Swift Current; together they had three children.

During the Second World War McIntosh served as a soldier in the Canadian army. He retired with the rank of Major, having served as deputy assistant adjutant and quartermaster general. After the war McIntosh owned and operated a furniture store in the city of Swift Current with his father until 1977.

His career in public life began in 1948–1949 as an alderman for Swift Current, and in 1955 he was elected mayor. In 1958 he was elected as Member of Parliament for the riding of Swift Current-Maple Creek. Jack was re-elected four times and served as an MP until his retirement in 1972. McIntosh remained very loyal to John Diefenbaker even when he was no longer the leader of the Progressive Conservative Party. However, he had strong disagreements with Tory leader Robert Stanfield over the direction he was taking the party. In his final years as an MP he did not attend caucus meetings or serve on any parliamentary committees. Throughout his career, Jack was always very interested in veterans' issues and foreign affairs. He served several times as a member of the Canadian delegation at the United Nations General Assembly.

Throughout his career Jack was a strong advocate for farmers in the area and was very involved with the community of Swift Current. His involvement included organizations such as the Shriners, the Society for the Prevention of Cruelty to Animals, the Royal Canadian Legion, the First United Church and the Canadian Cancer Society. Even after he retired from the furniture business he did not slow down. At age seventy-one McIntosh took up farming in order to explore his love of the outdoors.

TRENT EVANISKY, DIEFENBAKER CENTRE

## MCINTOSH, LACHLAN FRASER (1897–1962).
Founding minister of the department of Co-operation and Co-operative Development, Lachlan McIntosh's reforms led to an explosion of all types of co-operatives in Saskatchewan after 1944.

Born in Bottineau, North Dakota, on July 30, 1897, McIntosh moved to Canada in 1906. His parents settled in the Qu'Appelle district where McIntosh was educated and began farming. Moving to Prince Albert, he became intimately involved in the co-operative movement. In 1923 he helped to organize the Saskatchewan Wheat Pool and was the first Wheat Pool delegate from the Prince Albert region in 1924. McIntosh was involved in many local civic organizations such as the

Prince Albert Board of Trade and the Prince Albert Agricultural Society.

In 1944, McIntosh was elected as the CCF member representing Prince Albert. He was appointed to T. C. Douglas' first cabinet initially as minister of Public Works, but soon was asked to establish the new department of Co-operation because of his close involvement in the movement. The department set about facilitating the development of co-operatives and succeeded markedly in that respect by providing government incentives for their creation and by removing legal impediments to their development. Although relations between the co-operatives and government was not always harmonious, during his five years as minister, the number of co-operatives and credit unions in Saskatchewan increased significantly, as did their membership. This allowed the movement to expand even more during the fifties and early sixties.

McIntosh also served for a period as Agriculture minister after the resignation of George Williams. After re-election in 1948, he was also appointed as minister of Municipal Affairs, remaining minister of Co-operation until 1949 when he was relieved from that post. Serving as minister of Municipal Affairs, he implemented a program by which the province would pay half of the cost of upgrading 12,000 miles of the municipal grid road for all-weather travel. The program resulted in the graveling of most of Saskatchewan's grid road system.

After Woodrow Lloyd became premier in 1961, McIntosh was moved back into the Co-operation portfolio. He was still in office when he died suddenly on March 17, 1962.

BRETT QUIRING

FURTHER READING: Macpherson, Ian. 1985. "The CCF and Co-operative Movement in the Douglas Years: An Uneasy Alliance." In Building the Co-operative Commonwealth, ed. J. William Brennan, 181–203. Regina: Canadian Plains Research Center.

## MCISAAC, JOSEPH CLIFFORD (b. 1930).

J. Clifford McIsaac was born in Mt. Herbert, Prince Edward Island, on August 30, 1930, to parents Alexander and Barbara. He received his diploma from the Nova Scotia Agricultural College in 1950 and his Doctor of Veterinary Medicine from the Ontario Veterinary College in 1955. Following his graduation, McIsaac established a veterinary practice in Unity, Saskatchewan which he operated from 1955 to 1964. On July 29, 1953, he married Marie Vandervoort of Chelsey, Ontario, and they had six children, Catherine, Alexander, Mona, Christopher, Mark, and Marjorie.

McIsaac was actively involved in his community, serving as a member of the school board and a member of the Saskatchewan School Trustees Association. He was also active on the committee which led to the establishment of the College of Veterinary Medicine at the University of Saskatchewan. He was active in various cattle and farm organizations, as well as veterinary medical associations.

McIsaac was first elected to the Saskatchewan legislature as the Liberal candidate from the Wilkie constituency. He was re-elected in 1967 and again in 1971. He served in the cabinet of Ross Thatcher as minister of Municipal Affairs from July 1965 to November 1967, and as minister of Education and minister in charge of the Saskatchewan Transportation Company from November 1967 to June 1971.

As minister of Municipal Affairs, McIsaac oversaw the revision of municipal legislation in the province and the development of a road program and housing branch within the department. However, it was while serving as minister of Education that McIsaac faced a great controversy which divided the government and the educational community in the province. In 1967, Ross Thatcher announced that the government would take control of the large budget of the University of Saskatchewan and lessen the authority of the local school boards in the province to set salaries, school operating costs, and construction requirements. This announcement created a major controversy which united the educational sector against the government, eventually forcing Thatcher to back down on his demands. Although it was Ross Thatcher who set the policy and made the announcement regarding the educational sector, it was McIsaac who was forced to deal with the consequences of this action.

SAB R-A 15783

CLIFFORD McISAAC

In 1974, following his departure from the Saskatchewan legislature, McIsaac was elected to serve as a Member of Parliament in the Government of Canada for the Kindersley riding. He served as parliamentary secretary to the Ministry of Transport and the Department of Regional and Economic Expansion, chairing the committee on Regional and Economic Expansion. He also served as member of the House of Commons standing committees on Agriculture, Transport, Regional Economic Expansion and Management and Member Services, and as chief government whip. From 1981 to 1991 McIsaac served as a member of the Canadian Dairy Commission and from 1991 to 1996 served as chairman of the National Farm Products Marketing Council.

ROBERTA LEXIER, UNIVERSITY OF ALBERTA

BIBLIOGRAPHY: Eisler, Dale. 1987. *Rumours of Glory: Saskatchewan and the Thatcher Years*. Edmonton: Hurtig Publishers.

## MCKNIGHT, WILLIAM HUNTER (b. 1940).

Born July 12, 1940, in Elrose, Bill McKnight was a farmer and a Progressive Conservative Party activist who played a leading role as party president in the 1970s revival of the provincial party. He served in the House of Commons as MP for the Kindersley–Lloydminster riding for fourteen years, from 1979 to 1993, and was in the cabinet of Prime Minister Brian Mulroney for nine years, serving variously as minister of Labour, Indian Affairs and Northern Development, Housing, Western Diversification, National Defence, Agriculture, and Energy, Mines and Resources. He retired from politics in 1993 to become involved in consulting and business ventures from his base in Saskatoon. McKnight married Beverly Rae in 1961 and they have two children, Robert and Torrie.

It should not have been a surprise to anyone when Bill McKnight inherited the Defence portfolio in the federal cabinet just as the job was about to enter its most controversial phase in decades. He was handed the job in late 1988 and soon was leading the government charge to slash the defence budget in the interests of trimming a runaway national deficit. He closed armed forces bases, cut billions of dollars from planned defence spending and cancelled equipment contracts. Then came a standoff with Native warriors at Oka, Quebec, in 1990 that led to the largest domestic troop deployment since the 1970 separatist crisis in Quebec. In 1991 came deployment of

Canadian forces to the Gulf War, the largest deployment to military action since the 1950s. Suddenly, the cuts seemed ill-advised. McKnight was branded a "hatchet man" for the Progressive Conservative government. He disagreed, arguing he was merely doing the job assigned him by Mulroney. "Regardless of outside perceptions, I think I'm fulfilling my responsibilities in the way they were given to me. I'm part of a team." His assignments for the team often were difficult ones. His tenure at Indian Affairs and Northern Development (1986–1988) was dominated by the thorny issue of land claims and accusations from native leaders that the minister was not listening to them. In the Agriculture portfolio (1991–1993), he was involved in acrimonious negotiations with provincial governments and farmers over how to redesign farm income safety nets while the industry was buffeted by several years of drought and low grain prices brought on by an international export subsidy war. The Conservative government sent billions of extra dollars to the agricultural sector and, in retirement, McKnight called it his proudest achievement in politics.

As Agriculture minister, he also played the role of prophet by warning farmers that, because of world trade talks then unfolding, they likely would lose the prized Crow Benefit grain transportation subsidy that was considered a key ninety-year-old entitlement by prairie grain farmers. McKnight's prediction came true, but it was the successor Liberal government that killed the program in 1995. In 1991, while McKnight was Agriculture minister, son Robert decided he could not make a living from the family farm at Wartime and auctioned off the equipment.

BARRY WILSON, LOW, QUEBEC

**MCLAREN, LORNE AUBREY** (b. 1928). A cabinet minister in the Devine government, Lorne McLaren was best known for his central role in the Tory fraud scandals.

McLaren was born in Saltcoats on August 17, 1928. Raised on the family farm, he was employed with Morris Rod Weeder Co., Ltd., in 1951. Rising through the ranks of the Yorkton-based farm implement manufacturing company, McLaren entered management and became company president in 1979. Active in other aspects of the farm implement industry, McLaren also served as chairman of the Prairie Implement Manufacturers Association.

As an active member of the business community, he was courted by the Progressive Conservatives as the 1982 election approached. McLaren decided to run and defeated the NDP incumbent, Randy Nelson, in the general election. McLaren was appointed to the new government's first cabinet as minister of Labour. A strong opponent of trade unions, McLaren was charged with introducing the government's new labour legislation which sought to undo much of Saskatchewan's existing labour laws, making the province more business-oriented. However, McLaren's time in cabinet proved to be short-lived, as he was dropped from his position in 1985.

Re-elected in 1986, McLaren was appointed government caucus chair. Between 1986 and his political retirement in 1991, McLaren used his position to defraud taxpayers of over one million dollars through the filing of false expense accounts. After McLaren left politics, an RCMP investigation into the financial dealings of the PC caucus office uncovered McLaren's central role in the fraud scandal. McLaren was the first person charged in relation to the investigation. He eventually plead guilty to charges of fraud, theft and breach of trust. He was sentenced to three-and-a-half years in prison, the most serious sentence of all nineteen people convicted in the scandal.

BRETT QUIRING

## MCNAB, ARCHIBALD PETER (1864–1945).

A. P. "Archie" McNab was one of Saskatchewan's most popular Lieutenant-Governors. McNab was born with his twin brother, Neil, on May 29, 1864, in Glengarry, Ontario. Frustrated with their stony farm in Ontario, Archibald and Neil McNab left for Virden, Manitoba, to purchase a farm in 1882, at the age of eighteen. Five years later Archie quit farming and purchased grain for Ogilvie Flour Mills until he moved to Rosthern in 1902. At that time, married with three children, A. P. McNab invested in two grain elevators in Rosthern. He was quite successful in Saskatchewan; four years later he moved to Saskatoon where he founded a milling company, Dominion Elevator Company, and helped to found the Saskatchewan Central Railway Company and the Saskatchewan Power Company.

SAB R-B 3697

ARCHIBALD MCNAB

McNab first officially entered politics in 1908, winning the Saskatoon City seat for the Liberal Party in that year's provincial general election. He never lost an election, being MLA for Saskatoon City from 1908 to 1917, for Elrose from 1917 to 1921, and for Saskatoon City again from 1921 until he resigned to accept a position on the local government board in 1926. After being first elected in 1908, Premier Walter Scott named McNab the commissioner of Municipal Affairs. In 1912 he became minister of Public Works, overseeing the building of the Saskatchewan legislative buildings and countless other public buildings across the province. For most of the construction of the legislative building, he camped out in a tent on the grounds, in order to monitor the work closely. One of his greatest accomplishments, however, was acquiring the University of Saskatchewan for Saskatoon; he was first elected on the promise that he would resign his seat if Saskatoon did not get the university.

McNab sat on the local government board until he resigned in 1930 under accusations of impropriety. At that point, he entered retirement until he was appointed Lieutenant-Governor of Saskatchewan in 1936, at the age of seventy-two. Serving two terms, he was the last Lieutenant-Governor to reside in Government House. McNab quickly became known as a kind, down-to-earth man who preferred being called "Archie," allowed children to play on the grounds of Government House, and rode streetcars whenever possible. At the 1938 Regina Exhibition the Piapot Reserve named McNab an honorary chief, bestowing on him the name "Mayo Tayhay," or "Kind Heart." McNab resigned due to failing health in 1945, and died on April 29 of that year.

MARYANNE COTCHER, UNIVERSITY OF REGINA

**FURTHER READING:** Kerr, Don, and Stan Hanson. 1982. *Saskatoon: The First Half-Century*. Edmonton: NeWest Press.

## MEAKES, FRANK (1917–1989).

Frank Meakes was born February 20, 1917, in Punnichy. He was raised and educated near Lestock, where he would remain for most of his life. After completing his education he began farming near Lestock, growing wheat and breeding pure-bred cattle.

An adherent of the co-operative philosophy, Meakes was involved in many local co-operative ventures and in the Saskatchewan Farmers' Union. He served as president of the Lestock Co-operative Association from 1944 until 1957, as director of the local telephone board, on the Lestock Wheat Pool board and the board of the local Credit Union. He also was involved in local government, serving as municipal councillor and also on the local school board prior to his election to the legislature.

Active in the CCF since 1942, Meakes was instrumental in helping to found the party in his area, serving as president of the Touchwood CCF association for eight years. After CCF incumbent Tom Johnson retired from politics in 1956, Meakes was elected in his place. Re-elected in 1960, Meakes was named deputy Speaker in 1961 and was appointed minister of Co-operation in 1962, a position he held until the government was defeated in 1964. Narrowly defeated in the 1964 election, Meakes returned to Lestock. Contesting the 1967 campaign, Meakes was re-elected to the legislature and took a prominent position in the opposition as Agriculture critic.

WEST'S STUDIO, REGINA • SAB R-A 8346A-1

FRANK MEAKES

A mild-mannered, soft-spoken and well-read man, Meakes was clearly identified with the left wing of the CCF/NDP. Meakes was one of the few NDP MLAs who publicly supported the Waffle Manifesto. After his final re-election in 1971,

Meakes spent his time as chair of government caucus until he retired from the legislature in 1975. Still remaining active in public life, Meakes was elected mayor of Lestock in 1976 and was elected to the Parkland Regional Library Board in 1976. Retiring from public life for good in 1985, Meakes died in Lestock on July 8, 1989.

BRETT QUIRING

FURTHER READING: Saskatchewan Archives Board. Frank Meakes Papers. Memoirs.

## MELENCHUK, JAMES WILLIAMS (b. 1953).

Leader of the Saskatchewan Liberal Party, Jim Melenchuk's decision to join a coalition government with the NDP led to his dismissal as party leader and his eventual defection to the NDP.

Born June 24, 1953, in Regina, Melenchuk was educated at both the University of Regina and University of Saskatchewan. In 1980 he graduated medical school and established a private practice in Saskatoon. Active in the medical community, Melenchuk served in a variety of capacities for the Saskatchewan Medical Association, including president in 1994.

Active in the Liberal Party, Melenchuk served the party in a variety of positions before running for office. He first contested public office in the 1995 provincial election in the constituency of Saskatoon Northwest but was narrowly defeated. Entering the campaign with high hopes, the Liberals were disappointed with the election of only eleven MLAs. Melenchuk was one of the many Liberals critical of the performance of leader Lynda Haverstock, and he played a role in her removal as leader. In 1996, Melenchuk contested and won the party leadership, inheriting a fractured and internally divided party.

In the summer of 1997 talks began between the Liberals and the Progressive Conservative Party on forming a united opposition to the NDP government. Melenchuk was cool to the idea, but four of his MLAs went ahead and helped to form the Saskatchewan Party in August 1997. The Liberal's troubles continued as one MLA chose to sit as an independent and another joined the NDP, causing the party to lose its place as the Offical Opposition. Misfortune continued in 1998 when Melenchuk ran in a by-election in Saskatoon Eastview and was defeated by New Democrat Judy Junor.

Contesting the 1999 general election in the constituency of Saskatoon Northwest, Melenchuk was narrowly elected. Although his party only elected four MLAs, they held the balance of power. Melenchuk chose to enter a coalition with Roy Romanow's NDP minority government. As part of the coalition deal, Melenchuk was appointed minister of Education and MLAs Ron Osika and Jack Hilson were also brought into the government. Although the Liberal Party initially endorsed the coalition, party members soon became critical of the deal and he was removed as leader in 2001.

Melenchuk remained in cabinet as Lorne Calvert became premier, choosing to sit in the house as an independent. In 2003, Melenchuk became minister of Finance and later joined the NDP, winning the party nomination in Saskatoon Northwest. However, Melenchuk was narrowly defeated in the election later that year.

BRETT QUIRING

## MERCHANT, E.F. ANTHONY (b. 1944).
Although elected only for a single term, Tony Merchant has remained a flamboyant and controversial personality in Saskatchewan politics.

Merchant was born October 19, 1944, in Yorkton and was raised in a legal and very political family. His mother Sally Merchant was elected to the legislature in 1964 as a Liberal representing Saskatoon and his brother-in-law, Otto Lang, served as a federal cabinet minister in the Trudeau government. Consequently, Merchant took to politics early in his life. He attended the University of Saskatchewan, earning both a B.A. and a law degree. He established a law practice in Regina and was active in the Liberal Party.

In 1975 he first contested public office carrying the seat of Regina Wascana for the Liberals. Merchant quickly became one the Liberals' most prominent and vocal members, developing a keen ability to attract media attention. When party leader Davey Steuart was called to the Senate in 1976, Merchant ran for party leadership against fellow lawyer and Regina MLA Ted Malone. Merchant's campaign focused on radically changing the structure and policy of the party, which was on the verge of collapse. Although Merchant started as the front runner, many of the long-time members grew critical of Merchant's tactics of signing up large numbers of "24-hour Liberals," causing the leadership campaign to become increasingly bitter. Merchant lost the campaign and became critical of Malone's leadership.

Merchant did not seek re-election in 1978, opting instead to contest the 1979 federal election in the riding of Regina East. Merchant launched a massive campaign, spending over two years and $100,000 on the campaign—the most expensive campaign in Saskatchewan history. However, he finished third behind New Democrat Simon De Jong. Merchant contested the seat in 1980 but again finished third. Merchant would try to re-enter twice more, losing the federal Liberal nomination in Regina-Wascana in 1993 and then losing as the Liberal candidate in Palliser in 1997.

Merchant remained involved in his successful law firm in Regina, heading several high-profile class action law suits. In 2002, his wife Pana was appointed to the Senate.

BRETT QUIRING

## MERCHANT, SALLY MARIA MARGHARITA (née Smith) (b. 1919). Sally Merchant was born in Yorkton in 1919. Her father, Vincent, was a Liberal MLA for Yorkton. She attended school at the Loretto Convent in Sedley.

Merchant was involved in a number of careers that took her across the prairies and to Ottawa. She hosted a television interview program, worked for Census Canada, and served as a regional manager throughout the west for the Department of Consumer and Corporate Affairs. She also was a sessional lecturer at the universities of Alberta and Saskatchewan

In 1964, as a Liberal candidate, she was elected as MLA for the City of Saskatoon. In the multi-member constituency she was the only Liberal who was able to break the CCF's Saskatoon slate. She served only one term. She decided not to contest the 1967 election because of a rather strained relationship she had with the premier, Ross Thatcher.

In 1967, she was part of the Canadian delegation to the United Nations (Third Committee). From 1974 to 1978 she was a member of the University of Alberta senate and in 1983 she was appointed to the

WEST'S STUDIO, REGINA•SAB R-A 8404

SALLY MERCHANT

Canadian Radio and Television Commission. Merchant was also involved in numerous charity and community activities. She has served as the Saskatchewan chairperson of UNICEF, and on the boards of the Abilities Council, the Salvation Army Red Shield Campaign, and many others. She has also retained membership in the Consumer's Association of Canada, the Canadian Women's Press Club and the Liberal Party of Canada.

Merchant's son, Tony Merchant, later followed in his mother's footsteps when he was elected to the Saskatchewan legislature in 1975.

LEAH SHARPE, REGINA

## MESSER, JOHN RISSLER (b. 1941). As one of the key ministers of the Blakeney government, "Jack" Messer piloted many of the government's most controversial measures through the legislature.

Born May 26, 1941, Messer was raised in the Tisdale area. After completing his education, he moved to British Columbia and established a successful real estate business. He returned to school, attending both the University of British Columbia and the University of Saskatchewan before establishing a farm near Tisdale.

In 1967, Messer won the CCF-NDP nomination in the constituency of Kelsey that was held by long-time CCF MLA John H. Brockelbank. At the age of twenty-six, he was narrowly elected, becoming one of the youngest MLAs ever elected in Saskatchewan at the time. Messer's political talents quickly established him as a force within the Saskatchewan NDP. He was appointed to the important position of the party's Agriculture critic. Messer became part of a young group of

MLAs who were rising to prominence in the party that nearly elected Roy Romanow as leader in 1970.

After the Thatcher government was defeated in 1971, Messer was appointed to Blakeney's first cabinet as minister of Agriculture. Messer was given responsibility for the government's most controversial program, the Land Bank. The program endeavored to help young farmers through government-sponsored land purchases which would

JACK MESSER

then be leased back to the farmer at preferable rates. Messer helped to develop the structure of the program and tried to convince the public of the program's validity. The program, however, was highly controversial, many believing it was unwarranted tampering with the land tenure system. The program quickly became a liability in rural Saskatchewan, as the results of 1975 campaign indicated. After he was re-elected in 1975, Messer was moved out of the Agriculture portfolio and into Industry.

Messer remained as minister of Industry for only a year, when he was appointed minister of Mineral Resources. Messer was assigned this portfolio to tackle the difficult issue of uranium development in northern Saskatchewan. Messer was very supportive of the expansion of uranium mining and the exploitation of uranium reserves at Cluff Lake and Key Lake. The issue was politically sensitive, with large portions of the public and the New Democratic Party being opposed. Messer's

seeming disregard for an inquiry into the proposed development led to a great deal of criticism of him within his own party. However, the developments went ahead. As minister of Mineral Resources, Messer was also instrumental in the establishment of the Potash Corporation of Saskatchewan, serving on the corporation's first board and also serving on the cabinet committee that nationalized a large portion of the province's potash sector.

Re-elected for a final time in 1978, Messer resigned from the legislature in 1980 to return to business. Messer returned to politics in 1990 as the NDP provincial secretary, the party's highest administrative position. He ran the NDP's 1991 election campaign, which resulted in Romanow's election as premier. In 1991, he was appointed president of SaskPower. He remained as president until he resigned in 1998 amid controversy around the sale of one of SaskPower's subsidiaries, Channel Lake Petroleum.

Messer continued to maintain his large farm in Tisdale and in 2003 was elected president of Ducks Unlimited Canada.

BRETT QUIRING

## MICHAYLUK, DMYTRO ("DICK") (1912
–1990). Dick Michayluk was born in 1912 in Blaine Lake, the son of recent immigrants from the Ukraine. He was schooled at Krydor High School and upon graduation attended normal school in Moose Jaw. He began his teaching career in 1933 at the height of the Depression.

Upset with the conditions of the school system and concerned with the welfare of the community, he became involved in the Saskatchewan Teachers Federation, the cooperative movement and the CCF. Michayluk also devoted his time to a number of community organizations, including the Ukrainian Greek Orthodox Church, the Krydor Board of Trade and the board of the Redberry Credit Union. An avid outdoorsman, Michayluk sought to develop and promote the tourist potential of his area as the director of the Saskatchewan Fishing and Gaming League.

WEST'S STUDIO, REGINA•SAB R-A 8377

DICK MICHAYLUK

Michayluk was first elected to the legislature in 1960 for Redberry. He quickly developed a reputation as a fiery, passionate and forthright speaker who, when agitated, was known to periodically revert to speaking Ukrainian. After he was re-elected in 1964 he held a prominent role in Opposition as the CCF Education critic, but after the 1967 election he increasingly took a less active role in order for the party to showcase new younger MLAs. Michayluk was elected for the fourth time in 1971, and he retired from politics in 1975. Michayluk retired to Saskatoon, where he died on January 2, 1990.

BRETT QUIRING

**MILLAR, JOHN** (1866–1950). An early farm organizer, community leader and member of Parliament, John Millar exemplifies the connection between the farmer organizations and elected office in the early days of Saskatchewan politics.

Born in Woodstock, Ontario, on March 19, 1866, Millar was educated at the Woodstock Collegiate Institute where he received a teaching certificate. He taught school in Ontario for several years before coming to Saskatchewan in 1889 to teach in Moosomin. Early in the 1890s, Millar gave up teaching and began farming near Indian Head.

Millar was involved in the local agitation that helped force the federal government to pass the *Manitoba Grain Act*. Although the act more stringently regulated the railroad's obligations to farmers, Millar and others quickly became concerned about the government's willingness to enforce its new legislation. The situation came to head the next year in 1901 when a bumper crop paralyzed the grain transportation system across Saskatchewan, leaving many farmers unable to sell their grain. Millar and fellow farmer John Sibbold organized a meeting of farmers in the Indian Head district to discuss the growing crisis in the fall of 1901. The group decided to hold a public meeting later that year; on December 16, they gathered and formed the Territorial Grain Growers' Association (TGGA). Millar was elected the organization's first secretary-treasurer, a position he held until 1908. Early in 1902 Millar, along with Matthew Snow and William Motherwell, set out to build the TGGA, each organizing in different parts of the province. They tried to establish TGGA locals, creating a presence for the organization throughout the territory. Involved in the TGGA's landmark victory, "the Sintaluta case," in which the TGGA successfully convicted the Canadian Pacific Railroad for breach of the *Manitoba Grain*

SAB R-A 3283

JOHN MILLAR

*Act*, both the TGGA and Millar reached a new level of political prominence. The federal government appointed Millar chairman of the Royal Grain Commission in 1906, which investigated grain transport systems throughout the world and proposed several changes to Canadian legislation.

Also active in the local community, Millar was elected to the Indian Head town council in 1910, made mayor in 1914, and served on the public school board. After the First World War, Millar once again became active in politics as the Progressive candidate in the riding of Qu'Appelle in 1921. He was easily elected in the Progressive sweep. Once elected to parliament, Millar quickly became aligned with the moderate, pro-Liberal faction of the party led by Manitoba MP T. A. Crerar. Millar ran again as a Progressive candidate in 1925, but shortly after his election he chose to sit with the Liberal government and gave Prime Minster King his full support. Re-elected in 1926 as a Liberal-Progressive, Millar was nevertheless defeated by Conservative Ernest Perley in 1930.

Retiring to Indian Head, Millar died May 15, 1950. In 1955 the town of Indian Head unveiled a plaque commemorating Millar's contribution to the farmers' movement and the founding of the TGGA.

BRETT QUIRING

**MITCHELL, DON** (b. 1944). Don Mitchell was born in Souris, Manitoba, in 1944 and moved with his family to a farm outside of Moose Jaw at the age of three. He attended elementary and high school in Moose Jaw and graduated from Riverview Collegiate in 1962. He went on to obtain a Bachelor of Arts with a double major in Political Science and English from the University of Saskatchewan, Regina Campus, in 1969. During his time at university, he became very politically involved as editor of the student newspaper, president of the students' union, member of the Saskatchewan NDP provincial council, and vice-president of the Canadian Union of Students.

After university, Mitchell worked for the Saskatchewan and National Farmers Union. He was also active with the Saskatchewan branch of the Waffle movement which was seeking to transform the NDP into an increasingly left-wing and socialist party. In 1970, Woodrow Lloyd, who had supported the Waffle Manifesto at the 1969 federal NDP convention, resigned as leader of the Saskatchewan NDP. At the age of twenty-six, Mitchell, supported by the Waffle group and the Saskatchewan New Democratic Youth, ran as a candidate in the leadership race to replace Lloyd. In a province-wide leadership campaign, Mitchell advocated a more left-wing agenda for the Saskatchewan NDP, including expanded public ownership of the resource sector, improved labour standards through a new trade union act, and a Crown land assembly in which the government could take land in trust, thereby assisting farm families in passing it on from generation to generation. At the convention in July 1970, he won the support of 18 percent of delegates on the first ballot and 25 percent on the second ballot. Roy Romanow led on the first two ballots but on the final ballot most Mitchell supporters shifted to Allan Blakeney, who won a narrow victory over Romanow. Thus, Mitchell's candidacy helped ensure Blakeney's version of social democracy within the Saskatchewan NDP. At the time, Blakeney's leadership potential was considered by many on the left wing of the NDP as more progressive than Romanow's. The NDP government under Blakeney went on to introduce the "New Deal for People," including a "land bank" and policies for oil and potash emphasizing public ownership which were variations on Mitchell's platform in the leadership race.

After his leadership bid, Mitchell completed his Master's degree in political science in 1972 at the University of Regina. He expanded his Master's thesis into a book entitled *The Politics of Food* in 1975. He worked part-time as a sessional lecturer at the University of Regina from 1973 until 1998. Also, from 1975 to 1991, he worked as a manager of the Churchill Park Greenhouse Co-op, a small co-operative for disadvantaged workers in Moose Jaw. He continued to be politically active throughout this time, running for mayor of Moose Jaw in 1972. Further, in the late 1970s and early 1980s, he was involved in a research group dealing with agriculture issues called the RAE Group (Research, Action and Education) and wrote for a number of independent social-ist magazines such as *Next Year Country*, *Canadian Dimension*, *Last Post*, and *Briarpatch*. During the Devine era, he became involved again in the NDP at the community level as part of the Moose Jaw South constituency association.

In 1988, he was elected as a municipal councillor in Moose Jaw and then served as the mayor of Moose Jaw from 1991 to 1994. As a councillor, he helped to established advisory committees on social planning and the environment. As mayor, he struggled to maintain existing municipal services without increasing taxes in the face of drastic cutbacks in operating grants from the provincial government after 1991.

Since 1998, he has been a community development co-ordinator in the Moose Jaw area for the Regional Intersectoral Committee, a provincial government agency which funds community-based projects in human services.

He remains a community activist involved with the Saskatchewan branch of the Canadian Centre for Policy Alternatives, the Palliser federal NDP riding association, the New Politics Initiative, Saskatchewan Health Coalition, Transport 2000, and the Council of Canadians. He is married to Martha Tracey and they have two children, Dave and Tracey.

DAVID MCGRANE, CARLETON UNIVERSITY

FURTHER READING: Mitchell, Don. 1975. *The Politics of Food*. Toronto: James Lorimer & Company.

## MITCHELL, ROBERT WAYNE "BOB" (b. 1936).

Bob Mitchell, a former law partner of Roy Romanow, was a long-time cabinet minister for the NDP government who held a wide variety of posts. Mitchell began his long and varied political career as minister of Human Resources, then of Labour and Employment. He was also provincial secretary, minister of Labour, and minister of Post-Secondary Education and Skills Training. His main portfolio, however, was the Department of Justice, a post which he held from 1991 to 1995, and from which he temporarily resigned in 1995 amid a scandal concerning the Martensville sexual abuse trials.

Robert Wayne Mitchell was born on March 29, 1936, in Preeceville to Charles Stuart Mitchell and Beda Annette Abrahamson. He is of Native descent, as his great-grandmother was a Dakota Indian. He was raised on a farm near Sturgis. Mitchell went to the University of Saskatchewan and earned his Bachelor of Economics and Bachelor of Law degrees (1959). Bob married fellow lawyer Sandra Gail Stolson in 1968 and they have six daughters.

Mitchell was admitted to the bar in 1960 and practiced law in Saskatchewan from 1960 to 1970. From 1970 to 1973 he worked for the federal Department of Labour and the Department of Regional Economic Expansion. In 1974 he worked for the International Labour Organization in the Caribbean. From 1974 to 1979 he was deputy minister of Labour for Saskatchewan, and in 1979 he became a senior partner in the law firm of Mitchell Taylor Romanow Ching of Saskatoon. Mitchell was first elected in 1986, although he ran and was defeated in 1982.

SASKATCHEWAN NDP PHOTO ARCHIVES
BOB MITCHELL

In the years as an Opposition member, he was justice critic, trade critic, and potash critic. He was re-elected during the great NDP wave of 1991 as the member for Saskatoon Fairview. He ceased practicing law in 1991, when he joined cabinet as the minister of Human Resources, Labour and Employment.

As Justice Minister, Mitchell oversaw several high-profile cases, including the William Dove murder and the DNA testing in the David Milgaard case that led to Milgaard's release from prison and lawsuit against the Province of Saskatchewan. He also oversaw the Robert Latimer case, the Carnie Nerland inquiry, and the Martensville sexual abuse cases and aftermath. The Martensville sexual abuse case came back to haunt Mitchell in 1995 when, on a call-in radio show, he revealed the name of a young offender convicted in the case. Conservative Justice critic Don Toth revealed the slip in the legislature and Mitchell subsequently resigned his portfolio on February 20, 1995. News reports of the day called the resignation "unconditional," although at the time a return to cabinet was not dismissed if Mitchell's name was cleared by a police investigation. By March 28, 1995, an investigation, led by former Supreme Court justice William McIntyre, determined that although a crime had indeed been committed, charging Mitchell would not serve the public interest. Justice McIntyre determined that no undue burden was placed on the young offender that was not already borne by the young man. By April 5, 1995, Mitchell had resumed his position as Justice Minister and Attorney General, although his return to the portfolio was short. Mitchell was appointed minister of Post-Secondary Education and Skills Training in November 1995. Robert Wayne Mitchell resigned from cabinet in 1998, and he resigned his seat on January 18, 1999.

DANA TURGEON, REGINA

BIBLIOGRAPHY: Saskatchewan Archives Board. Robert Wayne Mitchell fonds. SAFA #3. Regina.

**MORE, KENNETH** (1907–1993). Kenneth More was born on May 25, 1907, in Qu'Appelle to Logan More and Edna (Hamill) More. After graduating from high school, he received his secondary education at Regina College followed by Teachers' College. He was married July 19, 1932, to Lillian Ruth of Estevan. Together they had three daughters. He taught school for two years in small Saskatchewan towns before moving to Estevan and then Regina, eventually becoming involved in a men's clothing business.

His life in the public service began in 1949 when he became a member of the Regina chapter of the Anti-Tuberculosis League, ten years after being diagnosed with that same disease himself. He was elected vice-president of the league in 1955 before becoming president in 1958. He was also president of the Saskatchewan Amateur Hockey Association from 1956 to 1958, president of the Regina Patricia Hockey Club from 1953 to 1957, president of the Western Canada Softball Association from 1947 to 1948, as well as a member of the Regina Chamber of Commerce.

In 1958, More was elected to Parliament for the Progressive Conservative Party in the riding of Regina City and went on to be re-elected a record three consecutive times in Regina before being defeated in 1968. His greatest victory came in 1962 when he defeated Tommy Douglas, federal NDP leader and former Saskatchewan premier, who had been favored to win.

Agricultural policies were always of prime concern for More during his time in Parliament. He was particularly concerned about the viability of small family farms in competition with larger operations. More believed in utilizing deficiency payments to benefit the family farm.

JASON CALDWELL, DIEFENBAKER CENTRE

**MORRISON, LEE GLEN** (b. 1932). Born in 1932 at Vidora, Lee Morrison is best known as a long-time critic of government and party politics in Canada. Election as a member of Parliament for Swift Current-Maple Creek in 1993 did not alter his opinion: "When strangers on airplanes ask me the inevitable question: 'What do you do?,' I usually tell them, quite truthfully, that I am a farmer and a retired engineer. I do not ordinarily mention this aspect of my life unless the conversation turns to politics."

Morrison's aversion to the practice of politics stems, in part, from his belief that the federal government is intrusive, costly and ineffective as far as westerners are concerned. This opinion explained his decision to join the Reform Party, a movement committed to securing a fair deal for western Canada from Ottawa, fiscal restraint and smaller government. A booster of the west, Morrison championed individual as opposed to group rights.

Characterizing himself a "redneck," a label he claimed "to wear with considerable pride," Morrison's achievements are not commonly associated with that term. He earned two degrees from the University of Saskatchewan: a B.A. in 1956 and a B.E. in Geology in 1957. After graduation, he became a consulting engineer for international mining and oil companies. During that time (eighteen years in all) he did work for the United Nations and the World Bank. Another ten years were spent as a mining exploration geologist.

In Parliament he criticized what he believed were the government's overreaching, self-serving policies. In 1995, with some publicity, he opted out of a pension plan for MPs that he considered indefensibly generous. Although the bulk of Morrison's critique was directed at the federal Liberals, his rebukes were not reserved for that government alone. He was also a fervent opponent of the United Alternative movement, which unsuccessfully sought to unite the Reform and Progressive Conservative parties.

After serving seven years in the House of Commons, Morrison quit politics in October 2000. In his farewell address, his comments were characteristically pointed. He said he did not regret leaving "a totally dysfunctional institution," and his last words, rare for a member of Parliament, were, "I shall not look back."

DAVID E. SMITH, UNIVERSITY OF SASKATCHEWAN

## MOTHERWELL, WILLIAM R.

(1860–1943). Ontario schoolboy, prairie homesteader, Saskatchewan dry farmer, provincial and federal minister of Agriculture, and eminent Canadian—William Motherwell was most aptly described as "first, last and always a farmer." Farming was indeed Motherwell's first love. Yet that experience with the enormous challenges of homesteading the southern Saskatchewan prairie was what pushed

SAB R-A 249

WILLIAM MOTHERWELL

him away from his model farmstead in Abernethy to serve in the Saskatchewan legislature for thirteen years, and in the Canadian House of Parliament for another eighteen. It spurred him on to be an advocate and a political voice for western Canada's farmers.

Born in Ontario on January 6, 1860, William Motherwell was the fourth son of his Irish father, John Motherwell, and English mother, Eliza (Janet) Motherwell. On the family farm where their ancestors had homesteaded in Lanark County near Perth, Motherwell's boyhood was spent in the pattern of rural Ontario life—attending the country school in the winter and working on the farm in the busy summer season. However, like many of the "younger sons" in land-restricted Ontario in the late 1800s, he was not likely to inherit land, and he sought his future elsewhere.

When the Ontario Agricultural College was founded at Guelph in 1879, Motherwell received one of the district scholarships offered to attract students. As he told a friend in later years, it was a Dr. Mills, the head of the College, from whom he had caught the vision of agriculture as a profession, and who inspired him to make it his life's work.

After graduating from the college, Motherwell headed west. On an exploratory venture at first, he set out with two classmates in the summer of 1881, reaching Portage La Prairie, Manitoba, where he found work. After returning home to Ontario for one last winter, Motherwell, then twenty-two, headed out to stay. From the end of the rail line at Brandon, Manitoba, he joined a caravan of Red River carts and wagons west. When they reached Fort Qu'Appelle, Motherwell engaged a land surveyor to go with him to locate a homestead in the Pheasant Valley, just northwest of present-day Regina.

In 1882, Motherwell was one of the first to select land in the Abernethy district. With a pair of oxen and a plough he broke the land and began to farm. A year later, he completed construction of a three-room log house in preparation for a new stage in his homestead experience. In December 1884 Motherwell married Adeline Rogers (1861–1905), daughter of Ontario parents who had settled near Carberry, Manitoba. William and Adeline lived together on the prairies for twenty-one years. Of their four children, Robert Talmage (1890–1957) and Eliza Alma (1892–1974) grew to adulthood.

By the time Motherwell made application for his homestead in 1889, he was able to report that he had broken 100 acres and had enclosed 75 acres. He then had thirty head of livestock. The Motherwells farmed and raised their small family in the log house for thirteen years until it was finally replaced in 1897 by an impressive stone house that stands to this day, now the centre of the Motherwell Homestead National Historic Site. Motherwell remembered those homesteading years in terms of the hard work and thrift that was required—how the wood and nails from packing boxes were used for the floors of his house; how he planted every tree in the surrounding shelterbelts; and how he collected every stone that went into building his house and barn.

The prairie landscape was a huge and imposing space. Dramatically different in climate, topography and soil composition from the farmlands of Ontario, southern Saskatchewan is a semi-arid plain. The homesteaders faced enormous difficulties living on the open landscape and making the land productive. They dealt with erratic rainfalls and periodic drought without irrigation, and the biting, eroding winds without trees for shelter. They fought weeds, insect pests and crop diseases at a time when herbicides and insecticides were almost non-existent. Acquiring good horses, equipment, and hired help for the low-tech, labour-intensive farming of the day was essential. Indeed, distance to markets, to rail lines, and even to nearest neighbours became a formidable barrier that could make or break a farmer's success.

Besides the considerable natural challenges of climate and geography, at the turn of the twentieth century there were also significant political barriers to getting crops to market in a context where the railways and elevator systems were owned and operated by interests in eastern Canada. Besides the CPR monopoly on rail transportation, farmers faced decades of depressed prices and the realities of Prime Minister Macdonald's national policies. Growing the crops and getting them to the rail lines, topped with such aggravations as inadequate numbers of rail cars and having no say as to price, grade or dockage of one's harvest, was too much for many to bear.

While around him many homesteaders quit their claims in the face of the myriad of difficulties, for Motherwell they were the catalyst for his entry to political life. As a co-founder and first president of the Territorial Grain Growers Association in 1901, Motherwell developed a deep conviction that solutions were to be found in pulling together and fighting for changes to the benefit of the farmers. Cooperative movements rather than rugged individualism would be the strategy for prairie agriculture. However, in the midst of Motherwell's growing interest in political activism and community service, for Adeline the years of hard work as a homesteader's wife and increasing bouts of asthma were proving too much. She died in the spring of 1905 at the age of forty-four, in the midst of Motherwell's successful campaign to enter provincial politics.

After Adeline's death Motherwell took on his duties in the Saskatchewan legislature and resided in Regina for three years with the children, who were fifteen and thirteen at the time of their mother's passing. Appointed Saskatchewan's first minister of Agriculture in 1906, he began making the changes he thought most essential to improving the lot of western Canada's farmers. However, the homestead in Abernethy, referred to as "Lanark Place," again became the Motherwell family's centre in 1908 when William Motherwell married Catherine Gillespie (1866–1952). Born and raised in Ontario, Catherine had moved west in her twenties to be a teacher and missionary to First Nations people in southern Saskatchewan. After seven years as principal of the File Hills Boarding School, north of Abernethy, Catherine turned her energies to the work of the family and farm, as Mr. Motherwell was often on duty at the legislature in Regina.

Motherwell set Saskatchewan's Department of Agriculture on the track of "scientific agriculture." As it played out in western Canada, scientific agriculture was built on the concept that there are laws, or certainties in nature, and that through discovery of these certainties and application of scientific techniques that work in sync with them, nature with all of its vagaries and apparent randomness can be conquered. The conviction that agricultural success on the dry prairies could be obtained with the right information directing careful application of very basic equipment and practices brought an urgency to get the information out. Thus Motherwell and others fervently "preached the gospel of dry farming," which was largely built around preserving soil moisture by the two key practices of summerfallowing and elaborate systems of soil tillage.

Motherwell's educational efforts were initiated on a multitude of fronts through lectures, agricultural societies, institutes, bulletins, and the Saskatchewan College of Agriculture which he co-founded in 1908. He even advocated that nature study and school gardening be introduced in the public schools. Through an extensive series of bulletins published by the Saskatchewan Department of Agriculture, Motherwell and the agricultural experts at the College widely distributed advice on all aspects of farm technique and farm life. Often in multiple languages, the bulletins were "how-to" manuals on such topics as summerfallowing, crop rotation, tree planting, farm diversification, co-operative associations, and dairying. Motherwell was convinced that such essential information could not be communicated only in verbal or written forms, but had to be demonstrated and seen by farmers. To that end a system of experimental farms, demonstration plots, and local fairs were established in Saskatchewan. The network of rail lines was also capitalized on as a vehicle for reaching farmers with demonstrations, lectures and exhibits inside special train cars known as the "Travelling Dairy," the "Special Seed Train," and the hugely successful "Better Farming Train." Motherwell's own homestead was arranged and run in a way that he consciously saw as a model for others to follow.

Motherwell resigned from his Saskatchewan cabinet post in 1917, and his seat in 1918 in protest to the provincial Liberals' pro-conscription stand during the World War I years, as well as their policy to curtail French language rights in the Saskatchewan public schools. But after only a few short years, Motherwell was again tempted back into public life. He was nearly sixty-two years old in 1921 when he ran for federal politics and was elected in the Regina constituency by a large majority. Prime Minister William Lyon Mackenzie King invited him to serve as Canada's minister of Agriculture, which he did from 1922 to 1925 and 1926 to 1930. After August 1930, Motherwell sat on the Opposition side of the House under Conservative Prime Minister R. B. Bennett until Mackenzie King's Liberals returned to office in 1935.

In Ottawa Motherwell worked to improve the quality and continuity of the exportable and home-consumed products through the standardization and grading of all forms of agricultural produce. He also worked to achieve rust-resistant varieties of wheat, and established the Dominion Rust Research Lab in Winnipeg in 1926. He is credited for helping Canada become the first country in the British Empire to adopt policies to curtail tuberculosis, by setting up "Restricted T.B. areas" and an Accredited Herd System. Motherwell championed the cause of the prairie farmer through endorsing government regulation and financial aid to prairie farmers, as well as participation in co-operative enterprises.

Motherwell's service in Ottawa required others to take up the day-to-day operations on the home front. He and his wife Catherine went back and forth to Ottawa when the House of Commons was in session, returning back to Lanark Place when the work schedules allowed. Nevertheless, it was often said that Motherwell was never far removed from his farming operation—at any time this "statesman in overalls" could report on the cycle and state of his crops, and on what agricultural methods were working for him at the time.

The 1935 federal election was Motherwell's last. He retired from politics in 1939, just before he reached the age of eighty, the "Grand Old Man of Canadian Agriculture," and died on May 24, 1943. Motherwell's legacy was, above all else, that of advocate and defender of prairie farmers. He had a deep conviction that agriculture—and, thus, the prairies—were the economic foundation of Canada, and should be guarded and appreciated as such. He was often called a "Laurier liberal" which means that he had a deep respect for the rights of minorities and for the common man, and their potential as citizens of the country. He fought not only for the doors of Canada to be open for immigration and settlement of the west, but for support of those newcomers, as their success was for the benefit of all.

W. R. Motherwell was designated an eminent Canadian for his contributions to the development of agriculture on the prairies, his activities as a farm activist and reformer, and his years of service as a provincial and federal minister of Agriculture. His homestead was designated a national historic site in 1966 because of its architectural interest and its historic associations with the career of W. R.

Motherwell, and as an illustration of a prairie homestead of western Canada's settlement period.

FRIEDA ESAU KLIPPENSTEIN, PARKS CANADA

**FURTHER READING:** Dick, Lyle. 1989. "Farmers 'Making Good': The development of Abernethy District, Saskatchewan, 1880–1920." *Studies in Archaeology, Architecture and History.* Ottawa: Parks Canada • Shepard, R. Bruce. 1997. "W. R. Motherwell and the Dry Farming Congress in Canada." *Saskatchewan History.* 49, no. 2: 18–27 • Turner, Allan Reaman. 1958. "W. R. Motherwell: The Emergence of a Farm Leader. *Saskatchewan History* 11, no. 3: 94–103 • Turner, Allan R. 1959. "W. R. Motherwell and agricultural education, 1905–1918." *Saskatchewan History* 12, no. 1: 81–96.

## MUNROE, FREDERICK (1881–1955).

Frederick Munroe, a Conservative from the constituency of Moosomin, served the minister of Public Health from 1929 to 1934 in the J. T. M. Anderson government.

He was born in 1881 in Moose Creek County, Ontario. By 1906 he had achieved his Master of Surgery degree from Montreal's McGill University. Three years later, he married Francis Jamieson with whom he raised four children. Prior to his election win in 1929, he had practiced medicine in Welwyn for twenty-two years.

In 1930 Munroe introduced a bill that established the *Saskatchewan Cancer Commission Act*, and was chairperson of the resulting commission from its inception to 1934. Cancer clinics opened in Regina (1931) and Saskatoon (1932). It is for his work as doctor and minister of Public Health that, in 1954, the Saskatchewan division of the Canadian Cancer Society honoured him with the creation of the annual Munroe Lectures.

During his time as minister, he established a psychopathic ward in the Regina General

Hospital. In 1949 the psychopathic division of the hospital was named the Munroe Wing. In July 1933, he amended the *Marriage Act* to require that, before legal recognition of any nuptial is granted, the male must produce a doctor's certificate verifying his good mental and physical health. He also oversaw regulatory changes to the sale and transportation of milk products.

After his defeat in 1934, Dr. Munroe established a large medical practice in Regina that he maintained until 1954. He died at his Regina home on November 19, 1955.

RYAN GRIFFITHS, UNIVERSITY OF REGINA

## NASSERDEN, EDWARD (b. 1919).

Edward Nasserden was born in Clark's Crossing on June 4, 1919. He attended school in Warman. Edward was married in July 1948 to Alma Rempel. They resided in Rosthern, where they raised a family of nine children.

Before entering politics, Edward worked as a farmer in the Rosthern area. He was also involved in various businesses, serving as president and director of Warman Telephone, and as director of the Saskatoon Cooperative Association and the district Credit Union.

Edward first ran for parliament for the Progressive Conservatives in Rosthern in 1953 but was defeated. He ran successfully in 1958 and represented Rosthern in the House of Commons until 1968. After redistribution, Nasserden chose to run in 1968 in the riding of Saskatoon-Biggar but lost the election. While in the House of Commons he served on several Parliamentary Committees including Agriculture, Immigration, Consumer Credit and Human Rights.

In 1970 he was chosen leader of the Progressive Conservative Party of Saskatchewan. He took over the reigns of the

party while it was still in the political wilderness. A provincial election took place in 1971. The party was not able to run a full slate of candidates and was shut out of the legislature. Liberal Party leader and former premier Ross Thatcher died suddenly after the 1971 election, opening a seat in the legislature. Nasserden ran under the Progressive Conservative banner in Thatcher's former constituency of Morse, but lost. Towards the end of 1971 Nasserden resigned as leader of the Progressive Conservative Party to facilitate the creation of a new party, which would have essentially been a merging of the Progressive Conservatives and the Social Credit Party of Saskatchewan. The merger was unsuccessful, and the PC Party acclaimed him as its leader. He continued on as leader of the party until 1972, when he retired in order to spend more time with his family.

In addition to his political and business interests, Nasserden served as a school board trustee, and was a member of the Aberdeen Angus Association, the United Farmers of Canada and the Saskatoon Dairy Pool.

TRENT EVANISKY, DIEFENBAKER CENTRE

## NICHOLSON, ALEXANDER MALCOLM ("SANDY") (1900–1991). Sandy Nicholson

was born on November 25, 1900, in Bruce County, Ontario. After childhood on the farm he decided on a career in the ministry and attended the University of Saskatchewan, where he studied theology.

Friendly, outgoing and unafraid of hard work, Nicholson soon became involved in the Student Christian Movement where he met his future wife, Marian Massey, and first heard J. S. Woodsworth speak about the socialist movement and the value of the political life. In 1928 he graduated, married Marian and began his ministry, first at St. Stephen's Presbyterian in Edinburgh, Scotland, and then at St. Stephen's United in Hudson Bay Junction, Saskatchewan, in 1930. Times were hard, but Nicholson traversed his large parish tirelessly, using his charismatic speaking and fundraising abilities to organise the community to care for and look after their poor as best they could.

Moved by a desire to improve the standard of living in his McKenzie constituency, Nicholson campaigned for CCF candidate George Stubbs in a 1934 provincial by-election. He sought the federal seat in McKenzie himself in 1935 but did not win it. Despite this loss he was encouraged by the financial contributions of his constituents and began to campaign, raise funds and educate them about the social movement in preparation for the next election. To facilitate this, Nicholson resigned from the ministry, citing as his reason his social conscience and his belief that he could do more to help his community from the political arena. He won the riding and sat as an Opposition member in Ottawa from 1940 to 1949 and again from 1953 to 1958. During this time he acted as the national treasurer for the CCF and advocated passionately in the House of Commons for his constituents as well as for access to universal health care and the rights of the poor, pensioners, women and farmers' groups.

In 1960 Nicholson was persuaded to run for the CCF in the Saskatchewan election. Medicare was the chief election issue. The CCF formed the new government. Sandy won his Saskatoon seat and took his place in T. C. Douglas's cabinet as the minister of Social Welfare and Rehabilitation. In this position

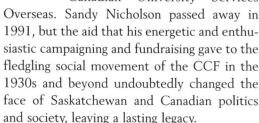

WEST'S STUDIO, REGINA•SAB R-A 8385

SANDY NICHOLSON

Nicholson worked hard to bring his social ideals into reality. He met with professionals to try to allay their fears as the CCF brought universal, publicly funded health care into legislation in 1962. In 1964 he again won his seat but the party did not fare so well. After three years as an Opposition member in the legislature, Nicholson was ready to retire. Although he ran again in 1967, he chose a riding that he was sure the NDP would lose and retired from political life when this prediction proved true.

Even in retirement Nicholson's social conscience moved him to employ his considerable skills and energy for his community's benefit. He performed extensive fundraising and leadership work for the Saskatchewan Association for Retarded Children and for the Canadian University Services Overseas. Sandy Nicholson passed away in 1991, but the aid that his energetic and enthusiastic campaigning and fundraising gave to the fledgling social movement of the CCF in the 1930s and beyond undoubtedly changed the face of Saskatchewan and Canadian politics and society, leaving a lasting legacy.

KYLE ULRICH, REGINA

FURTHER READING: Dyck, Betty L. 1988. *Running to Beat Hell: A Biography of A. M. (Sandy) Nicholson*. Regina: Canadian Plains Research Center.

## NIELSEN, DORISE WINIFRED (1902–1980).

Dorise Nielsen was the third woman to hold a seat in the Parliament of Canada. She was elected MP for North Battleford in 1940 by a grassroots coalition of CCF, Social Credit, and Communist Party supporters who called themselves the United Progressives.

Dorise Winifred Webber was born on July 30, 1902, in London, England, the youngest of five children in a middle-class family. After attending college and teaching in England, she emigrated to Saskatchewan in January 1927 to take up a teaching post near the present town of Spiritwood. She soon married a homesteader, Peter Nielsen, and gave birth to four children, one of whom died in infancy.

By 1935 both Peter and Dorise were staunch supporters of the new CCF Party. Soon, however, Dorise's politics moved even further left. A series of letters she wrote to the *Western Producer* reveal that by 1937 she was an admirer of the Soviet Union and believed that "the communists alone, because of their analysis of the cause, can supply us with the solution to our present difficulties." Nevertheless, she continued to work for the CCF, and along with many other members, pushed for a united front of all left-wing groups. She became a member of the Meadow Lake CCF executive and the Provincial Council of the CCF. In the 1938 provincial election she served as campaign manager for CCF candidate Robert Paul. Shortly after Paul's defeat, the Meadow Lake CCF executive joined with supporters of other groups to form the United Progressives. On March 26, 1940, as the United Progressive candidate, Nielsen defeated Cameron McIntosh, the Liberal incumbent since 1925.

Dorise Nielsen was one of many women and men who were politicized by the Great Depression which struck Saskatchewan longer and harder than any other part of Canada. Considered one of the best speakers in the House, she worked conscientiously to bring attention to the plight of the west. While the Communist Party was outlawed (1940–1942), she was spokesperson for its policies in Parliament, and active in the crusade to have its members released from prison. She also protested the internment of Japanese Canadians, advocated equal pay for women in the armed services, and proposed, successfully, that the new family allowance be payable the mother.

Following her defeat in 1945, she moved to Toronto and worked for the Labour Progressive (Communist) Party in various capacities. As the party dwindled, she sought other employment but could find very little that suited her abilities. Finally, in 1957 she moved to China, where she worked until 1980 as an English teacher and polisher of English texts for the Foreign Languages Press in Beijing.

FAITH JOHNSTON, WINNIPEG

**NILSON, JOHN THOMAS** (b. 1951). John T. Nilson held several ministerial positions in the New Democratic Party governments of Romanow and Calvert. Born in Saskatoon on July 9, 1951, Nilson was educated at Pacific Lutheran University, Tacoma, Washington, the University of Oslo, Norway, St. Olaf College, Minnesota, and the University of British Columbia in Vancouver. In 1977 he acquired a degree in law from the lattermost institution and was admitted to the British Columbia Bar in 1978. After admission into the Saskatchewan Bar in 1979, he practiced law and mediation in Regina with MacPherson, Leslie & Tyerman.

SASKATCHEWAN NDP PHOTO ARCHIVES

JOHN NILSON

In 1995 he ran for office in the general election. This first attempt in June 1995 earned him a victory in the constituency of Regina Lakeview. He was re-elected in that constituency in 1999 and again in 2003. Nilson was appointed minister of Justice and Attorney General in November 1995, a position he held until February 8, 1999, at which time he switched portfolios to the Crown Investments Corporation (CIC). From CIC, Nilson moved to Health in early 2001.

Nilson was Saskatchewan's minister of Justice in 1999 when David Milgaard's cash settlement from the government was negotiated. This was in compensation for Milgaard's material loss and immeasurable pain and suffering resulting from his 1970 wrongful conviction. While minister, Nilson advocated the use of restorative justice, which drew on aboriginal traditions of healing and reconciliation for victim and offender. Offenders are held accountable in broader ways than punitive segregation, and communication between offender and victim is encouraged in order to reach beyond punishment toward justice.

During his term as Crown Investments Corporation Minister, Nilson oversaw the implementation of the Saskatchewan Rate Review Panel, which is a body mandated to review the pricing structure among the Crown Corporations.

Nilson was minister of Health in April of 2001 when Kenneth Fyke, who had headed the Commission on Medicare, submitted *Caring for Medicare: Sustaining a Quality System*. The commission had been appointed by Premier Roy Romanow in June of 2000. In this period, the commission was one of several conducted nationally and provincially on medicare across Canada. The final report of the Commission on Medicare was followed by the provincial government's Action Plan for Saskatchewan Health Care. The result of this planning and research was, among other initiatives, the consolidation of thirty-two health districts into twelve Regional Health Authorities, and the creation of the Quality Council which ensures accountability in the system.

RYAN GRIFFITHS, UNIVERSITY OF REGINA

## NOLIN, JOSEPH OCTAVE (1868–1925).

Joseph Nolin was born in Botineau, North Dakota, on May 16, 1868, to Joseph Nolin (a Canadian) and Maryane Gaudry (a French-Canadian). He was of French, Scottish, Irish and Salteaux Indian ancestry. Nolin was educated in St. Anne des Chenes, Manitoba. He was a British subject though he was born in the United States, as his parents retained their British citizenship while living in the United States. He was married on February 6, 1891, to Marie Villeneuve and raised a family of thirteen children, of whom twelve survived.

SAB R-A 12967

JOSEPH NOLIN

Nolin was a trustee for the Nolin School District from September 25, 1903, to May 16, 1904. The country school had been named for his family and he had helped to organize the school district. As well, for ten years, Nolin was the captain of the Battleford steam ferry, which crossed the Saskatchewan river.

Joseph Nolin was a Justice of the Peace and was first elected in 1908 in the constituency of Athabaska with 469 votes to 23. He was a

Liberal, a Roman Catholic and one of Saskatchewan's first Métis members of the Legislative Assembly. He was re-elected in 1912, 1917, 1921, and in 1925 at Île-à-la-Crosse. Nolin rarely spoke in the legislature, though when he did, roads and railroads were favorite subjects when urging the needs of the north country. For seventeen years, Nolin was an MLA and spoke in English, French, German and a Native tongue. He was also an avid outdoorsman and, when in the north, frequently traveled by canoe, dog sled, horse and, in later years, automobile. He also assisted settlers in the Meadow Lake and Beaver Lake districts.

His uncle, Charles Nolin, was minister of Public Works and of Agriculture in the Norquay administration in Manitoba. Nolin's father was a clerk in the legislature at that time as well.

Joseph Nolin passed away in 1925 shortly after being re-elected to the legislature.

HEATHER WILSON

SOURCES: Saskatchewan Archives Board. Joseph Nolin. R-E2417 • Saskatchewan Archives Board. Nolin School District #903.

## NOLLET, ISIDORE CHARLES

(1898–1988). Long-time farm leader and politician Isidore Charles "Toby" Nollet was born on November 18, 1898, at Sentinel Butte, North Dakota. Toby received his education at St. Benedict's Academy and St. Thomas Military College in Minnesota. During the First World War he served overseas with the American Expeditionary Force and spent a year in Germany with the army of occupation.

SAB R-A 8371

ISIDORE NOLLET

Following his return from overseas service he came with his father to western Canada. After a careful survey of available lands they settled at Freemont, Saskatchewan, establishing a ranching operation stocked with Aberdeen Angus cattle. In 1957, the ranch was sold to a group of neighbours, who formed a cooperative venture known as the Neilburg Cooperative Grazing Association.

During his years as a rancher and farmer, Toby Nollet took a keen interest in community affairs. For three terms he was reeve of the rural municipality of Hillsdale and an active member of the United Farmers of Canada. He was a member of various cooperatives, including the Saskatchewan Wheat Pool, and helped to organize Canadian Cooperative Implements Limited in the area.

Toby Nollet's activity in the Farmer-Labour party led to membership and support of the Cooperative Commonwealth Federation (CCF) in the early 1930s. He was elected a member of the provincial legislature in 1944 and continued to represent the Cut Knife constituency for the CCF until his retirement from active politics in 1967.

He was Deputy Speaker of the Legislative Assembly from 1944 to 1946, when he became the minister of Agriculture, a post he held until 1964 when the CCF was defeated in a general election. With eighteen unbroken years as minister of Agriculture, Toby Nollet was the longest-serving minister of Agriculture in Saskatchewan's history. During his term as minister, he was responsible for many innovations in his department, all designed to improve the lot of the province's farmers.

Under his guidance, the Lands

Branch and the Conservation and Development Branch were established, the latter providing an engineering service to deal with soil and water problems, flood control, irrigation, and reclamation. Provincial community pastures were developed which now accommodate well over 100,000 head of cattle. Under an Earned Assistance Policy, hundreds of erosion control projects were undertaken, thousands of miles of field shelter belts were planted, and more than 100 community grazing associations were organized and assisted.

In 1958, a farm management service was added and a project which he had enthusiastically supported was launched with the signing of an agreement between provincial and federal governments to develop the South Saskatchewan River project, now completed and known as the Gardiner Dam and Diefenbaker Lake. In the early 1960s, Toby Nollet added to his department the Family Farm Improvement Branch and a crop insurance program, and an Economics and Statistics Branch was organized.

In 1975, Toby Nollet was inducted into the Saskatchewan Agricultural Hall of Fame in Saskatoon. He died on April 29, 1988, in Kelowna, British Columbia.

LISA DALE-BURNETT

**NYSTROM, LORNE** (b. 1946). Lorne Nystrom was born April 26, 1946, on the family farm near Wynyard. Initially trained to be a teacher, he graduated from the University of Saskatchewan in 1970. Active in the youth wing of the NDP, he served as leader of the Regina Campus NDP, president of the Saskatchewan New Democrat Youth and as a vice-president of the federal NDP (1967–1968). In 1968, while still a university student, he became a candidate for Parliament in the riding of Yorkton Melville and won at the age of only twenty-two. He won six more elections in a row. However, in 1993 Nystrom, like so many NDP MPs, went down to defeat and the NDP lost official party status in the House of Commons. Seeking alternate employment, Nystrom operated a political consulting firm often involving projects overseas. Still enthusiastic about a parliamentary career, Nystrom ran and won in 1997 in Qu'Appelle and again in 2000 in Regina–Qu'Appelle.

Nystrom has served as the NDP's parliamentary critic in a number of areas: most notably youth, agriculture and food, the constitution (during the proposed Meech Lake and Charlottetown Constitutional amendments), finance, banking, justice, and democratic reform. He has also served as NDP caucus whip and deputy House Leader.

Nystrom ran three times for the leadership of the federal NDP and came in third on each occasion. In the 1975 convention, the youthful twenty-nine-year-old lost to Ed Broadbent. Twenty years later, in 1995, the NDP opted for a hybrid election involving a direct vote by party members and a convention. While

Nystrom led in the regional, labour and combined primaries, the convention was another story. He came a close third (with 29.6 percent) in a three-way race and lost to Alexa McDonough. The 2002/2003 NDP leadership campaign involved a direct vote by all members and,

SASKATCHEWAN NDP PHOTO ARCHIVES

LORNE NYSTROM

despite his strong placement in the primary portion of the 1995 race, the Saskatchewan-based Nystrom was a distant third to the Toronto-based Jack Layton.

Nystrom sought to leave his mark in several policy areas. On the constitution, he differed with NDP leader Broadbent and favoured equality of all provinces. In 1992, he was appointed a co-chair of the Charlottetown Referendum Committee, a factor in being appointed to the Privy Council by Brian Mulroney. Believing that the NDP must not only win the voters' hearts but also their minds, Nystrom urged the party to convey that it was ready to govern by showcasing a platform of financial responsibility—a hallmark Saskatchewan style of social democracy. Exhibiting elements of prairie populism, Nystrom has called for a tax on all international monetary speculation (Tobin Tax—see his book on economics, *Just Making Change*) and been an articulate advocate of proportional representation. Nystrom's bilingualism has served him well in Parliament and on constitutional matters.

Nystrom has shown considerable electoral success (winning nine of eleven elections) since 1968 and has been one of several Saskatchewan MPs who have formed the core of the federal NDP caucus.

In 2004, Nystrom was narrowly defeated in Regina-Qu'Appelle.

ALAN WHITEHORN, ROYAL MILITARY COLLEGE

## OGLE, ROBERT JOSEPH "BOB" (1928–1998).

Father Bob Ogle was a priest and foreign missionary, an author and a member of Parliament. He was born on December 24, 1928, in Rosetown and was raised on a poor farm in a devout Irish Catholic family during the Great Depression.

He studied for the priesthood at St. Peter's Seminary in London, Ontario, and was ordained in May 1953. He then returned to Saskatoon where he became a parish priest, founded the Catholic Centre, and became the rector of St. Pius X Seminary. He later completed a Doctorate in Canon Law at the University of Ottawa.

Father Ogle was a man of great energy and drive who wanted to make a difference. In 1964 he volunteered as one of the founding members of a diocesan mission team sent to the poverty-stricken region of northeast Brazil. There he engaged in pastoral work, organized literacy activities, farming co-operatives, and medical programs. In 1969 he coordinated a relief operation and house-building program following disastrous floods near the mission. He was later to say that he was profoundly influenced by what he saw in Brazil and that it changed his life.

He returned to Saskatoon in 1970 and was installed in one of the city's largest parishes. He was a good pastor, especially skilled at getting people involved in projects, but he was restless. In 1976 he took a sabbatical and traveled the world, investigating Canadian international development projects. When he returned home, he wrote about it in a book called *When the Snake Bites the Sun*.

The very night that he delivered his manuscript in September 1977 he received a call from a member of the NDP constituency organization for Saskatoon East, asking him to consider becoming a candidate in the next federal election.

He had never belonged to a political party but he was ready for something big. It was unusual for a priest to engage in partisan politics, so he consulted with his bishop, other priests, parishioners, friends, and even Otto Lang, the Liberal incumbent.

Eventually he decided to do it and the Ogle legend began to take shape. He was a creative campaigner who placed brief handwritten advertisements in the local newspaper, and who mounted an Ogle sign on a moveable trailer, parking it in neighbourhoods whenever he was door knocking.

SASKATCHEWAN NDP PHOTO ARCHIVES

BOB OGLE

While Otto Lang went busily about his task as Transport Minister, Father Ogle became a well-known figure, riding a bicycle around the city to do his canvassing. He knocked on every door in the riding, many of them more than once. He used a low-key, one might say pastoral, approach on the doorstep, asking people about themselves and their problems rather than telling them what to think or how to vote.

He defeated Lang in 1979, entering the NDP caucus during the minority government of Joe Clark, and he won again in 1980. He served as the NDP critic for External Affairs, for the Canadian International Development Agency, and as the critic for Health, where he steadfastly refused to follow his party's position on abortion.

He loved being an MP and he approached that work on a pastoral basis as well, generally keeping a promise never to make personal attacks on political opponents. But his career was causing controversy within the councils of the church. By 1984 the Vatican had decided that parliament was no place for a priest, and despite the fact that he had already won his party's nomination as a candidate Father Ogle was instructed not to stand for election.

He agonized over the order and considered leaving the priesthood, but in the end he decided to obey and did not contest the 1984 election. He was quoted at the time as saying that he was a priest first and hoped to remain one for the rest of his life.

During his last fifteen years he was almost constantly ill. He was suffering from serious headaches and he developed a bleeding ulcer even before he left politics in 1984. About a year later he had a heart attack, and eventually he was diagnosed with a cancerous and non-operable brain tumour.

Those who knew him well said that his Job-like plague of afflictions often left him near despair, but he was a tenacious man who loved life and refused to give up. In those pain-filled years he wrote two more books, initiated a project called Broadcasting for International Understanding, and hosted a retreat series on television.

His projects kept him (and his friends) busy, and he never completely lost his sense of humour. His health continued to decline, however, and he died in Saskatoon on April 1, 1998, at age sixty-nine.

Father Ogle's work was recognized civilly in his appointment as an Officer of the Order of Canada in 1989, and his receiving the Saskatchewan Award of Merit in 1995.

DENNIS GRUENDING

FURTHER READING: Ogle, Father Bob. 1990. A Man of Letters. Ottawa: Broadcasting for International Understanding. • Ogle, Father Bob. 1987. North\South Calling. Saskatoon: Fifth House. • Ogle, Father Bob. 1977. When the Snake Bites the Sun. Saskatoon:Texchuk Enterprises.

**ORCHARD, DAVID HUGH** (b. 1950). A farmer, author and political activist, David

Orchard was born on June 28, 1950, into a middle-class farming family from Borden. He spent two years studying arts and sciences at the University of Saskatchewan (1968–1970) and then began a law degree there in 1971. However, despite being one of the top students in his class, he soon decided against a career in the legal profession and left the program after one year. Orchard spent the next several years drifting through a variety of jobs, including working as logger in British Columbia and a taxi driver in Saskatoon. Returning to Borden in 1975, he took over the family farm and converted it into an "organic" operation, a decision that represented but one manifestation of his early interest in environmental issues.

Orchard's formal involvement in political activism began in 1985, when he and a small group of others decided to act upon their growing concern over the proposed Canada-United States Free-Trade Agreement (FTA). Shortly after the initiation of negotiations were announced in September of that year, they founded Citizens Concerned About Free Trade (CCAFT). Orchard was president of this non-partisan group dedicated to communicating the case against the agreement to the public. The group also later campaigned to stop the North American Free-Trade Agreement (NAFTA) and the proposed Multi-Lateral Agreement on Investment (MAI).

In 1998, Orchard took his political activities a step further by running for the national leadership of the Progressive Conservative Party of Canada, ironically the very party that had negotiated the CUSFTA and that he had fought so hard against in the 1988 and 1993 federal elections. His goals included not only gaining a larger constituency for CCAFT, but also attempting to bring the Tory party back to its traditional roots of anti-continentalism and state-sponsored nation building. In the final results of the second ballot on November 14, Orchard finished as runner-up to former Prime Minister Joe Clark, garnering 22.5 percent support to Clark's 77.5 percent. While some were pleased with his ability to sign up new members and add excitement to an otherwise lacklustre campaign, others viewed Orchard as "an outsider," whose showing served as an indictment of the party's revamped process for electing a leader. Under its new system, the former method of electing delegates to the leadership convention was replaced by giving a direct vote to each party member, the winner being determined by tabulating a victor who would then "take all" of the riding's 100 convention points. Though he enjoyed at least some support in ridings across Canada, Orchard's campaign was particularly successful in Saskatchewan and British Columbia—provinces in which CCAFT had been strong as well. Not one to be deterred by critics, he went on to run as the Progressive Conservative candidate for the riding of Prince Albert in the 2000 federal election, this time finishing in fourth place with just over 12 percent of the popular vote.

Orchard ran for the Progressive Conservative Party leadership again in 2003. Finishing a strong third at the convention, he supported Peter MacKay on the condition that the PC Party run a candidate in every riding in the next federal election. MacKay soon after entered into talks with the Canadian Alliance and negotiated a merger of the two parties. Orchard fought ratification of the merger in both the party membership and in court, but both efforts failed.

Orchard continues to farm in the Borden area and serves as president of CCAFT. If success at the polls has eluded him thus far, a degree of political influence has not. In addition to authoring a best-selling book, he has written numerous articles on free trade, environmental issues and Canadian politics, and maintains a busy schedule as a guest speaker at various public forums.

TIM KRYWULAK, CARLETON UNIVERSITY

SOURCES AND FURTHER READING: Orchard, David. 1993. *The Fight for Canada: Four Centuries of Resistance to US Expansionism.* Toronto: Stoddart.

## ORMISTON, JAMES NORRIS (1915–1977).

James Ormiston was born in Regina on May 30, 1915, to Mr. and Mrs. George T. Ormiston. While still a child his family moved to Cupar, where he attended primary and secondary schools. Ormiston furthered his education in Scotland. Upon the outbreak of World War II, Ormiston joined the Canadian Army, where he became a member of the 14 Field Company, Royal Corps of Engineers. He served with the Corps until 1946, rising to the rank of Sergeant.

Upon his discharge from the army, James Ormiston returned to the Cupar area, where he farmed, raised Hereford cows and sold insurance for the Great West Life Insurance Company. In 1949 he married Isabel Turner, with whom he would have one daughter, Valerie.

Ormiston made his first foray into electoral politics with a run for the federal seat of Melville in 1953. Running against federal agriculture minister Jimmy Gardiner, he lost. Through his work in the provincial Progressive Conservative Party, Ormiston became close friends with provincial leader Alvin Hamilton. Ormiston carried the Progressive Conservative Party of Saskatchewan colors in Melville during the 1956 election. He lost. In the meantime, Ormiston's local prominence led local Conservatives to lobby him to seek the nomination in the federal election of 1957, but he again lost. Finally, however, in the 1958 election, Ormiston defeated Jimmy Gardiner.

Ormiston served as an MP until his defeat in 1968. Ormiston, a friendly extrovert, quickly became a popular member of the House of Commons, described by Paul Martin, Sr., as "the amiable member from Melville." Always a hard worker, Ormiston was keenly interested in veterans affairs, serving on the Veterans Affairs Parliamentary Committee, a committee that he would later chair. Ormiston was fluently bilingual; he was one of the first western MPs who spoke French.

Defeated by Lorne Nystrom in 1968, Ormiston returned to Cupar, where he became the town's mayor. He served in this capacity until his death in 1977.

In his leisure time, Ormiston was heavily involved with the Masons and Shriners. During the war, he had formed an affinity for the Salvation Army, an organization which he promoted throughout his life.

ROB PAUL, DIEFENBAKER CENTRE

## OSIKA, RON (b. 1939).

Ron Osika was born in Hafford and brought up in the Battlefords. He served as the MLA for Melville from 1995 to 2003.

Osika served with the Royal Canadian Mounted Police in Manitoba and northwestern Ontario for twenty-five years before he retired as a Staff Sergeant in 1981. He then took on management positions at the Saskatchewan Crop Insurance Corporation for over a decade.

In 1993, Osika first attempted to enter politics contesting the Reform Party nomination in Yorkton-Melville, but was defeated by Garry Breitkreuz. In June 1995, he was elected for the first time to the Saskatchewan

Legislative Assembly as a Liberal MLA for Melville. Following Lynda Haverstock's resignation in November of that year, he became the interim leader of the Official Opposition until the new leader was elected in November 1996.

Osika was one of only three Liberals elected to the 1999 government, but held the balance of power when the NDP failed to carry enough seats to form a majority government. Liberal leader Melenchuk took advantage of minority government to form a coalition government with the NDP. As part of the coalition deal Osika was appointed Speaker of the Legislative Assembly. In February 2001, Osika resigned as Speaker and was appointed minister of Municipal Affairs and Housing in Lorne Calvert's coalition government. He later took responsibility for the Saskatchewan Water Corporation and the Saskatchewan Liquor and Gaming Authority.

In October 2001, the Liberal Party elected David Karwacki leader and requested that Osika and Melenchuk leave the coalition cabinet. Both declined and sat as independents while remaining in Lorne Calvert's cabinet.

In 2002, Municipal Affairs and Housing was amalgamated with Aboriginal Affairs and Intergovernmental Affairs into the newly-formed Government Relations department of which Osika became minister. In February 2003, he added the minister responsible for Saskatchewan Property Management Corporation to his portfolio. Contesting the seat of Melville–Saltcoats as a New Democrat in the 2003 election, Osika was defeated.

JACQUELINE M. ROY, UNIVERSITY OF REGINA

**PANKIW, JIM** (b. 1966). Jim Pankiw was a highly controversial Reform and Canadian Alliance MP who was eventually expelled from the party for his comments on aboriginal people.

Born on August 7, 1966, Pankiw was raised on the family farm in Unity. He attended the University of Saskatchewan completing a degree in anatomy in 1988. He continued his education, studying to become a chiropractor. He earned a Doctorate of Chiropractic from the Canadian Memorial Chiropractic College in Toronto in 1992 and was trained as an acupuncturist at the International College of Acupuncture in Sri Lanka. In 1992, he established a chiropractic practice in Saskatoon where he worked until his election to the House of Commons.

In 1997, Pankiw first contested the riding of Saskatoon Humboldt for the Reform Party. Narrowly elected, Pankiw attracted some attention during the term for some of his comments regarding the government's affirmative action programs and for some of his criticisms of the Federation of Saskatchewan Indian Nations. Pankiw was re-elected for the Reform party's successor, the Canadian Alliance, in 2000. Shortly after the election, he made several more comments that many perceived as racist. In September 2001, he was suspended form the Canadian Alliance caucus as his party was eager to distance itself from Pankiw's comments. After caucusing for a year with the Democratic Representative caucus, a group of former Alliance MPs critical of Stockwell Day's leadership of the Alliance party, Pankiw was again on his own as he was not allowed to rejoin this party when the rest of the caucus rejoined the Alliance.

Sitting as an independent, Pankiw caused a controversy with a series of newsletters he sent to his constituents. Harshly critical of affirmative action programs, aboriginal crime rates, and First Nations government, Pankiw was once again in the national spotlight. His newsletters attracted a great deal of attention and sparked protests from a variety of community groups. Pankiw used the controversy as a basis to run for mayor of Saskatoon. Although he lost, he surprised many by garnering over 22 percent of the vote. He remained in the House of Commons as an independent. In the 2004 election, Pankiw finished a strong fourth, winning over 20 percent of the vote.

BRETT QUIRING

## PARKER, REGINALD JOHN MARSDEN

(1881–1948). R. J. M. Parker was born on February 7, 1881, at Liskeard, Cornwall, England, to John William Parker and Fanny Marsden Parker, who were both English. Parker was educated at Manammead School, Plymouth, Devon, England, and St. James College, Whitney, Oxfordshire, England, and was a member of the Church of England. He came to Canada in 1898 and on June 5, 1904, was married at Saltcoats to Cecil Margaret, daughter of James Henry Edward Mapleton of Shillingthorpe, Saskatchewan.

SAB R-A 636 (2)

R. J. M. PARKER

They raised a family of five children, four of whom achieved higher education and received university degrees.

Upon arriving in Canada, R. J. M. Parker worked as a farmhand for two years, earning five dollars a month. He then established his own homestead at Togo in the North-West Territories. He was the first councilor in the rural municipality of Cote from 1904 to 1910, when a local improvement district was organized, and was municipal reeve from 1906 to 1932. Parker was also a member of the Royal Arch Masons.

Originally a Conservative, R. J. M. Parker was elected to the Saskatchewan Legislative Assembly in June 1929 as a member for the Pelly constituency. From 1929 to 1934, Parker was a member of the Liberal opposition. Parker was re-elected in every election until Premier Patterson's Liberal Administration defeat. He was a member of cabinet during the depression and was appointed minister of Municipal Affairs in the Honorable James Garfield Gardiner's cabinet on July 19, 1934. This was a difficult position to hold during the depression years. He held this position until 1944 when his party was defeated by the CCF. He was re-appointed as a member of Honorable W. J. Patterson's cabinet on November 1, 1935, and was re-elected in the general election of 1938. However, Parker was defeated in the general election of 1944.

In 1945, the prime minister phoned Parker and offered him the position of Lieutenant-Governor. On June 25, he was sworn in as Lieutenant-Governor of Saskatchewan at the age of sixty-four. Mr. and Mrs. Parker quickly assumed the responsibilities of the position and in a very short time held dinners for three ambassadors. He died in office on March 23, 1948, six days after hosting a dinner for the High Commissioner of New Zealand. Parker was given a state funeral with a military procession through downtown Regina.

HEATHER WILSON

## PATRICK, THOMAS ALFRED (1854–1943). Thomas Alfred Patrick, physician and legislator, fought the election campaign of 1898 with buttons proclaiming "No

annexation to Manitoba." In that campaign he was the first to propose the present boundaries of Saskatchewan and Alberta—and was almost alone in wishing to extend the boundaries north to 60 degrees.

Born at Ilderton, Ontario, on December 23, 1864, he graduated in medicine from the University of Western Ontario in 1888. He practised medicine and surgery at Saltcoats until 1894 and in Yorkton until 1939.

COURTESY OF C. J. HOUSTON
AND C. S. HOUSTON

T. A. PATRICK

In an age when physicians tended to be over-represented in political office, Patrick was the first physician to seek office (1881) and the first to be elected (1897) to a legislature within the present boundaries of Saskatchewan, He sat in nine sessions of the Legislative Assembly of the North-West Territories, initially as an independent supporter of Premier Frederick Haultain, but always as one of the strongest proponents in the fight for a more responsible form of territorial government. His election campaign of 1898 helped turn the tide against the idea of one large prairie province, or of one southern ranching province and a northern mixed-farm province, or of making each of the four existing postal districts into provinces.

Patrick was an active promoter of Saskatchewan's third hospital, the Yorkton Queen Victoria Hospital. By chance, a few seconds after midnight on September 1, 1905, the day that Saskatchewan officially entered confederation (though the proclamation was not signed until September 5), he delivered the province's first baby. Jennie was born to Trintie and Thomas Luke Gibney. On February 1, 1928, four hours after the bells had rung to celebrate the assumption of city status by Yorkton, Patrick delivered Muriel, born to Roslyn and Mayme Young—assisted in the delivery room by Jennie Gibney, R.N.

Thomas Patrick died on September 8, 1943.

C. STUART HOUSTON, SASKATOON

REFERENCES: Houston, C. J., and C. S. Houston. 1980. *Pioneer of Vision: The Reminiscences of T. A. Patrick, M.D.* Saskatoon: Western Producer Prairie Books.

## PATTERSON, WILLIAM JOHN (1886–1976).

The response to two signal events in the history of Saskatchewan—the Great Depression of the 1930s and the Second World War—fell largely to the Liberal government of Premier William Patterson, which was in power from 1935, when James Gardiner departed to serve in the federal cabinet, until the landslide victory of the Co-operative Commonwealth Federation in the provincial election of 1944.

The sixth premier of Saskatchewan, Patterson was the first premier to be born in the province, the first to have seen military service, the first to take office as a bachelor—he did not marry until 1937. Patterson himself was described as a popular, if lacklustre, leader. His government was successful in obtaining financial assistance from Ottawa to fight the Depression, made a forceful contribution to the reappraisal of federal-provincial relations at the time of the Rowell-Sirois Report, and passed important legislation in areas such as health care, taxation and labour standards which helped to establish the legislative framework familiar to citizens of

Saskatchewan to this day.

Yet Patterson failed to make a strong or lasting impression as a public figure. Even at the time, he felt compelled to defend the record of what some called a "do-nothing government," and to point out that his government had managed to maintain public services and government credit in the face of adversity.

William Patterson was born

SAB R-A 629 (1)

WILLIAM PATTERSON

at Grenfell, in what was then the Assiniboia District of the North-West Territories. His father, John Patterson, a railway section foreman, began work on the Grenfell section of the CPR in 1882. His mother, Catherine Fraser, had traveled out from Scotland. They built a small house at Grenfell with lumber brought overland from the end of the railway line at Broadview, and William, the first of their five children, was born there on May 13, 1886.

After leaving school at the age of fifteen, Patterson worked in a bank, and then for the provincial Department of Telephones, before enlisting as a cavalry officer in 1916. He served in France, and was wounded in September of 1918, in the same week that two of his brothers were also wounded in action. Returning to Saskatchewan, he studied law for a year with Grenfell lawyer G. C. Neff, and then moved to Windthorst where he opened an insurance and financial agency.

Patterson had displayed a precocious interest in politics, attending the first provincial leadership convention in 1905 before he was old enough to vote. In 1921, he was elected as the MLA for the Pipestone constituency, and served in a number of cabinet portfolios in the Gardiner governments. He became leader of

the Liberal Party and premier of Saskatchewan in 1935.

Facing the serious crisis of the Depression, the Patterson government sought to preserve and extend social programs which would relieve the financial difficulties of citizens and municipalities, while at the same time protecting the fiscal reputation of the province. The government instituted a sales tax to assist the beleaguered education system, extended pension and debt relief legislation, and expanded publicly funded care for tuberculosis, cancer and polio. The government also enacted legislation supporting the establishment of credit unions, permitting workers to form and join trade unions, and improving labour standards with respect to such issues as hours of work and days of rest.

Though Patterson believed strongly in encouraging the initiative of individuals, he also believed that government could play a vital role in society, particularly in assisting those who faced difficulties as a result of financial adversity or ill health. He saw the taxation revenue necessary to support well-administered government programs as a good investment, and placed great importance on careful management of public resources.

Though the Patterson government, and Patterson himself, were respected as conscientious and fiscally-prudent stewards of provincial resources, the government faced growing competition from populist political parties based in western Canada, particularly the Social Credit Party and the Co-operative Commonwealth Federation. The CCF, under the leadership of Tommy Douglas, swept the Liberals from power in 1944.

Patterson stepped down as party leader in 1948, and resigned from the legislature in the same year to take up a post with the federal Board of Transport Commissioners. He was appointed as the first Saskatchewan-born Lieutenant-Governor in 1951, and served in that position until 1958.

Patterson faced straitened circumstances in his retirement, as there was no pension coverage for his years in the legislature. In March of 1958, Premier Douglas introduced a special bill which would provide a pension to Patterson at the maximum level provided under recently-passed legislation. Patterson lived in quiet retirement until his death on June 10, 1976.

BETH BILSON, UNIVERSITY OF SASKATCHEWAN

## PAULSON, WILHELM HANS (1857–1935).

On August 14, 1857, Wilhelm Paulson was born to Paul Erlendson Paulson and his wife (née Gundun) in Iceland. His ancestors were agriculturalists in the mountains of Northern Iceland.

Wilhelm Paulson came to Canada in 1883,  having never attended a structured school. He had been instructed by his parents and was also self-taught. On September 21, 1897, Paulson married Anna Kristin, a daughter of Nikulas Johnson of North Dakota. Paulson was a hardware merchant and member of the Lutheran church. He stood as a candidate for Gimli in the Manitoba legislature in 1910 but was unsuccessful. He and his wife raised a family of four children.

SAB R-A 670 (2)

WILHELM PAULSON

Paulson had a keen interest in the colonization of western Canada and devoted thirty years of his life to that work, only receiving pay as a Dominion government official for nine years, from 1896 to 1905. He made several trips to Europe and the United States on immigration work and was in favor of thoroughly Canadianizing every class of foreigners arriving in the country. He was first elected to the Saskatchewan legislature in 1912 for Wynyard and was re-elected in 1917. He did not run in the following election but was re-elected in a by-election on October 20, 1924, to fill the vacancy caused by George W. Robertson's resignation. He was re-elected in 1925 and 1929 for Quill Plains.

Wilhelm Paulson passed away in 1935.

HEATHER WILSON

## PEDERSON, MARTIN PEDER (1921–2001).

Martin Pederson was born on December 5, 1921, on his family's farm near Hawarden. He flew 92 missions with the Royal Air Force during World War II and after the war returned to Saskatchewan and farmed near Hawarden. He became involved in politics through the provincial Progressive Conservative Party and between 1950 and 1958 served terms as provincial president and national vice-president of the Young Conservative Association and president of the Saskatoon PC Association. These positions led to his selection as provincial PC leader in 1958.

In the 1956 provincial election the PCs received 2 percent of the popular vote and elected no members to the legislature, but Pederson was optimistic that he could improve the party's fortunes by capitalizing on the popularity of John Diefenbaker, the federal PC leader. Pederson was at least partially successful. He increased the party's share of the popular vote substantially in the 1960, 1964 and 1967 provincial elections and in 1964 was elected to the legislature in the constituency of Arm River. He was the first Conservative representative in the chamber since the party had been wiped out in the 1934 provincial election. Diefenbaker, however, never provided significant assistance to his provincial colleagues and the provincial Liberal leader Ross Thatcher also courted his tacit support. Pederson was the only Conservative elected to the legislature during this period and in the 1967 provincial election the PC's share of the popular vote declined compared to the 1964 contest. Pederson lost his seat and in 1968 resigned the party leadership.

During Pederson's tenure, Thatcher attempted to polarize all anti-CCF/NDP sentiment behind the provincial Liberal Party, a strategy that often made the PC Party's position difficult. While some Conservatives were attracted to Thatcher's ideological opposition to the CCF/NDP, many of the voters who supported Diefenbaker federally, and who Pederson hoped to attract to the provincial PC Party, were traditional CCF/NDP supporters. While Thatcher promoted cooperation between Liberals and Conservatives, Pederson's overall goal was to establish the PCs as a clear alternative to both the CCF/NDP and the Liberals. Despite his lack of electoral success, Pederson was credited with keeping the PC Party viable during the 1960s, which contributed to the party's revival in the 1970s.

In addition to politics and farming, Pederson pursued a career in business and

WEST'S STUDIO, REGINA•SAB R-A 8396

MARTIN PEDERSON

operated both trucking and insurance companies. Between 1983 and 1987, under the PC government of Grant Devine, Pederson served as chair of the Saskatchewan Liquor Board. In 1998, in one of his last public statements, he strongly criticized the four PC MLAs who joined with a number of Liberal MLAs to form the Saskatchewan Party. He argued that he had maintained the PC Party under far more difficult circumstances than these MLAs faced and felt the formation of the Saskatchewan Party was a betrayal. Pederson passed away on September 1, 2001.

MIKE FEDYK, REGINA

**FURTHER READING:** Eisler, Dale. 1987. *Rumours of Glory: Saskatchewan and the Thatcher Years.* Edmonton: Hurtig Publishers. • Wilson, Barry. 1980. *The Politics of Defeat: The Decline of the Liberal Party in Saskatchewan.* Saskatoon: Western Producer Prairie Books.

## PEPPER, JAMES AUBURN (1915–1985).

Auburn Pepper was born August 9, 1915, in Goodwater. He attended public school in the Delight rural school district and high school in Goodwater. He farmed in the Goodwater area. He served on the local school board, was a wheat pool delegate, a rural municipal councillor and a member of the United Church.

By 1940 Pepper was an active member of the CCF. He lived in the Weyburn provincial constituency which after 1944 was represented in the Saskatchewan legislature by Premier T. C. Douglas. He served as president of the constituency for several years and then was nominated to contest the Weyburn riding for the CCF in 1964, after Douglas had left the province to become national leader of the

New Democratic Party. Pepper won election and was re-elected in 1967, 1971, 1975 and 1978. From 1971 to 1982, during the years of the Blakeney government, he served as deputy Speaker of the Legislative Assembly and NDP caucus chairman.

Weyburn was never a safe seat for either the CCF or the NDP. In 1960 Tommy Douglas was elected by less than 600 votes. In 1961 a by-election was held in the riding to replace him after he went to Ottawa; it was won by the Liberals. This made Pepper's five consecutive victories that much more remarkable, especially considering that the 1964 and 1967 provincial elections were won by Ross Thatcher and the Liberal Party.

WEST'S STUDIO, REGINA•SAB R-A 8367

JAMES PEPPER

GEORGE HOFFMAN, UNIVERSITY OF REGINA

**PERLEY, ERNEST EDWARD** (1877–1948). Ernest Perley was a forceful advocate for the interests of western farmers in Ottawa and is particularly noteworthy because he was the only pre-Depression Conservative in Saskatchewan to politically survive the Depression.

Born November 23, 1877, in Maugerville, New Brunswick, Perley moved west with his parents in 1883 to settle on a farm near Wolseley. His father, William Dell Perley, a staunch Conservative, was elected to the Territorial Council, House of Commons and served as Saskatchewan's first Senator. He set the tone for Ernest Perley's eventual career in politics. Finishing high school, Ernest Perley continued his education at Wesley College in Winnipeg. He returned to Wolseley and took over his father's farm upon his death in 1909. Although operating a large farm and a grain elevator at Wolseley, Perley took an active interest in his community. In 1909 he was elected to the first council of the rural municipality of Wolseley and became involved in numerous community posts, serving as president of both the Wolseley Agricultural Society and the Wolseley Board of Trade.

In 1921 he made his first attempt at a seat in the House of Commons in the riding of Qu'Appelle, but was badly beaten in the Progressive sweep of that year. He returned to municipal politics and later that year was elected as the mayor of Wolseley, a post he would hold for two years. Perley continued to manage his farm until 1930 when he again attempted election in Qu'Appelle, this time successfully.

During the short life of the Bennett government, Perley was influential in the government's agricultural policy and helped to frame the 1935 *Canadian Wheat Board Act*. After the act passed he was appointed to the wheat board advisory committee where he fought to establish a constant price for wheat consumed within Canada. In 1935 the Conservatives received a thrashing at the polls, but Perley managed to narrowly survive the sweep. At the time of his re-election he was the only Conservative elected in Saskatchewan at either the provincial or federal level, and one out of only a handful of Conservatives from anywhere on the prairies.

Being Saskatchewan's lone Conservative conferred a leadership position on Perley, who began to spend more time rebuilding his party. He was again re-elected in 1940, but was defeated in 1945 by the CCF's candidate,

Gladys Strum. He spent the last days of his life farming and working towards rebuilding the Conservatives. He died while attending an executive meeting of the Saskatchewan Progressive Conservative Party on August 16, 1948.

BRETT QUIRING

## PERLEY, WILLIAM DELL (1838–1909). As an early pioneer and as both the first Member of Parliament and Member of the Senate representing Saskatchewan, William Perley played a leading role in the formation of many of the province's future institutions and was an early advocate for the future province.

Perley was born in Gladstone, New Brunswick, on February 6, 1838. He was schooled in the public school system and finished his education at Sackville Academy and the Baptist Seminary. He was exposed to politics at an early age through his father, William Edward Perley, who served over twenty years in the New Brunswick House of Assembly, seven of those years in cabinet. In 1860, Perley moved to Maugerville, New Brunswick, where he began farming. He entered into political life shortly thereafter, serving seven years on the County Council. In 1878, he first contested a seat in the House of Commons when he ran for the Conservatives in Sunbury. He was narrowly defeated and was again defeated in 1882.

In 1883, Perley moved to Wolseley where he established a farm and later the local grain elevator. He took an active part in organizing the first municipal council to which he was elected chairman. In 1885 and 1886 he was elected to the territorial council. He was a supporter of Dewdney's policy of discouraging immediate local authority and the gradual extension of power toward eventual province-

hood. Perley was part of a delegation to the federal government representing the council's territorial concerns.

When the territories were granted representation in the House of Commons in 1887, Perley contested Assiniboia East for the Conservatives and was elected handily. However, his term in the House of Commons was short when the minister of the Interior, Thomas White, suddenly died in 1888. Perley resigned his seat to create an opening for Edgar Dewdney, whom John A. Macdonald wanted to fill the vacancy. Later in the year Perley was called to the Senate, becoming the first Senator from the future province of Saskatchewan. In 1890, the government changed the procedure for the allocation of funds to the territories when it proposed to pass a line-by-line estimate for expenditures. This alarmed Perley, who worried that this threatened the power of the territorial council to allocate funds as they saw fit. Along with James Lougheed, Perley managed to stop the government plan and convinced the government to approve funds for the territories in a lump sum, allowing the local authorities to allocate the funds as they saw fit.

Perley remained active in the community, serving as the mayor of Wolseley during much of his time in the Senate and remaining there until his death on July 15, 1909.

BRETT QUIRING

FURTHER READING: Thomas, Lewis. 1978. *The Struggle for Responsible Government in the North-West Territories.* 2nd Ed. Toronto: University of Toronto Press.

## PETERSEN, SHERWIN HOLGER (b. 1953). Sherwin Petersen served two terms in the Conservative government in Saskatchewan during the 1980s. He was one of the Tories

charged during an RCMP investigation into the misuse of public money by MLAs and party officials.

Peterson was born near Rose Valley in 1953. He grew up on the family farm. After high school, he studied farm machinery mechanics at Kelsey Institute in Saskatoon. In 1975 he started his own farm in the Rose Valley area, and eventually branched out into the seed cleaning business. Petersen was elected to the Saskatchewan legislature in 1982, as the Progressive Conservative member for the rural constituency of Kelvington–Wadena. He served as legislative secretary to the minister of Agriculture from 1985 until 1989, when he was appointed minister of Highways and Transportation. He held that post until November 1, 1991. He ran in the October 1991 provincial election but lost his seat when the New Democratic Party, then led by Roy Romanow, defeated the Conservatives. In 1993, Petersen once more ran for public office as the Progressive Conservative candidate in the federal riding of Mackenzie, but finished a distant fourth.

In April 1995, Petersen was charged with two counts of fraud over $5,000 and one count of conspiracy to commit fraud. He was accused of using false expense claims to get cash, a video camera, a computer, and a computer hard drive. At the end of a lengthy trial, he was found guilty on one count of fraud, but was acquitted on the other two charges. He was given a discharge, ordered to do 240 hours of community service work and to pay restitution of $9,285. He was also placed on probation for three years. Petersen spent his 240 hours of community service work cleaning sewers and repairing waterworks.

GERRY JONES, REGINA

**PHELPS, JOSEPH LEE** (1899–1983). Joseph Phelps, minister of natural resources and industrial development (1944–1948) in the first Saskatchewan CCF government of Premier Tommy Douglas, was born in Belleville, Ontario, on August 12, 1899. He came west with his family in 1909 to a homestead north of Wilkie (NE quarter of section 26-41-19-W3), on land his father, George Phelps, had registered in 1905. Their first family home on the prairies was a wooden, one-room, twelve-foot by sixteen-foot lean-to shack, containing a small four-foot-high attic area which provided modest sleeping

SASKATCHEWAN NDP PHOTO ARCHIVES

JOE PHELPS

space for the children, Eva, Lulu, Don and Joe. In his mid-teens Joe Phelps took on the responsibility of operating the family farm while working for the Narrow Lake Telephone Company.

Joe Phelps' political career began when he was elected district director of the Saskatchewan Grain Growers Association at age seventeen in 1916. He participated in a convention in 1926 which merged the Farmers Union of Canada and the Saskatchewan Grain Growers Association into the United Farmers of Canada (Saskatchewan Section).

Joe Phelps was greatly influenced by listening to J. S. Woodsworth, founder of the Cooperative Commonwealth Federation (CCF), who later asked Phelps to join the Farmers Union and attend meetings with him. Joe Phelps played a major role in the formation of the Saskatchewan Farmer-Labour

Party, founded in Saskatoon in July 1932, which was a joining of the United Farmers of Canada (Saskatchewan Section), and the Saskatchewan Independent Labour Party.

In the 1938 Saskatchewan provincial election, Joe Phelps successfully entered politics as an elected CCF member from the Saltcoats constituency, holding the seat until 1943 as an Opposition MLA, and subsequently as a Government MLA. The CCF swept into power on June 15, 1944, and Phelps was a minister of the Crown from 1944 to 1948.

The election of a socialist government in Saskatchewan created much grist for the media mill all across North America. Comments ranged from anti-business sentiment to charges of a Russian communist connection. Undaunted, the CCF government set about putting their programs in place, with the initial thrusts being in health, farm security, labour, education and natural resources.

As minister of Natural Resources and Industrial Development in the new government, Joe Phelps was instrumental in establishing the Saskatchewan Fur Marketing Board, the Fish Marketing Board and the Timber Board, all created to facilitate the orderly marketing and conservation of these natural resources. Passage of the *Crown Corporations Act* in March 1945 established the framework for the Saskatchewan government's entry into business enterprise, which enabled Joe Phelps to spearhead the creation of Saskatchewan Clay Products, Saskatchewan Leather Products and Saskatchewan Wool Products in the summer of 1945. Other initiatives undertaken by Phelps were the Saskatchewan Air Ambulance Service, the Sodium Sulfate Plant at Chaplin, and Saskatchewan Government Airways. In his role as minister in charge of the Saskatchewan Power Commission, the forerunner of the

Saskatchewan Power Corporation, Phelps began the program which saw the electrification of rural Saskatchewan, and by 1958 47,000 farms had electrical power. Through his initiative, legislation was passed establishing the Western Development Museum on August 25, 1947, and he would later serve as chairman of the board from 1949 to 1961.

Joe Phelps' approach of tackling issues head on, and letting the chips fall where they may, became a political liability. This trait, combined with long absences from his Saltcoats constituency while working on so many provincial issues, probably led to his political defeat in June 1948.

It wasn't long before he was approached with the challenge of revitalizing the Saskatchewan Farmers Union. In 1949 the Saskatchewan Farmers Union, which was called at that time the United Farmers of Canada (Saskatchewan Section), had declined in number to a few hundred paid-up members and was $12,000 in debt. By 1954, Joe Phelps, as outgoing president, was able to report that membership in the Saskatchewan Farmers Union was over 100,000.

In 1952, the provincial government established a Royal Commission on Agriculture and Rural Life, whose mandate was to investigate social and economic conditions in rural Saskatchewan. Joe Phelps was appointed to the Commission and worked more or less co-operatively with the other members over a five year period, but in the end he could not come to total agreement with them on three areas: farm produce prices, rural depopulation, and farm organizations. He issued a Minority Report explaining his position.

At the Western Development Museum in Saskatoon in August 1982, Joe Phelps was inducted into the Saskatchewan Agricultural Hall of Fame in honour of his many accomplishments. At 81, Phelps was still organizing, now as vice-president of Action Now, a provincial senior citizens organization.

After a long, active and determined life, Joe Phelps died at age eighty-two on March 15, 1983, and is buried in the Wilkie cemetery.

DOUG CHARRETT, PRINCE ALBERT

**FURTHER READING:** Dobbin, Murray. 1981. One-And-A-Half Men: The Story of Jim Brady and Malcolm Norris. Vancouver: New Star Books.

**PICKERING, ROBERT HUGH** (b. 1932). Robert Pickering was among the handful of former Progressive Conservative Members of the Legislative Assembly who were cleared of charges resulting from an RCMP investigation. The investigation, known as Project Fiddle, looked into allegations of misuse of public money by Conservatives during the 1980s.

Pickering was born in Avonlea in 1932. He grew up in the area and eventually owned his own farm.

Pickering was elected to the Saskatchewan legislature in 1978 as the Progressive Conservative representative for the rural constituency of Bengough–Milestone, which includes Avonlea. When the Conservatives won government in 1982, under the leadership of Grant Devine, he was appointed to the cabinet. He served as minister of Rural Affairs from May 8, 1982, to May 5, 1983; minister of Rural Development from May 5, 1983, to July 14, 1983; and minister of Parks and Renewable Resources from July 14, 1983, to January 16, 1985. Even though he was dropped from Devine's cabinet in 1985, he ran for the Conservatives in the provincial election the following year and won. He did not seek re-election in the 1991 provincial election. In January 1997, Pickering was charged with defrauding taxpayers by submitting nearly $27,000 worth of false MLA expense claims through his communications allowance. He was accused of receiving cash for work that was not done. He chose trial by judge alone and was found not guilty.

GERRY JONES, REGINA

**PREBBLE, PETER W.** (b. 1950). Peter Prebble was born in Essex, England, on September 13, 1950. Educated in Prince Edward Island, he received a Bachelor of Administration from the University of Prince Edward Island in 1972. Coming to Saskatchewan, Prebble continued his education at the University of Saskatchewan, earning a Masters of Education in 1979.

Active in the environmental and anti-uranium movements, Prebble soon became involved in the Saskatchewan NDP and took part in the heated debates within the party over whether the government should encouragement development in Saskatchewan's uranium industry. In 1978 he won a hotly contested NDP nomination in Saskatoon University, which was largely waged over the uranium issue. Elected in the 1978 general election, Prebble continued to press the government on environmental issues and continued to be critical of its uranium policy.

Defeated in Grant Devine's sweep of 1982, Prebble returned to private life, but returned to the legislature again in 1986 when he was elected to represent the constituency of Saskatoon Greystone. Serving out the term in Opposition, Prebble faced strong competition in 1991 from Liberal leader Lynda Haverstock, and narrowly lost. Once again returning to private life, Prebble worked for a variety of community and environmental organizations in Saskatoon, including as the coordinator of the lobby group Saskatoon Communities for Children.

Prebble returned to politics again in 1999, winning back the seat of Saskatoon Greystone. During the term, he served most notably as co-chair of the Special Committee to Prevent the Abuse and Sexual Exploitation of Children Through the Sex Trade. The committee undertook extensive consultation throughout the province and made many recommendations on how to reform the provincial law. After Lorne Calvert became premier, Prebble's influence grew. He was appointed Legislative Secretary to the minister of Energy and Mines responsible for energy conservation. The position was responsible for helping Saskatchewan meet its emissions commitments under the Koyoto Accord. Under his guidance, Saskatchewan implemented a number of measures to reduce pollution, most notably through the construction of large-scale wind power generation. Shortly before the 2003 election, Prebble was promoted to minister of Energy Conservation.

Re-elected in 2003, Prebble was moved into the ministry of Corrections and Public Safety.

BRETT QUIRING

## PROCTER, ARTHUR THOMAS (1886–1964).

Although he served six years in cabinet, Arthur Procter is most noted for leading much of the Liberal Opposition to the first Douglas government.

Born in Oswald, Manitoba, in 1886, Procter was educated at St. John's College and later the University of Manitoba where he earned a Law degree in 1910. In 1911, he came to Moosomin where he established a law practice. He served as Crown prosecutor in the Moosomin district in 1914 and 1915 until

SAB R-A 8162

ARTHUR PROCTER

he enlisted in the Canadian Army. Serving with the Fort Garry Horse, Procter saw action in France and was wounded in combat. After the war he returned to Moosomin to resume his law practice.

Procter first came to public prominence in 1928 when he served as assistant counsel for the Royal Grain Commission. The next year he first contested the election for the Liberals in the constituency of Moosomin, but was defeated. Riding a wave of anti-government sentiment, Procter was narrowly elected in 1934. He was re-elected in 1938 and was appointed to cabinet as minister of Highways and Transportation after the defeat of Charles Dunn. In 1944, Procter was one of only five members of the Liberal government to be elected in the face of the CCF's electoral sweep. Along with former premier William Patterson, Procter was the only former minister who was re-elected. Procter played an important role in the Liberal Opposition, leading many of the Opposition's attacks on the policy of the Douglas government.

In 1948, Procter retired from politics and accepted an appointment to the Saskatchewan Court of Appeal where he remained until his retirement in 1961. He died in Regina on July 12, 1964.

BRETT QUIRING

## PROCTOR, DICK (b. 1941).

Dick Proctor was born in Toronto on February 12, 1941. He was educated at Carleton University, graduating in 1966 with a Bachelor of Journalism. After a brief term at the Edmonton *Journal*, he moved to the Toronto *Telegram* in 1966, where he co-wrote a popular consumer advocacy column, "Action Line." He left the paper in 1968 to work for the CBC and later the *Globe and Mail*, writing primarily on sports.

In 1978 he moved to Saskatchewan, accepting a job as Premier Allan Blakeney's press secretary, and figured prominently in the coordination of the NDP's 1978 election campaign. After briefly working as federal NDP leader Ed Broadbent's secretary, he was appointed to establish and run the Saskatchewan government's office in Ottawa in order to facilitate better communications between Saskatchewan and the federal government. In 1983 he was appointed research director for the National Union of Provincial Government Employees and in 1986 was appointed project co-odinator of the Canadian Labour Congress in Latin America.

In 1989 he was appointed Federal Secretary of the NDP, the party's top administrative position. Proctor moved back to Saskatchewan in 1992 to briefly take a position in the Department of Health. He had kept in close contact with the provincial NDP by co-ordinating publicity for the party in both the 1982 and 1986 election campaigns. In 1993 he ran the federal NDP campaign in Saskatchewan and afterward was appointed provincial secretary of the party, a position he held until 1996. In 1997 he won the hotly contested NDP nomination in the riding of Palliser and was elected later in the year.

Proctor has held several important positions within party caucus, serving as the party's critic for Agriculture and Defence, and was elected caucus chair in 1999. He received national attention in 1998 when, during a flight, he overheard a conversation between solicitor-general Andy Scott and a friend. In the discussion, Scott predetermined the outcome of the judicial inquiry into the RCMP's conduct at a 1997 meeting of APEC. Proctor made public the notes he recorded of the discussion, and the resulting political scandal forced Scott to resign from cabinet on November 28, 1998. In the 2000 election, Proctor was re-elected, but he was narrowly defeated in 2004.

BRETT QUIRING

## RAMSLAND, SARAH KATHERINE

(1882–1964). Sarah Ramsland, MLA for Pelly from 1919 to 1925, was Saskatchewan's first female MLA.

Sarah McEwen was born on July 19, 1882, in Minnesota, the granddaughter of a Democratic member of the state legislature. She taught school before her marriage to Magnus O. (Max) Ramsland. The Ramslands moved to Buchanan after 1905, where Max brokered real estate.

Max Ramsland was elected the Liberal MLA for Pelly in 1917 but died in the influenza epidemic of November 1918. The Liberals needed a candidate, and felt obliged to support his widow and three children. Following a

SAB R-A 7553

SARAH RAMSLAND

precedent set the previous year in British Columbia, they solved both problems by inviting Mrs. Ramsland to run in the by-election to fill her husband's seat.

Women's issues were not raised in the campaign. Sarah Ramsland's opponent was an independent with a platform similar to the Liberal platform. Ramsland made no claim to moral superiority and promised no political reforms. Neither her sex nor her widowhood made much difference to the voters, who elected her, although with a smaller majority than her husband had received.

Ramsland's performance in the legislature was clean but undistinguished. In her first session, Premier Martin invited her to second the throne speech, but she declined the honour, and rarely spoke. When the provincial franchise had been granted to women three years earlier, many people hoped that women's direct participation in politics would lead to more honest government and more progressive social legislation. But Ramsland was neither a feminist nor a social-reform activist. She was simply a loyal Liberal backbencher. Ironically, the election of Saskatchewan's first female MLA represented the triumph of traditional politics over the contemporary feminist notion that women had a special contribution to make to public life.

Ramsland was re-elected in 1921, though by a reduced margin, and was defeated by a Progressive candidate in 1925. Hours before her final legislative session ended, she introduced a resolution calling for an amendment to federal divorce laws that would permit women to apply for divorce on the grounds of a spouse's adultery, on equal terms with men.

After her defeat, Ramsland worked for the provincial library. She was active in several women's organizations, later married Regina businessman W.C.F. Scythes, and died on April 4, 1964. Not until the CCF victory in 1944 was another woman elected to the Saskatchewan legislature.

ELIZABETH KALMAKOFF, REGINA

BIBLIOGRAPHY: Kalmakoff, Elizabeth. 1994. "Naturally Divided: Women in Saskatchewan Politics, 1916–1919." *Saskatchewan History* 46 (2): 3–18. • Kalmakoff, Elizabeth. 1993. *Woman Suffrage in Saskatchewan.* Unpublished MA thesis, University of Regina.

**RICHARDS, JOHN** (b. 1944). Born in Exeter, England, in 1944, John Richards grew up in Saskatoon where his family emigrated after the war. He graduated from the University of Saskatchewan in economics in 1964. After further studies at Cambridge and at Washington University in St. Louis, he returned to the University of Saskatchewan as a visiting assistant professor in 1970. The university's decision not to re-appoint him led to a major student protest in 1971. That year, however, he was elected to the provincial legislature for the constituency of Saskatoon University. In the new NDP government he served as legislative secretary to the minister of Public Health, Walter Smishek. Richards prepared studies for the cabinet recommending a universal plan covering prescription drugs and the creation of a new department of the environment, which the government implemented.

In the summer of 1973 he resigned from the NDP caucus. While the left-wing Waffle had been expelled from the NDP in Ontario (in May 1972), in Saskatchewan it voted itself out of the party on the 1973 Thanksgiving weekend. While the intention of those who departed had been to create a new party to the left of the NDP, the loose association soon fell apart due to internal quarrels. As a result, in 1975 Richards ran as an independent candidate but was defeated. He returned to Washington University, completing a doctorate in economics. Since 1978, he has taught economics at Simon Fraser University, latterly in the Faculty of Business Administration, where he became a full professor.

PETER A. RUSSELL, OKANAGAN UNIVERSITY COLLEGE

**ROLFES, HERMAN HAROLD** (b. 1936). Herman Rolfes was a long-time New Democratic Party Member of the Legislative Assembly. He was a minister under Allan Blakeney and served again under Roy Romanow as Speaker of the Saskatchewan legislature.

Herman Rolfes was born in Humboldt on July 13, 1936, to Joseph and Josephine (Heckmann) Rolfes. He was educated at St. Peter's College in Muenster and went on to the Teacher's College in Saskatoon in 1955 and 1956. In 1960 he graduated from the University of Saskatchewan with a Bachelor of Arts, and in 1964 he received his Bachelor of Education degree. In 1971 he completed a Master's degree in guidance and counselling.

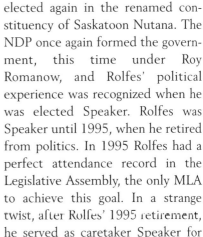

SAB R-A 24775
HERMAN ROLFES

Herman Rolfes married Myrna Josephine Hopfner in 1961. They have two children, Debora Lynne and Brian Joseph. Rolfes began a career in education after completing his degrees. He served as principal at St. Paul's North Elementary School, St. Charles' Elementary School, St. Philip's Elementary School, and Bishop Murray Elementary School, all in Saskatoon. He also served as the Director of Guidance at Holy Cross High School in Saskatoon.

In 1971 he became the MLA for Saskatoon Nutana South. Rolfes was re-elected in Saskatoon Buena Vista in 1975 and 1978. He was minister of Social Services from 1975 to 1979. From 1978 to 1979 he simultaneously held the portfolio of minister of Continuing Education. From 1979 to 1982 Rolfes held the portfolio of Health, and for a brief time in 1980 he was also minister of Culture and Youth. In the 1982 general election, however, Rolfes lost the seat of Saskatoon South in 1982 to Robert Myers of the Progressive Conservative Party.

In 1986, Rolfes regained his seat, winning a narrow victory over Myers in the Saskatoon South constituency. In 1991 he was elected again in the renamed constituency of Saskatoon Nutana. The NDP once again formed the government, this time under Roy Romanow, and Rolfes' political experience was recognized when he was elected Speaker. Rolfes was Speaker until 1995, when he retired from politics. In 1995 Rolfes had a perfect attendance record in the Legislative Assembly, the only MLA to achieve this goal. In a strange twist, after Rolfes' 1995 retirement, he served as caretaker Speaker for several months. Because MLAs had to elect a new Speaker before Rolfes could be released from his duties, Rolfes served as Speaker for a few months until a new session of the legislature could be called.

DANA TURGEON, REGINA

**ROMANOW, ROY JOHN** (b. 1939). Roy Romanow was born in Saskatoon on August 12, 1939. His parents were Ukrainian immigrants who had settled on the west side of Saskatoon. Despite English being his second language, Romanow performed well in school and entered the University of Saskatchewan in the fall of 1957 to study political science. After completing his first degree, he entered the university's College of Law, graduating in the spring of 1964. While at university, Romanow was heavily involved in student politics, becoming president of the Students' Representative Council. He was also an outspoken advocate of the provincial CCF and its introduction of medicare.

After graduating, Romanow began practicing law but had his eye set on politics. In 1966, he secured the CCF's nomination for the Riversdale constituency in Saskatoon and was successful in the provincial election the next year. Recognized as a top debater in the legislature, he was the natural leader of a new group of MLAs who encouraged him to run for leadership of the party when Premier Woodrow Lloyd resigned in 1970. The party establishment's surprise at his willingness to challenge the old guard turned into astonishment when Romanow forced the contest into a third ballot, almost beating former Lloyd cabinet minister Allan E. Blakeney. As a major asset in the NDP's election victory the following year, Romanow was appointed deputy premier, House Leader and Attorney General by Blakeney.

The 1970s were a time of innovation and expansion for the Saskatchewan government. Romanow initiated the province's first human rights code and accompanying commission, a new ombudsman office, the first provincial legal aid plan, the Indian constables program with the RCMP and the Meewasin Valley Authority to enhance Saskatoon's riverbank environment. By 1979, national unity had become a priority for the Blakeney government and Romanow became minister of Intergovernmental Affairs and one of the chief

OKTOBER REVOLUTION PHOTOGRAPHY

ROY ROMANOW

negotiators of a new constitution for Canada. The compromise "Kitchen Accord" bringing together all the provinces (except Quebec) and the federal government was handwritten by Romanow in an eleventh-hour set of negotiations involving federal Justice Minister Jean Chrétien and his provincial counterparts including Roy McMurtry of Ontario.

Many in Saskatchewan felt that the Blakeney government had been overly preoccupied with the constitution, and the NDP was routed in the provincial election of 1982. Narrowly defeated in Riversdale, Romanow used his time out of office to reflect on his career and he co-authored *Canada Notwithstanding*, a book about the making of the Canadian constitution. In 1986, Romanow re-entered political life, winning back the Riversdale constituency and taking over the leadership of the NDP after Blakeney resigned a year later. In Opposition, he fought against the privatization initiatives of the Conservative government led by Grant Devine. Then, on October 21, 1991, the NDP swept to a massive victory, setting the stage for a decade-long government headed by Romanow.

As premier, Romanow inherited a government that was almost bankrupt after years of fiscal mismanagement and a struggling agricultural economy. Tackling the debt crisis with a speed and commitment that surprised almost everyone, Romanow insisted on restoring the public's confidence in the ability of government to manage its finances. At the same time, his government pioneered major reforms in health care, including regionalization. By the mid-1990s, Saskatchewan was beginning to register budget surpluses, leading a trend that was soon followed by other jurisdictions in Canada. Health reform had also achieved some success although the closing and conversion of dozens of rural hospitals drew much criticism.

Romanow pursued an incremental economic strategy for the province that encouraged private sector initiative with only modest public investment in the 1990s, eschewing both the mega-development strategy pursued by Devine that had produced so much debt in the 1980s and the active expansion of the Crown corporation sector as had occurred under Blakeney in the 1970s. He initiated a major review of the future of the Crown sector that ultimately called for greater investment outside Saskatchewan and in a more competitive business and regulatory environment within the province. In agriculture, he favoured more market-sensitive safety nets that would encourage even greater diversification. He also pushed through a forest strategy that required partnerships with new Aboriginal businesses in the province. He also introduced welfare reforms aimed at encouraging independence through earned income supplements and training initiatives.

By his second term in government, Romanow was able to turn some of his attention to national issues. He was a leader in the social union negotiations that ultimately produced the National Child Benefit and the Social Union Framework Agreement (SUFA). He tirelessly fought against the threat of Quebec's secession in the federation, trying to forge a balance between Ottawa's centralism and the radical decentralism urged by Quebec and Alberta. He had Saskatchewan intervene in the Quebec secession reference before the Supreme Court of Canada to make it clear that decisions on the future of Canada triggered by Quebec's separation must involve provinces like his own, and he supported the federal government's Clarity Bill on the rules surrounding any future referendum on separation.

Romanow's government emerged with a minority in the provincial election of 1999. Years of budgetary constraint along with deteriorating relations with rural voters facing an increasingly uncertain future and organized labour following a bitter nurses' strike had taken their toll. Romanow initiated a coalition with the three sitting Liberal members to provide some stability for his government. Realizing that some of the dissatisfaction registered in the election, however, Romanow decided to announce his resignation one year later making way for a leadership convention. After Lorne Calvert was selected leader, Romanow left the premier's office in February 2001.

After only three months in retirement, however, Romanow was asked by Prime Minister Chrétien to become the sole chair of a Royal commission. He accepted on the condition that it would be directed from Saskatchewan, beginning an 18-month inquiry on the future of health care in Canada. Conducting multi-layered consultations that captured the attention of Canadians and the media, as well as initiating extensive research, he delivered his major report, *Building on Values*, in November 2002.

GREGORY P. MARCHILDON, UNIVERSITY OF REGINA

## ROSS, JAMES HAMILTON (1856–1932).

James Hamilton Ross was a rancher, politician, commissioner of the Yukon, Member of Parliament, and senator. During his nearly two decades in active politics, Ross played a key role in shaping the institutions that provided local government for western Canada. His work provided the foundation for Saskatchewan and Alberta's entrance into confederation as provinces. Ross was born in London, Canada West, on May 12, 1856, and moved with his family to Manitoba in the early 1870s. In 1882 he moved to the District of Assiniboia in what is now Saskatchewan and established the first mixed farming operation in the Moose Jaw district. He married Barbara Elizabeth McKay on November 23, 1886.

He was elected to the North-West Council in 1883, where he was an early and eloquent advocate of constitutional reform and western development through agriculture. He demanded that the federal Parliament give the North-West Territories all the rights and responsibilities of a province. Ross was elected to the Legislative Assembly of the North-West Territories which had succeeded the North-West Council in 1888. His colleagues selected him as Speaker in 1891, the highest office available to an MLA at the time. The issues surrounding responsible government came to a head in 1894 when Lieutenant-Governor Charles MacKintosh refused to accept the Territorial Executive Committee's proposed budget (it recommended each year's budget to the Governor). The committee resigned and the Lieutenant-Governor appointed a new Committee which submitted the Governor's budget to the legislature. Ross resigned the speakership and voted against the budget in the evenly divided Assembly, causing its defeat. Ross joined the original Executive Council, led by Frederick Haultain, shortly after it resumed office. There, he guided the Territories' first labour legislation through the Assembly.

Although a Liberal, he was an ardent supporter of Premier Frederick Haultain's plan to obtain provincial status for the Territories. When responsible government was granted to the North-West Territories in 1897, Ross entered the first cabinet as commissioner of Agriculture, commissioner of Public Works, and Territorial Secretary. He relinquished these positions in 1899 to become Territorial Treasurer. As Territorial Secretary and later Treasurer he showed tremendous administrative and political skill in keeping the North-West Territories solvent in the face of a deepening fiscal crisis (by 1897 the Territories had all the obligations of a province but few of the revenue-generating powers). He was instrumental in obtaining the federal grants necessary to keep the Territorial government afloat before 1901. In 1899 Ross was appointed a treaty commissioner. Ross personally led the negotiations with the Indian bands from Athabasca, in what is now Alberta. He assisted David Laird in negotiating Treaty Eight and traveled throughout the North-West to obtain riders to the original treaty.

Appointed commissioner of the Yukon Territory in 1901, Ross proved to be a talented administrator as he reorganized the civil service and sponsored legislation in a variety of fields. He was the first commissioner to reside in Government House in Dawson City. Despite suffering a paralytic stroke in 1902, he became the first Member of Parliament to represent the Yukon Territory in a by-election on December 2nd, 1902. Summoned to the Senate of Canada on October 30, 1904, he served there until his death in Victoria on December 14, 1932.

MICHAEL THOME, UNIVERSITY OF SASKATCHEWAN

**FURTHER READING:** Lingard, C. Cecil. 1946. *Territorial Government in Canada: The Autonomy Question in the Old North-West Territories.* Toronto: University of Toronto Press. • Thomas, Lewis Herbert. 1956. *The Struggle for Responsible Government in the North-West Territories, 1870-97.* Toronto: University of Toronto Press.

## ROUSSEAU, PAUL ÉMILE

(1929–2001). Paul Rousseau was born in Fort Frances, Ontario, December 20, 1929. He spent much of his childhood in Fort Frances but later lived in Winnipeg and Montreal. He came to Saskatchewan in 1958 with his family, briefly settling in Melville before finally settling down in Regina. After spending a couple of years as sales manager of Neil Motors, Rousseau purchased the dealership in 1960 and renamed it Crestview Chrysler, which developed into one of Regina's most successful car dealerships.

SAB R-PS 82-612-688

PAUL ROUSSEAU

He first entered politics running for the Progressive Conservatives in 1975 in the constituency of Regina South. Although he was defeated, he increased the PC vote significantly and finished a respectable second. Contesting the seat again in 1978, Rousseau was successful. His election carried some significance, for it showed that the Conservatives were successfully inheriting much of the beleaguered Liberal Party's former strength in south Regina and it marked the first time since 1929 that the Conservatives had elected a member to the legislature representing Regina.

As the only Conservative representing a major urban constituency, Rousseau became a prominent member of the Opposition, and upon his re-election in 1982, was appointed to the new Grant Devine government's first cabinet as minister of Industry and Commerce. A salesman by trade, his first job was to convince the business community that Saskatchewan's new government had completely abandoned the previous government's economic policies and that Saskatchewan was now "open for business." However, his lasting legacy is the

"Lights On for Life" campaign by Saskatchewan Government Insurance for which he was responsible. The safety campaign was the first of its kind in North America and advocated the use of headlights during the day to reduce the number of accidents. The campaign was a huge success and was adopted by many other jurisdictions across the continent.

In 1985, Rousseau left cabinet and chose not to contest the next election. After the election, he was appointed Saskatchewan Agent General in London, a position he held until 1991 when government fiscal restraints led to the abolishment of the position. He returned to Regina where he died on October 8, 2001.

BRETT QUIRING

## SCHMIDT, GRANT

(b. 1948). Grant Schmidt was born on July 21, 1948, in Balcarres to George Schmidt and Helen Banerd. He attended high school at Melville High School, and then the University of Saskatchewan where he completed an undergraduate and law degree.

Schmidt was well-known during his tenure as a member of the legislature for his outspoken nature and controversial views on welfare, legal aid, and women's issues. He once quipped that reporters would wait outside his office for stories. Despite the fact that his controversial views were a lightning rod for the media, Grant quickly rose through the ranks of the Tory government to become a senior member of cabinet and veteran member of the Devine government. First elected in 1982, then re-elected in 1986, Schmidt was a member of the cabinet from 1985 to 1991, holding a series of portfolios which included Social

Services, Labour, and Economic Development.

In 1989 it was announced that Saskatchewan Government Insurance (SGI) would be privatized. A cabinet shuffle moved Schmidt into the position in charge of SGI's privatization. The Devine government of that period felt that Saskatchewan's salvation rested in the divestiture of its Crown corporations, a stark contrast to past New Democrat Keynesian economic policies. Schmidt and the government sought to create a spinoff company called SGI Canada. SGI Canada's function was to find and invest in opportunities that would grow its parent company, SGI. However, the government proposed to privatize SGI Canada, and place its parent company, SGI, under SGI Canada's control. Despite the opposition of the New Democrats and the labour movement, the government concluded that SGI needed to grow its business in order to be viable and therefore they would pursue with its privatization. This was met with ferocious opposition and led to a Court of Queen's Bench decision against the government by trying implement this change without legislative approval.

In the 1991 provincial election, Grant Schmidt fell victim to the New Democrat sweep of the legislature. Following the defeat of the Progressive Conservative government, Grant Devine stepped down as leader. The battered Progressive Conservatives hoped that a new leader would rejuvenate the party, which was reduced to a small fraction of seats in the legislature. Grant Schmidt entered the leadership race but was defeated by Bill Boyd, who held a seat in the legislature. After his defeat Schmidt retired from politics but resurfaced in political circles again in 2003.

Musing for a number of weeks that he was prepared to throw his hat into the ring again as a candidate in the 2003 provincial election, Schmidt surprised Saskatchewan Party officials by defeating Bob Bjornerud, a sitting member of the legislature and founding member of the Saskatchewan Party, for the nomination in the new constituency of Melville-Saltcoats. Hundreds of people attended the nomination meeting where Schmidt supporters edged out Bjornerud at the end of the night. This outraged veteran Saskatchewan Party MLA Dan D'Autremont and former MLA Bill Boyd, who quickly sought to have Schmidt's nomination overturned by the party's executive committee.

Since their formation in the spring of 1997, the Saskatchewan Party had gone to great lengths to demonstrate that they did not have any ties to the Devine Tories. Allowing Schmidt to run as a candidate under their banner would have undermined those efforts. The executive committee did indeed overturn the nomination result. Schmidt then appealed to a higher decision-making body within the party: the nine-member executive council. However, the council upheld the decision of the executive committee. Seeing no other alternative, Schmidt chose to run in the riding of Melville-Saltcoats as an independent.

The constituency of Melville-Saltcoats became a hotly contested seat. Among the candidates were Bob Bjornerud, the man Schmidt had defeated for the Saskatchewan Party nomination, and Ron Osika, a former Liberal coalition member who was running as a New Democrat. In the end, Schmidt received only 18 percent of the vote, finishing behind both Osika and Bjornerud, who held the seat. Schmidt has since launched a lawsuit against the Saskatchewan Party, seeking reimbursement for electoral expenses he incurred during his Saskatchewan Party nomination.

HEATH PACKMAN, REGINA

**SCOTT, GEORGE ADAM** (1874–1963). George Scott was born in Portage La Prairie, Manitoba, on December 11, 1874. He was educated in Manitoba and taught school before moving to Davidson to begin farming in 1903. In 1905 his cousin, Walter Scott, was elected premier and their close relationship prompted George Scott's move into politics. In 1908 Scott was elected to the legislature representing the constituency of Arm River. Although he never held any cabinet position, Scott exercised some influence over Walter Scott who consulted him on many matters of political importance.

Scott fell out of favour with Walter Scott's successor, William Martin, over Martin's support for Robert Borden's Unionist government. Scott was among the few members of the provincial government who remained loyal to Wilfird Laurier and refused to join with the feder-

SAB R-A 35

GEORGE SCOTT

al Conservatives over the conscription issue. In 1919 Scott was elected Speaker of the legislature, a position he held until his political retirement in 1928. In 1928, he resigned his seat when he was appointed income tax inspector for Regina. Upon retirement in 1943, he moved to Alberta and died in Calgary in 1963.

BRETT QUIRING

**SCOTT, THOMAS WALTER** (1867–1938). Walter Scott was born on a farm near Ilderton, Ontario, on October 27, 1867. In 1885, he moved west to Portage La Prairie and worked with C. J. Atkinson, owner and editor of the Manitoba *Liberal*. This was the beginning of his career as a journalist. In 1886, Scott followed Atkinson to Regina where he worked for the Regina *Journal* before buying half of the Regina *Standard* and all of the Moose Jaw *Times*. In 1895, he bought the Regina *Leader* from Nicholas Flood Davin. Scott supplemented his income with land speculation in and around Regina, a common pursuit for those times. Walter Scott married Jessie Read and they adopted Dorothy, Jessie's niece. They had no children of their own.

Walter Scott was first elected to the Canadian House of Commons in 1900 for the constituency of Assiniboia West, defeating the incumbent Nicholas Flood Davin. Scott represented his constituency in the North-West Territories as a backbencher in the Wilfrid Laurier government and was re-elected in the general election of 1904. Scott and the minister of the Interior, Clifford Sifton, influenced the development of the autonomy bills which created the two new provinces of Alberta and Saskatchewan. Three controversial issues arose: one province or two; should the provinces have control of the mineral rights; and should there be separate schools. Two provinces were created; the two provinces did not gain the right to control their own mineral rights until twenty-five years later; and separate schools were allowed but within one public school system. On

SAB R-A 245

WALTER SCOTT

September 4, 1905, Saskatchewan became a province.

Lieutenant-Governor Amédée Forget chose Walter Scott as the first premier. The first general election was on December 13, 1905. Under the campaign slogan "Peace, Progress and Prosperity," the Scott government won a majority. Scott and his government were re-elected in 1908 and 1912. As premier, minister of Public Works and, later, minister of Education for eleven years in total, Scott led his government in building a public administration and infrastructure for the new province. He supervised the construction of the legislative building in Regina and opened the University of Saskatchewan in Saskatoon. Agriculture was the cornerstone of the new government, and the University of Saskatchewan became the first university in Canada to have a College of Agriculture alongside the other professional colleges.

From 1905 to 1916, the Scott government used the co-operative model to assist farm families to build and maintain a rural telephone system and the Saskatchewan Co-operative Elevator Company. The government provided financial backing, but the farmers were required to invest some of their own money in the co-operative and thus had a voice in its operation. The Scott government set a bold social policy by banning the bar and establishing government-controlled liquor stores. This was a step toward full prohibition, which came under the leadership of Scott's successor, William Martin. In 1916, the Scott government passed legislation to provide the franchise to women.

Throughout his premiership, Scott suffered from manic depression and was absent from his office up to six months of each year. With extra effort during his days of good health and with loyal support from James Calder, his deputy premier, Scott was able to lead an active and progressive government. By 1916, two problem areas began to weigh heavily on Scott. Reverend Murdock MacKinnon, a Presbyterian minister in Regina, launched a public campaign against the Scott government for its legislative amendments to the School Act which, according to MacKinnon, encouraged the Catholics to establish their own school system. At the same time, the Scott government was accused of graft in the letting of contracts for public projects. Several members of the Scott government were accused of accepting bribes in a vote concerning the distribution of liquor licenses. Full investigations cleared Scott and his cabinet of any wrongdoing, but the charges and the battle with MacKinnon were enough to force Scott to resign in ill health on October 20, 1916.

The Scotts retired to Victoria, but his health never did recover to the point that he was able to return to his career in journalism. In 1935, Scott was committed to the Homewood Sanitarium in Guelph, Ontario, where he died in 1938.

Walter Scott's legacy was assisting in the creation of Saskatchewan by building its public administration and civil service, fostering a public infrastructure with a legislative building and a provincial university, and promoting an agricultural industry and a rural way of life for thousands of new settlers. To assist the farming population, under a co-operative model, the Scott government led the way in the establishment of an elevator system and rural telephone companies. Scott was a man of the people and won all five elections he contested with ever larger majorities. His social policies of closing the bars and granting the vote to women were progressive for the time. Under Scott's leadership, the provincial Liberal Party became a strong force that stayed in office continuously from 1905 to 1944, with one exception from 1929 to 1934.

GORDON L. BARNHART, UNIVERSITY OF SASKATCHEWAN

---

**FURTHER READING:** Barnhart, Gordon. 2000. *"Peace, Progress and Prosperity": A Biography of Saskatchewan's First Premier, T. Walter Scott.* Regina: Canadian Plains Research Center.

**SERBY, CLAY** (b. 1950). Clay Serby held several important cabinet posts, including deputy premier, in the NDP governments of Roy Romanow and Lorne Calvert.

He was born on February 15, 1950, on his family's farm near Theodore, which he later owned and operated with his brother. He completed a certificate in Social Work and was employed as a social worker in Prince Albert and Yorkton. He held leadership positions in several community-service organizations in Yorkton and was an alderman there between 1986 and 1991.

SASKATCHEWAN NDP PHOTO ARCHIVES

CLAY SERBY

Serby won the constituency of Yorkton as a New Democrat in the 1991, 1995, 1999, and 2003 provincial elections. After the 1995 election, he was appointed to cabinet as the minister responsible for three government agencies. He was then given more significant portfolios as minister of Highways and Transportation (1997), Health (1997–1998), and Education (1998–1999). In these areas, he managed the consequences of deep spending cuts made during the Romanow government's first term, rather than putting forward major new initiatives.

As minister of Municipal Affairs, Culture and Housing (1999-2000), he was at the centre of the provincial government's drive to merge Saskatchewan's many small, fragmentary rural municipalities into larger, and arguably more efficient, administrative units. Municipal politicians and others in rural Saskatchewan vehemently opposed such amalgamation. After Serby endured the brunt of their criticism, the Romanow government withdrew its plans to rationalize local government in Saskatchewan.

Serby was one of only two NDP candidates elected in rural Saskatchewan in 1999, excluding the two northern seats. In 2000, Romanow appointed him minister of Agriculture and Food. In 2001, Calvert added the posts of deputy premier and minister responsible for Rural Revitalization to Serby's portfolio in an effort to convey that the provincial government would prioritize rural issues and interests.

In these positions, he sought greater federal assistance for Saskatchewan farmers. Generous American and European farm subsidies reduced the world prices at which Saskatchewan's agricultural products were sold. Serby argued that the government of Canada's responsibility for international trade compelled it to address this inequity by increasing Canadian farm subsidies. The federal government provided only limited new assistance, responding that agriculture was only partly a matter of federal jurisdiction, that foreign subsidies were only a contributory factor in the long-term decline of Canadian farming, and that, in any case, Canada could not afford to subsidize its agriculture as intensively as the more industrialized American and European economies could.

Serby also sought federal assistance to compensate Saskatchewan for the impact of severe prairie drought on crop production and the discovery of BSE, or "mad cow" disease, in Canada on livestock production. His management of these crises earned widespread respect and co-operation, even from his partisan opponents.

On balance, Serby will likely be remembered as a versatile minister who performed competently in a wide variety of challenging portfolios in rapid succession, rather than as a leading exponent of any particular policy initiative or political position.

ERIN M. K. WEIR, UNIVERSITY OF CALGARY

## SHILLINGTON, EDWARD BLAIN ("NED") (b. 1944).

A key member of both the Blakeney and Romanow governments, Ned Shillington held eleven different cabinet posts and was one of the chief legislative technicians of both governments.

Born August 28, 1944, in Moose Jaw, Shillington was raised on a farm south of the city. After completing high school, he attended the College of Law at the University of Saskatchewan. Graduating in 1968, he articled in Regina before joining a practice in Moosomin.

SASKATCHEWAN NDP PHOTO ARCHIVES

NED SHILLINGTON

Shillington first became actively involved in politics in 1968 when he helped NDP MLA Ed Whelan research changes to the insurance act brought forward by the Thatcher government. Together their critique of the bill forced the repeal of the proposed legislation.

In 1971, Shillington carried the NDP banner in the constituency of Moosomin and narrowly lost the election, which was a considerable feat since the CCF/NDP had never won the seat. Shortly after the election he became an assistant to Attorney-General Roy Romanow, a position he held until winning the NDP nomination in Regina Centre. Contesting the 1975 election, Shillington was easily elected and by the end of the year was appointed to cabinet as minister of Consumer Affairs. As minister, he was charged with introducing the government's rent control legislation to deal with skyrocketing rents. However, Shillington's main contribution to the Blakeney government was behind the scenes with legislation. For much of the period he served as deputy government House Leader and chair of the legislative review committee.

Leaving cabinet in 1980, Shillington returned to practicing law. In 1982, he was one of only eight New Democrats to survive the Conservative sweep and took on significant critic duties. Shillington was re-elected in 1986 and 1991. In 1992 he was re-appointed to cabinet as associate minister of Finance as the depth of the province's financial crisis became clear. His role was to assist Finance Minister Ed Tchorzewski to deal with this crisis by helping develop the budget and by playing a key role as vice-chair of the treasury board. He was further responsible for piloting the government's agenda through the legislature and resumed his former position as chair of the legislative review committee. While holding a variety of cabinet posts in the Romanow government, Shillington's main contribution was again in committees and in the legislative process.

Re-elected for the last time in 1995, Shillington left cabinet in 1998 and resigned his seat shortly before the 1999 election to become a consultant. He later moved to

Calgary to establish a consultancy firm, where he continues to reside.

BRETT QUIRING

## SIMARD, (ROSE MARIE) LOUISE (b. 1947).

Louise Simard orchestrated one of the largest changes in Saskatchewan health care since the advent of Medicare. While she was minister of Health from 1991 to 1995, Simard ushered in the "wellness" approach to health care, a process which involved sweeping reforms to the health care system, including massive hospital closures in rural Saskatchewan and the establishment of health districts and boards.

Simard was born on April 17, 1947, in Val d'Or, Quebec, and was raised in Meadow Lake. She attended the University of Saskatchewan, receiving a Bachelor of Arts in philosophy and a degree in law. Simard articled as a lawyer with the firm McPherson, Leslie and Tyerman, and was admitted to the bar in 1971. She worked as an assistant to Garnet Holtzman, Legislative Council, from 1973 to 1974.

Louise Simard was the first woman ever to hold the position of Legislative Council and Law Clerk for the province of Saskatchewan, a position she held from 1974 to 1978. In 1978 she left that position to found her own law firm. Simard was a member of the Attorney General's committee on the consolidation of the Queen's Bench and District Courts in 1979. She was also a board member of the Medical Council of Canada and the Canadian Nurses Association, as well as a vice-chairperson of the Saskatchewan Human Rights Commission and a consumer representative on the Council of the College of Physicians and Surgeons.

Simard was previously married to Linton Smith, a fellow lawyer whom she met during university. They had two children, Paul and Marin, before divorcing. The Legislative Assembly briefly became the site of gossip when Simard married fellow cabinet member Dwain Lingenfelter in 1994.

Louise Simard was elected as the MLA for Regina Lakeview in 1986, a position she held until 1991. During those years, Simard was the Opposition Health Critic, as well as the critic for women's issues, the Saskatchewan Power Corporation, the Human Rights Commission and the Ombudsman. In 1991 she became the MLA for Regina Hillsdale. When the NDP formed the government in 1991, Simard became the minister of Health and minister responsible for the Status of Women. She held these portfolios from November 1, 1991, until February 3, 1995.

SASKATCHEWAN NDP PHOTO ARCHIVES

LOUISE SIMARD

In 1995 Simard resigned from cabinet and declined to run in the general election of 1995. She joined the law firm of McPherson, Leslie and Tyerman in April 1995. In 2000, she was hired as the CEO of the Saskatchewan Association of Health Organizations (SAHO). SAHO is a non-profit, non-governmental umbrella group representing 180 health organizations in the province of Saskatchewan, including the thirty-two health districts, and is the employer representative for provincial health care employee contract negotiations.

DANA TURGEON, REGINA

**BIBLIOGRAPHY:** Saskatchewan Archives Board. Rose Marie Louise Simard fonds. SAFA # 15. Regina.

## SMISHEK, WALTER EDMUND

(b. 1925). Walter Smishek served in a number of high-profile positions in the Government of Saskatchewan. As such, he played an important role in the province's life during almost two decades of elected service.

Smishek was born in Poland on July 21, 1925. He started training to be a teacher and attended Teachers' College in Saskatoon. Deciding that six weeks would not equip him to be a good teacher he left teachers' college to work for Western Grocers. Smishek became active in the trade union movement and served as a representative for the Retail Wholesale and Department Store Union. He became Executive Secretary of the Saskatchewan Federation of Labour in 1960, and further served on the political action committee of the Canadian Labour Congress and as a vice-president of the Saskatchewan Federation of Labour. He also represented Labour on the University of Saskatchewan senate for six years and on the Senate Executive Committee for three years.

Smishek has had a long-time interest in improving life for all, and in building a stronger and more caring society. In 1961, as a member of the Advisory Planning Committee on Medicare, he wrote a dissenting report which opposed user/deterrent fees. He also expressed several other reservations which are even now being acted upon. Smishek was concerned with what he considered the overemphasis on fee-for-service as the means of physician remuneration. He opposed the establishment of an independent commission to operate Medicare. He opposed the imposition of personal premiums as a means of financing Medicare and recommended income and

WEST'S STUDIO, REGINA•SAB R-A 8382

WALTER SMISHEK

corporate tax as the most effective and fair means of financing the program. Later, as minister of Health, Smishek acted to remove these premiums.

Smishek was first elected to the Saskatchewan legislature as the member for Regina East in 1964 and represented this area of the city through five elections until 1982. Following the election of the NDP as the government in 1971, Smishek was appointed to a number of high profile portfolios. He served as minister of Health from 1971 to 1975; minister of Finance from 1975 to 1979; and minister of Urban Affairs from 1979 to 1982. He also served as a member of the Saskatchewan Treasury Board, and as its chairperson from 1975 to 1979. From 1978 to 1982 Smishek served as chair of a Special Cabinet Committee on Social Policy and was the minister-in-charge of the Social Policy Secretariat. Smishek was best known for his leadership in health programming. During his period as minister of Health, the province abolished medicare and hospital premiums; abolished medical and hospital user fees; introduced the children's School Dental Program and the Prescription Drug Plan; and established programs to provide aids to assist the disabled in independent living. During this time the department of Health also joined with the departments of Education and Social Services in establishing core services, an agency designed to provide integrated and coordinated services to the disabled.

After Smishek was defeated in the 1982 election, he went to work for the federal government in the department of Indian and Northern Affairs.

ALEX. TAYLOR, REGINA

## SNYDER, GORDON TAYLOR

(b. 1924). A twenty-two-year veteran of the Saskatchewan legislature, Gordon Snyder's most memorable contribution is the overhaul of the province's labour legislation while he was minister during the Blakeney government.

Born September 17, 1924, in Moose Jaw, Snyder was educated at the Moose Jaw Technical School. Snyder enlisted in the Royal Canadian Airforce in 1942, serving in Canada. After being discharged, he began working for the Canadian Pacific Railroad as a fireman and was eventually promoted to engineer in 1956. Active in the railroad unions, he served in a variety of posts in the Brotherhood of Firemen and Engineers.

Snyder's father had been very active in the CCF, and this influenced Snyder's first involvement in the party's youth wing. In 1960 he was first elected to the Saskatchewan legislature, replacing long-time CCF MLA and railroader Dempster Heming. He represented the dual-member constituency of Moose Jaw. Re-elected in 1964, Snyder had a relatively low profile during his first two terms until he was elected again in 1967 for the new single-member constituency of Moose Jaw North. In 1967, he and several newer MLAs were brought to the NDP's front benches in order to give the party a new face. Snyder was appointed to the high-profile critic portfolio of Health.

Re-elected in 1971 in Moose Jaw South, he was appointed to the new Blakeney government's cabinet as minister of Labour, a post he held for eleven years until the government's defeat. Snyder's first priority was to reverse much of the Thatcher government's legislation, repealing the controversial *Emergency*

WEST'S STUDIO, REGINA•SAB R-A 8366

GORDON SNYDER

*Services Act* and removing barriers for the creation of trade unions. In Snyder's term as minister, the province completely overhauled the scope of labour legislation. Also during his tenure, the first forty-hour work week was established in Canada, the Occupational Health and Safety board was strengthened, more stringent safely legislation was introduced and the Workers' Compensation Board was expanded. The Minimum Wage Board was re-established to develop a process of constant review of the minimum wage, tying it to a percentage of the average industrial wage. This decision saw the minimum wage rise from $2.25 to $4.25 during Snyder's term as minister, the highest in Canada. Also during his tenure, the role of the Womens' Bureau, the forerunner of the Womens' Secretariat, was greatly expanded. In 1972 the province was the first in Canada to introduce legislation insuring equal pay for similar work.

Re-elected in 1975 and 1978, Snyder was narrowly defeated in 1982 and retired from public life.

BRETT QUIRING

FURTHER READING: Shaak, L. 2002. *Without Regrets: Gordon Snyder's Reflections.* Moose Jaw: On Stage Consulting. • Snyder, Gordon. 1997. "Social Justice for Workers." In *Policy Innovation in the Saskatchewan Public Sector, 1971–1982,* ed. Eleanor Glor. North York: Captus Press.

## SOLOMON, JOHN LEWIS

(b. 1950). John Solomon was born on May 23, 1950, in Dauphin, Manitoba. In 1972, he graduated from the University of Manitoba with a Bachelor of Arts degree in economics and political science and later took one year of graduate studies in the Master of Business Administration program.

In 1973, Solomon came to Saskatchewan and married Janice Lee Bench in 1974. They have two children, Jennifer Nicole and Mathew John.

Solomon was first elected to the Saskatchewan legislature on October 17, 1979, as the New Democratic Party representative for Regina North West after defeating the leader of the Liberal Party, Ted Malone, in a by-election. Solomon was defeated in the 1982 provincial election by Progressive Conservative Bill Swenson, but was re-elected to the legislature as the NDP representative for Regina North West in 1986 and 1993. He served as a Member of the Legislative Assembly until 1993, when he was elected to the House of Commons.

As an MLA, Solomon served as the chair of the Legislative Standing Committee on Crown Corporations. While serving as an Opposition MLA from 1986 to 1991, he was the critic for Energy and Mines, the Saskatchewan Oil and Gas Corporation and Revenue. Solomon was also Opposition co-ordinator for the Crown Corporations Committee.

Solomon has held several positions within the NDP. From 1973 to 1975, he served as Director of Education and Policy Development as well as provincial secretary in 1978. From 1975 to 1978, he worked as the executive assistant to the minister of Northern Saskatchewan. He has also been president of the Regina West federal NDP and vice-president of the Regina North West NDP. Solomon was the tour co-ordinator for former Manitoba premier Ed Schreyer in the 1977 Manitoba general election and for former Saskatchewan premier Allan Blakeney in the 1978 provincial election. He has worked on numerous campaigns throughout the years.

Solomon has worked as a small business owner, a consultant and as a member of Parliament's assistant. He was also a CNR trainman in Winnipeg for three years and a member of the United Transportation Union for seven years. He has previously served as an executive assistant with Northern Saskatchewan Minister Ted Bowerman. At the time of Solomon's election to the legislature, he was a corporate planner with SaskTel in Regina.

In 1993, Solomon was elected to the House of Commons as an NDP representative for Regina–Lumsden. He was re-elected in 1997 representing Regina–Lumsden–Lake Centre and was defeated in 2000. As an MP, Solomon served as the NDP whip as well as the critic for Co-operatives, Western Economic Diversification, Atlantic Opportunities Agency, Federal Office of Regional Development-Quebec, Industry, Science, Research and Development, Natural Resources, Small Business, Consumer Affairs, Tourism and Crown Corporations. He was also a member of numerous committees.

Actively involved in his community, Solomon has been a member of several co-operative, church and business organizations, including Sherwood Credit Union, the Co-op, Normanview West Community Association, St. Peter's Catholic Church, the Canadian Federation of Independent Business (CFIB), the Saskatchewan Roughriders and the Association of United Ukrainian Canadians.

JENN RUDDY, REGINA

**SONNTAG, MAYNARD** (b. 1956). Maynard Sonntag was born in Goodsoil on January 31, 1956. He began working as a Credit Union manager in 1980, managing the branch in Goodsoil and then becoming an assistant manager in Meadow Lake.

Sonntag was first elected to the Saskatchewan legislature for the constituency of Meadow Lake in 1991, and has retained the same seat since that time. Due to the consistent urban/rural party split in the legislature, Sonntag was the NDP's lone rural MLA in 1999.

After several years as a backbencher, Sonntag became the youngest member named to cabinet by the Romanow government when he was named minister for the Saskatchewan Property Management Corporation in 1997. He held numerous roles in cabinet, including the portfolios of Post-Secondary Education and Skills Training (1998–1999), Highways and Transportation (1999–2001, 2004), Energy and Mines (2001) and Crown Investments Corporation (2001–2003).

Sonntag was one of seven challengers to succeed Roy Romanow as NDP leader in 2001, his platform focussing on youth and Aboriginal issues. He withdrew from the race after the second ballot, having received only 8.8 percent of the vote despite receiving the endorsement of defeated Labour minister Joanne Crofford.

Sonntag successfully defended his seat in the 2003 election. After the election, Sonntag was appointed minister of Aboriginal Affairs and minister responsible for SaskTel.

GREG FINGAS, REGINA

## SPARROW, HERBERT ORVAL (b. 1930).

Herbert Orval Sparrow—senator, farmer, businessman, and soil conservation advocate— was born on January 4, 1930, to a farm family in the Vanscoy area. Sparrow took his primary and secondary schooling in Saskatoon.

As a young man he moved to North Battleford, where he set up a fast-food business and also acquired a farm. He married Lois

Irene Perkins. These were busy years for Sparrow, who, in addition to having the normal responsibilities of a growing family, was active on city council (1957–65) and was president of the Saskatchewan Liberal Party. In both 1964 and 1967, Sparrow contested the provincial constituency of The Battlefords for the Liberal party, but was defeated both times by Eiling Kramer.

In 1968 Sparrow was appointed by Lester B. Pearson to the Canadian senate, making him one of the youngest senators at thirty-eight years of age. Sparrow has served on numerous Senate committees, establishing a reputation as an environmental advocate. While chair of the senate Agriculture, Fisheries and Forestry Committee, he oversaw publication of "Soils at Risk: Canada's Eroding Future," one of the most popular federal government publications in recent history. After publication of this report he toured extensively, speaking about soil conservation in Canada and abroad. He even addressed the United Nations Environment Program (UNEP) in Australia where he received the UNEP Medal and certificate of Distinction for Soil Conservation.

His tireless efforts to inform Canadians about the dangers of soil degradation won him wide recognition. He is an honorary life member of the Agricultural Institute of Canada, and an honorary member of the Soil Science Society of Canada. He has received the Soil Conservation Society of America honour award for Soil Conservation and the H.R. MacMillan Laureate Award in agriculture at the University of Guelph for the most significant contribution to agriculture in the years 1984 to 1989. In 1988 McGill University conferred on him an honorary doctor of science degree for his efforts on behalf of soil conservation.

One of the longest-serving senators in

Canada, Sparrow has also gained a reputation for voting with his conscience, often to the dismay of his party leaders. Whether the issue was the Pearson Airport deal, gopher control, or urban reserves, Sparrow has never been reticent about clearly stating his opinions.

Sparrow has continued to contribute to his local community, supporting the Battlefords boys' and girls' school lunch program to aid underprivileged children. In 1990 he was named Battleford and District's Citizen of the Decade. In 2000 he was inducted into the Saskatchewan Agricultural Hall of Fame.

LISA DALE-BURNETT

## SPENCE, GEORGE (1880–1975). George Spence was born in the Orkney Islands off the north coast of Scotland on October 25, 1880. He received his public school education in England, and attended the Leith Academy Technical College in Scotland, where he studied electrical engineering.

In 1900, he came to Canada and spent three years in the gold fields of the Klondike. He then farmed in Manitoba, and spent some time with the Canadian Pacific Railway, working on survey parties. In 1912, he settled on a homestead at Monchy, south of Swift Current, right on the United States border. His experiences as a homesteader in one of the driest parts of the Canadian prairies left a lasting impression on the man who in later years was to become one of Canada's staunchest advocates of soil and water conservation by every possible means.

George Spence entered politics in 1917, and was elected to the Saskatchewan legislature, then re-elected in 1921 and 1925. In

SAB R-B 434

GEORGE SPENCE

that year he resigned his seat, and was elected as a Member of Parliament. Two years later he returned to provincial politics, and in succession was appointed minister of Labor and Industries, minister of Highways, and minister of Public Works. During the period 1927 to 1938 he was influential in the building of ten branch railway lines in southwestern Saskatchewan, and in the early beginnings of the present-day numbered highway system.

George Spence's greatest contribution to the welfare of western Canadian agriculture was made during his nine years as director of the Prairie Farm Rehabilitation Administration, set up to deal with the problems created by the drought of the 1930s. He was appointed to the post in 1938, and during his regime the engineering and financing of joint federal, provincial and local conservation schemes such as the St. Mary River and Bow River projects were concluded. He was also responsible for much of the planning of the South Saskatchewan River project, which, combined with the others in Alberta would, in his words, "put a green belt from the Rocky Mountains to the Lake District in Manitoba."

His early experience as acting chairman of the Better Farming Commission in 1920 provided him with a vast understanding of the problems of dryland farmers, especially those in the arid southwest corner of the province. The Commission's findings led to the establishment of the Swift Current Research Station, where such problems have been intensively studied since 1921. The findings of the Commission tied in closely with the ultimate objectives of PFRA.

Following his retirement from PFRA in 1947, George Spence

served for ten years on the International Joint Commission, the authority which deals with the allocation of water from sources shared by Canada and the United States. Among many awards and recognitions, he was made a Commander of the British Empire in 1946; in 1948 he received an Honorary Doctor of Laws degree from the University of Saskatchewan. He was author of a book "Survival of a Vision," published in 1967, also of a treatise on the growing of tender roses. Following a brief illness, George Spence died in Regina on March 4, 1975.

LISA DALE-BURNETT

**FURTHER READING:** MacEwan, Grant. 1958. "Crank about Conservation." In *Fifty Mighty Men*. Saskatoon: Western Producer Prairie Books. 241–246.

## STEUART, DAVID GORDON (Davey) (b. 1916).

David (Davey) Steuart was the deputy premier of Saskatchewan, the leader of the Official Opposition in Saskatchewan and eventually a senator representing Saskatchewan.

Steuart was born in Moose Jaw on January 26, 1916. His family moved around the province a number of times and eventually ended up in Prince Albert. In 1951 he ran for city council in Prince Albert and was elected. He served for most of the next decade on city council and eventually served two terms as mayor of Prince Albert. He was also elected as the president of the Saskatchewan Urban Municipalities Association.

In 1958 Steuart was a member of the Liberal Party executive and was instrumental in Ross Thatcher's

WEST'S STUDIO, REGINA•SAB R-A 8362

DAVID STEUART

successful bid for the leadership of the Saskatchewan Liberals. Steuart was elected party president at the same convention in 1959. He ran for the Saskatchewan legislature in the general election of 1960 and was unsuccessful, but was elected two years later in a by-election in Prince Albert.

In the general election of 1964, not only was Davey Steuart re-elected, but the Liberal Party formed the government of the province. Steuart was given a number of high-profile cabinet assignments. He was the first Liberal minister of Health, and was given responsibility for implementing the government's controversial user fees program. He then went on to be the minister of Natural Resources, and eventually, in June of 1965, he was appointed deputy premier. In 1967 Thatcher ceased to be his own Finance Minister and gave that portfolio to his deputy. The day that Steuart delivered his first budget was called "Black Friday" by the Opposition due to the combination of spending restraints and tax hikes. This budget is often pointed to as the beginning of the end of the Thatcher government. In the general election of 1971 the Liberals were defeated and the NDP once again formed government. Even with the change in government, Steuart was re-elected in his own Prince Albert West seat and moved across the house to sit in opposition. Steuart's analysis of why the Liberals lost the election was often quoted and repeated, "If we missed making enemies of anyone, it was because we hadn't met them."

Very shortly after the election, Ross Thatcher died of a heart attack and left the Liberal party without a leader. Steuart was elected by his fellow caucus members to be the interim leader of the party and a leadership race was underway. On September 17, 1971, Steuart became the first person to declare his intentions to run for leader of the Liberal Party. Eventually two other contenders would emerge and there was a leadership convention on December 11, 1971. Steuart won on the second ballot with 535 ballots and became the leader of the Saskatchewan Liberals and the leader of the Official Opposition.

After four years as leader of the opposition, Steuart was given his chance to form a government when the NDP called an election for June 11, 1975. The results of this election were not good for the Liberals as they only won fifteen seats but, more importantly, the upstart Conservative Party won seven. Thus, it looked as if there was a new alternative to the NDP and the Liberals never recovered from the outcome of the 1975 election. Steuart was largely blamed for the poor showing and two days after the election he stepped down as Liberal leader.

On December 11, 1976, Steuart was replaced by Ted Malone as the leader of the Liberal party. Steuart announced at the convention that he had been asked by PrimeMinister Pierre Trudeau to serve as one the senators from Saskatchewan. He was appointed to the senate that December and served there for fifteen years until his retirement in 1991.

STEVEN LLOYD, SASKATOON

## STEWART, ALAN CARL (1893–1958).

Alan Carl Stewart, soldier, lawyer, politician and first mayor of Yorkton, was, as T. C. Douglas said in his eulogy, a "political stormy petrel" and a "doughty fighter who feared no foe."

Born at Moosomin on September 27, 1893, Stewart attended public and high school there. His studies in law at the University of Manitoba were interrupted by the outbreak of the First World War. Serving overseas with the First Canadian contingent, he was invalided home after sustaining nearly fatal injuries at Passchendaele; these left him with a metal plate inside and a life-long scar on the outside of his skull.

SAB S-B 3963

CARL STEWART

He studied law in Moosomin, extramurally, with the firm of Brown, Proctor and Mundell, before joining the firm of Wilson and Graham in Yorkton. In 1922, he married Gladys McDougall of Winnipeg. They had four children: Bruce, Brent, Barry and Carla Ann. He was a brilliant criminal lawyer, serving many years as Yorkton's city solicitor, and was president of the Yorkton Branch of the Canadian Legion. While president of the Yorkton Board of Trade, he brought to Yorkton a number of commercial firms and warehouses; this earned him in 1958 the Yorkton Enterprise designation of "Yorkton's greatest citizen." He founded the Yorkton Terriers senior hockey club, and helped Yorkton get its first curling rink. On his farm he bred prize livestock.

His thirty years of active political life began with his election as a town councillor and his becoming the first mayor when Yorkton was elevated to city status in 1927. He ran for the provincial legislature four times, twice successfully, and for the federal parliament three times, once successfully. He fought every election "in a rough and tumble manner," speaking without notes. Under the Progressive banner, he was narrowly defeated in the provincial election of 1925 and again in the federal election of 1926. In 1929, he won election to the Saskatchewan legislature. He led the five successful Independent candidates, who voted with the Conservatives led by Dr. J. T. M. Anderson to make a stable coalition government possible. As minister of Highways, Stewart launched an unprecedented $20 million construction program, laying out for the first time a system of numbered highways that criss-crossed the settled portions of the province.

Defeated in the provincial Liberal landslide of 1934, he was then elected as a Unity candidate in 1938. To avoid a wartime election, he moved a successful motion that the legislature sit for an additional sixth year. The unpopularity of this extension may have helped the cause of T. C. Douglas in the 1944 CCF landslide. Stewart then turned his attention to federal politics; he was defeated as an Independent Liberal in 1945 before attaining success as a Liberal in 1949. Following that four-year term in Ottawa, war-related ill health forced his retirement; he died in Long Beach, California, on July 26, 1958.

C. STUART HOUSTON, SASKATOON

**STONE, ARTHUR** (1897–1988). Arthur Stone, long-time CCF backbencher, represents the party's connection to the small yet influential labour movement.

Born in Croydon, England, on October 18, 1897, Stone was educated in Britain before coming to Canada in 1913. In 1914 he arrived in Winnipeg and accepted a job with what would later become the Canadian National Railway (CNR). Apprenticing as a skilled machinist, he was first exposed to trade unions—an association which he would continue for his entire life. The most formative political event of his life was the 1919 Winnipeg General Strike. During the strike, he became acquainted with and sympathetic to the philosophy of strike leaders such as John Queen, J. S. Woodsworth and William Ivens.

After completing his apprenticeship, he was stationed at the CNR yards in Saskatoon. He continued his involvement in the International Association of Machinists and trade union movement more generally. He served for ten years on the executive of the Saskatoon Trades and Labor Council, serving as vice-president for four of those years. He also served as the vice-chairman of the CNR's Saskatchewan Machinists' Association.

In 1944, he first contested a seat in the Saskatchewan legislature in the constituency of Saskatoon and was elected in the CCF sweep. He was re-elected four times until he retired from politics in 1964. Although he never held a cabinet post, he was influential, along with C.C. Williams and Dempster Heming, by providing the government with a strong link to the labour movement. As well, Stone was influential in helping shape the major labour reforms the CCF enacted, cementing the position of trade unions in Saskatchewan and improving the conditions of workers.

Stone remained active in the NDP after his retirement, routinely attending party conventions and events. He grew

SAB R-B 5445-12

ARTHUR STONE

critical of the NDP establishment for what he saw as the NDP's abandonment of core principles and actively supported the waffle, one of few former MLAs to do so.

BRETT QUIRING

**STURDY, JOHN HENRY** (1893–1966). Teacher, school administrator, founding member of the Saskatchewan Teachers' Federation (STF) and CCF cabinet minister for sixteen years, Jack Sturdy instituted many reforms that altered the way the Saskatchewan government administered its programs.

Born on January 27, 1893, in Goderich, Ontario, Sturdy came to Saskatoon in 1912. He was educated at the University of Saskatchewan and the Saskatoon Normal School. He began a teaching career but then enlisted in the Canadian Expeditionary Force and saw action in France at the Battle of Somme. Upon returning to Saskatchewan, he farmed for a short period of time before accepting a position as principal of Fort Qu'Appelle school. He became active in both the newly formed STF and within the CCF's precursor, the Farmer-Labour Party (FLP). He contested the 1934 election for the FLP in Qu'Appelle-Wolseley, but was badly defeated. In 1935 he was elected to the executive of the STF and later that year was appointed general secretary, the organization's top administrative position. In 1940 he left the STF to take a position as the overseas assistant director of educational services for the Canadian Legion. He returned to Saskatoon in 1944 to contest the election as the CCF candidate in Saskatoon City and was easily elected.

Sturdy was appointed to T. C. Douglas'

SAB R-B 5445-18

JOHN STURDY

first cabinet as minister of Reconstruction and Rehabilitation. Although he never had the profile or the influence of other cabinet colleagues, like Corman, Brockelbank or Fines, he nevertheless spearheaded many social reforms. Under his term as minister, the government took on more responsibility for welfare and social justice programs, greatly expanding their scope. As minister in charge of the penal system, the province's jails began to practice a restorative model of justice. After re-election in 1948, 1952 and finally in 1956, he was appointed as minister-without-portfolio acting as special advisor to the premier on minority groups. In 1956, Sturdy chaired the Committee on Indian Affairs, which recommended that the provincial franchise be extended to First Nations people, that they no longer be restricted to reserves and that they be allowed to purchase liquor. The committee's report marked an important shift in how the Douglas government dealt with First Nations issues and set the tone for government policy until the CCF was defeated in 1964.

Sturdy retired from politics in 1960 and moved to Victoria, British Columbia, where he died September 20, 1966.

BRETT QUIRING

**SWENSON, RICHARD ("RICK")** (b. 1952). Rick Swenson, born in 1952, was raised in the Baildon district near Moose Jaw. He pursued his post-secondary education at the University of Saskatchewan and the University of Regina, majoring in political science and history. He has farmed full-time since 1974 and has been active in promoting new crop varieties and irrigation projects. He has served on the boards of the Saskatchewan Alfalfa Growers and the Canadian Wheat Growers Association. In 1985 he was elected for Thunder Creek in a by-election to replace Colin Thatcher. A member of the Progressive Conservative government, he served as legislative secretary to the minister of Agriculture, then as minister of Energy and Mines (1989), minister of Indian and Métis Affairs (1991), and as acting leader of the Opposition (1993–1994). In the latter capacity he was also Opposition finance critic and chair of the Public Accounts Committee. As a minister, his major accomplishment was the signing of the memorandum of understanding on Treaty Land Entitlement, the culmination of years of negotiation between the province and the First Nations authorities. Rick retired from political life in 1995 following his decision not to seek re-election.

PETER A. RUSSELL, OKANAGAN UNIVERSITY COLLEGE

## JAMES GORDON TAGGART (1892-

1974). James Gordon Taggart made significant contributions to Canadian agriculture in his roles as public servant, agricultural researcher, educator and politician. Born on September 28, 1892, Taggart grew up on a farm near Truro, Nova Scotia. His formal education in agriculture took place at the Provincial Agricultural College in Truro, and the Ontario Agricultural College in Guelph. After working as a district representative for the Guelph agricultural college, he moved west to Alberta where he taught and was later principal of the Vermilion School of Agriculture.

SAB R-A 2823

JAMES TAGGART

In 1921, Taggart moved to Regina where he demonstrated tractors for the Ford Motor Company. Later that year, he became the first superintendent of the Dominion Experimental Farm in Swift Current. The Farm, in the heart of the dryland area known as the Palliser Triangle, was destined under the guidance of Gordon Taggart and his successors, to show that farming was not only possible but could be made profitable in the area if proper cultural methods were used to make the most of a difficult combination of soil and moisture conditions.

After thirteen years at the Experimental Farm, Taggart entered provincial politics, winning the Swift Current seat for the Liberals in 1934. Taggart served as Saskatchewan's minister of Agriculture from 1934 to 1944, first under Gardiner, and then Patterson. Starting in 1939, Taggart held a number of appointments related to the war effort, including food administrator with the federal Wartime Prices and Trade Board and chairman of the Meat Board. When the Patterson Liberals were defeated in 1944, Taggart moved to Ottawa, where he continued to work on various boards, and later provided post-war guidance to the Agricultural Prices Support Board. In 1949, Taggart had a second chance to work under Jimmy Gardiner, when he was appointed federal deputy minister of Agriculture. He held this post until 1959.

To Gordon Taggart much credit must be given for his successful efforts to focus the attention of federal authorities on the importance of Prairie agriculture to the nation's economy, and on the lack of federal policies designed to give western farmers a reasonable chance of success in their difficult calling. For his success in these endeavours he was made a Commander of the British Empire; his professional colleagues elected him a Fellow of the Agricultural Institute of Canada, and several universities gave him honorary degrees.

Gordon Taggart died on June 11, 1974.

LISA DALE-BURNETT

**FURTHER READING:** "Bluenose Deputy." 1949. *The Country Guide.* May: 7, 60-63.

## TAYLOR, LEONARD WILLIAMS (b. 1952)

As a city councillor, MLA, and MP, Len Taylor has represented the people of North Battleford at every level of government.

Taylor was born January 19, 1952, in North Battleford. After completing a Bachelor of Arts degree at the University of Saskatchewan in 1974, he returned to North Battleford where he established a small business and worked as a journalist.

In 1988, Taylor was first elected to the House of Commons in the riding of The Battlefords–Meadow Lake as a New Democrat. During his first term, he served as his party's critic for the Environment, Aboriginal Affairs and Northern Development. In 1993, Taylor was re-elected, which was a sizeable feat as the NDP dropped from forty-four to only nine seats. In the much smaller caucus, Taylor played a larger role, taking on many more critic duties and serving as the NDP House Leader from 1994 to 1996.

In 1997, Taylor again sought re-election but was defeated in the redistributed riding of Battlefords–Lloydminster. After defeat, he returned to private life, working as a financial consultant and real estate agent. He remained involved in the community, serving on the

LEN TAYLOR

board of the local Chamber of Commerce and as director of both the local tourism authority and United Way. In 2000, Taylor returned to politics when he ran for a seat on the North Battleford city council. He was easily elected, leading the city-wide ballot.

Taylor made the jump into provincial politics in 2003, running in the constituency of The Battlefords. Taylor was again easily elected, defeating Jack Hilson, the incumbent Liberal MLA. Immediately after the election, Taylor was appointed to cabinet as minister of Government Relations.

BRETT QUIRING

## TCHORZEWSKI, EDWIN LAURENCE (b. 1943).

Ed Tchorzewski was an MLA for over twenty-five years and an important cabinet minister in both the Blakeney and Romanow governments. However, he is best known as minister of Finance for the Romanow government who reined in the province's sizeable deficit.

Born April 22, 1943, in Alvena, Tchorzewski completed his secondary schooling in Hudson Bay. Afterward, he attended the University of Saskatchewan, completing a B.A. in political science. Tchorzewski accepted a position in Humboldt with the separate school system, teaching until his election to the legislature.

Active in politics at an early age, Tchorzewski won the NDP nomination for the constituency of Humboldt in 1969 at the age of twenty-six, and was easily elected in the 1971 general election. He was appointed to cabinet in 1972 as minister of Culture and Youth and as minister of Consumer Affairs. Tchorzewski quickly rose up the ranks in Allan Blakeney's cabinet, moving into Education in 1975, Health in 1977 and Finance in 1979. Besides holding these important cabinet posts, Tchorzewski also served as one of Blakeney's top political lieutenants advising the premier on political issues within the Saskatchewan NDP.

ED TCHORZEWSKI

In 1982, Tchorzewski lost in Humboldt as the Blakeney government was swept out of office. Moving to Regina, he again ran for office in the constituency of Regina North East after the seat became vacant. Tchorzewski easily won the 1985 by-election, capturing over seventy percent of the vote. Re-elected in 1986, Tchorzewski was appointed deputy leader and widely touted as a possible successor to Allan Blakeney's leadership of the NDP. However, Tchorzewski chose not to run and Roy Romanow was acclaimed leader.

In 1991, the NDP was returned to power and Tchorzewski was easily re-elected in the new constituency of Regina Dewdney. He was appointed to Romanow's first cabinet as minister of Finance, the position he held in the Blakeney government when it was defeated in 1982. Tchorzewski was confronted with the daunting task of balancing the budget after years of deficits incurred by the Devine government. In the 1992 budget, Tchorzewski introduced increases in taxation and cut government spending, both of which led to significant opposition, but ultimately balanced the provincial books in 1993.

Finance took a toll on Tchorzewski, who left the portfolio shortly before the 1993 budget to take the less taxing position of provincial secretary. Later in 1993, he took on the responsibility for Education for several months and in 1995 took over as minister of Municipal Government. Re-elected in 1995, Tchorzewski left cabinet after the election and served his last term as a government backbencher.

Tchorzewski was elected president of the federal NDP in 1997, and in 1999 he resigned from the legislature to become chief of staff to federal NDP leader Alexa McDonough. Still active in provincial politics, Tchorzewski returned to Saskatchewan to be the NDP's campaign manager in 1999. In 2002, Tchorzewski was hired as special advisor to newly elected Premier Lorne Calvert.

BRETT QUIRING

**THATCHER, WILBERT COLIN** (b. 1938). Son of premier Ross Thatcher, Liberal and Progressive Conservative MLA, and provincial cabinet minister, Colin Thatcher's notoriety is linked to his sensational trial and subsequent conviction for the murder of his ex-wife, JoAnn Wilson.

Colin Thatcher was born August 25, 1938, in Toronto, and raised in Moose Jaw and also at the nearby family ranch. He was introduced to politics at an early age as his father, Ross Thatcher, was intimately involved in Saskatchewan politics throughout most of Colin's childhood. He was educated in Moose Jaw, and after high school studied at the University of Saskatchewan for two years before transferring to the agricultural program at Iowa State

University. While in Iowa he met and married JoAnn Geiger.

After completing university, he returned to Moose Jaw and managed his father's ranching operation near Caron. After his father's death in 1971, Thatcher contested but lost the Liberal nomination in Ross Thatcher's former seat of Morse. In 1974, Thatcher again contested public office, winning the Liberal nomination in the constituency of Thunder Creek. Narrowly elected in the 1975 general election, Thatcher quickly developed a reputation as a volatile and maverick MLA. Constantly feuding with his party's MLAs and with the federal Liberals, Thatcher left the party in 1977 to join the rising, Dick Collver–led, Progressive Conservatives. Easily winning re-election in Thunder Creek as a Conservative, Thatcher was named Opposition House Leader, but his relationship with his colleagues proved to be just as poor as it had been with the Liberals.

In August 1979, Thatcher's wife JoAnn left him, beginning a long and bitter divorce. On May 17, 1981, JoAnn was shot in her home by a sniper, but survived. Many, including JoAnn, suspected that Thatcher was behind the shooting.

In 1982 Thatcher was re-elected and appointed minister of Energy. During his term as minister, he was widely regarded as a successful, competent minister. He tried to increase oil drilling in the province by lowering royalty rates and providing incentives to attract oil companies to the province. However, Thatcher continued to have a stormy relationship with his colleagues, remaining aloof from cabinet and rarely attending. His erratic and confrontational behaviour led to his dismissal from cabinet in January 1983.

Later in the month, JoAnn was brutally beaten and shot to death in her garage.

Thatcher was immediately the prime suspect. After a lengthy investigation, Thatcher was charged with JoAnn's murder in May 1984. The trial attracted a great deal of media attention and scrutiny from around the world. On November 6, 1984, a jury found Thatcher guilty of first-degree murder and he was sentenced to twenty-five years without the possibility of parole.

While in prison, Thatcher remained in the public eye as he wrote his memoir. Several books were written about the murder, and the story was made into a TV movie that was aired across Canada, the United States, and Great Britain.

BRETT QUIRING

## THATCHER, WILBERT ROSS (1917–1971).

There are two drastically different and enduring images of Ross Thatcher that serve as bookends to the core years of his career in Saskatchewan public life. One is of a confident and determined politician who seized the moment and infused his party with hope and high expectations. The other is of a man unable to disguise his desperation, a spent political figure nearing not only the end of his time as premier of Saskatchewan, but also his life. Both scenes are set in Saskatchewan community halls, places that echo to this day with the voices of the province's rich political history.

Thatcher was born on May 24, 1917, in Neville. Thatcher's father, Wilbert, was a businessman who went into the hardware business in the Moose Jaw area during the 1920s. He was successful and his chain of stores expanded even during the depth of the Depression. While attending school Ross Thatcher helped out in his father's stores and established his business skills. Thatcher was a serious and ardent student and was able to graduate from high school at the age of fifteen. He attended Queen's University, graduating with a Bachelor of Commerce at the age of eighteen. After graduation Thatcher landed a job as the executive assistant to N.J. MacLean, vice-president of Canadian Packers in Toronto. Thatcher enjoyed his experience working at the top level of Canadian business, but by the late thirties his father called him home to work in the family business. As the decade progressed, Thatcher's father fell ill and the running of the businesses fell on Ross.

WEST'S STUDIO, REGINA•SAB RA 8359

ROSS THATCHER

Thatcher had an early interest in politics. Although he had a businessman's outlook, he soon became involved with the CCF. He was attracted to the CCF's activism and its interest in economic development. Thatcher believed that private business was not spurring the type of economic development that Saskatchewan needed, so the government had to step in. In 1942, he contested his first election, running for Moose Jaw city council on a labour-reformist slate. After a two-year term on council, Thatcher won the CCF nomination in the riding of Moose Jaw, winning the seat in 1945.

From the beginning, Thatcher was not a natural fit with the CCF. As an MP, Thatcher was clearly on the right wing of the CCF caucus. His interest in business and the importance of the profit motive were so clearly dominant that his relationship with the party was uncomfortable. In 1955 he broke from the CCF over its policy on corporate tax rates. After initially sitting as an independent, Thatcher contested the 1957 election campaign as a Liberal in the riding of Assiniboia. During the campaign Thatcher attacked the Saskatchewan CCF's record in creating crown corporations. The attack upset Premier T. C. Douglas who challenged Thatcher to a debate. Thatcher accepted, and the debate took place in May 1957 in Mossbank and was broadcast across Saskatchewan. The debate itself was largely regarded as a draw; however, the mere fact that Thatcher stood toe-to-toe with Douglas was a victory. It gave Liberals a hope that they had found someone who could finally challenge Douglas.

Thatcher lost to CCF candidate Hazen Argue in the 1957 election and again in 1958, but he was viewed by many as the possible saviour of the Saskatchewan Liberal Party. After leader Hammy McDonald was forced out of his position in the summer of 1959, Thatcher contested the party leadership and easily won on the first ballot. Thatcher brought to the party the zeal of a convert in attacking his former party. It was just the energy the Liberal party had been looking for. Thatcher first led the party into the 1960 election where he fought Douglas over the issue of Medicare. Although he increased support for his party, he failed to defeat the CCF.

The Liberals were gaining momentum, and the opposition and protest to Medicare helped to solidify anti-CCF opposition. Thatcher also worked to incorporate many Conservatives and Socreds into his party in order to defeat the CCF. Gaining momentum, he won three by-elections during the term, turning all three seats from the CCF to the Liberals. In 1964, Thatcher's work paid off as he defeated the CCF for the first time in twenty years.

Thatcher believed that government needed to control spending by reducing what he saw as waste and inefficiency while at the same time cutting taxes. He reduced taxes and sold several of Saskatchewan's crown corporations. He further set out to promote that Saskatchewan was "open for business" to outside investors who, he believed, had been scared away by twenty years of socialism. He attracted investment that resulted in the rapid expansion of the potash industry and provided subsidies for the development of pulp mills in the north.

Thatcher's relationship with the federal Liberals was a stormy one. He demanded complete control over the party in Saskatchewan and resented both Pearson's and Trudeau's attempts to establish a separate federal organization in the province. Further exacerbating the difficulties were disagreements over federal agriculture policy, which upset many farmers and hurt provincial Liberal fortunes.

Thatcher was re-elected in 1967, but shortly afterward his government began an unannounced austerity programme that caught even senior ministers off guard. In the 1968 budget, Thatcher cut government programmes, raised taxes, and introduced widely unpopular utilization fees on medical procedures. The cuts were accompanied by a downturn in the agricultural and potash industries. Thatcher became increasingly combative with friends and foes alike. His government became isolated and increasingly vulnerable. In 1971 he was defeated by the Allan Blakeney–led NDP.

On July 22, 1971, three weeks after the election, Thatcher died of a heart attack at his Regina home.

BRETT QUIRING

FURTHER READING: Eisler, Dale. 1987. *Rumors of Glory.* Edmonton: Hurtig Publishers. • Smith, David. 1975. *Prairie Liberalism: The Liberal Party in Saskatchewan 1905-1971.* Toronto: University of Toronto Press.

## THAUBERGER, JOSEPH (1909–1998).

Despite living in a province that has typically been resistant to Social Credit ideas, Joseph Thauberger worked tirelessly for more than six decades to improve the lives of Saskatchewan residents.

Thauberger, who was born on August 26, 1909, in Bessarabia (now Moldova) and came to Saskatchewan at the age of two, was a farmer at Vibank when he joined the provincial Social Credit Party in 1935. He quickly became active in the party, running in his first provincial election in June 1938 in the Qu'Appelle–Wolseley constituency. But, as he would find for much of his career, it was a difficult task for Social Credit to make a dent in the popularity of the CCF and the Liberals in Saskatchewan. Despite coming in third in that election and the next four elections in the Humboldt constituency (his best result was 32 percent of the vote in 1952), Thauberger's conviction in his beliefs was not diminished.

His commitment to Social Credit led him to a leadership role in the party: he was elected its first president in 1949 and acclaimed as the president of the Social Credit league in 1952. These positions gave Thauberger a political platform for speaking out against what he felt were the greatest flaws in the system—namely control of the economy by the government and the banks. During the 1950s he was a vocal critic of the CCF for their emphasis on collective ownership rather than private entrepreneurship. He believed that this was the cause of the province's lack of economic growth, as Saskatchewan's debt was increasing by ten million dollars per year at that time. Thauberger also pointed out that in Social Credit-governed Alberta, roughly the same number of farms had been electrified as in Saskatchewan but at lower cost to the farmer because of private utility ownership.

Thauberger was also opposed to personal politics throughout his career and urged people to consider issues rather than individual and party loyalties. As an example of this principle, it was his policy to vote for any bill brought forward by either the CCF or the Liberals which he believed would be good for the people of the province.

After 1956 Thauberger did not run in any more provincial elections, but he continued to teach Social Credit policy and take on other endeavours. A devout Catholic, Thauberger was elected president of the Catholic section of the Saskatchewan School Trustees Association for the academic year of 1964/65.

In 1972 he also wrote a short book called *Will Inflation Ruin Us?*, which explained his economic ideas in layman's terms.

During the 1980s Thauberger parted ways with the Social Credit Party, believing that it had become too radical. However, he was not ready to leave politics just yet. As a result, he founded the Canada Party, a federal party which embodied many of the same ideals as Social Credit did at the height of its popularity. Thauberger ran in the 1993 federal election as its leader at the age of eighty-four.

He did not have any desire to be prime minister, but rather ran out of principle. "I have dedicated my life to trying to change this wicked system. For my family, for my children," he said. "I'm going to give it all I've got—this is my legacy."

Although he received just a few hundred votes in the Regina Qu'Appelle riding, Thauberger remained characteristically positive, saying that the Liberal victory was a step in the right direction for Canadians. He announced his retirement from politics following the election. Thauberger passed away in Regina on April 21, 1998.

STEPHANE BONNEVILLE

FURTHER READING: Thauberger, J.A. 1972. *Will Inflation Ruin Us?* Regina: New World Publishing Company.

## THIBAULT, ARTHUR JOSEPH (1914–1983).

WEST'S STUDIO, REGINA•R-A 8393

ARTHUR THIBAULT

Arthur Thibault was born February 21, 1914, in Bonne Madone. He was educated in Kaminka School and in 1941 established a grain and livestock farm in Tarnopol. Thibault's first elected position was in municipal government, serving on the local school board for twelve years and as reeve of the rural municipality of Invergordon from 1952 until 1959. Thibault was also active in many local organizations, particularly the local chapter of the Saskatchewan Farmers' Union and in the co-operative movement.

Thibault took to politics at an early age. He first became involved in the CCF during the 1938 election and worked for the party continuously until his death. First active in his local constituency, he ran for office in 1959 after the resignation of his local MLA, Henry Begrand, created a vacancy in the constituency of Kinistino. Thibault won the hotly contested by-election that first featured the CCF plan to introduce medicare, and was re-elected a year later in the 1960 general election. Narrowly re-elected in 1964 when the CCF lost government, Thibault took on greater responsibility as one of the Opposition's primary critics. He was re-elected in 1967 and 1971 in the new constituency of Melfort–Kinistino. In 1973, Thibault was appointed chairman of the Special Committee on Highway Traffic and Safety. A subject close to the heart of Thibault, the committee, which functioned until 1975, brought forward several key changes to highway safety. The committee recommended the highly controversial step of making it mandatory to wear seat belts. Thibault also became an early advocate for the strengthening of laws against drinking and driving.

Elected for the last time in 1975, Thibault retired from politics in 1978. He worked in the St. Louis Alcoholism Rehabilitation Centre from 1978 until 1981. In retirement, Thibault was involved with the Prince Albert Council on Alcoholism and Drug Abuse and continued to lobby the government on safety issues. Thibault died on February 22, 1983.

BRETT QUIRING

**THOMSON, ANDREW** (b. 1967). Andrew Thomson was born on July 16, 1967, in Kindersley. Both his parents were teachers. In 1979, his family moved to Prince Albert where he continued his studies and in 1985 he graduated from Carlton Comprehensive High School. He went on to attend the University of Saskatchewan and received a Bachelor's degree in political studies in 1990. While at university, he served on the university's Council, Senate, and Board of Governors, and was president of the students' union in 1991.

After university, he worked for the newly elected Romanow government as an assistant to the premier and various ministers before joining the civil service. In government, he worked on reform of the province's gaming regulations and was a co-architect of an initiative to involve First Nations governments in regulating and operating casino gaming.

In June 1995, at age twenty-seven, he was elected as the NDP MLA for Regina South. During his first term, he chaired the government's caucus committee on employment and economy, and served as a member of the legislature's public accounts committee. Thomson was re-elected in 1999 and became chair of the legislature's Crown Corporations Committee. That same year, Premier Romanow appointed him to the Cabinet Committee on the Economy, even though he was not yet in cabinet.

Premier Calvert appointed him to cabinet in October 2001 as minister of Energy and Mines. Accordingly, he served on the Treasury Board, led Saskatchewan's response to the Kyoto Accord, and initiated a review of Saskatchewan's oil and gas royalties. He also developed the Saskatchewan government's "GreenPrint for Ethanol Production" and introduced the first legislation in Canada requiring the use of ethanol-blended gasoline.

In March 2002, the government was re-organized and Thomson was appointed minister of the new department of Corrections and Public Safety and chair of the Cabinet Committee on Public Security that co-ordinated Saskatchewan's emergency planning and counter-terrorism initiatives. He was also appointed minister responsible for Information Technology, minister responsible for the Saskatchewan Property Management Corporation and a member of the Planning and Priorities Committee of Cabinet and the Investment Attraction Council. Re-elected in the 2003 election, Thomson was appointed minister of Learning.

DAVID MCGRANE, CARELTON UNIVERSITY

**TKACHUK, DAVID** (b. 1945). Senator, schoolteacher and businessman, David Tkachuk was born in Saskatoon on February

18, 1945 and grew up in the rural community of Weirdale. Tkachuk earned a B.A. in history and political science from the University of Saskatchewan in 1965, and a teaching certificate from the College of Education the following year. Active in student politics, Tkachuk sat on the university's student council. After completing university studies, Tkachuk worked in business and later began a brief teaching career (1972–1974), but resumed his active interest in politics when he joined the Saskatchewan Progressive Conservative Party in 1974. Thereafter, he played a major role in bringing that party out of political obscurity to defeat Allen Blakeney's New Democratic Party in the 1982 provincial election.

The newly elected Progressive Conservative government rewarded Tkachuk's largely behind-the-scenes party work by naming him Principal Secretary to Premier Grant Devine (1982–1986). Tkachuk also spent one year in British Columbia working for that province's Social Credit Party. In the late 1980s, Tkachuk, through his company Strategic Direct Marketing Inc., offered direct mail and telemarketing services to, among other clients, the government of Saskatchewan. Turning his attention to the federal stage in the early 1990s, Tkachuk contributed to the Progressive Conservative Party of Canada's efforts to rebuild itself after its disastrous electoral defeat in the 1993 federal election, which left the party with only two seats in the House of Commons. Since his appointment to the Senate by Brian Mulroney in 1993, Tkachuk has served on several Senate committees, including the Aboriginal Peoples Committee, the Agriculture and Forestry Committee, the Banking, Trade, and Commerce Committee (deputy chair), and the Special Senate Committee on Bill C-36 regarding terrorism. He also served as chair of the National Finance

Committee (1993–1997) and as member of the Special Inquiry into the Pearson Airport Agreements (1995). More recently, Tkachuk has been a vocal proponent of the so-called "unite the right" movement, which advocated a coalition of the Progressive Conservative and Canadian Alliance parties at the federal level. One of Senator Tkachuk's notable contributions to Saskatchewan and Canadian history was the securing of considerable funding for the Diefenbaker Canada Centre at the University of Saskatchewan, which houses the former prime minister's papers. Tkachuk currently serves as a board member at Calian Technology, Ltd., as chairman and board member of Blackstrap Hospitality Corporation, and as an honorary patron of Bosco Homes in Alberta.

ERIC STRIKWERDA, YORK UNIVERSITY

## TOTH, DON JAMES (b. 1948). Don Toth
was a founding member of the Saskatchewan Party and the party's most experienced parliamentarian. Born May 31, 1948, in Kipling, Toth was raised on the family farm near Langbank. He attended the University of Saskatchewan for a year, studying agriculture, and then attended the Full Gospel Bible Institute in Eston. Upon graduation in 1971, he returned to Langbank to establish a farm.

Toth was heavily involved in the community, serving on several local boards. He was first elected to public office as councillor of the rural municipality of Silverwood in 1985, serving until his election to the legislature. Active in the Progressive Conservative Party of Saskatchewan, he was involved in the local constituency association, serving as its president from 1978–1981. In 1986, Toth first contested a seat in the Saskatchewan legislature, running in the constituency of Moosomin for the Progressive Conservatives. Easily elected, he served the Devine government as the legislative secretary to the minister of Health and as chair of the Crown Corporation Committee from 1989 to 1991.

Narrowly re-elected in 1991, as the Devine government was defeated, Toth played an important role as the party's Justice critic. Toth was elected again in 1995 as the Progressive Conservatives were reduced to only five MLAs. The party's poor showing forced Toth to take on more critic duties and he became one of the party's most visible spokesmen.

In 1997, Toth joined with three other Progressive Conservative MLAs and four Liberals to form the Saskatchewan Party. As a prominent member of the new caucus, Toth served as the party's deputy House Leader and as deputy whip, as well as holding several critic duties. In 1999 and 2003, Toth was re-elected in Moosomin with large majorities.

BRETT QUIRING

## TOTZKE, ALBERT FREDERICK (1882–1951).

A. F. Totzke was Saskatchewan's second non-Anglo-Saxon and non-Francophone MLA, symbolic of Saskatchewan's growing multicultural base during the time of western settlement. Born in Kitchener, Ontario, on December 20, 1882, Albert Totzke's parents were immigrants from Germany. Totzke was educated in Ontario, gaining his Bachelor of Pharmacy and

SAB S-B 676

ALBERT TOTZKE

becoming a pharmaceutical chemist and a pharmacist.

After completing his education, Totzke moved to Vonda and quickly became prominent in the community. In 1906 he was appointed overseer of Vonda, and in 1907 he became its secretary-treasurer. In the 1908 provincial general election, Vonda elected Totzke—running for the Liberal Party—as its Member of the Saskatchewan Legislative Assembly. At that time he was only twenty-six years old, and had just married Evelyn Lynch of Ontario the year before. In 1913 Totzke became the government whip, a position he held until he left the legislature in 1917. In the federal general election held on October 29, 1925, Totzke was elected as Humbolt's Member of Parliament. He was re-elected in 1926 and 1930. In 1926 he became a member of the Liberal Party's caucus, where he remained until he left Parliament in 1935. Albert Totzke died on October 17, 1951.

MARYANNE COTCHER, UNIVERSITY OF REGINA

## TREW, BEATRICE JANET (née Coates) (1897–1976).

Beatrice Trew, a leader in farm organization, rural women's organizations, politics, and church groups, was born on December 4, 1897, in Coates Mills, New Brunswick. She received teacher training in Fredericton, New Brunswick, and taught for two years in that province before moving west in 1917 to a school at Manor, Saskatchewan. The following year she moved to a teaching position at Lemsford, and it was here that she met and married J. Albert Trew, a district farmer.

When the Lemsford Homemakers Club was formed in 1920, she was elected first secretary-treasurer. She later rose to the presidency of the Swift Current district

Homemakers. She resigned this position in 1944 when she was elected Member of the Legislative Assembly for Maple Creek. Defeated on her bid for re-election as an MLA in 1948, she returned to her active role in Homemakers and the local church. She received a life membership in the Lemsford Home-makers Club.

BEATRICE TREW

In addition to serving one term as MLA, Trew was a member of the national council of the Co-operative Commonwealth Federation (CCF) for eleven years and vice-president of the Saskatchewan section of the party for eight years.

When the Saskatchewan Farmers Union was organized in 1950 she and her husband joined. She became women's district director in 1953. In 1958 Trew was elected women's president of the provincial farm union, a post she held for five years. She represented farm union women at three meetings of the Associated Country Women of the World, at Edinburgh, Scotland, in 1959, at Melbourne, Australia, in 1962, and in Michigan in 1965.

Trew was a member of the Thompson Advisory Planning Committee on Medical Care which, in 1961, laid the groundwork for Canada's first universal medical care plan. The committee study took her to England, Holland, Norway, Sweden, and Denmark.

Beatrice Trew died in a traffic accident on June 4, 1976.

LISA DALE-BURNETT

**TREW, KIM DALE** (b. 1953). Kim Trew was born in Kyle on June 7, 1953. He was raised on the Beechy Co-op farm and graduated from Beechy High School. While growing up, Trew spent two years living in Guyana, South America, with his family. He later graduated from the University of Regina with a certificate in Personnel Administration. On December 27, 1975, he married Lorna Ivy Brasseur. They have two sons and a daughter.

Trew was raised in a politically involved family. His grandmother, Beatrice Trew, was a founding member of the Co-operative Commonwealth Federation (renamed the New Democratic Party) and in 1944 she was the first elected woman CCF MLA.

Trew was first elected to the Saskatchewan legislature on October 26, 1986, as a New Democratic Party representative for the Regina North constituency. He was re-elected in 1991 (Regina Albert North), 1995 (Regina Coronation Park) and in 1999 (Regina Coronation Park).

During his first term as an MLA, Trew was the NDP critic for Saskatchewan Government Insurance (SGI), during which time he successfully led the fight to stop the privatization of SGI. He was also the NDP critic for Saskatchewan Transportation Company (STC), and broke the Conservative Eagle Bus of Texas scandal, in which the Grant Devine Progressive Conservatives purchased Eagle buses for STC at considerably higher prices than necessary.

Trew served as deputy Speaker of the Legislative Assembly from 1999 to 2001. In February 2001, he was appointed to Premier Lorne Calvert's cabinet as minister of Labour and minister responsible for Gaming. On October 12, 2001, he was appointed minister responsible for Saskatchewan Property Management Corporation and served as such until March 26, 2002. Trew has also served on several committees during his career as an MLA.

Prior to entering politics, Trew worked at the Saskatchewan Wheat Pool for twelve years, eight of which he served as a Safety Officer. While working at the Wheat Pool, he was also involved in the Grain Services Union, serving as a member of its bargaining team. He is a current member of the Sherwood Co-op, the Page Credit Union and the Saskatchewan Safety Council. He is also a past executive member of the Grain Services Union and a past member of the Canadian Society of Safety Engineering.

Trew was re-elected in Regina Coronation Park in 2003.

JENN RUDDY, REGINA

## TUCKER, WALTER ADAM

WEST'S STUDIO, REGINA•SAB R-A 8051-1

WALTER TUCKER

(1899–1990). Walter Adam Tucker was born in Portage la Prairie, Manitoba, on March 11, 1899. At the age of eighteen Tucker graduated from the University of Manitoba with a Bachelor of Arts degree. In 1923 he attended the College of Law at the University of Saskatchewan, where he graduated with not only a degree in law, but with high academic standing. In 1925 Tucker began practicing law in Rosthern.

Walter Tucker's political career began ten years later when the people of the constituency of Rosthern elected him to the House of Commons. He served in this capacity until 1948 when he resigned to lead the Saskatchewan Liberals in their provincial election battle against the CCF. For Tucker, a man once described as a "maverick Liberal, strongly of the left wing flavor of Liberalism, an agrarian radical, but one who is opposed to the inhibiting, narrowing doctrines of statism and socialism," his years as Saskatchewan Liberal leader were filled with frustration.

From the time Tucker took over as party leader in 1946 he battled internal party divisions. Some viewed him as left-wing, while others saw him as "Gardiner's chore boy." To complicate matters even more, he was leading a Liberal Party attempting to not only rebuild itself after a disastrous defeat in 1944, but a party taking on a new identity, that of the defender of capitalism. In a predominantly agrarian province convinced it was being exploited by the eastern Canadian monopolies, this was not a recipe for success. Externally, Tucker and the Liberals were battling a CCF party now firmly entrenched in the political landscape of the province. Tucker, who was a competent politician in his own right, proved to be no match for T. C. Douglas. After two consecutive election defeats Tucker resigned as leader of the provincial Liberals.

In 1953 Tucker resigned his seat in the Saskatchewan legislature and was again successfully elected to the House of Commons as the representative for the riding of Rosthern. Between the years 1945 and 1948 Tucker was Parliamentary assistant to the minister of Veterans Affairs. He was once quoted as saying that during his time as an MP his proudest moment came in 1946 when the Veterans Charter was created. Tucker, himself a veteran of both world wars, was instrumental in leading the federal committee that pushed to have the bills passed which provided for the rehabilitation of veterans of World War II. Tucker retired from politics in 1958.

During the years 1958 to 1963 Tucker practiced law in Saskatoon. In August of 1963 he was appointed to the Court of Queen's Bench where he served until 1974. His first judicial assignment was in Yorkton. During the swearing-in ceremony, Tucker's "outstanding work and experience as a lawyer, parliamentarian, [and] leader of a provincial party" were recognized. Walter Adam Tucker passed away September 19, 1990.

DWAYNE YASINOWSKI

FURTHER READINGS: Smith, David E. 1975. *Prairie Liberalism: The Liberal Party in Saskatchewan 1906-71.* Toronto: University of Toronto Press. • Kritzwiser, H.H. 1946. "The Liberals choose a proven leader" in *Western Business and Industry.* 20 (8).

## TURGEON, WILLIAM FERDINAND-ALPHONSE (1877–1969).

William Turgeon was Saskatchewan's most prominent francophone politician. He was Attorney General from 1907 to 1921, when he became a Court of Appeals judge. He became the Chief Justice in 1938 and retired from the bench in 1941. He then served as an ambassador, retiring in 1956. He served on more Royal Commissions than any other person. To Fransaskois, however, Turgeon is best remembered as a champion of francophone rights.

William Ferdinand-Alphonse Turgeon was born on June 3, 1877, in Petit-Rocher, New Brunswick, and raised in New York. In 1893 he attended the Collège de Lévis in Quebec, and then Laval, where he received a Bachelor of Arts in 1900. He apprenticed at a law firm in St. John, New Brunswick. His father Onésiphore, a member of

SAB R-A 251

WILLIAM TURGEON

Parliament and a senator, introduced him to Sir Charles Fitzpatrick, Sir Wilfrid Laurier's Solicitor-General. Fitzpatrick encouraged him to go to Prince Albert, then the judicial centre for the North-West Territories. He moved in 1903 with his new bride, Gertrude (Boudreau), and founded a law practice. He soon came to the attention of John Henderson Lamont, opposing counsel in his first case. Lamont, impressed with the young man, invited him to become a Crown prosecutor.

Lamont was politically connected, and Turgeon was soon befriended by prominent members of the Liberal Party. His mentor Lamont replaced Senator Thomas O. Davis as the controller of the Territories' "Liberal Machine." Turgeon was also friends with Monsignor Albert Pascal, bishop of Prince Albert. Lamont became Attorney General of Saskatchewan in 1905; by 1907, he left to take his seat as the Member of Parliament for Saskatchewan. Premier Walter Scott needed a politically well-connected replacement for Lamont who could carry the Roman Catholic and, if possible, the francophone vote for the Liberals. Turgeon was his best option.

Turgeon was appointed Attorney General in 1907, a position he held until 1921. In that time he spearheaded a number of important initiatives; the provincial telephone system, the University of Saskatchewan, and co-operative elevators all exist today because of W. F. A. Turgeon's efforts. His most notable achievement, however, came in the field of francophone rights.

Turgeon's tenure as Attorney General occurred at a very difficult time for the Fransaskois. The *Saskatchewan Act* of 1905 had given some rights to minority groups: children could receive primary education in another language where numbers warranted, as well as one hour of language instruction per day and a half-hour of religious education at the end of the school day. Growing nativist sentiment after World War I undermined these rights, however. There were public demands to eliminate education in languages other than English. To consolidate his hold on power, Premier William Martin began to erode francophone education rights. Turgeon nearly resigned his post as Attorney General in disgust, but stayed on to broker a compromise: the first year of primary education in French, as well as one hour per day in French in other grades and half an hour of religious education (also in French). The bargain was not great, but it was more than other groups were able to ensure. Francophone groups still hold W. F. A. Turgeon in high esteem for his efforts.

In 1921, Turgeon accepted a seat on the Saskatchewan Court of Appeals. He rose to the position of Chief Justice before his retirement from the bench in 1941. During these years, he also set a benchmark no one else has yet surpassed: the most Royal Commissions ever served upon by one person (twelve). Instead of retiring, Turgeon then began his diplomatic career. By the time he retired in 1956, he had served as the ambassador for Argentina, Mexico, Belgium, Ireland and Portugal, and was the first Canadian ambassador to Chile.

W. F. A. Turgeon's first wife passed away in 1944. They had five children together. He remarried in 1946 to Alvine Fleury De La Gordeniere, who passed away in 1951. He retired to Prince Albert, where he died on January 11, 1969.

Over the years, W. F. A. Turgeon received many honours, including the Order of Canada, and had a street in Regina and a school in Prince Albert named for him. His former residence in Regina was saved from the wrecking ball in 1983 and was moved to its present location. Now known as the Turgeon International Hostel, it is a provincial heritage site.

DANA TURGEON, REGINA

BIBLIOGRAPHY: Morrissette, Pierre. 1976. "La carriere politique de W. F. A. Turgeon, 1907–1921." Unpublished M.A. thesis, University of Regina.

## TURNBULL, OLAF ALEXANDER (1917–2004).

Olaf Turnbull, prominent activist in the Saskatchewan Farmers' Union, MLA, cabinet minister and co-operator, was born north of Kindersley in 1917. Raised on a fairly prosperous farm, Turnbull inherited much of his political beliefs from his father, who was a voracious reader and regularly attended meetings held by travelling lecturers. After completing high school, he joined a band that toured much of the west. In 1939, Turnbull attended the University of Saskatchewan's agricultural economics program. After completion of his degree in 1943, he returned to the farm where he continued to farm for the next sixteen years.

Shortly after returning to farming, Turnbull became active in the Saskatchewan Farmers' Union (SFU) at the local level but quickly became more involved within the organization. He was elected vice-president of SFU; during this time Turnbull and Stuart Thessin were the organization's main policy drafters and the pair wrote many of the organization's briefs presented to government. Turnbull represented Saskatchewan farmers on the Interprovincial Farmers' Union Council, a leading force in the national farmers' union organization and undertook many initiatives to change and shape provincial and federal agricultural policy. Turnbull was particularly keen on establishing a floor price for agricultural products and managed to exert pressure on the government to work towards this goal. In 1957, he was appointed to the Price Stabilization Board's advisory committee, by the Diefenbaker government, that made recommendations to the minister on this matter. In 1959, he was elected chairman of the farmers' trek to Ottawa to demand deficiency payments on wheat from the federal government.

Although courted by several political parties, Turnbull ran for the CCF in the 1960 election. He had tremendous respect for T.C. Douglas after attending a meeting with him as a young man and was a strong supporter of the Medicare system proposed by the CCF; therefore, he decided to contest the election as a CCF candidate. Elected in the constituency of Elrose, Turnbull was immediately appointed to cabinet as minister of Co-operation due to his high profile as a farm leader. Turnbull contested the party's leadership within in a year of being elected when Douglas moved on to lead the federal NDP. He lost to long-time MLA Woodrow Lloyd, but managed to garner a third of the convention delegates. After the election, Lloyd appointed Turnbull minister of Education, where he introduced several important reforms. Firstly, he phased out the normal school's role in training teachers, transferring responsibility to the universities, and, secondly, he made it possible for the separate school system to fund its high schools through the property tax system. The change in the position of the separate schools created a great deal of controversy, which led many to note

SASKATCHEWAN NDP PHOTO ARCHIVES

OLAF TURNBULL

that it was a major cause of the CCF's electoral defeat in 1964.

In the 1964 election, Turnbull was narrowly defeated and once again returned to farming. In 1965, he took a job as an instructor with the Co-operative College in Saskatoon. In 1972 he was appointed executive director of the college, a position he held until his retirement in 1982.

Olaf Turnbull passed away in Saskatoon on March 15, 2004.

BRETT QUIRING

**UHRICH, JOHN MICHAEL** (1877–1951). John Uhrich was born on June 7, 1877, in Formosa, Ontario. He was schooled in Walkerton, Ontario, where upon graduation he began a short career teaching. In 1902 he enrolled in Northwestern University in Chicago in the faculty of Medicine. While at university, Uhrich first came to Saskatchewan to teach school on his summer breaks. He graduated from medical school in 1907 and in 1909 established a medical practice in Hague.

Uhrich was approached by the Liberals to run for election in 1917, but turned down the opportunity. However, the Liberals did succeed in convincing him to contest the 1921 election in Rosthern in which he was successful. Uhrich was appointed to cabinet as provincial secretary after Charles Dunning became premier in 1922. Uhrich was unofficially appointed to represent the French and Catholic communities in cabinet after William Turgeon vacated the post in 1921. In 1923 Uhrich was given the added responsibility of minister of Public Health upon the department's creation. During his tenure as minister, the provincial government significantly expanded its role in health care. The provincial government's role in the municipal hospital system increased and the number of hospitals across the province expanded. However, Uhrich's greatest contribution was in the field of preventive medicine. Under his stewardship public inspection of water and milk supplies began, as well as immunization programs for smallpox and diphtheria. In 1929 he enacted legislation clearing the way for the provincial government to assume the cost of treatment for tuberculosis in the province. This policy, once implemented, caused a drastic decline in the number of cases of the disease in Saskatchewan.

Uhrich was re-elected in the 1925 and 1929 elections. The defeat of the Gardiner government in 1929 relegated Uhrich to the Opposition benches for the first time in his career, where he pressed the government's record on public health. When the Liberals returned to power in 1934, Uhrich assumed his former role as minister of Public Health and in 1938 he was given the added responsibility for Public Works. In recognition of his service to public health in Saskatchewan, in 1940 the Canadian Public Health Association granted Uhrich a lifetime membership. Due to ill health, Uhrich retired from politics in 1944.

Upon the unexpected death of Lieutenant-Governor Reginald Parker in 1948, Uhrich was called upon to fill the position. He served as Lieutenant-Governor until his own death on June 15, 1951.

BRETT QUIRING

## VALLEAU, OAKLAND WOODS (1892–1976).

Oakland Valleau was born in 1892 in Lennox and Addington County, Ontario. In 1912, he moved to Saskatchewan and homesteaded in the Moose Range district, later farming in the Hanley, Kenaston, and Aylsham areas. Valleau quickly became involved in a variety of farmer associations and was an active member in the United Farmers of Canada Saskatchewan Section, the Canadian Seed Growers' Association, the Saskatchewan

SAB R-A 10894-2

OAKLAND VALLEAU

Wheat Pool and the co-operative movement. He was first elected to represent the Melfort constituency in the provincial legislature in 1938, a seat he held until his defeat in 1948. With his election in 1938, Valleau was one of ten CCF members who formed the Official Opposition.

Valleau represented the left wing of the CCF Party and was a key figure in the pacifist movement in the party. He was a candidate in 1942 for the leadership of the Saskatchewan CCF and was seen as a member of the "old guard" of the party. After he lost his leadership bid to Tommy Douglas, Valleau pledged Douglas the loyalty of the CCF members of parliament. When the CCF formed government in 1944, Valleau was re-elected in his Melfort constituency and was chosen for a key role in Douglas' cabinet. Valleau was sworn in as provincial secretary and was responsible for establishing two major initiatives: the development of a separate Department of Social Welfare and the creation of the Saskatchewan Government Insurance Office (SGIO). He introduced legislation to create the Department of Welfare and became its first minister. One of the first acts he introduced was free hospitalization for the old age pensioners. In 1944, Valleau introduced the *Saskatchewan Government Insurance Act* which created the SGIO. He was the first chairman of the board of the SGIO and also purchased the first policy ever issued by SGIO on May 1, 1945.

During the years from 1945 to 1948, Valleau's son Delmar was elected to the legislature and the two became the first father and son members to serve in the Saskatchewan legislature at the same time. Valleau was defeated in the 1948 general election by a mere thirty votes. The main reason for his defeat was the agreement between the Liberals and Conservatives, who only ran one candidate in the constituency in an attempt to oust the CCF.

After his defeat, Valleau was chairman of the Worker's Compensation Board until 1962 and served on a variety of other boards. O. W. Valleau died on March 6, 1976.

JAY KASPERSKI, REGINA

## VAN MULLIGEN, HARRY (b. 1947).

Harry Van Mulligen has been a significant figure in Saskatchewan politics since 1979. After years as a municipal councilor and a backbench MLA, he rose to become the most important provincial cabinet minister other than the premier.

Van Mulligen was born in Dwingeloo, the Netherlands, in 1947 and emigrated to Canada with his family at the age of nine. He was raised in Brandon, Manitoba, and earned a Bachelor of Arts at the University of Brandon. In the 1968 federal election, he ran for the NDP in Brandon-Souris but was defeated. Van Mulligen moved to Regina in 1974 and completed a Bachelor of

SASKATCHEWAN NDP PHOTO ARCHIVES

HARRY VAN MULLIGAN

Social Work at the University of Regina. While serving on Regina's City Council from 1979 through 1985, he opposed the right-wing policies of Mayor Larry Schneider and Premier Grant Devine.

In the 1986 provincial election, he won the constituency of Regina Victoria and became an MLA in the NDP opposition to Devine's government. As chair of the Public Accounts Committee, he was a leading critic of Devine's financial management, which was widely seen to be imprudent and unaccountable.

He was re-elected from Regina Victoria in 1991, 1995, and 1999 as part of Roy Romanow's government, and from Regina Douglas Park in 2003 as part of Lorne Calvert's government. Despite being one of the more experienced and astute members of the NDP caucus, his status as one of many MLAs from the NDP stronghold of Regina meant that there was no political imperative to appoint him to cabinet. Instead, he served as deputy Speaker of the Legislative Assembly and was nearly elected Speaker.

Between 1998 and 2001, Van Mulligen was minister of Social Services in the Romanow and Calvert governments. He also served as deputy government House Leader and minister responsible for Disability Issues during these years. His main task in Social Services was to finish implementing "Building Independence," a set of welfare reforms to encourage people to move off social assistance into the workforce. Certain welfare benefits, especially those for children, were extended to low-income workers to eliminate disincentives to employment and to ease the transition into the labour force.

After removing Van Mulligen

from cabinet in 2001, Calvert appointed him minister of Finance and government House Leader immediately after the 2003 election. Both posts entailed substantial challenges since the government of Saskatchewan faced a significant deficit in its finances and held a majority of only one seat (excluding the Speaker) in the legislature.

In addition to his political career, Van Mulligen was a social worker, an adult educator, and a real estate agent.

ERIN M. K. WEIR, UNIVERSITY OF CALGARY

---

**FURTHER READING:** MacKinnon, Janice. 2003. *Minding the Public Purse: The Fiscal Crisis, Political Trade-offs, and Canada's Future.* Montreal & Kingston: McGill-Queen's University Press.

## WALKER, ROBERT "BOB" (1916–1989).

Robert Walker was born in Regina on March 16, 1916, but was raised on the family farm near Mazenod. Upon completion of high school, Walker enrolled at the normal school in Moose Jaw and began a short teaching career. In 1942 he enlisted in the RCAF as a wireless operator. Walker began his political career while still in uniform, when, in 1945, he ran unsuccessfully for the Ontario legislature as the CCF candidate in Leeds County. After he was discharged from the RCAF, Walker enrolled in the University of Saskatchewan, College of Law, where he obtained his degree and was called to the bar in 1951.

In 1948 Walker was first elected to the Saskatchewan legislature in the constituency of Hanley. He was re-elected in 1952 and in 1956. From 1951 until 1956 Walker served in the legislature with his brother Ed Walker, who represented the constituency of Gravelbourg for the CCF, making them the only siblings to serve concurrently in the Saskatchewan legislature. He was appointed to cabinet in 1956 as Attorney General and a year later also took on the portfolio of provincial secretary, holding both positions until the CCF's defeat in 1964. During his term as Attorney General, he oversaw an overhaul of judicial procedure in the province, established small claims courts and expanded the services of legal aid. He was a vigorous opponent of the Diefenbaker government's attempts to repatriate the Constitution under the proposed Fulton-Favreau amending formula, which he believed would provide an obstacle to enacting progressive legislation.

Walker was re-elected in 1964 by two votes, but the result was controverted by the court and a by-election was held where he won easily. However, in 1967 Walker was defeated and returned to his law practice in Saskatoon. After defeat, Walker continued to be involved within the NDP. He was elected to

WEST'S STUDIO, REGINA•SAB R-A 8378

ROBERT WALKER

the NDP's provincial executive in 1969 and grew increasingly critical of party president, Bev Currie's, affiliation to the Waffle, a movement with the party which promoted a socialist and nationalist agenda. Walker created a stir when he accused Currie and the party's youth wing of authorizing the use of party funds for Waffle events and campaigns. Walker's criticism of Currie and the Waffle quickly turned into an attack on party leader Woodrow Lloyd. In a joint caucus-executive meeting Walker confronted Lloyd, claiming that he had become a liability to the party's success. The chain of events that followed from Walker's comments directly led to Lloyd's resignation as leader in 1970. Walker once again ran for the NDP nomination in Hanley for the 1971 election but was defeated by a single vote, ending his political career.

Continuing his law practice in Saskatoon, Walker served five years on the University of Saskatchewan Board of Governors. Walker retiring to Victoria, British Columbia, in 1984 and died March 29, 1989.

BRETT QUIRING

**WEIR, ROBERT** (1882–1939). As federal minister of Agriculture during much of the depression, Robert Weir faced many challenges trying to improve the conditions of prairie farmers. He instituted anti-drought measures and led the federal government into the orderly marketing of agricultural produce.

Weir was born in Wigham in Huron County, Ontario, on December 5, 1882. Working his way through normal school, Weir continued his education in his spare time, earning a degree in physics from the University of Toronto. Weir came to Saskatchewan before the First World War, accepting a position teaching mathematics at Regina Collegiate. He enlisted in the Canadian Army shortly after war was declared in 1914, quickly rising to the rank of Major. Wounded during the battle of Passchendaele, Weir finished the war in a military hospital in London. He returned to Saskatchewan in 1919 as a school inspector, but on doctor's advice quit and began farming in an attempt to improve his health.

Investing in the farm economy during the post-war depression, he acquired a substantial mixed farming operation near Melfort. He

SAB R-B 11272

ROBERT WEIR

further established a successful breeding program for purebred horses, and later expanded into the breeding of cattle, sheep and swine. By 1930, he had established a successful farming operation that was recognized as a prime example of modern scientific farming methods, making Weir a recognized leader in the local and provincial farming community.

He was courted by all political parties leading up to the 1930 federal election but, being a lifelong Conservative, decided to carry that party's banner in the riding of Melfort. Despite the riding's poor Conservative history, Weir won and was quickly appointed minister of Agriculture in the new R. B. Bennett government.

Taking office at the beginning of the Depression, the most difficult time for prairie agriculture, left Weir with an impossible task. Drastically falling prices and severe drought created hardship for nearly all Saskatchewan farmers, and they looked to the federal government for answers. Weir tried to alleviate the worst effects of these problems. When the prairie wheat pools could not make payments for wheat contracts, the federal government took control over wheat sales, which led to the re-establishment of the Canadian Wheat Board in 1935. Weir further attempted to expand compulsory orderly marketing with the *Natural Marketing Act* in 1934, which was part of the Bennett New Deal and, like much of its sister legislation, was later found unconstitutional.

To address the growing drought problems and problems of shifting top soils, Weir promoted the growing of hedgerows and trees around fields. To this end he provided the foundation for the *Prairie Farm*

*Rehabilitation Act* in 1935 that sought to promote agricultural land improvement to help alleviate the effects of the depression and to provide work for unemployed labourers.

As the federal minister from Saskatchewan, Weir along with Railway Minister R. J. Manion, was appointed to negotiate for the federal government with the On-to-Ottawa trekkers. The talk resulted in a brief stalemate, allowing the trek leaders to meet with R. B. Bennett and the federal government paying for the basic needs of the trekkers. Relations broke down between the government and the trekkers, leading to the Regina Riot.

Weir was defeated in the 1935 election with many other members of the Bennett government. He returned to his farm where he remained until March 7, 1939, when he was killed in a farm accident.

BRETT QUIRING

**FURTHER READING:** Abel, P. M. 1930. "Saskatchewan's Cincinnatus." *Country Guide.* September. • Howard, Victor. 1985. *"We Were the Salt of the Earth!": The On-To-Ottawa Trek and the Regina Riot.* Regina: Canadian Plains Research Center.

## WHELAN, EDWARD CHARLES ("ED") (b. 1919).

Long-time Regina MLA and CCF activist, Ed Whelan was one of the foremost forces within the CCF-NDP during the sixties and seventies.

Born in Essex County, Ontario, on August 6, 1919, he was educated at Amherst and at the Toronto Technical School. A machinist by trade, Whelan worked in Windsor until coming to Saskatchewan in 1946. Doing fieldwork for the Co-operative Union of Saskatchewan,

WEST'S STUDIO, REGINA•SAB R-A 8370

ED WHELAN

Whelan began his close association with the province's co-operative movement. He served as a director of both the Sherwood Co-op and the Sherwood Credit Union, serving as the latter's vice-president from 1958 to 1960. In 1956, Whelan was appointed chairman of the provincial Mediation Board, a position he held until his election.

Active in the CCF since his time in Ontario, Whelan and his wife, Pemrose, became very involved in the local CCF association. Serving in a variety of capacities, he ran the CCF campaign in Regina in 1956 and was elected president of the Regina CCF in 1959. Nominated as one of the four CCF candidates in the multimember constituency of Regina in 1960, Whelan was easily elected. In 1962 he agreed to run the campaign for federal party leader T. C. Douglas, who failed in his attempt to capture the federal riding of Regina. Re-elected in Regina North in 1964, Whelan was promoted to the position of CCF whip.

An active participant in party debates, his boisterous personality created a great deal of animosity between himself and the left wing of the party particularly the Waffle. While in Opposition, Whelan and Pemrose were closely tied to the daily operations of the party. Pemrose served on the party executive and ran a failed bid for the party presidency. She also served as president of the federal and provincial women's organizations. An opponent of the Waffle, Whelan was closely involved in many of the policy debates of the period and was one of the most outspoken members of caucus within the party.

Re-elected in Regina Northwest in 1971 and 1975, Whelan was appointed to cabinet as minister of Mineral Resources immediately after the 1975 election. Whelan was appointed to the cabinet committee that formulated the government's policy on potash, which led to the creation of the Potash Corporation of Saskatchewan. Moved into the Consumer Affairs portfolio in 1976, Whelan was elected a final time in 1978. In 1979, Whelan resigned from cabinet and the legislature after a dispute with Premier Allan Blakeney over the purchase of art for government buildings.

Whelan retired to Regina and published two books with Pemrose on CCF history: one on T. C. Douglas and the other on former Attorney General Jack Corman.

BRETT QUIRING

## WILLIAMS, CHARLES CROMWELL

(1896–1975). Charlie Williams, long-time Regina politician, spent thirty-six years in elected office at both the municipal and provincial levels. He served twenty years as minister of Labour, the longest any Saskatchewan cabinet minister has served in one portfolio, and left an indelible mark on the direction of labour legislation in the province and across Canada.

Williams was born in Moosomin on February 9, 1896. He went to school in Wapella where his family had moved when Williams was young. He took one year of arts education at Brandon College before accepting a job as a telegraph operator with the Canadian Pacific Railroad in Manitoba. It was there that he first joined the Order of Railroad Telegraphers and became active in the labour movement.

He enlisted in the Canadian Army in 1915 and saw service overseas. He served on the front lines in both France and Belgium before being wounded by a grenade at the Battle of Amiens in August 1918. Returning to Canada, he was employed by the Grand Trunk Railroad as a station agent and was stationed at numerous places across the prairie provinces. He was finally stationed in Regina in 1931, where he would spend most of the rest of his life. He became active in the Regina labour community, serving as his local's president for six years, as secretary of the provincial Committee of Railway Brotherhoods and in the Trade and Labour Congress (TLC).

In 1937 he first ran for office, winning a spot on the Labour-dominated Regina City Council. In 1938 he ran for the CCF in the Regina by-election, but was badly beaten by both the Liberal and Conservative candidates. In 1939, Williams was defeated in a re-election bid for City Council when the entire Labour slate was defeated. He ran for mayor for the first time in 1940 but was again defeated; he was successful on his second try in 1941. He was re-elected mayor twice until he was successfully elected to the Saskatchewan legislature in 1944.

Williams was included in Tommy Douglas' first cabinet in 1944 as minister of Labour. Along with former Regina city councillor C.M. Fines and former Moose Jaw Mayor Jack Corman, Williams brought to the cabinet table a great deal of experience, which has been credited for much of the CCF government's early success. As minister of Labour, Williams piloted a series of major reforms in labour legislation in the province. He introduced mandatory two-week holidays,

SAB R-A 2886-3

CHARLES WILLIAMS

expanded the number of statutory holidays, and introduced workers' compensation. Under his leadership, Saskatchewan became the first province to guarantee the right to collective bargaining.

However, Williams' appointment to cabinet created considerable tension within Saskatchewan's labour movement. The Canadian Congress of Labour (CCL) was upset with the appointment of Williams because of grievances the labour group had with Williams during his time as mayor, and because it was seen as the Douglas government's endorsement of the CCL's rival labour organization, the TLC. This tension between the CCL and the TLC would provide constant irritation for Williams, and the CCF generally, until the unions began merger talks in the late fifties.

Williams spent twenty years as minister of Labour and was re-elected to the provincial legislature four times, each time topping the ballot of the multi-member constituency of Regina. He retired from provincial politics in 1964, but contested the 1965 Regina municipal election and served on council until his final retirement from politics in 1973. He died while on vacation in Vancouver on January 31, 1975.

BRETT QUIRING

## WILLIAMS, GEORGE HARA (1894–1945).

Agrarian socialist George Hara Williams was born November 17, 1894, at Binscarth, Manitoba, of United Empire Loyalist stock. After service in World War I he attended the Manitoba Agricultural College and in 1920 was appointed director of livestock and equipment for Saskatchewan with the Soldier Settlement Board.

In 1921 Williams began farming at Semans

under the Canadian Government Soldier Settlement Program. He soon became very active in the farm movement, joining the farmers union in 1923 and serving on the United Farmers of Canada executive from 1927 to 1931. Positions included vice-president in 1928 and president from 1929 to 1931. Williams also served for a short time as secretary of the Marxist Farmers' Educational League and was founder and secretary of the short-lived Farmers' Political Association formed in 1924.

George Williams was a prominent figure in the organization of the Farmer-Labor Group. Williams and M. J. Coldwell co-chaired the 1932 convention that brought delegates from the United Farmers of Canada together with members of the Independent Labour Party to form a new party, the Farmer-Labor Group. In 1934 this group, which members insisted was not a political party, was renamed the Cooperative Commonwealth Federation (CCF). Williams contributed his understanding of rural problems to this new party, and tirelessly campaigned throughout Saskatchewan in the 1934 provincial election.

Williams, elected in the Wadena Constituency, was one of five successful CCF candidates in the 1934 provincial election. M. J. Coldwell, CCF party leader, was not among those successful candidates. A rivalry that had been brewing between the two men surfaced when Williams argued forcefully against the proposal that one of the CCF members of the legislature resign

SAB R-A 723-1

GEORGE WILLIAMS

to allow Coldwell to take over a seat. Williams remained floor leader of the CCF group in the legislature, and leader of the Opposition. When Coldwell was elected in a federal election in 1935, Williams became leader of the provincial CCF. He served as secretary, office manager and party organizer during 1935, and as party president, organizer and leader from February 1936 to July 1941.

After the Second World War was called, Williams tried to join up, but was rejected by army medical officers because of an injury he'd received in World War I. He persisted, and by 1941 Williams had taken up active military duty. Williams' participation in the armed forces highlighted an issue that had exacerbated poor relations between Williams and some members of the CCF: the question of national neutrality.

Concerned by Williams' absence, his uncompromising personality and his dogmatic espousal of Marxist socialism, which party members felt alienated many farmers and exacerbated factionalism within the CCF, Tommy Douglas was courted to become leader of the Saskatchewan CCF. Douglas had successfully defeated Williams as party president and Williams' position as party leader became severely undermined. Although Williams did not seek re-election, Williams backed Tisdale MLA John H. Brockelbank, who was widely seen as a place holder for Williams until he returned from the war. However, at the CCF annual convention in 1941 Douglas was elected leader over Brockelbank and Williams' influence over the Saskatchewan CCF was greatly diminished.

Just before the 1944 election, Williams was discharged from the army and returned from overseas service. He worked loyally in the 1944 campaign, and was instrumental in rallying rural support for the CCF. Williams'

unswerving dedication to his beliefs, which in his case was demonstrated by his military service, and his grasp of farm issues undoubtedly led to his re-election in Wadena. Tommy Douglas appointed Williams the minister of Agriculture, a post that he filled until February 1945 when failing health forced him to resign. He died on September 12, 1945, in Vancouver.

LISA DALE-BURNETT

**FURTHER READING:** Steininger, Friedrich. 1976. "George H. Williams: Agrarian Socialist." Unpublished M.A. thesis. University of Regina.

## WILLIS, CLARENCE GEORGE (1907–1984).

Born in Dauphin, Manitoba, on November 11, 1907, George Willis came to Saskatchewan while he was in high school. He finished his schooling at Nutana College in Saskatoon, after which he attended the University of Saskatchewan for one year before receiving a teaching certificate from the Saskatoon Normal School. In 1931, he began teaching school at Resource and continued until 1944. In that year he was rejected from military service for health reasons, whereupon he began farming to improve his health.

Willis was an early convert to the CCF, first becoming involved with the party prior to the 1944 election and serving on many party bodies before his election to the legislature. In 1945, he was elected to his first public post as a trustee of the Melfort Larger School Unit, a position he held until 1951. He also became involved in the co-operative movement and in the Melfort Agricultural Society of which he was president from 1948 to 1951. In 1952, Willis won the CCF nomination in Melfort-Tisdale and was elected in the same year, defeating the Liberal incumbent. He was re-elected in 1956 and was appointed to cabinet as minister of Public Works. After he was again elected in 1960, Willis took over administration of the Highways Department. During his time as minister he largely continued the policy of his predecessor, John T. Douglas, and continued with the expansion and paving of Saskatchewan's highway system. Also, during his term as minister the province began the construction of its first four-lane highway in Saskatchewan, Highway 6 from Regina to Lumsden.

In 1964 Willis was re-elected, but the defeat of the Lloyd government relegated him to the Opposition benches. Re-elected in 1967, Willis retired from politics in 1970 after resigning his seat due to ill health. Willis retired to British Columbia, where he died on February 14, 1984.

BRETT QUIRING

## WILLOUGHBY, WELLINGTON BARTLEY

(1859–1932). Wellington Bartley Willoughby was born on July 10, 1859, in Charlton, Peel County, Ontario. After completing high school in Hamilton he attended the University of Toronto and graduated with a Bachelor of Arts and a degree in law. He was called to the Ontario Bar in 1886 and practiced law in Toronto for more than ten years. Willoughby followed the family tradition of political activism and Conservative Party membership in his twenties and he ran unsuccessfully for the party in the 1896 federal election. After his defeat Willoughby sought new challenges, and in 1897 he moved to Moose Jaw, one of the fastest growing settlements in the North-West Territories. He

SAB R-A 28210
WELLINGTON WILLOUGHBY

established his own legal practice, specializing in the booming real estate business, and developed a wide range of other business interests. In 1908 he was appointed city solicitor for Moose Jaw.

Willoughby found his new home to be a more fruitful arena for his political ambitions, and he quickly established himself as one of the leading figures in the local Conservative Party organization. In 1908 he became the MLA for Moose Jaw and he was re-elected in 1912 and 1917. These were difficult times, however, as the Liberals held an overwhelming majority of the seats in the legislature and opposition forces were fragmented. During his first term, Willoughby worked hard to unite members of the federal Conservative Party and supporters of the loose Provincial Rights grouping to form the beginnings of a provincial Conservative Party under the leadership of F.W. Haultain in 1911. When the party did not improve its standing in the 1912 election (winning only 8 seats to the Liberals' 46), Haultain stepped down and was replaced as leader of the Opposition by Willoughby.

In his capacity as leader of the provincial Conservative Party, Willoughby first focussed on improving the organizational structure of his fledgling party, ensuring that every community established riding committees to oversee membership recruitment and fund-raising. He also proved to be an effective leader in the legislature and, though hamstrung in some respects by his promise of full support for the government's efforts in World War One, he did succeed in maintaining a clear ideological alternative to the Liberals. Especially on the controversial issue of education, Willoughby continued to oppose those provisions of the School Act which catered to minority religious, linguistic, or cultural sensibilities. By insisting that schools should serve primarily as vehicles of Canadianization, Willoughby ensured his party support from many of the Ontario Protestant and British-origin segments of the population. However, in the process he also reinforced the perception that his party was hostile to non-British immigrants and cemented their allegiance to the Liberals.

These political cleavages were far more beneficial for the Liberals than the Conservatives, as was evidenced in the 1917 election when Liberal support increased to fifty-one seats and the Conservatives lost one seat. Although Willoughby held his seat in Moose Jaw, it was clear that there were limits to his abilities as a leader and in 1917 he was persuaded by Prime Minister Borden to accept a seat in the Canadian senate to make way for Donald McLean from Saskatoon as the new Conservative Party leader. Willoughby served briefly as Conservative leader in the senate until his death on August 1, 1932.

MICHAEL COTTRELL, UNIVERSITY OF SASKATCHEWAN

## WILSON, JAMES ROBERT (1866–1941).

James Wilson was an early industrialist, first mayor of Saskatoon, MP and federal cabinet minister. Born September 16, 1866, near Almonte, Ontario, he moved west with his parents in 1883, being among the first to settle in the Dundurn district. Wilson served for a short time in the medical corps during the 1885 Riel Rebellion. An entrepreneur by inclination, Wilson tried various enterprises from farming to railroad contracting before starting a successful general store in Saskatoon in 1899. In 1902, he opened a flour mill in Saskatoon and later expanded into a grain company, both of which he eventually sold to Quaker Oats.

As the prominent business interest in Saskatoon, Wilson soon gravitated towards local politics. Elected Overseer for the Village of Saskatoon in 1903, he guided the community through the growth that would lead to the community's incorporation as a city in 1907. Serving as the city's mayor from 1907 to 1908, Wilson used his personal wealth to guarantee loans for the city to build its basic sewer infrastructure. Wilson's first foray in politics beyond the municipal level occurred in 1908 when he unsuccessfully contested the provincial election for the Conservatives in Saskatoon. Returning to municipal politics, Wilson was elected to Saskatoon city council in 1914 and remained there until 1919.

Wilson's public profile made him the obvious candidate to carry the Unionist banner for the government in 1917, and he was elected in a landslide victory in the riding of Saskatoon. Upon the appointment of Saskatchewan's minister, James Calder, to the Senate, Wilson was brought into the cabinet in 1921 as minister-without-portfolio. A few months later he was badly defeated in the Progressive sweep of the province. Wilson's support for the Meighen government and, more importantly, his support for its protective tariff, doomed his political career.

After his defeat he remained involved in many community causes, including being a vocal proponent of the Hudson's Bay Railroad, a perennial issue for Saskatchewan's farming and business communities. Wilson also served as chair of the Dominion Farm Loans Board before his death on April 3, 1941.

BRETT QUIRING

**FURTHER READING:** Kerr, Don, and Stan Hanson. 1982. *Saskatoon: The First Half-Century*. Edmonton: NeWest.

**WOLFE, JOHN THOMAS** (1955–1995). Although he was a provincial minister, veterinarian and community leader, Jack Wolfe is probably best remembered for the tragic circumstances around his death.

Born in Killdeer on May 2, 1955, Wolfe was educated in Rockglen before attending university. In 1979, he graduated from the University of Saskatchewan with degrees in biology and veterinary medicine. The following year he returned to Rockglen to establish his veterinary practice. Involved in numerous local community organizations, Wolfe first sought elected office in a 1988 by-election in Assiniboia-Gravelbourg as a Progressive Conservative. Winning the seat, he was quickly appointed to cabinet as associate minister of Health in 1989 and a year later was appointed minister of Urban Affairs.

Narrowly defeated in the 1991 election, Wolfe returned to his veterinary practice in Rockglen. In the following years, however, it came to light that a number of former members of the Devine government had been submitting fraudulent expense forms. The resulting RCMP investigation called into question Wolfe's purchase of a computer through the Progressive Conservative caucus office. Wolfe denied having committed any wrongdoing. He was called to testify at the preliminary hearing of John Scraba. Convinced that the crown prosecutor and the RCMP did not believe him, Wolfe grew increasingly depressed about the situation. On May 2, 1995, he shot himself in his veterinary clinic, leaving behind a pregnant wife and three small children.

BRETT QUIRING

**FURTHER READING:** Jones, Gerry. 2000. *Saskscandal.* Calgary: Fifth House.

**WOOD, EVERETT IRVINE** (1910–1983). Everett Wood was born October 4, 1910, on a farm northeast of Swift Current. After completing high school in Swift Current he attended the Canadian Pentecostal Bible College in Winnipeg for two years, but was forced to leave before his studies were complete due to the Depression. In 1931, Wood was appointed to the Pentecostal Assembly at Spy Hill, but his clerical career came to an end the next year when he took charge of the family farm after his father fell ill.

WEST'S STUDIO, REGINA•SAB R-A 8368

EVERETT WOOD

Wood was involved in many local agricultural associations, in the Saskatchewan Wheat Pool and in several local advocacy groups. He was first elected to public office in 1947 when he was elected councilor of the rural municipality of Saskatchewan Landing, a position he held until 1950. In 1952 he was elected reeve of Saskatchewan Landing, which he held until his election to the legislature.

He was exposed to the CCF through his involvement in the farmers' organization, and he joined the party in the early forties. Wood held numerous party positions until he was elected to the legislature representing the constituency of Swift Current in 1956. After re-election in 1960, Wood was elected Speaker of the legislature; however, he stepped down less than a year later when he was appointed to Woodrow Lloyd's first cabinet as minister of Municipal Affairs. He remained minister until the government was defeated. Wood served the next two terms in Opposition until

1971 when the NDP returned to power. Wood was appointed to Blakeney's first cabinet, once again as minister of Municipal Affairs. As one of only three ministers with previous ministerial experience, Wood provided the government with much-needed governmental experience during its first term.

Wood did not seek re-election in 1975 and retired from politics. He died in 1983.

BRETT QUIRING

**WOOFF, ROBERT HANSON** (1900–1992). Robert "Bob" Wooff was born in Yorkshire, England, in 1900 and came to Canada with his parents in 1906. After originally settling in the Moosomin area, the family later settled near Cleaves, becoming one of the first families to settle in the region of northwestern Saskatchewan. Wooff was schooled at Emmaville and in 1925

WEST'S STUDIO, REGINA • SAB R-A 8380
ROBERT WOOFF

received a certificate in Agriculture from the University of Saskatchewan. An active advocate for education, Wooff first became involved in politics as a school board trustee and, unlike many of his fellow trustees, was a strong advocate for the introduction of larger school districts. Wooff's career in the Saskatchewan legislature began when he was elected in Turtleford in 1944. Wooff's political career was marked by a series of narrow wins and defeats. He was defeated in 1948, re-elected in 1952, and defeated again in 1956. In the 1960 election, he was elected again only

to have the result contraverted by the court and lost the subsequent by-election. In 1964, with the defeat of the Lloyd government, Wooff was again returned to the legislature and played a prominent role in Opposition as the party's primary agricultural critic. After narrowly achieving victory in the 1967 election, Wooff voluntarily relinquished his prominent role in favour of promoting some of the NDP's younger MLAs before retiring from politics in 1971. He continued to stay active within the community and within the NDP until his death on March 23, 1992.

BRETT QUIRING

**WYLIE, DAVID JAMES** (1859–1932). David James Wylie was an influential pioneer, agricultural promoter, rancher, and politician. Born in 1859 in Shrewsbury, England, Wylie was educated at Cheltenham College, an English public school. Shortly after his twenty-first birthday Wylie emigrated to Canada and settled first in Winnipeg and then in Medicine Hat, in the administrative district of Alberta. Shortly afterwards, he moved to Maple Creek, in the administrative district of Assiniboia (what is now Saskatchewan).

With the outbreak of the 1885 Riel Rebellion many in the Cypress Hills region feared an Indian invasion. Wylie, like many single ranchers, went west to Fort Macleod and joined the Rocky Mountain Rangers, a hodgepodge of "irregulars" who sought to fight alongside General Strange's forces against Riel. Led by ex-army officer John Stewart, the Rangers never saw battle and were disbanded shortly after the skirmish at Duck Lake. Shortly after returning to Maple Creek, Wylie took up the position of foreman on Sir John Lester Kaye's farm. In 1896, Wylie organized the Maple Creek Cattle Company and was quickly recognized as an authority on ranching.

Wylie supported Frederick Haultain's non-partisan system of government. He ran for the Legislative Assembly of the North-West Territories as a Haultain supporter in the 1902 general election but was defeated by Horace Greeley. In Saskatchewan, he was elected in 1905, 1908 and 1912 as a supporter of the Provincial Rights Party and then the Conservative Party. During Haultain's period in opposition, Wylie was his most consistent and passionate supporter of non-partisan government within the Territories. Switching to the Conservatives in 1912 after Haultain's resignation, Wylie was defeated in 1917 by Liberal A. J. Colquhoun. He unsuccessfully contested the federal election of 1921 for the Conservatives.

Wylie's legacy is the passion and energy he emoted while promoting western agriculture, both within the legislature and without. He campaigned with Haultain against the terms of union that brought Saskatchewan into Confederation without control over natural resources. While an MLA, Wylie was a passionate advocate for Saskatchewan ranching and agriculture. He was an active member of the standing committees of agriculture and education. After his defeat, Wylie became president of the Saskatchewan Stock Growers Association. In this role, Wylie is best remembered for his response to the 1921 collapse in beef prices, when he presented a petition to Prime Minister Arthur Meighen proposing longer leases and lower rentals on ranchland.

While not distinguishing himself in the legislature, Wylie gained his reputation as a skilled farmer, rancher and businessman. He wedded western ranching to the Conservative party as Saskatchewan ranching's first and most ardent defender. He helped set a precedent for agriculturalists in western politics.

Wylie passed away in 1932.

MICHAEL THOME, UNIVERSITY OF SASKATCHEWAN

FURTHER READING: MacEwan, Grant. 1948. "Dreadnought Joe Wylie." In The Sodbusters, 185–189. Toronto: Nelson.

## YOUNG, ALEXANDER MCGILLVRAY

(1878–1939). Alexander Young was born in Millsville, Nova Scotia, on July 30, 1878. After growing up in Nova Scotia, he attended McGill University, completing a medical degree. In 1907 he came to Saskatoon and set up a medical practice. Young quickly became involved politics and was elected to Saskatoon City Council in 1913. Political tensions within the city grew as the previous decade's boom of development began to wane. The crisis brought Young into conflict with developers who wanted the city to relax building standards to keep their buildings profitable. They also conflicted over the city's proposed construction of an oil pipeline. Although Young lost both of these battles, he established himself as a prominent force in Saskatoon city politics.

Young first contended Saskatoon's mayoralty in 1914, but lost. He contested the position again in 1915 and again lost, but was narrowly successful in 1916. Young tried to redefine the role of mayor, resulting in sharp opposition from city commissioner C. J. Yorath. Young believed that being mayor was a full-time position. He attempted to introduce a salary for the position and also attempted to expand the mayor's power at the expense of the city commissioner. Young was re-elected in 1917 and 1918 before his defeat to political adversary Frank MacMillan, who would contest Young in all but one of his subsequent election campaigns. Young returned to the mayor's office in 1920 and 1921.

In 1925 Young contested the riding of Saskatoon for the Liberal Party, narrowly beating the Conservative Party candidate, MacMillan. Retaining his seat in the 1926 election, Young was a strong advocate for lowering the tariff on finished goods, a position dear to the heart of Saskatchewan farm movements. MacMillan defeated Young in 1930 as R. B. Bennett swept to power, but Young successfully regained his seat in 1935 when the Bennett government was defeated. Shortly after his election, Young developed a brain tumor and on July 7, 1939, died in surgery.

BRETT QUIRING

**FURTHER READING:** Kerr, Don, and Stan Hanson. 1982. *Saskatoon: The First Half-Century*. Edmonton: NeWest Press.

**ZAZELENCHUK, JO-ANN** (b. 1958). Jo-Ann Zazelenchuk, MLA for Saskatoon Riversdale (1982–1986), was the youngest member ever elected to the Saskatchewan Legislative Assembly. Born in Saskatoon on October 19, 1958, she completed a Bachelor of Arts in economics at the University of Saskatchewan and studied certified management accounting at the University of Calgary. As the twenty-three-year-old Progressive Conservative candidate in Riversdale, she narrowly defeated the New Democratic incumbent and future premier, Roy Romanow, in the 1982 provincial election. Romanow had been the most prominent cabinet minister in Allan Blakeney's government and was a visible national figure in the landmark constitutional negotiations that preceded the 1982 election. This humiliating ejection of a star NDP politician from a traditionally safe NDP seat by a young political neophyte epitomized and reflected the extent of the Conservative electoral sweep in 1982, which produced the largest government caucus in Saskatchewan history. Romanow soundly defeated Zazelenchuk in the 1986 election, ending her political career. She went on to work in Saskatchewan's non-profit sector.

ERIN M. K. WEIR, UNIVERSITY OF CALGARY